Psychology
FOR **A2**-LEVEL
Student
Workbook

Hugh Hillyard-Parker
Mike Cardwell

Collins

An imprint of
HarperCollins*Publishers*

Contents >> Psychology for A2-level: Student Workbook

USING THE BOOK

This book is designed to be used alongside *Psychology Third Edition* and *Psychology for A2-level Third Edition*, both by Cardwell, Clark and Meldrum, published by Collins. Those books – which we refer to throughout this workbook as 'the textbook' – provide a detailed coverage of all aspects of the A2 psychology course offered by the Assessment and Qualifications Alliance (AQA), Specification A.

This workbook will help you prepare for the A2 examination by providing a wealth of additional resources:

- structured activities to help with understanding, note-taking and summarizing the large volume of information in the textbook
- sheets to help with planning your work and revising – see 'Keeping track' on p. iv
- hundreds of exam-orientated activities and questions, giving you plenty of practice at writing exam answers
- separate example worked answers to the kinds of question set in the exam
- detailed guidance on answering all types of exam question.

How this workbook relates to the textbooks

This workbook is divided into twelve units, each corresponding to one unit in the textbooks. You will notice that this workbook uses a dual numbering system:

- The first number, always in blue, refers to the unit of the same number in *Psychology for A2-level Third Edition*.
- The second number, always in brown, refers to the unit of the same number in *Psychology Third Edition*.

So, depending on which textbook you are using, you should follow either the blue or brown numbers.

Every section from AQA modules 4 and 5 is represented in the workbook. The table below shows which sections from each module are covered:

AQA Module 4

Social Psychology
Unit 2/10   Relationships
Unit 3/11   Pro- and anti-social behaviour

Physiological Psychology
Unit 5/13   Biological rhythms, sleep and dreaming

Cognitive Psychology
Unit 8/16   Perceptual processes and development

Developmental Psychology
Unit 10/18   Cognitive development
Unit 11/19   Social and personality development

Comparative Psychology
Unit 15/23   Evolutionary explanations of human behaviour

AQA Module 5

Individual Differences
Unit 17/25   Psychopathology
Unit 18/26   Treating mental disorders

Perspectives

Unit **19**/27 Issues in psychology

Unit **20**/28 Debates in psychology

Unit **21**/29 Approaches in psychology

Key features

- Like the textbook, each unit is divided into *topics*. Each topic covers a distinct part of the AQA (A) specification.
- A *preview* at the start of each unit enables you to check quickly the topics covered and the pages of the textbook you'll need to use.
- The *introduction* at the start of each unit includes a diagram showing where the unit fits into the A2 qualification.
- *Understanding the specification* at the start of each topic provides an extract from the AQA specification with detailed notes explaining what the AQA (A) expects of you. More advice about understanding the specification is given on the right.
- A *topic map* gives you a visual picture of the content of each topic.
- *Keeping track* is a table that enables you to assess your progress in each topic. See right for guidance on using this feature.
- *Activities*, within each topic, are designed to help you understand and absorb all the information in the textbook. Some activities are simple question-and-answer type exercises, but many of them will help you with note-taking and summarizing of key points. This will be very useful both for initial understanding and later revision.

  Many of the activities are based around example exam questions and will give you invaluable practice at writing good, concise answers to the sorts of questions you will meet in the exam. Special *AO2 activities* will focus on the skills you need for the evaluation, or AO2, parts of questions.

  For most of the activities, space is left for you to write your answers in the book. Sometimes, though, you will be asked to use separate paper or to write your answer on a PC. Where relevant, *answers to activities* are included at the end of each topic.

- Each topic contains several *example examination questions* to give you a clear idea of the kinds of questions you can expect in the exam. This includes all types of exam questions.
- There is at least one *sample answer* per unit, with commentary, showing you clearly how to tackle exam questions. You will also find questions for you to try youself, called *One for you to try ...*, together with advice on tackling them.
- The *Check your understanding* section at the end of each topic corresponds to the feature of the same name in the textbook. This workbook provides feedback to the questions in the textbook.
- *Hints* are scattered through the topics, explaining difficult terms or giving useful bits of exam advice.

Keeping track

Planning and progress-checking are important parts of work. The *Keeping track* feature is designed to help you with these aspects of your work:

- In the 'Where is it?' column, you note down the relevant page numbers of the textbook.
- When you have finished your work on the topic, go through the checklist and tick the appropriate column according to how well you have mastered the subject matter. This will highlight any areas you need to go back over or do more work on.
- Alternatively (or in addition), use the checklist as a revision guide, ticking the final column only when you have revised the topic and are sure that you are completely on top of the subject matter.

Understanding the specification

A summary of the requirements of the AQA (A) specification is included in the textbook – see the Introduction, p. vii/x.

Words are used quite precisely in the specification and it is important to understand what they tell you.

- Where you see the word '*including*' in the specification, it means that questions can be set specifically on the items mentioned. For example, the paragraph on Biological rhythms includes the following: 'Research studies into circadian, infradian, and ultradian biological rhythms, *including* the role of endogenous pacemakers and exogenous zeitgebers'. This means that there could be an exam question asking you specifically about endogenous pacemakers or exogenous zeitgebers (see Example Exam Question 3 on p. 141/409).
- Where items are preceded by '*e.g.*', that means those items are only examples of appropriate subject matter. Exam questions *cannot* ask you specifically about those items.

Do, please, let us know what you think of the book. Feedback from users is enormously helpful and we shall pay close attention to it when we come to update this *Student Workbook*.

Hugh Hillyard-Parker, Mike Cardwell

AQA address

AQA
Stag Hill House
Guildford GU2 5XJ
www.aqa.org.uk

Relationships

There are three topics in this unit. You should read them alongside the following pages in the Collins *Psychology for A2-level/Psychology* textbook:

Topic	Psychology for A2	Psychology
1 Attraction and the formation of relationships	pp. 38–48	pp. 306–16
2 Love and the breakdown of relationships	pp. 48–56	pp. 316–24
3 Cultural differences in relationships	pp. 56–67	pp. 324–35

INTRODUCTION

Social Psychology is one of five sections in Module 4 (AQA Specification A), as the diagram below shows. This section is further divided into three sub-sections – 'Relationships' is the second of these.

Read the Preview and Introduction on p. 36/304 of the textbook now. This will give you an overview of what's in the unit.

Where this unit fits in to the A-level qualification

Module 4

- Section A: **Social Psychology**
- Section B: Physiological Psychology
- Section C: Cognitive Psychology
- Section D: Developmental Psychology
- Section E: Comparative Psychology

- • SOCIAL COGNITION
- • **RELATIONSHIPS**
- • PRO- AND ANTI-SOCIAL BEHAVIOUR

- a Attraction and the formation of relationships
- b Love and the breakdown of relationships
- c Cultural differences in relationships

In the Module 4 exam, there will be a total of 15 questions, three relating to each Section (i.e. one per sub-section). You have to answer **three** questions, from at least **two** sections.

HINT

2006 AQA Specification

The details given here refer to the AQA specification for 2006 onwards. If you are working to a different specification, you will need to check that carefully.

Social relationships make up an integral part of everybody's lives. As the unit introduction in the textbook explains (p. 36/304), relationships offer us some of our happiest – and saddest – experiences. In its penultimate paragraph, the unit introduction also poses several questions about relationships. This topic seeks to answer several of them. What attracts us to other people? What factors help us to decide whether or not to embark on a relationship? What have researchers found in their investigations into attraction and relationship formation?

UNDERSTANDING THE SPECIFICATION

Here is what the AQA (A) specification says about this topic. It forms part of A2 Module 4, Section A: Social Psychology.

There are two distinct, yet at times overlapping segments in this division: interpersonal attraction and the formation/maintenance of relationships.

In the former, you are required to describe and evaluate explanations (two are enough, and might include evolutionary explanations and the matching hypothesis) and research studies. For the latter, you are only required to cover theories, although studies can be effectively utilized as AO2 commentary. It is important to distinguish between 'interpersonal attraction' (what leads one person to be attractive to you rather than another person) and the 'formation/maintenance of relationships' (moving from being attracted to forming a relationship). However, the subtle distinction between theories that explain the formation of relationships (e.g. reward/need satisfaction) and those that explain their maintenance (e.g. equity theory) is not one you need worry about, as either or both are acceptable.

Relationships

a. **Attraction and the formation of relationships**

Explanations and research studies relating to interpersonal attraction (e.g. evolutionary explanations, matching hypothesis). Theories relating to the formation/maintenance of relationships (e.g. reward/need satisfaction, social exchange theory).

HINT

2006 AQA Specification

If you are using the 2004 version of the textbook, you will notice that 'Maintenance of relationships' (pp. 45–8/313–16) is now part of Topic 1 in the 2006 AQA specification (not Topic 2, as in the textbook). For that reason, we include it here in this topic.

TOPIC MAP

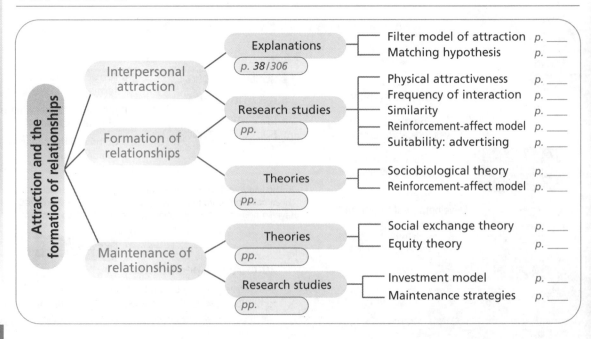

Attraction and the formation of relationships

- **Interpersonal attraction**
  - Explanations *p. 38/306*
    - Filter model of attraction p. ___
    - Matching hypothesis p. ___
  - Research studies *pp.*
    - Physical attractiveness p. ___
    - Frequency of interaction p. ___
    - Similarity p. ___
    - Reinforcement-affect model p. ___
    - Suitability: advertising p. ___
- **Formation of relationships**
  - Theories *pp.*
    - Sociobiological theory p. ___
    - Reinforcement-affect model p. ___
- **Maintenance of relationships**
  - Theories *pp.*
    - Social exchange theory p. ___
    - Equity theory p. ___
  - Research studies *pp.*
    - Investment model p. ___
    - Maintenance strategies p. ___

Topic map

Look through pp. 38–48/306–16 of the textbook to see where the items shown in the topic map are covered. Note down the relevant page numbers in the spaces left on the topic map. For example, explanations of interpersonal attraction are covered on p. 38/306 (that has already been written in).

KEEPING TRACK

Use the table below to keep track of your work on this topic and plan your revision. See p. iv of this workbook (Introduction) for guidance on filling it in.

Attraction and the formation of relationships		Tick if you ...		
What I need to learn	Where is it?	could make a basic attempt	could make a good attempt	have complete mastery of this
Explanations of interpersonal attraction				
Description of the filter model of attraction				
Description of the matching hypothesis				
Theories of relationship formation				
Description of sociobiological theory				
Evaluation of sociobiological theory				
Description of the reinforcement-affect model				
Evaluation of the reinforcement-affect model				
Research studies of interpersonal attraction and relationship formation				
Description of research into interpersonal attraction and the formation of relationships				
Evaluation of research into interpersonal attraction and the formation of relationships				
Theories of the maintenance of relationships				
Description of social exchange theory				
Description of equity theory				
Evaluation of social exchange and equity theory				
Description of research into maintenance strategies				

EXPLANATIONS OF INTERPERSONAL ATTRACTION

This topic starts with two explanations of interpersonal attraction (see p. 38/306):

- *a filter model* – the idea that we use social and personal filters to narrow down the 'field of eligibles' with whom we might form a relationship

- *the matching hypothesis* – the idea that we tend to be attracted to people who are similar to us in terms of physical attractiveness, intelligence, athleticism, etc.

Two explanations of interpersonal attraction

Read through the descriptions of the two explanations of attraction given on p. 38/306. Summarize each model by answering the questions on the next page.

Filter model of attraction

1 Who proposed the explanation?

2 What is the basic idea behind this model?

3 Why are different types of variable important at different stages?

4 What five main criteria are important during this process?

Matching hypothesis

1 Who proposed the explanation?

2 What is the basic idea behind this hypothesis?

3 What factors or attributes are important in this process?

4 What happens if partners are mismatched?

Organizing the information: AO1 and AO2

A key feature of the textbook is that it helps you target your studies towards meeting the demands of the AQA exam. One way it does this is by giving example exam questions in every topic. For example, in this topic, five exam questions are given on p. 44/312.

Even at an early stage in your studies, it's a good idea to understand how exam questions are structured. Just as at AS-level, exam questions at A2-level are designed to test different types of skill:

- AO1 = description and information-giving
- AO2 = evaluation and commentary.

ACTIVITY

AO1 and AO2 skills at A2

Read pp. 668–71/936–9, 'AO1 and AO2' and 'Question-setting'. Then look at Example Exam Question 1 on p. 44/312.

1 What does this question demand, in terms of AO1 and AO2 skills?

2 How many marks are available for AO1?

How many marks are available for AO2?

You would have 30 minutes to answer this question. This is enough time to write about 600 words. Half of this time would be spent on AO1 and half on AO2.

3 If you decided to write about two explanations, how many words of AO1 description would you need to write on each?

4 How many minutes would you have to describe each explanation?

Check your answers by looking at p. 8 of this book.

The text on p. 38/306 all counts as description, i.e. AO1 in terms of the AQA exam. There are 419 words describing the filter model of attraction and 280 words describing the matching hypothesis. So, if you decided to answer Example Exam Question 1 on p. 44/312 with reference to two explanations, you would have to summarize (or précis) the key points in far fewer words.

ACTIVITY

Précis-ing the explanations

Write a 150-word précis of each of the two explanations on p. 38/306. Do this on your PC, using the Word Count tool to check the number of words you produce.

Evaluating explanations of interpersonal attraction

If all the text on p. 38/306 is AO1, what can you use for the evaluation – or AO2 – part of exam questions about explanations of interpersonal attraction? The answer is research studies: you can use research findings as effective AO2 evaluation by commenting on whether the research supports the theory or highlights problems with it.

Three of the criteria listed on p. 38/306 have been extensively researched (although it is worth noting the age of some of the research), i.e. physical attractiveness, frequency of interaction/proximity and similarity. The results of this research are described in the textbook on pp. 41–2/309–10.

 **ACTIVITY**

Research into interpersonal attraction

Read the text on pp. 41–2/309–10, up to the heading 'The reinforcement-affect model'. Draw up a table, following the format shown below. Note down the names of relevant researchers, together with the key points of their research studies. In the final column, note down how you could use this as AO2 commentary in an essay discussing interpersonal attraction.

Aspect of attraction	Researcher	Key points	How to use as AO2 commentary
Physical attractiveness	● Murstein (1972)	●	●
	● Walster *et al.* (1966)	●	●

Look again at Example Exam Question 1 on p. 44/312. In an answer to this question, you would spend half your time writing A02 evaluation – that's about 300 words. If you decided to answer this question with reference to two explanations (filter model and matching hypothesis), you could draw your commentary from the points listed in the table you completed in the last activity.

 **ACTIVITY**

Evaluating explanations of interpersonal attraction

Write a 300-word evaluation of the two explanations of interpersonal attraction described on p. 38/306, i.e. the filter model and matching hypothesis. Do this on your PC, using the Word Count tool to check the number of words you produce.

If you add this to the 300 words you wrote to précis the two explanations (see activity on p. 4 of this book), then you have a complete answer to Example Exam Question 1 on p. 44/312.

THEORIES OF RELATIONSHIP FORMATION

Two theories of relationship formation are covered in the textbook: sociobiological theories (p. 39/307) and the reinforcement-affect model (p. 40/308).

Sociobiological theory

ACTIVITY

Understanding sociobiological theory

Read the whole of p. 39/307 and then answer the following questions

1 What is the underlying proposition of the sociobiological model?

2 Wilson (1975) argues that men and women 'bargain' in their sexual relationships. What form might that 'bargaining' take?

3 Why does the sociobiological model have problems explaining homosexual relationships?

4 In what way could the theory be seen as supporting divisive gender stereotypes?

The text in the top half of p. 39/307 describes sociobiological theory and could be used as AO1 description in answering exam questions on theories of relationship formation. The panel at the bottom of p. 39/307 headed 'AO2 Evaluation' contains a number of points that you could use as AO2 commentary.

AO2 ACTIVITY

Evaluating sociobiological theory

Look again at the text under 'Innovative and effective AO2' on p. 669/937 of the textbook. There it makes the point that AO2 evaluation is not just a case of 'slagging off' a particular theory or piece of research. Effective criticism involves pointing out both the positive aspects as well as any negative ones.

Now look again at the 'Evaluation' on p. 39/307. Four main points of commentary are listed. Which are positive (i.e. provide support for the theory) and which are negative (i.e. argue against the theory)?

There are 350 words in the Evaluation panel. Write 150 words of AO2 commentary on sociobiological theory, again using your PC to check your word count.

In addition to the points made in the Evaluation panel, you can also use research findings as AO2, by commenting on whether research supports the theory or identifies problems with it. Several pieces of relevant research are described on p. 42/310 of the textbook (right-hand column).

AO2 ACTIVITY

Research support for sociobiological theory

Read the paragraphs under the heading 'Suitability: advertising for a mate' on p. 42/310. Draw up a table, using the format shown below. For each researcher, note down the key points of their research studies. In the final column, note down how you could use this as AO2 commentary in an essay discussing sociobiological theory.

Researcher	Key points	How to use as AO2 commentary on sociobiological theory
Cameron *et al.* (1977)	•	•

Reinforcement-affect model

ACTIVITY

Understanding the reinforcement-affect model

Read the whole of p. 40/308 and then answer the following questions.

1 What is the central proposition of the reinforcement-affect model?

2 According to this model, what roles are played by
(a) classical conditioning
(b) operant conditioning?

3 According to Argyle, what is the importance of non-verbal signals?

4 In what way, according to Argyle, do social relationships help to satisfy individual needs?

When it comes to exam questions, the text in the top two thirds of p. 40/308 could be used as AO1 description, while the panel at the bottom of the page contains useful points for AO2 commentary.

There is also important AO2 material on p. 42/310 under the heading 'The reinforcement-affect model', which looks at some research support for the model.

Evaluating the reinforcement-affect model

Complete the table below, which summarizes points to make when evaluating the reinforcement-affect model. If you need more space than is given here, draw up your own version of the table on a separate sheet of paper.

Evaluative point	Researcher	Group(s) of people studied	Argues for or against the model?
●	May and Hamilton (1980)		
● value may be given as much to rewarding others as to rewarding self	Hays (1985)		Against
●	Hill (1970)		
●	Lott (1994)		

Answering exam questions on relationship formation

Having done all the activities above, you are now well prepared to tackle questions on theories of relationship formation, such as Example Exam Question 4 on p. 44/312. This question tells you exactly how many theories you should refer to (i.e. two), which means you can break your answer down into four 'chunks' of 150 words, as shown in the table below.

Writing an example exam question

On your PC, write an answer to Example Exam Question 4 on p. 44/312, following the structure shown in the table below.

	AO1 (description)		AO2 (commentary)	
Theory 1: sociobiological theory	150 words	p. 39/307 (top)	150 words	p. 39/307 (bottom) p. 42/310 (2nd column)
Theory 2: reinforcement-affect model	150 words	p. 40/308 (top)	150 words	p. 40/308 (bottom) p. 42/310 (1st column)

RESEARCH STUDIES OF INTERPERSONAL ATTRACTION

Pages 41–3/309–11 of the textbook give description and evaluation of several research studies investigating attraction and relationships. You have already looked at how you can use research findings as AO2 commentary in some exam questions. Sometimes, however, questions will be set that ask you to describe the research studies themselves for AO1 and then evaluate them for AO2. Example Exam Question 5 on p. 44/312 is exactly one such question. In answering this question, you could use any of the research studies described on pp. 41–2/309–10.

Evaluating research studies

When it comes to evaluating research studies, there are many factors that you can consider, such as:

● the age, nature and location of the research studies
● the types and numbers of participants
● validity, reliability and bias
● ethical issues.

The Evaluation panel on p. 43/311 lists several issues relevant to this area of research.

Evaluating research into interpersonal attraction

If, in the exam, you were asked to describe and evaluate research into interpersonal attraction, you could use the research into physical attractiveness by Walster *et al.* (1966) and Murstein (1972), described on p. 41/309. In evaluating these pieces of research, think about which of the criticisms listed on p. 43/311 would be particularly relevant. (You could also include other, more general criticisms in the AO2 part of your answer.)

EXAMPLE EXAM QUESTIONS

In your work on this topic, you have already looked in detail at two possible exam questions (Example Exam Questions 1 and 4 on p. 44/312) – and answered them! Here is another one for you to try.

ACTIVITY

One for you to try ...

Discuss psychological research (explanations and/or studies) into interpersonal attraction. (24 marks)

This question gives you the choice of writing about explanations of interpersonal attraction or about research studies, or about both. It really is your choice – this is not a trick question! When choosing your approach, bear two things in mind.

1 Is the material you're using really about interpersonal attraction or relationship formation? The distinction between these is not always that clear, but you should at least try to use the right material.

2 Whatever approach you choose, is there enough AO2 material available for your commentary?

With these questions in mind, one possible solution is to use studies alone for the answer. Remember that studies can be a useful source of AO2 material for explanations, but if you use them as AO1 *and* AO2

material, you must be prepared to pass comment on the studies themselves.

A suitable route through this question would use the following material drawn up into four paragraphs of about 150 words each (pp 41–3/309–11):

● AO1 – e.g. studies of the role of physical attractiveness and frequency of interaction

● AO1 – e.g. studies of the role of similarity and suitability

● AO2 – e.g. commentary on the artificiality of research in this area, lack of emphasis on change and variability, nature of personal characteristics

● AO2 – e.g. commentary on the influence of others, overemphasis on physical attractiveness, does familiarity always lead to liking?

ANSWERS TO ACTIVITIES

AO1 and AO2 skills at A2, p. 4

1 The way this question is phrased makes it easy to work out what is demanded in terms of AO1 and AO2. The AO1 part is to *describe* one or more explanations of interpersonal attraction. The AO2 part involves *evaluating* the explanation(s) you have described.

2 There are 12 marks available for the AO1 description and 12 marks for the AO2 evaluation.

3 You would have time to write about 150 words of AO1 description on each of the two explanations.

4 You would have at most 7.5 minutes to describe each explanation (including thinking time).

CHECK YOUR UNDERSTANDING

When you have finished working through this topic, try the questions in 'Check your understanding' on p. 43/311 of the textbook. Check your answers by looking at the relevant parts of the textbook or this workbook, listed below.

1 textbook p. 38/306; workbook p. 4 (activity)
2 textbook p. 38/306; workbook p. 4 (activity)
3 textbook p. 38/306; workbook p. 4 (activity)
4 textbook p. 38/306; workbook p. 4 (activity)
5 textbook p. 43/311
6 textbook p. 39/307

7 textbook pp. 39/307 and 42/310; workbook p. 6 (activity)
8 textbook p. 40/308
9 textbook pp. 40/308 and 42/310
10 textbook pp. 40/308 and 42/310; workbook p. 7 (activity)

Topic 2 >> Love and the breakdown of relationships

Topic 1 looked at what attracts people to each other and brings them together; this topic continues the story by looking at love and how psychologists have sought to explain this strange and powerful phenomenon. Sometimes, however, love isn't enough and relationships break down. This topic also examines what happens when things begin to fall apart and people decide to end their relationship.

UNDERSTANDING THE SPECIFICATION

Here is what the AQA (A) specification says about this topic. It forms part of A2 Module 4, Section A: Social Psychology.

The specification entry for this topic requires you to cover at least *two* psychological explanations of love. Two example explanations are given in the specification, although these are just that, examples, and you can cover completely different explanations. It is imperative, however, that whatever explanations you choose, they are *psychological* and are concerned with the explanation of *love* (and not just attraction). The example given 'love as attachment' should not dwell solely on early attachment bonds, but should examine the link between early attachment and the development of romantic relationships in adulthood.

Relationships

b. Love and the breakdown of relationships

Psychological explanations of love (e.g. triangular theory, love as attachment). Explanations (e.g. Lee, Duck) and research studies relating to the breakdown of relationships.

The same advice (i.e. more than one explanation) applies to the specification entry on the breakdown of relationships. You should cover explanations and research studies separately, and be prepared to cover AO1 and AO2 content for both. Some questions may offer you the opportunity to link explanations (as AO1) and research studies (as AO2), but explanations and research studies can constitute complete exam questions in their own right.

TOPIC MAP

The diagram below gives you an overview of what you are about to study.

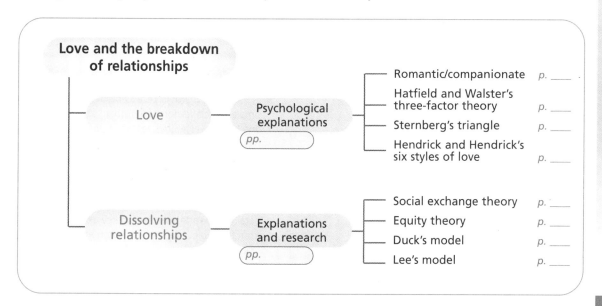

Love and the breakdown of relationships
- Love → Psychological explanations (pp. ___)
  - Romantic/companionate — p. ___
  - Hatfield and Walster's three-factor theory — p. ___
  - Sternberg's triangle — p. ___
  - Hendrick and Hendrick's six styles of love — p. ___
- Dissolving relationships → Explanations and research (pp. ___)
  - Social exchange theory — p. ___
  - Equity theory — p. ___
  - Duck's model — p. ___
  - Lee's model — p. ___

Unit 2/10 // Relationships

9

Topic map

Look through pp. 45–54/313–22 of the textbook to see where the items shown in the topic map are covered. Note down the relevant page numbers in the spaces left on the topic map.

KEEPING TRACK

Use the table below to keep track of your work on this topic and plan your revision. See p. iv of this workbook (Introduction) for guidance on filling it in.

Love and the breakdown of relationships		Tick if you ...		
What I need to learn	Where is it?	could make a basic attempt	could make a good attempt	have complete mastery of this
Psychological explanations of love				
Description of romantic and companionate love				
Description of Hatfield and Walster's three-factor theory				
Description of Sternberg's 'triangular theory'				
Description of Hendrick and Hendrick's six styles of love				
Evaluation of psychological explanations of love				
Theories and research relating to the breakdown of relationships				
Description of factors contributing to the ending of relationships				
Description of Duck's model				
Description of Lee's research and model				
Description of research into the ending of relationships				
Evaluation of research into the ending of relationships				

PSYCHOLOGICAL EXPLANATIONS OF LOVE

'What is this thing called love?' Songwriters and poets have plenty to say on the topic. Psychologists have also devoted a great deal of energy to trying to explain it. Read from the top of p. 52/320 up to and including the activity at the top of p. 54/322. Try that activity and see if your answers agree with the ones given on p. 69/337.

Explanations of love

Write 150-word summaries of the explanations of love offered by: Hatfield and Walster (1981), Sternberg (1986, 1988), and Hendrick and Hendrick (1986). These summaries would count as AO1 descriptions in questions asking you to outline explanations of love.

It is possible that an exam question might ask you to 'describe and evaluate **one** psychological explanation of love'. To prepare for this eventuality (however unlikely), you should also prepare a 300-word descriptive summary and a 300-word evaluation of your favourite explanation as indicated above.

Describing explanations of love

● In the exam, it would be acceptable to draw a simple sketch version of Sternberg's triangle, but don't then waste time describing the diagram in words. For example, there's no need to say 'The triangle has three points, with passion at one point ...', as the diagram shows that already!

● Don't try to reproduce the whole of Table 2.4/10.4 in the exam. That is far too much detail! It is worth memorizing key examples from the table – such as 'consummate love', 'companionate love' and 'infatuation' – which would allow you to make comparisons and draw contrasts.

Answering exam questions on love

There are no example exam questions relating to psychological explanations of love in the textbook, but a typical question would be the following:

> Outline and evaluate **two or more** psychological explanations of love. *(24 marks)*

If you decided to limit your answer to two explanations, then you could divide your answer conveniently into four 150-word 'chunks'. The first chunk is the AO1 component of the first explanation and the second its corresponding AO2 component.

You can then repeat this for the second explanation, making this a far less daunting question to answer.

You can use two of your summaries from the last activity as your two AO1 chunks.

Evaluating explanations of love

There is nearly a full page's worth of good evaluative material on p. 54/322 of the textbook – nearly 550 words of it, in fact. The challenge you face in writing the AO2 part of your essay is twofold:

1 presenting the key points in about half that number of words

2 relating the evaluation effectively to the AO1 material you have included.

With regard to the second point, if you described Sternberg's triangle of love as part of your AO1, you could make several evaluative points, based on the bullet points in the Evaluation panel on p. 54/322:

- A limitation of Sternberg's approach is that it describes types of love, but doesn't really explain their origin.
- Sternberg's approach is top-down (theoretical); other researchers (e.g. Fehr) have taken a 'bottom-up' approach, starting from people's own experiences and beliefs.
- Other researchers still (e.g. Westbay) have tried to synthesize these two approaches.

AO2 ACTIVITY

Evaluating Hendrick and Hendrick's six styles of love

What evaluative points could you make with regard to Hendrick and Hendrick's 'six love styles' explanation? You might like to think about the following aspects.

- The nature of their approach – is it top-down or bottom-up?

- Sub-cultural differences in love styles

- Cultural differences in notions of love, romance and sexual motivation

- Other points

THE BREAKDOWN OF RELATIONSHIPS

Psychologists have tended to focus on two main aspects of the breakdown (or dissolution) of relationships,

- the *reasons* for relationships ending – what causes relationships to break down
- the actual *process* of dissolution – what happens when relationships fall apart and how those involved deal with it.

The textbook includes material about both.

Reasons for breakdown

Why do relationships break down? Some of the many factors that may contribute to relationships breaking down are listed in Table 2.3/10.3 on p. 48/316. This is followed by further explanation of some of the most important factors, including maintenance difficulties and rule violation.

Why do relationships break down?

Read the text on pp. 48–9/316–17 under the heading 'Why do relationships break down?' and summarize the main points made by the following researchers:

Researcher	*Main points of their research*
Duck (1981)	
Shaver *et al.* (1985)	
Argyle and Henderson (1984)	

Economic theories of relationships, described earlier in the topic, also provide explanations for why relationships break down.

Economic explanations for relationship breakdown

Re-read the text on pp. 45–6/313–14 of the textbook, which discuss social exchange theory and equity theory. Using a PC, write 150 words on each, describing how the theory explains why relationships break down. Because the emphasis here is on the ending of relationships, you should pick out material that relates specifically to that aspect of relationships.

For example, in describing social exchange theory, the text about the four stages of long-term relationships (shown in Table 2.2/10.2) will be much less relevant than the text about comparison levels.

The 300 words you have just written would provide the first half of an answer to Example Exam Question 3 on p. 55/323.

If you were writing an essay about the reasons why relationships end, you would need to make points of AO2 evaluation. These could include comments about:

- the relative importance of different factors

- differences between relationships in Western and non-Western cultures
- differences between the sexes regarding what they view as important factors
- other individual differences, e.g. age differences.

Evaluating reasons for relationship breakdown

In the space below, note down four points you could make when evaluating reasons for relationship breakdown, along with a summary of the relevant research. The Evaluation panel on p. 50/318 and the Expert interview on p. 51/319 will provide plenty of material for this activity. Remember that for a point to be evaluative, it should not simply be descriptive but should form part of a sustained critical commentary on the material being evaluated.

Key AO2 point	*Relevant research*
1	
2	
3	
4	

The process of breakdown

The textbook includes two models that seek to explain the process of relationship breakdown, those of Duck (1988) and Lee (1984). Both divide the process into stages or phases, but emphasize different aspects of the process. (Note: pointing out similarities and differences would gain AO2 credit in an exam answer.)

ACTIVITY

Duck's model of relationship dissolution (1988)

1 What is meant by the following terms:

(a) 'intra-psychic'

_____

(b) 'dyadic'?

_____

(Try looking these terms up in a dictionary.)

2 Summarize Duck's model of relationship breakdown in the form of a diagram, similar to Fig. 2.2/10.2 on p. 50/318. This will help you to memorize the key stages. (Draw your diagram on separate paper.)

3 What does Steve Duck say about this model in his 'Expert interview' on p. 51/319?

_____

_____

_____

_____

_____

_____

_____

_____

HINT

When answering exam questions, you can refer to any of Steve Duck's comments in the Expert interview. If you do mention them, you can cite the reference 'Duck (2004)'.

Answering exam questions on the breakdown of relationships

Example Exam Questions 3 and 4 on p. 55/323 are typical questions that could be asked about the breakdown of relationships. For Question 3, you have a lot of choice as to which theories to include. You could focus either on explanations of causes of relationship breakdown (social exchange or equity theory) or on the process of breakdown (Duck 1988 or Lee 1984). Alternatively, you could mix the two:

- For part (a) of Example Exam Question 3, you could describe one theory relating to the causes of relationship breakdown (e.g. social exchange theory) and one theory relating to the process of breakdown (e.g. Duck's 1988 model).

- For part (b), you need to evaluate the two theories you have just described in terms of research studies. For the social exchange theory, you could use Rusbult's investment model (see Key research, p. 46/314). You could evaluate Duck's model by referring to Lee's research, bringing out the similarities and differences.

ACTIVITY

Planning your answer

Plan a possible answer to Example Exam Question 4 on p. 55/323. Key questions to consider are:

1 Will you focus on theories* or on studies?

2 How many theories/studies will you focus on? The fact that the question uses the plural ('theories/studies') means you have to include at least two, but two would be enough.

3 What points of criticism/evaluation will you make?

Draw up an outline plan for your essay (similar to the one on p. 7) showing the different 'chunks' you could divide your essay into.

*Note that the specification for 2006 onwards refers to 'explanations', rather than 'theories', so exam questions from 2006 will also use the term 'explanations', rather than 'theories'.

EXAMPLE EXAM QUESTION

Look at Example Exam Question 4 on p. 55/323. Specific advice on how to answer this question can be found below it. The answer on the following page has been constructed in a very simple four-paragraph layout, with the first two paragraphs making up the AO1 component of the answer and the last two paragraphs making up the AO2 component of the answer. You do not have to construct all your answers like this, but it does make for more effective use of your time and knowledge. It also ensures that you balance both skill components in your answer. The material for this answer can be found on pp. 48–51/316–19 in the textbook.

Discuss research (explanations and/or studies) relating to the breakdown of relationships.

(24 marks)

Duck (1981) claimed that there were a number of different reasons for the breakdown of a relationship. These included conflict between the partners, boredom with the relationship, or an attractive alternative relationship. Duck suggested that the causes for relationships breaking down could be divided into two categories. These were predisposing personal factors, such as distasteful personal habits, or precipitating factors, such as exterior influences (e.g. the presence of a rival) and the nature of the relationship as it developed (e.g. the relationship was going nowhere). Other psychologists (e.g. Shaver *et al.* 1985) have focused on maintenance difficulties, particularly when living or working apart, as a primary cause of relationship breakdown. Day-to-day maintenance strategies can become more difficult and place greater strain on the relationship. Argyle and Henderson (1984) found that rule violation was important in relationship breakdown. The most critical of these rule violations were jealousy, being intolerant of other relationships and disclosing confidences.

Duck (1988) proposed a four-phase model of the termination of close relationships. In the intra-psychic phase, one partner becomes increasingly dissatisfied with the relationship. If this dissatisfaction is strong enough, it leads to the next phase. In the dyadic phase, the other partner is involved. If the difficulties aren't resolved, this leads to the social phase of the breakdown. In this phase, the break-up is made public and any social implications are negotiated. In the final phase, the grave-dressing phase, partners begin publicizing their own accounts of the breakdown, and developing their own versions of where the blame lies. Lee (1984) surveyed the break-up of pre-marital romantic relationships, and found evidence for five distinct stages. Partners go from initial dissatisfaction to the more intense stages of exposure and negotiation, where this dissatisfaction is first aired and then negotiated with the other partner. They then try to resolve the difficulties, but terminate the relationship if this attempt is unsuccessful. In some cases, usually when the relationship was less intimate, individuals go straight from the dissatisfaction stage to the termination stage.

Moghaddam *et al.* (1993) believe that Western and non-Western relationships have different concerns and features in the breakdown process. They argue that North American relationships are mostly individualistic, voluntary and temporary, whereas most non-Western relationships are collective, obligatory and permanent. Duck (2004) believes that in cultures with a strong collective group responsibility, social networks play a different kind of role in the breakdown of relationships, for example offering more relational support to help the couple work through problems. Although research has found some evidence to suggest men and women have different approaches to the breakdown of relationships, it has not found evidence for significant differences in the reasons for relationship breakdown. Argyle and Henderson's research has, however, discovered important gender differences in attitudes to rule violation in friendships: women see lack of emotional support as a critical factor in relationship breakdown, whereas men say that absence of fun is a more important reason.

Duck's and Lee's views of relationship breakdown share some similarities; they both see breakdown as going through a number of stages before termination, rather than seeing it as a single step. The main difference is one of emphasis. Lee's model emphasizes the early stages of the process, particularly the painful stages of exposure and negotiation. Duck's model, however, focuses on the beginning and end of this process, particularly on how people might react after the relationship is over. Akert's research into the impact of relationship dissolution (Akert 1992) found that the role people played in ending the relationship was the biggest factor in predicting how the break-up would affect them. Akert discovered that the partner who did not initiate the break-up was generally the most miserable, with high levels of loneliness, depression and anger in the weeks after the end of the relationship. Those who initiated the break-up found the end of the relationship less upsetting and less stressful, and had fewer negative symptoms, compared to partners who were less responsible for the break-up of the relationship.

CHECK YOUR UNDERSTANDING

When you have finished working through this topic, try the following questions in 'Check your understanding' on p. 56/324 of the textbook. Check your answers by looking at the relevant parts of the textbook, listed below.

5 textbook p. 48/316 (Table 2.3/10.3)
6 textbook p. 49/317
7 textbook p. 50/318
8 textbook pp. 52–3/320–1
9 textbook p. 53/321
10 no – see textbook p. 54/322

Most of the research in Topics 1 and 2 has a very particular focus: it was carried out in the West by White, predominantly male, heterosexual psychologists, focusing on face-to-face relationships between men and women in the Western world. Perhaps the psychologists carrying out the research considered those to be the relationships most worth studying. However, that has meant that other types of relationship have been relatively ignored or sidelined. Among these 'understudied' relationships are those between same-sex partners (gay men and lesbians) and those that take place 'in the ether', i.e. via computers or mediated through other forms of electronic device rather than in person. This topic looks at these two areas of relationships.

UNDERSTANDING THE SPECIFICATION

Here is what the AQA (A) specification says about this topic. It forms part of A2 Module 4, Section A: Social Psychology. As with many areas of the A2 specification, there is a specific requirement to cover more than one 'explanation' and more than one 'research study' in this topic area. The labels 'Western' and 'non-Western' are fairly broad, and can be taken to mean European/North American and the rest of the world. Another way of distinguishing between Western and non-Western cultures is along the individualist/collectivist continuum and this is the basis of most social psychologists research in this area. Questions may be totally focused on the Western/non-Western distinction, so it is important to be armed with both AO1 *and* AO2 material for this type of question. The term 'understudied relationships' is not a precise

Relationships

c. Cultural differences in relationships

Explanations and research studies relating to the nature of relationships in different cultures (e.g. voluntary/involuntary, permanent/impermanent types of relationships). 'Understudied' relationships such as gay and lesbian, and mediated relationships (e.g. relationships formed on the Internet and text [SMS] relationships).

academic topic, but can be interpreted as meaning any relationship that is not romantic, heterosexual or face to face. Thus, non-heterosexual relationships, relationships formed on the Internet (computer-mediated communication or CMC) and relationships based on text-messaging would all qualify as 'understudied'. Questions often ask for 'two or more' types of understudied relationship. Remember that gay and lesbian relationships are different in many ways, and can be presented as such in your answer.

TOPIC MAP

The diagram below gives you an overview of what you are about to study.

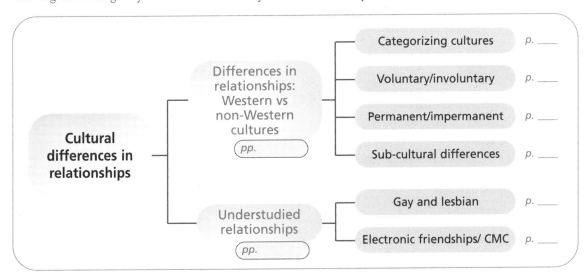

Topic map

Look through pp. 56–66/324–34 of the textbook to see where the items shown in the topic map are covered. Note down the relevant page numbers in the spaces left on the topic map.

KEEPING TRACK

Use the table below to keep track of your work on this topic and plan your revision. See p. iv of this workbook (Introduction) for guidance on filling it in.

Cultural differences in relationships		Tick if you ...		
What I need to learn	*Where is it?*	could make a basic attempt	could make a good attempt	have complete mastery of this
Differences in relationships between Western and non-Western cultures				
Explanations and research into categories of culture				
Explanations and research into voluntary and involuntary relationships				
Explanations and research into divorce (permanent and impermanent relationships)				
Explanations and research into sub-cultural differences in relationships				
Evaluation of these explanations and research studies				
Understudied relationships				
Theories and research relating to gay and lesbian relationships				
Theories and research relating to electronic friendships and computer-mediated communication (CMC)				
Evaluation of these theories and research				

DIFFERENCES IN RELATIONSHIPS BETWEEN WESTERN AND NON-WESTERN CULTURES

For this topic it is important to understand the difference between the terms 'culture' and 'sub-culture'.

Cultures and sub-cultures

Start by reading the text on p. 56/324. Then answer the following questions.

1 What is the difference between a 'culture' and a 'sub-culture'?

2 According to Moghaddam *et al.* (1993), what qualities characterize relationships:

(a) in Western cultures?

(b) in non-Western cultures?

Categorizing cultures

In this topic, there is an assumption that any differences in relationships between different cultures reflect – and can be explained by – more fundamental differences in the nature of those cultures. That assumption is not explicitly stated in the textbook, but it is worth making it clear if you are writing an essay about explanations for differences in relationships. That would then lead neatly into a discussion of differences between cultures.

In a large-scale study, Hofstede (1994) examined cultural differences between people in 50 countries. His analysis provides a very useful model for analysing differences between cultures. One of the key categories he explored was the distinction between individualism and collectivism.

ACTIVITY

Individualism/collectivism

Summarize the main points given in the text on p. 57/325 about individualism/collectivism. Note down the key features of individualist and collectivist countries, giving examples of countries that scored highly on each end of the scale (as shown in Table 2.5/10.5). In the final column, suggest ways in which this might influence the relationships of people living in those cultures.

Key features	Examples of countries	Influence on relationships
● Individualism emphasizes		
● Collectivism emphasizes		
● Individualism values autonomy; collectivism ...		
●		
●		

ACTIVITY

Other categories

Draw up similar tables to summarize the main features of the other dimensions identified by Hofstede (power-distance, masculinity/femininity, etc.). As above, suggests ways in which each factor might influence the relationships of people living in those cultures.

 ACTIVITY

Evaluating Hofstede's research

Evaluation involves both positive and negative 'criticism'. The four points in the Evaluation panel on p. 58/326 highlight possible problems with Hofstede's model. What points of *positive* evaluation could you make about his research?

As you might expect with such an ambitious study, Hofstede's work has been criticized on a number of counts, to do with the origin and nature of the research. Read the Evaluation panel on p. 58/326 to find out what those criticisms were and then do the activity on the right.

Voluntary and involuntary relationships

The distinction between voluntary and involuntary relationships mirrors the individualist/collectivist distinction. In other words, the power to choose a spouse or partner is linked to Western, individualist cultures.

Voluntary and involuntary relationships

Read the text under this heading on pp. 58–9/326–7 and then answer the following questions.

1 Worldwide, what is the most common form of marriage?

2 What observation do Rosenblatt and Anderson make about voluntary/involuntary marriages?

3 What is the 'Cupid's arrow' model of love?

4 What trend did Simpson *et al.* uncover in their research into the importance of love in Western marriages?

5 What significant points did Ghuman (1994) uncover in a study of Sikhs, Hindus and Muslims living in Britain and Canada?

The bride-price and dowry systems

One feature of arranged marriages is the payment of goods or money by the family of either bride or groom. Read the panel on p. 58/326 and then answer the following questions.

1 What is the difference between a 'bride-price' and a 'dowry'?

2 What do the bride-price and dowry systems imply about the status of women in the cultures that operate them?

3 Why would such systems be uncommon in individualist cultures?

Permanent/impermanent relationships

Impermanence is also suggested as a feature of Western, individualist relationships. This is logical, as having the power to choose a partner also implies that you have the power to reject that partner if the relationship doesn't work out as you want it to.

Permanent/impermanent relationships

Read the text under this heading and then consider the following questions:

1 Is divorce a universal phenomenon?

2 What are the most common grounds for divorce?

3 Why is there a higher divorce rate in Western, individualist cultures than in non-Western collectivist cultures?

4 What factors contribute to there being low rates of divorce in collectivist cultures?

5 How does the changing role of women in some cultures explain a higher divorce rate?

Cross-cultural variation

Several interesting pieces of research into divorce rates are described in the text, highlighting cross-cultural variations in attitudes towards divorce. Summarize the key points in the table below.

Country/culture	Key point	Researcher
● Poland	Low divorce rates. Women usually initiate divorce.	Goodwin (1999)
●		
●		
●		

Answering exam questions on cultural differences in relationships

In answering questions on cultural differences in relationships, you have to look carefully at the wording of the question. If we take Example Exam Question 1 on p. 67/335, you will see that both 'explanations' and 'differences' are in the plural. That means you need to write about at least two differences in relationships (e.g. individualist/collectivist and permanent/impermanent) and offer more than one explanation for these differences.

The textbook has mentioned several possible explanations for differences in relationships, including:

- the *influence of culture* on relationships – as discussed in the textbook, Western, individualistic cultures seem to encourage different sorts of relationship from non-Western, collectivist cultures

- the *changing role of women* – linked to social change and the movement (especially in Western cultures) towards recognition of women's equality and women's rights

- *economic factors* – see, for example, Goodwin's analysis on p. 57/325, first column

- other factors, such as *religion* or even *climate* – again, see Goodwin's analysis.

ACTIVITY

Outlining explanations for cultural differences

On your PC, write 300 words outlining two or more explanations of cultural differences in relationships between Western and non-Western cultures. Use any of the information in the topic so far.

When it comes to the AO2 or evaluation part of this question, you could, for example:

- make comments about the validity or accuracy of cultural categories used by psychologists (as outlined in the Evaluation panel on p. 58/326)

- use research studies to evaluate the explanations you described in the first half of your essay, examining whether research supports or challenges the explanation (plenty of research studies are described throughout pp. 56–60/324–8).

Evaluating explanations for cultural differences

On your PC, write a further 300 words evaluating the explanations of cultural differences in relationships that you described for the last activity.

Adding these two answers together will give you a complete answer to Example Exam Question 1 on p. 67/335.

UNDERSTUDIED RELATIONSHIPS

The second section of this topic focuses on types of relationships that psychologists have hitherto not paid much attention to. These include gay and lesbian relationships, and computer-mediated or 'electronic' friendships, such as those formed on the Internet.

Gay and lesbian relationships

In examining gay and lesbian relationships, particular questions arise:

1 In their relationships, to what extent do gay men and lesbians share experiences in common with heterosexuals?

2 What particular difficulties do gay men and lesbians face in their relationships?

3 How do they try to deal with or overcome those difficulties?

The text on pp. 60–2/328–30 considers these questions. It looks in turn at forming relationships, maintaining relationships and the particular difficulties gay men and lesbians have to face in their relationships.

Forming and maintaining gay and lesbian relationships

Most of the research into forming and maintaining relationships discussed in Topics 1 and 2 was based exclusively on heterosexual men and women. We don't, therefore, know how well it describes the needs and experiences of gay men and lesbians. We might assume that homosexuals' experience of interpersonal attraction is the same as, or similar, to that of heterosexuals, but without the research to back it up, we cannot be sure. Hence the relevance of the term 'understudied'.

Personal advertisements can be a revealing source of information about what different people seek from a potential mate or partner. What does research tell us about the qualities sought by gay men in comparison to straight men? Or lesbians in comparison to straight women? Try the activity at the top of the next page.

What people seek in a partner

Read p. 42/310 (second column) and then p. 61/329 (second paragraph). Complete the table below, summarizing the similarities and differences between what men and women of different orientations seek in a partner.

	Similarities between gay and straight	Differences between gay and straight
Men	●	●
	●	●
Women	●	●
	●	●

Difficulties faced by gay men and lesbians in relationships

Much of the text on pp. 60–2/328–30 focuses on the particular difficulties faced by gay men and lesbians in their relationships as a result of the continuing prejudice and discrimination they encounter, even in the 'liberal' West. Summarize these difficulties in a table, as below. Use the central column to describe possible strategies for overcoming these difficulties. In the final column, note down the name of any relevant researcher.

Difficulty	Strategies for overcoming difficulties	Relevant research
e.g. recognizing each other	gay-specific venues, e.g. cafés, bars	Shaw (1997)

Answering exam questions on gay and lesbian relationships

The textbook includes two questions on understudied relationships (see p. 67/335, Example Exam Questions 4 and 5). Read through these and the guidance notes given underneath each.

For both of these questions, you could use research studies as the basis for your answer. For AO1, you would need to describe the studies and their findings. For the AO2 part, you would need to focus your evaluation on the nature of the research and issues arising from it. The 'Commentary' panel on p. 62/330 contains many useful points which you could give a research-based focus:

● *Heterosexual bias* – Researchers use assumptions more appropriate to heterosexual relationships (consider, for example, the emphasis on reproduction in sociobiological theory of relationships – see p. 39/307).

● *Tendency to overstate differences* – Researchers may unwittingly display bias in looking for and overstating differences between heterosexuals and homosexuals, where there is actually far greater similarity than difference (see the bullet point 'Shared social worlds' on p. 62/330).

● *Need for more research* – Some initial research has identified areas where there are interesting

differences between heterosexuals and homosexuals that merit further research (see the bullet point 'After the relationship is over').

● *Western bias* – All the research discussed is based in Western societies, where more liberal attitudes have made it possible for gay relationships to flourish. Such research would not actually be possible in many countries in the world, where homosexuality is still illegal and in many cases punishable by death.

Outline essay plan – gay and lesbian relationships

Imagine you are about to answer Question 5 on p. 67/335. You decide to use gay and lesbian relationships as one half of your answer (the other half will be on 'electronic' friendships). This means writing about 150 words of AO1 as half your answer to part (a) and 150 words of AO2 as half your answer to part (b).

Draw up an outline of your answer, making a note of the key points and key research you will mention, together with the points of evaluation you will make.

ELECTRONIC FRIENDSHIPS AND COMPUTER-MEDIATED COMMUNICATION (CMC)

Electronic friendships and computer-mediated communication (CMC) are relatively new areas of research, because the technology that enables them to take place is itself relatively new. However, there is already plenty of fascinating research into these forms of communication, considered on pp. 62–6/330–4 of the textbook. Your challenge, when it comes to exam questions, is knowing how to organize the information.

For the AO1 (description) part of questions, one useful way of organizing the information is by outlining:

- the different forms that electronic friendships and CMC take
- the nature and characteristics of CMC relationships
- research into different aspects of electronic friendships and CMC.

ACTIVITY

Nature of computer-mediated communication (CMC)

Make notes on the textbook under the following headings:

1 The different forms of computer-mediated communication (CMC)
2 The main characteristics of CMC relationships.

ACTIVITY

Research into electronic friendships and CMC

Read the text on pp. 62–6/330–4. Draw up a table using the format shown below, by noting down the key points of the research studies listed.

Aspect of CMC	Researcher	Key points
● Lack of physicality	Van Gelder (1985)	● Individual has high level of control over what they reveal about themselves
● Issues of trust		

Evaluating electronic friendships and CMC

There are several effective ways of writing AO2 evaluation and the textbook is rich in material that you could draw upon. You could, for example:

- point out the similarities or parallels between CMC and face-to-face communication (see, for example, the text on gay men and CMC on pp. 64–5/332–3)
- highlight differences between these different forms of communication (see, for example, the Commentary panel on p. 64/332)
- explore the advantages of electronic friendships and CMC (see, for example, the text on initiating friendships on p. 64/332 and the Evaluation panel on p. 65/333)
- highlight problems that arise in electronic friendships and CMC (see Evaluation panel on p. 65/333, as well as the panels 'Joan' on p. 63/331 and 'Abuse on the Internet' on p. 66/334).

ACTIVITY

Outline essay plan – electronic friendships and CMC

Returning to Example Exam Question 5 on p. 67/335, now plan the second half of your answer (the first half was about gay and lesbian relationships). You need to write another 150 words of AO1 (for part (a)) relating to research into electronic friendships/CMC and another 150 words of AO2 (for part (b)).

Draw up an outline of your answer, making a note of the key points and key research you will mention, together with the points of evaluation you will make.

EXAMPLE EXAM QUESTIONS

In your work on this unit, you have already written a complete answer to Example Exam Question 1 on p. 67/335 and planned your answer to Question 5. Here is another question for you to try, along with some ideas about how to go about answering it.

ACTIVITY

One for you to try ...

(a) Outline two theories relating to the formation of relationships. **(12 marks)**

(b) To what extent have research studies demonstrated differences in relationships between Western and non-Western cultures. **(12 marks)**

Read the advice on answering this question on p. 67/335 of the textbook. In order to answer the first part of this question you will need to draw on material from Topic 1 of this workbook. This first part of the question is worth 12 marks, so should occupy approximately half of your answer. As the question asks for an outline of two theories relating to the formation of relationships, you should aim to spend more or less the same amount of time on each, although it is acceptable to have one theory slightly more detailed than the other. Practising your précis skills will pay off in questions such as this, leaving the first part of your answer as follows:

● Précis of theory 1 (approximately 150 words)

● Précis of theory 2 (approximately 150 words).

Part (b) of the question requires a quite different approach. This is the AO2 component of this question, and so it is essential that you do more than just describe differences between Western and non-Western relationships. Material on pp. 56–60/324–8 of the textbook can be used for your answer to part (b), but you must focus more on the evaluative aspect of this material. For example, you might briefly introduce a claim from the AO1 material on these pages, and then comment on this claim using the appropriate AO2 material. Remember, you will need to be highly selective when choosing material for this second part of the question. Therefore, your last two paragraphs (each of approximately 150 words) might start some thing like this.

Moghaddam et al. (1993) draw a distinction between social relationships in Western cultures, which tend to be individualistic, voluntary and temporary, and those in non-Western cultures, which tend to be collective, obligatory and permanent. This would suggest, therefore, that much of what we know about relationships is not relevant to non-Western cultures. Schwartz (1997), however, argued that these distinctions are not so clear cut and that there are many variations within, as well as between, cultures ... (etc.)

Almost all cultures now permit some form of divorce, although there is greater stigma attached to divorce in cultures with traditional arranged marriages. However, this shift to more impermanent relationships in the West is relatively recent, coinciding with increasing urbanization and mobility ... (etc.)

CHECK YOUR UNDERSTANDING

When you have finished working through this topic, try the questions in 'Check your understanding' on p. 66/334 of the textbook. Check your answers by looking at the relevant parts of the textbook or this workbook, listed below.

1 textbook p. 57/325

2 textbook pp. 57–9/325–7

3 textbook p. 60/328

4 textbook pp. 60–2/328–30

5 textbook p. 61/329

6 workbook p. 20 (activity)

7 textbook pp. 63–4/331–2

8 textbook p. 64/332 (Commentary panel)

9 textbook p. 65/333 (Evaluation panel)

10 textbook p. 65/333 (Evaluation panel)

PRO- & ANTI-SOCIAL
Behaviour

PREVIEW

There are three topics in this unit. You should read them alongside the following pages in the Collins *Psychology for A2-level*/*Psychology* textbook:

Topic	*Psychology for A2*	*Psychology*
1 Nature and causes of aggression	pp. 72–81	pp. 340–49
2 Altruism and bystander behaviour	pp. 81–94	pp. 349–62
3 Media influences on pro- and anti-social behaviour	pp. 95–104	pp. 363–72

INTRODUCTION

Social Psychology is one of five sections in Module 4 (AQA Specification A), as the diagram below shows. This section is further divided into three sub-sections – 'Pro- and anti-social behaviour' is the second of these.

Read the Preview and Introduction on p. 70/338 of the textbook now. This will give you an overview of what's in the unit.

Where this unit fits in to the A-level qualification

Section A:
Social Psychology

Section B:
Physiological Psychology

Module 4

Section C:
Cognitive Psychology

Section D:
Developmental Psychology

Section E:
Comparative Psychology

- SOCIAL COGNITION
- RELATIONSHIPS
- **PRO- AND ANTI-SOCIAL BEHAVIOUR**

a Nature and causes of aggression

b Altruism and bystander behaviour

c Media influences on pro- and anti-social behaviour

In the Module 4 exam, there will be a total of 15 questions, three relating to each Section (i.e. one per sub-section). You have to answer **three** questions, from at least **two** sections.

The effects of anti-social behaviour are all too obvious – the top photo on p. **71/339** shows one common example of anti-social, aggressive behaviour. But what makes behaviour anti-social? And what causes it? Explanations are many and varied. Some would argue that humans are programmed biologically to be aggressive in certain situations. This topic looks at attempts to explain aggressive behaviour from a social point of view, i.e. looking for the root causes in the way that human beings relate to each other. It also considers the effects of environmental stressors, such as temperature and crowding, and their link to aggressive behaviour.

UNDERSTANDING THE SPECIFICATION

Here is what the AQA (A) specification says about this topic. It forms part of A2 Module 4, Section A: Social Psychology.

The words 'social psychological' at the beginning of this specification entry should exclude 'biological' explanations of aggression, but could include 'psychological' theories such as frustration-aggression theory and excitation-transfer theory, as well as the social psychological theories given as examples. The only requirement is that you cover at least two of these theories, and are able to offer a complete 600-word (approx) discussion of one of your chosen theories, as well as a 300-word each (approx) version of two.

Environmental stressors include the three examples given. Two examples are covered fully in the textbook

Pro- and anti-social behaviour

a. Nature and causes of aggression

Social psychological theories of aggression (e.g. social learning theory, deindividuation, relative deprivation). Research into the effects of environmental stressors (e.g. heat, noise, crowding) on aggressive behaviour.

(heat and crowding) and you should have plenty to write about them, so it is not particularly effective trying to fit material from another topic (e.g. media effects) into an answer to a question on this topic.

Questions often ask you to discuss 'research (theories and/or explanations)...', which gives you the opportunity to write about the effects of environmental stressors from either a theoretical and/or a research study context.

TOPIC MAP

The diagram below gives you a visual 'map' of the content of this topic.

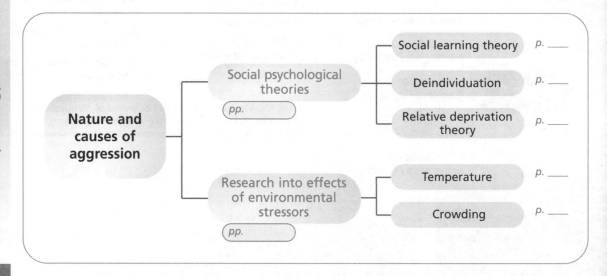

Nature and causes of aggression

Social psychological theories
pp.
- Social learning theory   *p.* ___
- Deindividuation   *p.* ___
- Relative deprivation theory   *p.* ___

Research into effects of environmental stressors
pp.
- Temperature   *p.* ___
- Crowding   *p.* ___

Topic map

Look through pp. 70–103/338–71 of the textbook to see where the items shown in the topic map are covered. Note down the relevant page numbers in the spaces left on the topic map.

KEEPING TRACK

Use the table below to keep track of your work on this topic and plan your revision. See p. iv of this workbook (Introduction) for guidance on filling it in.

Nature and causes of aggression		Tick if you ...		
What I need to learn	*Where is it?*	*could make a basic attempt*	*could make a good attempt*	*have complete mastery of this*
Social psychological theories of aggression				
Description of social learning theory				
Evaluation of social learning theory				
Description of deindividuation				
Evaluation of deindividuation				
Description of relative deprivation theory				
Evaluation of relative deprivation theory				
Effects of environmental stressors on aggressive behaviour				
Description of the relationship between temperature and aggression				
Evaluation of the relationship between temperature and aggression				
Description of the relationship between crowding and aggression				
Evaluation of the relationship between crowding and aggression				

SOCIAL PSYCHOLOGICAL THEORIES OF AGGRESSION

Aggressive behaviour takes many forms and the topic begins, on p. 72/340 of the textbook, with three definitions of aggressive behaviour. We are mainly concerned with the first type, succinctly described by Penrod (1983). Another similar definition is given by Aronson (1999): 'intentional behaviours aimed at causing either physical or psychological pain'.

Social learning theory

Read through the description of social learning theory on pp. 72–3/340–1 and then do the following activities.

ACTIVITY

Social learning theory

1   What is the basic proposition of the social learning theory explanation of aggression?

2   In what two ways do humans learn aggression?

3   What is meant by 'reinforcement'?

4   What, according to Huesmann (1988) is the link between media violence and aggressive behaviour?

Rewards and inhibitions

The textbook mentions several factors that influence whether or not people are likely to show aggressive behaviour. Make a list of factors that reward – and hence encourage – aggressive behaviour and, on the right, note down factors that make it less likely that we would behave aggressively.

We are more likely to behave aggressively if:	*We are less likely to behave aggressively if:*
●	●
●	●
●	●

Research related to social learning theory

Observational studies have been used extensively by researchers investigating aggression. Bandura's Bobo doll studies, described in the Key research panel on p. 73/341, helped him and his team develop his social learning theory.

Using research studies

Questions in this part of the 2006 AQA specification will be phrased in terms of social psychological *theories*; they will not ask you specifically about *research studies*. However, you can use the findings of research studies to illustrate your description of theories (for AO1) and can cite limitations in the research in your AO2 evaluation of the theories (see 'Methodological problems' in the Evaluation panel on p. 74/342).

Bandura's Bobo doll studies

Briefly explain why Bandura's Bobo doll studies support the notion of reinforcement.

_____
_____
_____
_____
_____
_____
_____
_____
_____
_____
_____
_____
_____
_____

Theories in précis

Read the panel 'Theories in précis' on p. 77/345 of the textbook, which offers excellent advice on tackling exam questions on social learning theory.

Following the bullet points in the right-hand column, write 150 words of description and 150 words of evaluation of the social learning theory of aggression.

When it comes to writing your AO2, the Evaluation panel on p. 74/342 contains about 350 words. As you have less than half that number to play with, take care to pick out only the most pertinent points.

The 300 words you write altogether would form half of an answer to Example Exam Question 2 on p. 81/349.

Deindividuation

The second social psychological theory of aggression explains it in terms of people losing their sense of 'individuality' and being freed from social norms that normally discourage 'anti-social behaviour'. The following activities explore this idea.

Individual and deindividuated behaviour

Read the text from the heading 'Deindividuation' to the end of the first paragraph on p. 75/343. Then answer the following questions:

1 What, according to Zimbardo, are the characteristics of:

(a) individual behaviour?

(b) deindividuated behaviour?

2 Describe three factors that might explain why being in a crowd might diminish awareness of individuality.

-
-
-

3 What features of Zimbardo's prison experiment could be said to have reduced individuality?

Milgram's obedience studies and deindividuation

In Stanley Milgram's studies into obedience, participants ('teachers') in the study were ordered to give supposed electric shocks to a 'learner' (Milgram's accomplice). Obedience levels varied depending on various factors. Look at the table on the right.

Do Milgram's findings support the notion that deindividuation can lead to anti-social or aggressive behaviour? Discuss this question with other students studying this unit.

Variation	Obedience rate
>> Original experiment	65%
>> Teacher and learner in the same room	40%
>> Teacher had to force learner's hand on to plate to receive shock	30%
>> Teacher given support from two other 'teachers' (confederates) who refuse	10%
>> Experimenter left the room and instructed the teacher by telephone from another room	20.5%
>> Teacher paired with an assistant (confederate) who threw the switches	92.5%

The 'baiting crowd'

Read the top right-hand paragraph on p. 75/343, and then answer the following questions.

1 What is a 'baiting crowd'?

2 What three features, according to Mann, are likely to lead to a baiting crowd?

-
-
-

A précis of deindividuation

Again following the guidance in the panel 'Theories in précis' on p. 77/345 of the textbook, write 150 words of description and 150 words of evaluation of the deindividuation theory of aggression. The Commentary panel on p. 75/343 contains nearly 470 words of evaluation, so you really have to be strict in reducing the number to 150 words.

Relative deprivation theory

The third social psychological theory of aggression focuses on conflict resulting from people's experiences of frustration, injustice or deprivation. Read the text on pp. 75–6/343–4 and then do the following activities.

Relative deprivation theory

1 What, according to this theory, is the cause of conflict and aggression?

_____

_____

2 Why is relative deprivation a subjective idea, rather than one that is objectively measurable?

_____

_____

3 Give an example from recent British history of aggression resulting from unequal social conditions. (Think about how you would explain this event in terms of relative deprivation theory.)

_____

_____

4 Runciman differentiates between egoistic and fraternalistic relative deprivation. Define these, giving an example, and describe how each might result in aggressive behaviour.

Egoistic relative deprivation =

_____

Example:

Effect on behaviour:

_____

Fraternalistic relative deprivation =

_____

Example:

Effect on behaviour

_____

A précis of relative deprivation theory

Again following the guidance in the panel 'Theories in précis' on p. 77/345 of the textbook, write 150 words of description and 150 words of evaluation of the relative deprivation theory of aggression.

You have now précis-ed all three social psychological theories described in the textbook. Putting two of them together would provide a complete answer to Example Exam Question 2 on p. 81/349.

THE EFFECTS OF ENVIRONMENTAL STRESSORS ON AGGRESSIVE BEHAVIOUR

Start your work on this part of the topic by trying the activity on p. 77/345 of the workbook. As you do this, you will think about three aspects of our environment – temperature, noise and crowds – and the stress they can cause This topic looks in detail at two of these aspects: temperature and crowds.

Temperature

The AQA specification mentions the word 'research', so to answer questions in this area, you need to focus on the findings of studies into the relationship between temperature and aggression. The following activity will help you with this.

Summarizing research studies

Read the text about temperature and aggression on pp. 77–8/345–6 including the Commentary panel. Draw up a table to summarize the findings of the research described there. Use the format shown below. In the final column, add any AO2 (evaluative) points, e.g. refer to research mentioned in the Commentary panel at the bottom of p. 78/346.

Researcher	Key points	Evaluative point
e.g. Anderson (1989)	● Hotter regions have more aggression	● see Moghaddam's warning
	● Hotter years/seasons/day also have more aggression	– climate not the only factor in explaining differences in rates of violent crime

Crowding

Crowding, too, can result in anti-social or aggressive behaviour. Stokols (1976) links the negative effects of crowding to a loss of control, but other researchers have investigated other aspects, such as crowding in nightclubs, whether there are gender differences and different types of crowding.

ACTIVITY

Crowding

Read through the text relating to 'crowding' on p. 79/347 and then answer the following questions.

1 How does crowding produce a state of psychological discomfort?

2 In what ways do people react to this discomfort? Cite any relevant research studies.

3 What is the difference between 'high social density' and 'high spatial density'?

Which produces negative effects more consistently?

4 What three ways of explaining the effects of crowding did Stokols (1976) suggest?

●

●

●

ACTIVITY

Crowding and gender

Several researchers have noted differences between the genders in how they respond to crowding. Comparing the responses of males and females is one way of providing AO2 evaluation for some exam questions. On separate paper, note down the key points of comparison covered in the textbook (p. 79/347), together with the names of the relevant researchers. You should be able to locate at least four relevant points.

ACTIVITY

Answering exam questions on environmental aggressors

Having completed the activity above, you should now be able to tackle questions on the anti-social effects of environmental stressors. One such question is Example Exam Question 5 on p. 81/349. Read the guidance notes given underneath the question and then plan your response.

If you limit your answer to two environmental stressors (only two are covered in the textbook, but you could research other stressors, such as noise, on the Internet), then your response will be divided into four 150-word chunks, as shown below.

	AO1 (description)		AO2 (commentary)	
Theory 1: temperature	150 words	7.5 minutes	150 words	7.5 minutes
Theory 2: crowding	150 words	7.5 minutes	150 words	7.5 minutes

Using your PC, draw up a list of the key points (and research studies) you will include for each 'chunk'.

EXAMPLE EXAM QUESTIONS

In your work on this unit, you have already written a complete answer to Example Exam Question 2 on p. 81/349 and planned a complete response to Question 5. Here is another question for you to try, along with some ideas on how to go about answering it.

ACTIVITY

One for you to try ...

Describe and evaluate one social psychological theory of aggression.

(24 marks)

Questions that focus on just one theory are relatively rare, but can appear, so it is best to be prepared for them. The most common response to this question is to focus on social learning theory, but it is easy to come unstuck if you have not carefully planned your response. Many students spend more time describing studies related to the social learning theory of aggression than they do describing the assumptions of the theory itself. The Bobo doll studies are certainly important in the development of this theory, but should not be used in lieu of a description of the theory itself.

In the textbook you are advised to plan your response along the by now familiar 4 × 150-word paragraph plan. Assuming that you have chosen social learning theory (although deindividuation and relative deprivation theory would be just as appropriate), the plan for your answer might look a little like this:

- the nature of social learning theory as an explanation of the development of aggressive behaviour – for example, learning by direct experience, learning by vicarious experience, reinforcement of aggressive behaviour

- media violence and aggressive behaviour – for example, the development of aggressive 'scripts' and the relationship between the observation of aggressive behaviour and subsequent aggressive behaviour

- a very brief outline of the main findings of the Bobo doll studies indicating that there is an important distinction to be drawn between learning and performance in these studies. Methodological problems with the Bobo doll studies

- further evaluation of the social learning theory – including explanation of inconsistencies in aggressive behaviour and commentary on social learning or biology as the primary causal agent.

HINT

2006 AQA Specification

For the 2006 specification, Example Exam Questions 3(b) and 4 will no longer be phrased in the way they are in the textbook. Research studies cannot be specified in an exam question on social psychological theories of aggression, although you can still use them as part of your evaluation.

CHECK YOUR UNDERSTANDING

When you have finished working through this topic, try the questions in 'Check your understanding' on p. 80/348 of the textbook. Check your answers by looking at the relevant parts of the textbook or this workbook, listed below.

1 textbook p. 70–1/338–9
2 textbook p. 72/340
3 textbook p. 72/340
4 workbook p. 27
5 workbook p. 27

6 textbook p. 76/344
7 textbook p. 76/344
8 textbook pp. 77–8/345–6
9 textbook p. 79/347; workbook p. 29

Pro-social behaviour is any act that helps or benefits others. This topic investigates two types of pro-social behaviour: altruism, where people act to help others without considering their own needs, and bystander behaviour, the way people respond to emergency situations they find themselves witnessing. It seems that, in such situations, some people are more likely to help than others. This topic will help you to discover why. The final section of this topic looks at whether people display helping behaviour differently according to their culture (e.g. collectivist–individualist) and whether the same is true of sub-groups within the same culture (e.g. men–women, urban–rural communities).

UNDERSTANDING THE SPECIFICATION

Here is what the AQA (A) specification says about this topic. It forms part of A2 Module 4, Section A: Social Psychology. Although there is a difference between human altruism and bystander behaviour, this distinction is quite a fine one, and many textbooks do not treat these as separate areas. This is reflected in the specification entry 'human altruism/bystander behaviour', which means that the explanations and research studies can apply to human altruism and/or bystander behaviour. The first explanation given as an example (empathy altruism) is an explanation of altruism, whereas the second (Latané and Darley's decision model) is an explanation of bystander behaviour. The only requirement is that you study two or more explanations in total, and two or more research studies. It is also a good idea to study research studies that support or challenge these explanations. This gives you the opportunity to use

> ### Pro- and anti-social behaviour
>
> **b. Altruism and bystander behaviour**
>
> Explanations (e.g. empathy-altruism, Latané and Darley's decision model) and research studies relating to human altruism/bystander behaviour. Cultural differences in pro-social behaviour.

these research studies as part of your evaluation of your chosen explanations. You must, however, be able to offer AO1 *and* AO2 content for *both* explanations *and* research studies. The same goes for the final part of this topic – cultural differences in pro-social behaviour. You may be asked to comment on cultural differences in pro-social behaviour as the AO2 component of a question, but you may also be asked to 'discuss' cultural differences, in which case you would have to provide both AO1 and AO2 material relevant to that topic.

TOPIC MAP

The diagram below gives you an overview of what you are about to study.

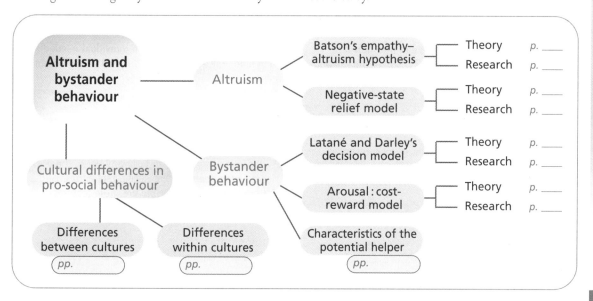

Topic map

Look through pp. 81–93/349–61 of the textbook to see where the items shown in the topic map are covered. Note down the relevant page numbers in the spaces left on the topic map.

KEEPING TRACK

Use the table below to keep track of your work on this topic and plan your revision. See p. iv of this workbook (Introduction) for guidance on filling it in.

Altruism and bystander behaviour		Tick if you ...		
What I need to learn	*Where is it?*	*could make a basic attempt*	*could make a good attempt*	*have complete mastery of this*
Altruism				
Description of Batson's empathy–altruism hypothesis				
Description of research studies relating to this hypothesis				
Evaluation of this hypothesis and relevant research				
Description of the negative-state relief model				
Description of research studies relating to this model				
Evaluation of this model and relevant research				
The influence of others (bystander behaviour)				
Description of Latané and Darley's decision model				
Description of research studies relating to this model				
Evaluation of this model and relevant research				
Description of the arousal : cost–reward model				
Description of research studies relating to this model				
Evaluation of this model and relevant research				
Cultural differences in pro-social behaviour				
Description of differences between cultures				
Description of differences within cultures				
Evaluation of cultural differences				

ALTRUISM

To start your work on this topic, read question 3 in 'Getting you thinking ...' on p. 71/339 of the textbook. Then read the case study of Kitty Genovese on p. 81/349. In both situations, an individual needed life-saving help, but the two situations had very different outcomes.

Understanding altruism

1 Why did the two situations (involving Lenny Skutnik and Kitty Genovese) have such different outcomes? What do you think were the key factors or differences?

Now read on up to and including Fig. 3.3/11.3 on p. 82/350.

2 According to Walster and Piliavin (1972), there are certain features that distinguish 'altruism' from mere 'helping'. What are these features?

Understanding altruism continued

3 Why might it be hard to distinguish an act of altruism from an act of egoism?

_____

_____

_____

4 As outlined by Batson, what is the key difference between 'empathic concern' and 'personal distress'?

_____

_____

_____

5 Study Fig. 3.3/11.3. Think of at least two situations where you have responded (a) with empathic concern and (b) with personal distress. What were the situations and what were the crucial differences between them?

(a) Situation where you felt empathic concern:

_____

_____

(b) Situation where you felt personal distress:

_____

_____

(c) Difference between situations:

_____

Research studies relating to the empathy–altruism hypothesis

In exam questions on altruism, you may be asked explicitly to discuss research studies, as the specification includes the word 'studies' – look, for instance, at Example Exam Question 3 on p. 94/362. Batson et al.'s (1981) research into the 'empathy condition' would be an obvious study to choose (see Key research panel on p. 83/351).

One good way of organizing your answer is to use the 'APFCC' method (Aims–Procedures–Findings–Conclusions–Criticisms), which you should be familiar with from AS-level psychology.

Batson et al.'s (1981) research into altruism

In the table below, write a summary of Batson and colleagues' research, using trigger phrases, mnemonics or whatever will help you to memorize the important features. Under 'Findings', note down key figures contained in Fig. 3.4/11.4 on p. 83/351. Under 'Criticisms', use the two columns to list separately those arguments that support Batson's hypothesis and those that present challenges to it.

KEY STUDY textbook p. 83/351

Researchers	Batson et al. (1981)	Findings
Title		
Aims		
Procedures		Conclusions

Criticisms – Support for the model	Criticisms – Challenges to the model

ACTIVITY

Other research into empathy and altruism

Further research studies are discussed on pp. 82–4/350–2 (including in the Commentary panel on pp. 83–4/351–2). These give further insight into whether people do act out of truly altruistic motives or not. Draw up a table, using the format shown below, to summarize the key points. Use the final column to indicate whether the research study supports Batson's empathy-altruism model or challenges it.

Researcher	Key features/findings	Conclusions	For/against Batson's model?
• e.g. Fultz et al. (1986)	High-empathy condition = ... Low-empathy condition = ...	When empathy aroused ... When no empathy ...	

The negative-state relief model

This model, developed by Cialdini *et al.* (1987), focuses on the egoistic motives we may have for helping people.

ACTIVITY

The negative-state relief model

Think back to the situations you described in the activity on p. 33. Feed these two situations into the diagram in Fig. 3.5/11.5. How well do they fit?

Does the negative-state relief model offer a more convincing explanation of your behaviour in the situations?

Two important research studies that provide support for the negative-state relief model are described in the textbook at the top of p. 85/353.

ACTIVITY

Research studies into the negative-state relief model

Write summaries of the two studies by Cialdini *et al.* (1987) and Manucia *et al.* (1984). Again, use the APFCC model to organize the information, i.e. summarizing Aims, Procedures, Findings, Conclusions and Criticisms. Use trigger phrases, mnemonics or whatever will help you to memorize the important features. Follow the format shown on p. 33, but write your summary directly into a PC word-processing program.

Under 'Criticisms', use the two columns to separate positive points and negative points. Here, you could refer to any of the points made in the Commentary panel (pp. 85–6/353–4).

ACTIVITY

Explanations of altruism

You have looked in some detail at two explanations of altruism. The activities above should have given you enough information to tackle questions such as Example Exam Question 1 on p. 94/362. Read the guidance notes given underneath the question and then plan your response. As your answer should be based on two explanations, it could be divided into four 150-word chunks:

	AO1 (description)		AO2 (commentary)	
Theory 1: empathy–altruism	150 words	7.5 minutes	150 words	7.5 minutes
Theory 2: negative-state relief model	150 words	7.5 minutes	150 words	7.5 minutes

For the AO2 part of your answer, a good strategy would be to consider research studies that either support or challenge the theory. There is plenty of good material in the textbook, both in the summaries of research studies and the Commentary panels. For AO2, however, don't just describe research studies (that would be AO1), but use their findings/conclusions to make evaluative points about the model.

Using your PC, draw up a list of the key points (and research studies) you will include for each 'chunk'.

THE INFLUENCE OF OTHERS (BYSTANDER EFFECTS)

The most disturbing feature of the murder of Kitty Genovese is the fact that so many people witnessed her struggle, but no one intervened. Psychologists have sought to explain the inhibiting effect that other people's presence can have on our behaviour. Foremost among these researchers are Latané and Darley.

Latané and Darley's cognitive model

Read the textbook from the main heading on p. 86/354 to the end of p. 87/355 and complete the following activity.

ACTIVITY

Latané and Darley's cognitive model

1 Explain what is meant by 'diffusion of responsibility':

_____

_____

2 Explain the basis of 'pluralistic ignorance':

_____

_____

_____

_____

3 Think of a mnemonic or other technique to help you remember Latané and Darley's five-stage decision model. For example, you could create an acronym based on key words from each stage, e.g. NIAKI = Notice ... Interpret ... Write down your mnemonic here:

_____

_____

_____

_____

4 Why might someone reach Stage 5 of the decision model, but still decide not to help?

_____

_____

_____

_____

You may be asked in the exam to describe one or more research studies relating to bystander behaviour (as 'studies' are mentioned in the specification). Latané and Darley's laboratory research is an obvious choice here – try the next activity.

ACTIVITY

Latané and Darley's research studies

Write a summary of Latané and Darley's research studies into bystander behaviour. Again, use the APFCC model to organize the information, using trigger phrases, mnemonics or whatever will help you to memorize the important features. Follow the format shown on p. 33, but write your summary directly into a PC word-processing program. Under 'Findings', note down key figures contained in Table 3.1/11.1 on p. 87/355.

ACTIVITY

Other research into Latané and Darley's cognitive model

The Commentary panel on p. 87/355 includes several other pieces of research that have given insight into the thought processes of bystanders considering whether to help. Draw up a table to summarize the key points. List each researcher and note down their key findings and conclusions. In a final column, indicate whether the research supports the cognitive model of Latané and Darley or challenges it.

The arousal : cost–reward model

Piliavin *et al.* (1981) developed a model of bystander behaviour that included a strong physiological element in addition to cognitive, or thought, processes. Read through the text on p. 88/356 up to the heading 'Research studies ...'. Then do the next activity.

ACTIVITY

Summary of the arousal : cost–reward model

It's often easier to remember things if we can picture them as a diagram. The diagram on the next page illustrates the main stages in Piliavin *et al.*'s arousal : cost–reward model. Complete the diagram by filling in the boxes with the key points described on p. 88/356.

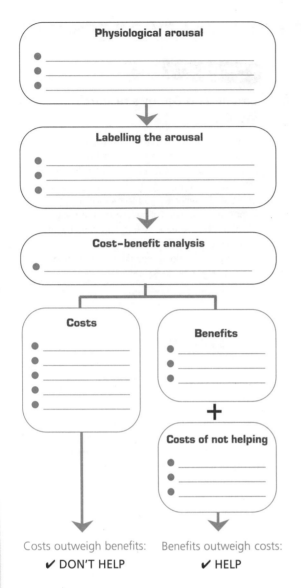

Physiological arousal
- _____
- _____
- _____

↓

Labelling the arousal
- _____
- _____
- _____

↓

Cost–benefit analysis
- _____

Costs
- _____
- _____
- _____
- _____
- _____

+

Benefits
- _____
- _____
- _____

Costs of not helping
- _____
- _____
- _____

Costs outweigh benefits:
✔ DON'T HELP

Benefits outweigh costs:
✔ HELP

In the exam, you may be asked to describe **one or more** research studies relating to bystander behaviour. Piliavin and colleagues' 'Subway Samaritan' study is a classic one that helped them develop their arousal : cost–reward model.

ACTIVITY

The 'Subway Samaritan' study

Write a summary of Piliavin and colleagues' research into bystander behaviour. Again, use the APFCC model to organize the information. Follow the format shown on p. 33, but write your summary directly into a PC. Include the findings of Piliavin and colleagues' later research into the characteristics of the person in need (see p. 89/357). Under 'Criticisms', include relevant points from the Commentary panel on pp. 89–90/357–8.

Other researchers have built on Piliavin and colleagues' research and investigated aspects of helping behaviour, especially those factors that might make a potential helper more or less likely to help.

ACTIVITY

Characteristics of the potential helper

Read the text under the heading 'Characteristics of the potential helper' on p. 89/357. Summarize the key points, highlighting what factors are involved, whether they promote or inhibit helping and what research demonstrated this.

CULTURAL DIFFERENCES IN PRO-SOCIAL BEHAVIOUR

Differences between cultures

Helping is a social behaviour. Since there are differences in types of society (e.g. individualist–collectivist), that would imply that people from those societies should display differences in helping behaviour. Research has indeed highlighted differences.

The Key research on p. 91/359 gives further insights into differences between individualist and collectivist cultures, although the results are not as clear cut as the researchers predicted.

ACTIVITY

Individualism and collectivism

Read the text under this heading on p. 90/358 and summarize the findings of the various pieces of research mentioned there. Create a three-column table, using the headings: Researcher, Culture studied and Findings/conclusions.

ACTIVITY

Reward allocation in the UK & Russia

Read the Key research on p. 91/359 and then answer the questions in the activity on p. 90/358. In addition, make sure you know the difference between an equity rule and an equality rule.

Differences within cultures

As well as differences between cultures, psychologists have investigated differences between sub-groups of the same culture. Two of these sub-cultural differences have been paid a lot of attention: gender differences and urban–rural differences.

ACTIVITY

Differences within cultures

Read through the text on pp. 92–3/360–1, including the Commentary panel, and then think about the following statements.

1 Women are more likely to give and receive help than men.

2 People living in rural communities are more likely to give and receive help than those living in urban communities.

Do you agree with them? Write 100 words commenting on each statement, citing relevant research studies to support your argument.

EXAMPLE EXAM QUESTIONS

In your work on this unit, you have already planned a complete answer to Example Exam Question 1 on p. 94/362. Here is another question for you to try, along with some ideas about how to go about answering it.

ACTIVITY

One for you to try ...

Discuss cultural differences in pro-social behaviour. (24 marks)

It is important to remember that there is both an AO1 and an AO2 component of this question. Although there is a temptation merely to describe cultural differences without commenting on them (and thus only providing AO1), the material on pp. 90–3/358–61 should make the process of answering this question that much easier. You will, however, need to be selective when deciding what will constitute the AO1 and AO2 content of your answer. You might draw upon differences between cultures for the first paragraph of your answer, and differences within cultures for the second paragraph. The commentary on pp. 92–3/360–1 could then constitute the last two paragraphs. You could weave some research support from the Tower *et al.* study into this commentary, but it is important that you do this in an effective manner. For example, you might state that:

'The proposed difference between members of individualist and collectivist cultures is supported by research from Tower et al. (1997), who found evidence that members of collectivist cultures do not apply the equality rule to people outside their own group ...'

An outline of the answer could be as follows:

- differences between cultures (individualism and collectivism, pro-social behaviour and the regulation of social relationships)

- differences within cultures (gender differences, urban–rural differences)

- commentary on research support (e.g. Tower *et al.*, laboratory and field study differences)

- further commentary (short- and long-term help, urban–rural differences).

CHECK YOUR UNDERSTANDING

When you have finished working through this topic, try the questions in 'Check your understanding' on p. 93/361 of the textbook. Check your answers by looking at the relevant parts of the textbook or this workbook, listed below.

1 textbook p. 70/338

2 textbook p. 82/350

3 workbook p. 34 (activity)

4 textbook p. 85/353 (Commentary panel)

5 textbook pp. 83–4/351–2; workbook pp. 33–4 (activities)

6 textbook p. 86/354

7 textbook pp. 86–90/354–8; workbook pp. 35 and 36 ('APFCC' activities)

8 textbook pp. 92–3/360–1

9 textbook pp. 92–3/360–1

10 textbook pp. 90–3/358–61

Topic 3 >> Media influences on pro- and anti-social behaviour

The role of the media in influencing the behaviour of people – especially children – has been a hot debate ever since the 1950s and 60s, when TV equipment started becoming more affordable and people began watching lots of television. Add in video, DVD and computer games, and the debate becomes even more topical and heated. This topic examines the arguments around the view that media violence promotes aggressive and anti-social behaviour, as well as considering the arguments that the media can be a force for good – that they can actually promote pro-social views and behaviour.

UNDERSTANDING THE SPECIFICATION

Here is what the AQA (A) specification says about this topic. It forms part of A2 Module 4, Section A: Social Psychology.

This should be one of the most straightforward areas of the specification, yet many students appear totally unprepared for at least half of the topic areas below. The specification is split into two distinct areas – media effects on *pro-social* behaviour, and media effects on *anti-social* behaviour. Each of these areas is as likely to be questioned as the other, yet students tend to be far better prepared for the latter rather than the former, and often present material on the media's anti-social effects even when the question is clearly on the pro-social effects of the media. Likewise, the specification clearly states the requirement to cover *explanations* relating to media influences, yet it is relatively rare to find students who can offer the same

> ### Pro- and anti-social behaviour
>
> c. **Media influences on pro- and anti-social behaviour**
>
> Explanations and research studies relating to media influences on pro-social behaviour.
>
> Explanations and research studies relating to media influences on anti-social behaviour.

depth of coverage for explanations as for research studies. The textbook is neatly divided into explanations and research studies for each of media influences on pro and anti-social behaviour (pp. 95–103/363–71), so this should not be a problem for you.

TOPIC MAP

The diagram below gives you an overview of what you are about to study.

> ### ACTIVITY
>
> **Topic map**
>
> Look through pp. 95–103/363–71 of the textbook to see where the items shown in the topic map are covered. Note down the relevant page numbers in the spaces left on the topic map.

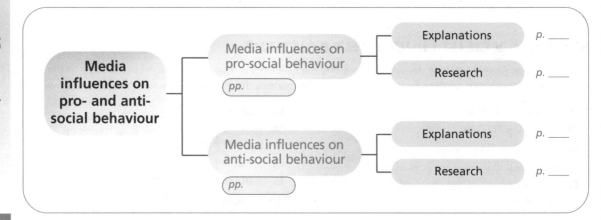

KEEPING TRACK

Use the table below to keep track of your work on this topic and plan your revision. See p. iv of this workbook (Introduction) for guidance on filling it in.

Media influences on pro- and anti-social behaviour		Tick if you ...		
What I need to learn	*Where is it?*	*could make a basic attempt*	*could make a good attempt*	*have complete mastery of this*
Media influences on pro-social behaviour				
Description of explanations of media influences on pro-social behaviour				
Evaluation of explanations of media influences on pro-social behaviour				
Description of research into media influences on pro-social behaviour				
Evaluation of research into media influences on pro-social behaviour				
Media influences on anti-social behaviour				
Description of explanations of media influences on anti-social behaviour				
Evaluation of explanations of media influences on anti-social behaviour				
Description of research into media influences on anti-social behaviour				
Evaluation of research into media influences on anti-social behaviour				

MEDIA INFLUENCES ON PRO-SOCIAL BEHAVIOUR

Perhaps because of the anxieties about the effects of violence in the media, research studies have tended to focus on the anti-social influences of the media. However, a number of studies have suggested the media's potential as a source of pro-social influences.

Explanations of media influences on pro-social behaviour

The textbook examines three aspects of how and why the media might influence pro-social behaviour:

1 *exposure to pro-social messages* – what types of message are there and how frequent are they compared to anti-social messages?

2 *social learning theory* – what is the mechanism by which pro-social messages might be learned and acted upon?

3 *development trends in pro-social influence* – how does a child's stage of development affect the way in which it might understand and absorb a pro-social message?

ACTIVITY

Summarizing explanations

Read through the text on p. 95/363 up to the Commentary panel. This contains nearly 500 words describing explanations of media influences of pro-social behaviour. This text would all count as description, i.e. AO1 in terms of the AQA exam. In the exam, however, you would have to present the gist of these explanations in far fewer words. Look at Example Exam Question 1 on p. 104/372, for example. You would have 30 minutes to answer this question, enough time to write 300 words outlining the explanations (AO1) and another 300 words evaluating them (AO2).

To practise constructing exam answers, do the following:

1 Summarize the key points of the explanations covered on p. 95/363 in a series of bullet points.

2 Using a PC, write 300 words of continuous prose outlining the explanations. Make sure that the words are your own, i.e. don't just copy chunks of the textbook.

The Commentary panel on pp. 95–6/363–4 presents a large number of evaluative points that you could use when discussing media influences on pro-social behaviour. In fact, each of the three bullet points in the panel could be broken down into several further bullet points. For example, the first bullet point, about pro-social messages, makes points about:

- research evidence showing that pro-social messages do influence children's values and behaviour
- children's lack of ability to generalize to new situations
- criticism of the quality of specially constructed pro-social programmes
- need for opportunities to model pro-social behaviour.

Evaluating explanations

Using a PC, write 300 words of continuous prose evaluating the explanations you described in the activity on p. 39. This will provide the second part of your answer to Example Exam Question 1 on p. 104/372. Again, make sure that the words are your own, i.e. don't just copy chunks of the textbook. (Note: You will find it useful to tackle the activity below first.)

Evaluating explanations of media influences on pro-social behaviour

Read through the Commentary panel on pp. 95–6/363–4 and draw up a list of all the key points made. You will need to divide each of the three bullet points into further sub-points, as we have shown above. Present this information in the form of a table, as shown below.

Explanation	Key point	Researcher
Exposure to pro-social messages	• Pro-social messages (e.g. Sesame Street) do influence children's values & behaviour	Hearold (1986) Mares (1996)
	•	

Research into media influences on pro-social behaviour

Researchers have investigated three types of television programme to find out which has the most positive effect, i.e. those using the following strategies:

- modelling pro-social behaviours only
- pro-social conflict resolution
- conflict without resolution.

Television programmes can portray quite different types of pro-social behaviour. Researchers have also investigated how individuals respond to seeing these different types of pro-social behaviour.

ACTIVITY

Strategies for modelling pro-social behaviour

Read from halfway down p. 96/364 to the end of the first paragraph on p. 97/365. Then read through the points in the Evaluation panel on pp. 97–8/365–6. For each of the three strategies, make notes on the following questions:

- What is the basis of the strategy being used (i.e. why would programme-makers choose this approach rather than the others)?
- When is this strategy most effective?
- What are the limitations of the strategy?

ACTIVITY

The effectiveness of pro-social messages in the media

Read the text on p. 97/365 about Hearold's (1986) meta-analysis and the comments in the Evaluation panel on p. 98/366 on the findings of both Hearold and Mares (1996). Consider the following questions and note down the points you would make in answering them. Include references to any relevant research.

- On what categories of people do pro-social messages have the strongest effect? (Think about gender, age, etc.)
- What advice would you give to programme-makers about the most effective ways of presenting pro-social messages, if they want to promote pro-social behaviour in viewers?

Meta analysis by Mares (1996)

Read the text on p. 97/365 about the meta-analysis of media influences on pro-social behaviour.
Complete the following table to analyse the results of Mares' meta-analysis of 39 different studies.

Category of behaviour	Examples of behaviour	Effects on children	Effect size
Positive interaction	● Friendly/non-aggressive interactions	● Promoted positive interactions	● Moderate
Altruism			● Smaller, when ...
Self-control			
Anti-stereotyping			● Larger, when ...

MEDIA INFLUENCES ON ANTI-SOCIAL BEHAVIOUR

As the introduction to this section of the textbook says (p. 98/366), many psychologists accept as undeniable truth the claim that 'media violence causes aggression, crime and violence'. As you will discover, however, the real truth is far from clear-cut. Indeed, some argue that media violence is largely irrelevant in the overall debate about delinquent behaviour (see final question in the Expert interview on p. 102/370).

Research into media influences on anti-social behaviour

A great deal of research has been done in this area, both experimental and non-experimental.
Pages 98–100/366–8 summarize some of the most significant studies, grouped according to the type of research.

Studies into the effects of exposure to TV violence

Read through the description of the six areas of research discussed on pp. 98–100/366–8. Summarize the key points of each area, noting down:

1 what overall conclusion can be drawn from this type of research into TV violence

2 details of relevant research, including procedures, findings and conclusions

3 the strengths and weaknesses of this type of study.

One possible format is shown on the next page – this takes the form of a 'revision card' which will help you with your revision of this area.

In thinking about the strengths and weaknesses of different types of research, you might find it useful to review your studies of research methods at AS-level (see *Psychology for AS-level* Unit 6/14).

Correlational studies

Overall conclusion	Viewing and/or preference for violent television is related to aggression.
Relevant research	Atkin et al. (1979)
● Procedures	9–13 year olds given situations to respond to
	Options = physical/verbal aggression, reduce/avoid conflict
● Findings	Heavy viewers of violence = 45% aggressive responses
	Little TV violence = 21% aggressive responses
● Conclusions	Correlation between viewing of violence and aggressive responses
Strengths/weaknesses	Relationship is correlational, not causal.

ACTIVITY

Problems with research studies

In several places in the topic, weaknesses in the research into anti-social behaviour are highlighted. Some are considered in the Evaluation panel on p. 101/369. These include:

● incomplete understanding of the nature of the audience

● methodological problems with the studies themselves.

Guy Cumberbatch mentions other problems, especially methodological issues, in the Expert interview on p. 102/370.

Make a complete list of problems with research studies into anti-social behaviour and the media. Use bullet points grouped under headings.

Explanations of media influences on anti-social behaviour

The textbook examines four different explanations of media influences on anti-social behaviour.

ACTIVITY

Explanations of media influences on anti-social behaviour

Read the text under this heading on p. 100/368 and the Commentary panel on p. 101/369. Then answer the following questions:

Cognitive priming

1 What, according to Huesmann, is a 'problem-solving script'?

2 What is the role of such scripts in the possible link between media violence and anti-social behaviour?

Observational learning

3 In what two ways might television influence the form that aggressive behaviour takes?

●

●

4 Give two arguments challenging the 'observational learning' explanation:

●

●

Desensitization

5 What are the main arguments of the desensitization explanation?

●

●

6 Summarize two research studies that challenge the desensitization hypothesis:

- _____
  _____

- _____
  _____

Justification

7 The justification explanation suggests a vicious cycle of violence, which is fed by watching media violence. Complete the diagram below to outline the stages of this cycle.

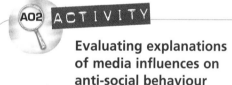

Child behaves aggressively

TV _____

Child feels _____

Consequence

_____

Justification

Explanations of media influences on anti-social behaviour

The text on p. 100/368 under this heading would count as description, i.e. AO1 in terms of the AQA exam. You could use it to answer questions such as Example Exam Question 4(a) on p. 104/372. You would have 15 minutes to answer this part of the question, enough time to write 300 words.

To practise constructing exam answers, do the following.

1 Summarize the key points of the explanations covered on p. 100/368 in a series of bullet points.

2 Using a PC, write 300 words of continuous prose outlining **two or more** explanations. If you restrict yourself to two explanations, that would be about 150 words on each. If you were to cover three, that would mean 100 words of explanation on each. Make sure that the words are your own, i.e. don't just copy chunks of the textbook.

The Commentary panel on p. 101/369 presents a large number of evaluative points that you could use when discussing media influences on anti-social behaviour. There is also plenty of excellent material in the Expert interview on p. 102/370 and in Table 3.3/11.3 on p. 103/371.

Evaluating explanations of media influences on anti-social behaviour

Start by carrying out the activity on p. 101/369 of the textbook. This will help you to pick out some of the most important points of the interview with Guy Cumberbatch. Then, using a PC, write 300 words of continuous prose in answer to Example Exam Question 4(b) on p. 104/372. Again, make sure that the words are your own, i.e. don't just copy chunks of the textbook.

EXAMPLE EXAM QUESTIONS

You have already planned and written complete answers to Example Exam Questions 1 and 4 on p. 104/372. On p. 44 is a complete sample answer to Question 2. A question such as this takes a bit of thinking about, and demands careful time planning. First, there are two parts to the question, each worth 12 marks. Second, there is an AO1 component and an AO2 component to each part, each worth 6 marks. Third, there is an instruction to write about *one or more* studies of pro-

social behaviour (in part a) and anti-social behaviour (in part b). A common mistake is to write *general accounts* of pro-social behaviour (e.g. about human altruism) instead of *media influences* on pro-social behaviour. This question makes specific demands, so should be answered in a highly focused manner. Is more than one study better than just one? That depends on how much you know about one study. In the sample answer, we make use of material from pp. 95–103/363–71.

(a) Outline and evaluate one or more studies relating to media influences
on pro-social behaviour.   (12 marks)

(b) Outline and evaluate one or more studies relating to media influences
on anti-social behaviour.   (12 marks)

(a) One of the first meta-analyses of the effects of pro-social behaviour was carried out by Hearold (1986). Hearold analysed 230 studies of the effects of the media and found that while fewer studies existed on pro-social effects, the effect size was much larger than for anti-social effects, and was consistently higher for both boys and girls. A more recent meta-analysis in this area was carried out by Mares (1996). Mares included four different categories in her analysis of 39 different studies. She found that children who viewed positive and altruistic interactions in the media tended to act more positively and altruistically compared with those who viewed neutral or anti-social content. Mares also found that programmes specifically designed to reduce stereotyping and prejudice were moderately successful, with a much larger positive effect when part of an extended programme of classroom activities designed to reduce stereotyping.

Hearold's findings might be explained by the fact that pro-social messages are generally designed to have an influence on viewers, whereas anti-social messages are not specifically designed for that purpose (Comstock 1989). Also, in these studies, the measures of pro-sociality are generally taken in an artificial and contrived environment, so their application to children's behaviour in real-life settings is limited. In both Hearold's and Mares's analyses, most of the studies examined were not broken down by sex. However, in those that were, more positive effects were discovered for girls, which is consistent with Hearold's findings. Many studies have found that pro-social effects were limited to situations which were similar to the pro-social act seen in the television programme. This contrasts with the typical finding that viewers are able to generalize anti-social behaviours from one context to another.

(b) Early correlational studies (e.g. Atkin *et al.* 1979) showed that physical or verbal aggression tended to be positively correlated with exposure to television violence. Although these studies did not suggest a causal link between television violence and anti-social behaviour, experimental studies (e.g. Liebert and Baron 1972) have shown that an increase in aggressive behaviour tends to follow even a fairly brief exposure to televised violence. This was also the conclusion from a field study (Parke *et al.* 1977), although in this study only children who were initially aggressive were affected by exposure to violent media. A meta-analysis of media violence research (Paik and Comstock 1994) also provided clear evidence that brief exposure to violent television or film caused short-term increases in aggressive behaviour, particularly among pre-school children, and more so for males than females. A more recent natural experiment found no evidence of an increase in anti-social behaviour following the introduction of television to the island of St Helena, and even found increases in some aspects of pro-social behaviour (Charlton *et al.* 2000).

Freedman (1996) argues that the correlations between aggression and exposure to violence tend to be quite small, accounting for less than 10 per cent of individual differences in the aggressiveness of children. Freedman (1992) also claims that many participants in experiments in this area display demand characteristics by simply providing the responses they believe the researcher wants. Livingstone (2001) extends this point, arguing that the more naturalistic a research design, the less likely it is that any effects will be observed. This suggests that any behaviours learned under experimental conditions could not be generalized to viewer's everyday lives. Cumberbatch (2004) claims that the view that media violence does cause violent behaviour is 'based on findings which appear weak, inconsistent and even contradictory', and which often gloss over non-significant findings which would weaken this point of view. Research by Hagell and Newburn (1994), for example, found that young offenders had less access to technology and watched less television and video than young non-offenders, and had no particular interest in violent programmes.

CHECK YOUR UNDERSTANDING

When you have finished working through this topic, try the questions in 'Check your understanding' on p. 103/371 of the textbook. Check your answers by looking at the relevant parts of the textbook or this workbook, listed below.

1 textbook p. 95/363

2 textbook p. 95/363

3 textbook p. 96/364

4 textbook p. 97/365; workbook p. 41

5 textbook p. 97/365

6 textbook pp. 99–100/367–8

7 textbook p. 100/368

8 textbook p. 103/371

9 textbook p. 103/371

10 textbook p. 101/369

BIOLOGICAL RHYTHMS
Sleep & Dreaming

PREVIEW

There are three topics in this unit. You should read them alongside the following pages in the Collins *Psychology for A2-level*/*Psychology* textbook:

Topic	*Psychology for A2*	*Psychology*
1 Biological rhythms	pp. 136–42	pp. 404–10
2 Sleep	pp. 142–50	pp. 410–18
3 Dreaming	pp. 150–58	pp. 418–26

INTRODUCTION

Physiological Psychology is one of five sections in Module 4 (AQA Specification A), as the diagram below shows. This section is further divided into three sub-sections – 'Biological rhythms, sleep and dreaming' is the second of these.

Read the Preview and Introduction on p. 134/402 of the textbook now. This will give you an overview of what's in the unit.

Where this unit fits in to the A-level qualification

Section A:
Social Psychology

Section B:
Physiological Psychology

Module 4

Section C:
Cognitive Psychology

Section D:
Developmental Psychology

Section E:
Comparative Psychology

● BRAIN & BEHAVIOUR

● **BIOLOGICAL RHYTHMS, SLEEP & DREAMING**

● MOTIVATION & EMOTION

a Biological rhythms

b Sleep

c Dreaming

In the Module 4 exam, there will be a total of 15 questions, three relating to each Section (i.e. one per sub-section). You have to answer **three** questions, from at least **two** sections.

Topic 1 >> Biological rhythms

Most living organisms are subjected to rhythmic variation in their physiology and behaviour. These rhythms include the basic 24-hour rest-and-activity cycle which we experience as sleep and wakefulness. Other rhythms last for periods more than or less than 24 hours, and serve to regulate specific bodily systems over shorter or longer periods. Of key importance in our cycle of sleep and wakefulness are the endogenous pacemakers (the body 'clock'), which is fine-tuned every day by exogenous zeitgebers such as daylight. If so much of our physiology is dictated by biological rhythms, what happens if these rhythms are disrupted?

UNDERSTANDING THE SPECIFICATION

Here is what the AQA (A) specification says about this topic. It forms part of A2 Module 4, Section B: Physiological Psychology.

The term 'research' is a fairly friendly instruction to write about explanations and/or studies relating to each of the named biological rhythms. The three biological rhythms mentioned here are prescribed, i.e. you must cover all three and be prepared to present an exam answer that covers any one or (more usually) a combination of two or more of these.

Endogenous pacemakers (such as the suprachiasmatic nucleus and pineal gland) function as a 'body clock' that serves to regulate the 24-hour circadian rhythm, whilst the main exogenous zeitgeber is daylight. Questions usually ask you to discuss the role of endogenous pacemakers and exogenous zeitgebers,

> ### Biological rhythms, sleep and dreaming
>
> **a. Biological rhythms**
>
> Research into circadian, infradian and ultradian rhythms, including the role of endogenous pacemakers and of exogenous zeitgebers. The consequences of disrupting biological rhythms (e.g. shiftwork, jet lag).

so you should be clear about the distinction between them and be able to offer an informed description and commentary on each.

Although the consequences of disrupting biological rhythms usually constitute the AO2 component of a question on this topic, it is possible for a question to focus entirely on the disruption of biological rhythms, in which case a description and critical commentary would be necessary.

TOPIC MAP

The diagram below gives you an overview of the content of this topic.

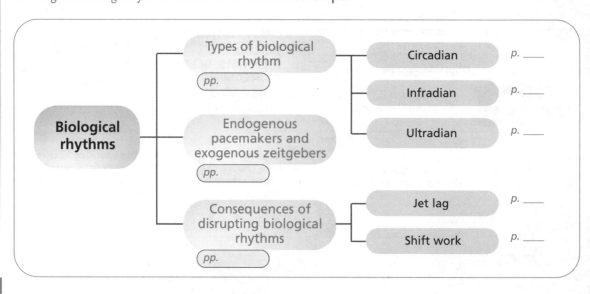

Topic map

Look through pp. 136–40/404–8 of the textbook to see where the items shown in the topic map are covered. Note down the relevant page numbers in the spaces left on the topic map.

KEEPING TRACK

Use the table below to keep track of your work on this topic and plan your revision. See p. iv of this workbook (Introduction) for guidance on filling it in.

Biological rhythms		Tick if you ...		
What I need to learn	Where is it?	could make a basic attempt	could make a good attempt	have complete mastery of this
Different types of biological rhythm				
Description of research into circadian, infradian, and ultradian biological rhythms				
Description of research into endogenous pacemakers and exogenous zeitgebers				
Evaluation of research into biological rhythms				
Consequences of disrupting biological rhythms				
Description of research into the effects of jet lag				
Description of research into the effects of shift work				
Evaluation of research into the consequences of disrupting biological rhythms				

DIFFERENT TYPES OF BIOLOGICAL RHYTHMS

Topic 1 begins by describing some of the types of rhythm to be found both in the natural world, in humans and in non-human animals. Read the first half of p. 136/404 for a good introduction to this topic. There then follows a description of the various types of biological rhythm. In the exam, you may be asked to describe or outline a number of these rhythms, as for instance in Example Exam Question 4 on p. 142/410. The next activity will help you collect and organize the information you need to answer such a question.

Different types of biological rhythm

What is meant by the following terms?

Rhythm	Definition	Examples
● Circadian		
● Infradian		
● Circannual		
● Ultradian		

Research into Seasonal Affective Disorder (SAD)

Winter depression is an interesting example of a circannual rhythm. It is discussed on p. 137/405, and also in Unit 17/25 on p. 500/768. Read those paragraphs now and then complete the following activity.

Winter depression is an interesting example of a circannual rhythm. It is discussed on p. 137/405, and also in Unit 17/25 on p. 500/768.

ACTIVITY

Seasonal Affective Disorder (SAD)

1 Define Seasonal Affective Disorder (SAD):

2 What factors are thought to be important in the cause of SAD?

3 What treatments have been found to be effective for people suffering from SAD?

4 Make a list of research studies relating to SAD described in the textbook:

Researchers	Key finding

ENDOGENOUS PACEMAKERS AND EXOGENOUS ZEITGEBERS

Biological rhythms seem to be determined by a combination of internal 'body clocks' and external factors. It is important to understand not only the difference between the two, but also the way in which the two work together.

ACTIVITY

Terminology

Define each of the following terms and give an example of each:

1 Endogenous pacemakers

Definition:

Example:

2 Exogenous zeitgebers

Definition:

Example:

The role of brain structures

The textbook discusses two brain structures in detail: the pineal gland and the suprachiasmatic nucleus (SCN). These are endogenous pacemakers, but they are heavily influenced by one particular external (exogenous) factor: light.

The various pathways involved are described in detail on p. 138/406 of the textbook. Don't be put off by the long names and the biological terms – the diagrams that follow summarize the information in a more memorable form.

The various pathways involved are described in detail on p. 138/406 of the textbook.

EXAM HINT

Using diagrams

Diagrams are an excellent way of remembering details – especially of processes and how things relate to each other. In the exam, however, you should generally write in continuous prose as you will be given a mark for 'Quality of Written Communication'. You can use diagrams such as those shown above, but you should offer some written description as well.

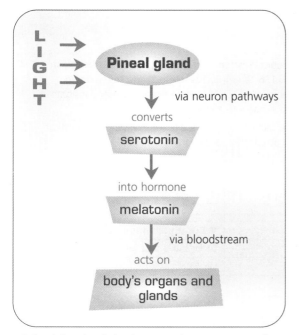

Role of the pineal gland as an endogenous pacemaker

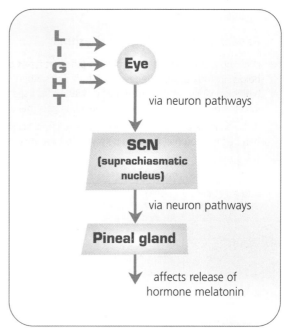

Role of the SCN as an endogenous pacemaker

ACTIVITY

Understanding the role of brain structures

Read through the text on p. 138/406, up to the heading 'Removing exogenous zeitgebers', and study the diagrams above. Then answer the following questions.

1 Which hormone seems to be responsible for the rhythmic nature of activities in both human and non-human animals?

_____

2 The diagrams show how light is linked to the production of this hormone. How does light reach the relevant part of the brain in:

● birds and reptiles

_____

_____

● mammals, including humans

_____

_____

3 What role does the bloodstream play in the process?

_____

_____

_____

Answering exam questions on biological rhythms

Exam questions may well ask you to describe and evaluate research into particular types of biological rhythm. See, for example, Example Exam Questions 1 and 2 on p. 141/409, where you are asked to consider research into two biological rhythms.

To prepare for such questions, it is important to have summaries of a range of different research studies relating to different biological rhythms. The next activity will help you with this.

EXAM HINT

Examples in exam questions

Example Exam Question 1 on p. 141/409 gives three examples of biological rhythms (in brackets), but asks you to outline and evaluate only two. Don't be misled by the number of examples – they are there just to remind you what you might include. Remember, too, that circannual rhythms, although not mentioned specifically in the specification, are examples of infradian rhythms.

Unit 5/13 // Biological rhythms, sleep & dreaming

Research into biological rhythms

Draw up a summary of research into different types of biological rhythm, using the column headings shown below. Include any of the research studies described on pp. 136–9/404–7. The research into free-running biological clocks at the bottom of p. 138/406 is especially important, as it provides extremely useful insights into the relationship between endogenous pacemakers and exogenous zeitgebers.

(NB: you have already summarized research into Seasonal Affective Disorder (see p. 48), so don't include that here, unless you feel it would help you to have a complete 'master list' of research studies.)

Researcher	Type of rhythm investigated	Method	Findings/conclusions
Zucker et al. (1983)	Circannual	Measured activity levels, reproductive cycles and body weight in ground squirrels	• Lesions in the SCN disrupted circadian, but not circannual rhythms • Circannual rhythms involve an endogenous pacemaker other than the SCN

Sleep as an ultradian rhythm

In Topic 2 you will learn that the alternation between different sleep stages is an example of an ultradian rhythm, so research related to this area would also be relevant to questions about research into biological rhythms. Read the text on pp. 142–3/410–11 under 'Types and stages of sleep' and add the research of Dement and Kleitman (1957) to the summary of research you compiled for the last activity.

If you were answering Example Exam Question 1 on p. 141/409, then you would need to provide 300 words of AO2 evaluation of research. The Evaluation on p. 139/407 gives four excellent points that you could include in your answer. In order to elaborate your evaluation for this question, you could make use of the material on the consequences of disrupting biological rhythms. Although this material is presented descriptively in the textbook, it does not take much 'tweaking' to turn this into AO2 commentary. You might practise your AO2 skills by including phrases such as 'This claim is supported by research which shows that...' and 'The importance of exogenous zeitgebers in maintaining a circadian rhythm was demonstrated by...'.

CONSEQUENCES OF DISRUPTING BIOLOGICAL RHYTHMS

If we rely on the coordination of internal clocks and external factors to keep our biological rhythms running smoothly, what happens when the coordination is disrupted. The textbook looks at two reasons why this might happen: jet lag and shift work.

Jet lag

Read the text under this heading on p. 139/407 of the textbook and then answer the following questions.

1 What is jet lag and what are its effects?

2 What is meant by the following terms?
● Phase delay
● Phase advance

3 What is the best way of coping with jet lag?

4 What hormone offers a possible treatment for jet lag?

Shift work

Read the text under this heading on pp. 139–40/
407–8 of the textbook and then answer the following
questions.

1 What is shift work and what are its effects?

_____

_____

_____

2 Why is moving back a shift harder to adjust to
than moving forward a shift?

_____

_____

_____

3 Research has suggested ways of minimizing the
effects of shift work? What are these?

_____

_____

_____

_____

4 Why, according to Coren (1996), is disruption of
biological rhythms more common nowadays in the
world of work than, say, 100 years ago?

_____

_____

_____

_____

Sleep deprivation

Topic 2 includes discussion of another, even more
extreme example of disruption of biological
rhythms: complete sleep deprivation. Read the text
on pp. 145–6/413–4 under the heading 'Horne's
(1988) core sleep/optional sleep model' and also
the second question and its answer in the
Expert interview on p. 148/416.

Summarize the research by Horne (1988, 2004) and
Dement (1978). In particular, note down:

1 the consequences of disrupting this important
biological rhythm

2 how subjects recovered after sleep deprivation

3 what this tells us about the nature and purpose
of sleep.

Answering exam questions on disruption of biological rhythms

Example Exam Questions 2 and 5 on pp. 141/409 and
142/410 show possible questions on disruption of
biological rhythms.

- In Question 2, disruption of biological rhythms is
brought in to part (b) and is specfically AO2-
oriented. The guidance given on p. 141/409
suggests various ways in which you could answer
this question. The studies of sleep deprivation from
Topic 2 would be good for comparing differences in
the degree of disruption, while the studies of shift
work would allow you to discuss the contrast
between phase-advance and phase-delay methods
of changing shifts.

- In Question 5, disruption of biological rhythms is
the focus of the whole question, which means
writing 300 words of description (AO1) and 300
words of evaluation (AO2).

When answering questions such as these, dividing your
answer into 'chunks' is a good way of ensuring that you
include the right kinds of information in the right
proportions.

Take Example Exam Question 5 on p. 142/410. In this
question, the number of types of disruption is not
specified, so you could restrict your answer to just one
type (e.g. jet lag) or you could include others (e.g. shift
work, sleep deprivation studies).

If you decided to include all three types of disruption,
your answer might break down into six chunks of
100 words, as follows:

	AO1 (description)	AO2 (commentary)
Consequences of:		
1 jet lag	100 words	100 words
2 shift work	100 words	100 words
3 sleep deprivation	100 words	100 words

Planning your answer

Plan your answer to Example Exam Question 5 on p. 142/410. Following the pattern shown at the bottom of p. 51, plan what points you would include in each chunk of 100 words. Do this in the form of bullet points, using your PC. Think, in particular, about what evaluative points you would make – the guidance on p. 142/410 will be useful in this regard.

When you are satisfied with your outline, write a complete answer to the question, limiting yourself to the 600 or so words you would have time to write in the actual exam.

If you would prefer to write about fewer types of disruption (e.g. just jet lag and shift work), then repeat this planning process, breaking your answer down into four chunks of 150 words each.

EXAMPLE EXAM QUESTIONS

In your work on this unit, you have already planned and written a complete answer to Example Exam Question 5 on p. 142/410. Here is another question for you to try.

One for you to try ...

Discuss the role of endogenous pacemakers and exogenous zeitgebers in biological rhythms. (24 marks)

For this question, careful planning is essential in order to ensure that you respond to all the required components. The question requires you to offer AO1 and AO2 material relevant to both endogenous pacemakers and exogenous zeitgebers. Despite the use of the plural in each of these, there would be no need to discuss more than one form of pacemaker and more than one form of zeitgeber. There is, however, a plurality requirement to discuss both pacemakers and zeitgebers rather than just one of these. This can be tricky to plan effectively, as these work together to sustain circadian rhythms. Making sure that you cover both in sufficient detail, and that you address both in a descriptive and evaluative way, should do the trick. These do not have to be balanced in terms of length (there is much more you can write about endogenous pacemakers than there is about exogenous zeitgebers) so do not worry about making each paragraph the same length.

One possible route through this question is suggested below. Each of these paragraphs would be approximately 100 words. The first three paragraphs constitute the AO1 component of your answer and the last three paragraphs the AO2 component. You would need to ensure that whatever material you use

for the AO2 part of your answer, it is part of a critical commentary, i.e. is used to support or challenge claims about the role of endogenous pacemaker and exogenous zeitgebers. The material to support this answer can be found on pp. 137–40/405–8:

- role of the pineal gland as an endogenous pacemaker
- role of the suprachiasmatic nucleus as an endogenous pacemaker
- results of removing exogenous zeitgebers (including description of research by Siffre, and Aschoff and Weber)
- evaluation of the role of endogenous pacemakers and exogenous zeitgebers (e.g. research findings, generalizability of research, individual differences and methodological problems associated with sample size)
- consequences of disrupting biological rhythms (interaction of exogenous pacemakers and exogenous zeitgebers in jet lag)
- consequences of disrupting biological rhythms (interaction of exogenous pacemakers and exogenous zeitgebers in shift work).

CHECK YOUR UNDERSTANDING

When you have finished working through this topic, try the questions in 'Check your understanding' on p. 141/409 of the textbook. Check your answers by looking at the relevant parts of the textbook, listed below.

1 textbook pp. 136–7/404–5

2 textbook pp. 136/404 and 137/405

3 textbook pp. 136–7/404–5

4 textbook pp. 137/405 and 500/768

5 textbook p. 138/406

6 textbook p. 138/406

7 textbook pp. 138–9/406–7

8 textbook p. 139/407

9 textbook pp. 139–40/407–8

10 textbook pp. 139–40/407–8

Topic 2 >> Sleep

Everyone sleeps. This fundamental activity takes up a quarter to a third of our lifetimes. At times, the urge to sleep overcomes all other needs. But what does sleep do for us? What is the reason for it? What happens when you are deprived of it? Why we sleep is still a matter of debate, although it is clear that most animals will go to great lengths to ensure they get sleep in one form or another.

UNDERSTANDING THE SPECIFICATION

Here is what the AQA (A) specification says about this topic. It forms part of A2 Module 4, Section B: Physiological Psychology. Here, the specification topic prescribes a number of required areas for you to study.

1 You should be able to offer both AO1 and AO2 content for *ecological* and *restoration theories* of sleep. Questions vary here, but it is possible that you might get a question that is just on ecological theories or just on restoration theories, or on both. Does the use of the plural 'theories' mean that you must cover at least two ecological theories and at least two restoration theories? Not necessarily, but it pays to be safe, and having more than one theory for each will give you more to write about if a question covers only one account (i.e. ecological or restoration).

2 You should also be able to provide AO1 and AO2 content for *research studies* in each of these areas. Remember that simply describing research studies counts as AO1, but building them into a critical commentary (e.g. showing how they support or

> ### Biological rhythms, sleep and dreaming
>
> **b. Sleep**
>
> Theories and research studies relating to the functions of sleep including ecological (e.g. Meddis) and restoration (e.g. Oswald, Horne) accounts. The implications of findings from studies of sleep deprivation for such theories.

challenge a theoretical perspective) would count as AO2. In this way, research studies can also be useful as part of the evaluation of theories of sleep.

3 The specification has, as a separate entry, the implications of *studies of sleep deprivation* for such theories. Strictly speaking, you should be able to describe studies of sleep deprivation for AO1, and then comment on their implications for understanding the functions of sleep as AO2. This may also function as the AO2 component of a question divided into parts, where the first part of the question is an outline of a theory or theories of sleep.

TOPIC MAP

The diagram below gives you an overview of what you are about to study.

> **ACTIVITY**
>
> ### Topic map
>
> Look through pp. 142–9/410–7 of the textbook to see where the items shown in the topic map are covered. Note down the relevant page numbers in the spaces left on the topic map.

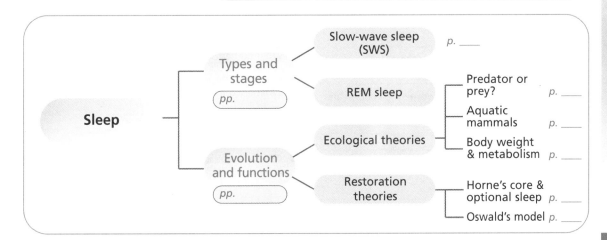

KEEPING TRACK

Use the table below to keep track of your work on this topic and plan your revision. See p. iv of this workbook (Introduction) for guidance on filling it in.

Sleep		Tick if you ...		
What I need to learn	Where is it?	could make a basic attempt	could make a good attempt	have complete mastery of this
Types and stages of sleep				
Description of types and stages of sleep				
Evolution and functions of sleep				
Description of ecological theories of sleep				
Description of research studies relating to ecological theories of sleep				
Evaluation of ecological accounts of sleep				
Description of restoration theories of sleep				
Description of research studies relating to restoration theories of sleep				
Evaluation of restoration theories of sleep				
Description of studies of sleep deprivation				
Assessment of the implications of findings from studies of sleep deprivation				

TYPES AND STAGES OF SLEEP

The 24-hour cycle of sleeping and waking is an example of a circadian biological rhythm. Sleep itself, however, is not a single unchanging event; as we sleep, we pass through various stages in regular cycles and these stages form an ultradian rhythm. The stages are described in detail on pp. 142–3/410–11.

In the exam, you will not be asked specifically to describe the types and stages of sleep, as that is not mentioned in the AQA specification. However, it is important to understand the characteristics of the different stages of sleep, especially SWS and REM. One reason for this is that the theories of the functions of sleep discussed in this topic make different claims about what the purpose of each type of sleep is.

ACTIVITY

SWS and REM sleep

Read through pp. 142–3/410–11 and then answer the following questions.

1 What is slow-wave sleep (SWS)?

2 How many stages of SWS are there?

3 What is the difference between synchronized and unsynchronized EEG activity?

4 What are the characteristics of 'alpha waves' and when do these occur?

5 What are the characteristics of 'delta waves' and when do these occur?

6 What do hertz (Hz) measure?

7 What are the main characteristics of REM?

8 At what stage in the cycle of sleep does REM occur?

A2 Physiological Psychology

EVOLUTION AND FUNCTIONS OF SLEEP

As the introduction to this section says, sleep is universal to birds, mammals and reptiles alike (although it is hard to recognize in reptiles). It must, therefore, have some vital function. The textbook considers two theories as to what that function is: ecological theories and restoration theories.

Ecological theories of sleep

Read the text under the heading 'Ecological theories' on p. 143/411 and the first two paragraphs on p. 144/412. Then complete the following activity.

ACTIVITY

Ecological theories of sleep

1 What is the basic proposition of the ecological explanation of sleep?

_____

_____

2 What is meant by the term 'ecological niche' and what aspects of animals' existence does it refer to?

_____

_____

_____

3 Name three differences in aspects of the sleep of mammals.

● _____

● _____

● _____

4 What variables contribute to these differences?

_____

_____

_____

ACTIVITY

Aspects of the ecological account

The textbook considers four aspects of animals' existence which might provide support for the ecological account, as well as highlighting possible problems with it. Read through the rest of the text on p. 144/412 and the top of p. 145/413, and then complete the following table:

	Key point	Problems?	Relevant research
● Lifestyle – predator or prey?			
● Environment – aquatic animals			
● Body weight and metabolism			
● Types of sleep			

In the exam, you may be asked to write a complete answer on one theory of sleep – this is the case with Example Exam Question 1 on p. 149/417, which explictly states just one theory of sleep. A complete answer is about 600 words, so for Question 1, you would have to write 300 words of AO1 description and 300 words of AO2 evaluation.

A good way of approaching the AO1 part of your answer would be to identify key points relating to the theory of the functions of sleep. Then, for each point, you could provide further detail either through the use of research studies or examples of animal behaviour. The last activity will help you do this.

Unit 5/13 // Biological rhythms, sleep & dreaming

A précis of the ecological account

Imagine you were answering Example Exam Question 1 on p. 149/417 with reference to the ecological theory of sleep. As the guidance below the questions explains, you would need to write 300 words of AO1. Using a PC, write a 300-word description of the ecological theory, following the approach suggested above.

Research on the Internet

Search on the Internet for more research into ecological theories of sleep and note down:

- a short description of the research
- the findings and conclusions of the research
- whether it provides support for the ecological theory, or challenges it.

A shorter précis of the ecological theory

In other exam questions, you may be asked to write about more than one theory of the functions of sleep. That is the case with Example Exam Question 3 on p. 150/418, where your answer would be divided equally between the ecological and restoration theories of sleep. Obviously, you would need to reduce the length of your description accordingly.

Again using a PC, make a copy of the 300-word description you wrote for the last activity, but this time reduce it to a 150-word summary. This is about as much as you could write in 7.5 minutes and would provide an answer to the 'outline' part of Example Exam Question 3(a) on p. 150/418. As you write this shorter précis, think carefully about the essential points that you want to include.

Evaluating the ecological account

The Evaluation panel on p. 145/413 contains 331 words of 'evaluation', focusing mainly on problems with the ecological account. In any evaluation, it would also be important to assess the strengths of this explanation of the functions of sleep.

There are other points in the text that you could use as evaluation:

- *predator or prey* – Do prey animals sleep less because it's dangerous or because they need to spend more time eating? It is difficult to untangle the importance of different variables.
- *body weight and the giant sloth* – The example of this large, 'lazy' animal (it's not called a sloth for nothing!) seems to undermine the argument that large animals, with slower metabolisms, need less sleep. The evidence is not consistent.

Exam questions may ask you specifically to describe and/or evaluate *research studies* relating to the ecological account of sleep. See, for example, Example Exam Question 4 on p. 150/418. Your answer to this question would clearly be different from one asking for a more general description or outline of a theory – here, the answer should be research-focused. The next activity will help you prepare the information for such an answer.

Summarizing research studies

Read through pp. 143–5/411–3 and summarize the research studies mentioned, making a note of the key points of each. Two are considered in some detail:

- Indus dolphin – Pilleri (1979), Carlson (1994)
- bottlenose dolphin – Mukhametov (1984).

Evaluating the ecological account

1 Imagine you were answering Example Exam Question 1 on p. 149/417 with reference to the ecological theory of sleep. You would need to write 300 words of AO2 evaluation (in addition to the 300 words of AO1 description you wrote earlier). Using a PC, write a 300-word evaluation of the ecological theory, remembering to include an assessment of both the strengths and weaknesses of this theory.

2 Now make a copy of your 300-word summary, but this time reduce it to a 150-word summary. This is about as much as you could write in 7.5 minutes and would provide an answer to the 'evaluate' part of Example Exam Question 3(a) on p. 150/418.

Restoration theories of sleep

Read the paragraph under the heading 'Restoration theories' on p. 145/413. Then do the following activity.

p. 145/413

ACTIVITY

Restoration theories of sleep

1 What is the basic proposition of restoration theories of sleep?

_____

_____

_____

2 Summarize the link between growth hormone and sleep.

_____

_____

_____

_____

The textbook discusses two main restoration theories of sleep: those of Horne (1988) and Oswald (1980).

ACTIVITY

Comparing two restoration theories

Read the text from the heading 'Horne's (1988) core sleep/optional sleep model' on p. 145/413 to the end of p. 146/414. Then read the Expert interview with Jim Horne on p. 148/416 and answer the following questions.

1 What are the key points of Horne's core sleep/optional sleep model?

_____

_____

_____

2 What are the key points of Oswald's model?

_____

_____

_____

3 What are the major similarities and differences between the models?

Similarities	Differences

ACTIVITY

Summarizing the restoration theory

1 Imagine you were answering Example Exam Question 1 on p. 149/417 with reference to the restoration theory of sleep. Using a PC, write a 300-word description of this theory.

2 Again using a PC, make a copy of your 300-word description and now reduce it to a 150-word summary. This would provide an answer to the 'outline' part of Example Exam Question 3(b) on p. 150/418.

Evaluating restoration theories

The textbook has done a lot of the evaluative work for you, by including lots of points for and against restoration theories of sleep in the panel on p. 147/415. With over 700 words of evaluation, your task in an exam would be to present a pithy summary of these points, relating them clearly to the points you made in the AO1 description.

AO2 ACTIVITY

Evaluating the restoration theory

1 Following on from the last activity, write a 300-word evaluation of restoration theories of sleep. Make sure your answer links clearly with the 300 words of description you wrote for the last activity. You could tackle this in two ways:

(a) Write a single chunk of 300 words to follow on directly from the AO1 description.

(b) Weave your evaluative comments into the AO1 description you wrote earlier. If you do this, you could use a different colour for the AO2 material, so that you can see clearly which is which. This would be useful later on when you come to revise for the exam and start looking back over your work

2 Again using a PC, make a copy of your 300-word evaluation and reduce it to 150 words. This would provide an answer to the 'evaluate' part of Example Exam Question 3(b) on p. 150/418.

Studies of sleep deprivation

Exam questions may ask specifically about studies of sleep deprivation, as that is included in the AQA specification for this topic. See for example, Question 5 on p. 150/418. The textbook contains details of a number of studies that investigated sleep deprivation:

- Randy Gardner's sleep deprivation record (Dement 1978)
- Everson *et al.*'s research into sleep deprivation of rats
- studies of fatal familial insomnia.

You could also use these studies in your answer to questions such as Example Exam Question 2(b) on p. 150/418. Here, the wording refers to 'research studies relating to the restoration account', but studies of sleep deprivation can come under that heading. In your answer, you would earn AO2 credit either by evaluating the individual studies (e.g. in terms of the stressful procedures used to prevent sleep, or the difficulty of generalizing from studies with few participants), or by assessing the degree of support they offer to restoration accounts.

ACTIVITY

Studies of sleep deprivation

For each of the three studies into sleep deprivation listed above, note down:

1 the key features of the study (procedures and findings)

2 how findings supported restoration theories

3 challenges or problems arising from the study's findings.

	Key features	Support for restoration theories	Challenges to restoration theories
• Randy Gardner (Dement 1978)			
• Rats and sleep deprivation (Everson *et al.*)			
• Fatal familial insomnia			

EXAMPLE EXAM QUESTIONS

In your work on this unit, you have already planned and written two different complete answers to Example Exam Question 1 on p. 149/417, as well as a complete answer to Question 3 on p. 150/418.

The following question is one of the more challenging questions that you might face in this topic area, so we have taken material from the textbook (pp. 145–8/413–6) to construct an answer for you.

Discuss the implications of findings from studies of sleep deprivation for theories of the functions of sleep.

(24 marks)

Sleep deprivation studies have provided much of the evidence for restoration theories. Dement (1978) reports the case of a 17-year-old schoolboy, called Randy Gardner, who stayed awake for 264 hours in 1964. He developed blurred vision and incoherent speech, some perceptual disturbances, and a mild degree of paranoia. The effects seemed mild compared to the degree of sleep deprivation. However, he recovered quickly when he eventually slept. The first night he slept for 15 hours and only recovered about a quarter of his overall lost sleeping time during the nights that followed. Recovery was specific to particular stages, two-thirds of Stage 4 SWS and a half of REM sleep were recovered, but little of the other stages of SWS. Some humans suffer from a rare inherited condition, 'fatal familial insomnia'. They sleep normally until middle age, but then simply stop sleeping, a condition which leads to death within two years.

In a review of the effects of sleep deprivation, Horne (1988) concluded from a number of controlled laboratory studies that sleep deprivation in normal participants produces only mild effects, together with some sleep recovery concentrated mainly in Stage 4 SWS and REM sleep. Although the effects of sleep deprivation were not dramatic, they did involve some problems with cognitive abilities, such as perception, attention and memory, while the recovery of Stage 4 SWS and REM sleep suggests that these are the critical phases. Stern and Morgane (1974) also found that after REM sleep deprivation, participants show 'REM rebound', an increase in REM sleep when they are allowed to sleep normally. This suggests that REM rebound is necessary to restore neurotransmitters lost during REM sleep deprivation. In animal studies, prolonged sleep deprivation in rats appears to cause them to increase their metabolic rate, lose weight and die within an average of 19 days (Everson *et al.* 1989). Allowing these animals to sleep within that time prevents their death.

Sleep deprivation studies have generally failed to provide conclusive evidence that sleep is necessary to keep the body functioning normally. In Horne's review of sleep deprivation studies, he found that very few of these reported that sleep deprivation had interfered with the participants' ability to perform physical exercise, nor was there any evidence of a physiological stress response to the sleep deprivation. Horne therefore concluded that as total sleep deprivation produces few obvious effects on the body, body restoration is not the purpose of sleep. Studies such as Dement's study of Randy Gardner lack the control of later laboratory studies, and therefore fail to provide conclusive evidence of the effects of sleep deprivation for the restorative process. Likewise, although cases of fatal familial insomnia support restoration accounts of sleep, they are very rare and such patients clearly have brain damage, making it difficult to generalize the findings.

Although animal studies involving sleep deprivation have suggested that sleep is essential for body restoration, these studies do not allow us to separate the effects of sleep deprivation from the methods used to keep the animals awake. In order to keep animals awake, they must be constantly stimulated, and hence stressed. It is most likely that sleep deprivation in animals interferes with the immune system, which then leads to death. It is also possible that sleep provides the only opportunity for tissue restoration in some species. Rats, when awake, spend all their time foraging for food, seeking mates or avoiding predators. Humans, on the other hand, are capable of resting during the day. Our metabolic activity when we are in a state of quiet restfulness is only 9 per cent higher than it is when we are asleep. Deprivation of sleep, therefore, may not have the same restorative consequences for humans as it does for other species.

CHECK YOUR UNDERSTANDING

When you have finished working through this topic, try the questions in 'Check your understanding' on p. 149/417 of the textbook. Check your answers by looking at the relevant parts of the textbook, listed below.

1 textbook p. 143/411
2 textbook p. 143/411
3 textbook pp. 143–4/411–12
4 textbook pp. 143–5/411–13
5 textbook pp. 145–7/413–15

6 textbook pp. 146–7/414–15
7 textbook p. 146/414
8 textbook pp. 146/414, 148/416
9 textbook p. 147/415
10 textbook p. 147/415

Dreams can be baffling, uplifting – even terrifying. So why do we dream? Does dreaming have a purpose, or is it simply a case of the mind randomly running through various images and feelings stored away somewhere? This topic looks at the nature of dreams – their content, duration and different types – and the relationship between dreaming and the stages of sleep. It then considers theories of dreaming, divided into two main approaches: neurobiological theories and psychological theories.

UNDERSTANDING THE SPECIFICATION

Here is what the AQA (A) specification says about this topic. It forms part of A2 Module 4, Section B: Physiological Psychology.

The term 'research' in this specification entry is usually repeated in examination questions with the amplification that it includes theories and/or studies relating to the nature of dreams.

Therefore, it would be acceptable to talk either about *theoretical accounts* of the nature of dreams (e.g. the proposal that lucid dreams exist or that some dreams are prophetic in nature) or *studies* of the nature of dreams (e.g. the work of Aserinsky and Kleitman). As this part of the specification deals with the *nature* of dreams, it would not be acceptable to include theories that are more concerned with the *function* of dreams.

Biological rhythms, sleep and dreaming

c. **Dreaming**

Research related to the nature of dreams (e.g. content, duration, types of dream). Theories of the functions of dreaming, including neurobiological (e.g. Hobson and McCarley, Crick and Mitchison) and psychological (e.g. Freud, Cartwright) accounts.

The second part of this specification entry does deal with the function of dreams. There are two distinct areas to study here: *neurobiological* theories (i.e. those based on the brain's physiological activity during REM sleep) and *psychological* theories (i.e. those theories that take the dream imagery itself as the issue to be explained). You should endeavour to cover at least two theories in each of these categories.

TOPIC MAP

The diagram below gives you an overview of what you are about to study.

Topic map

ACTIVITY

Look through pp. 150–7/418–25 of the textbook to see where the items shown in the topic map are covered. Note down the relevant page numbers in the spaces left on the topic map.

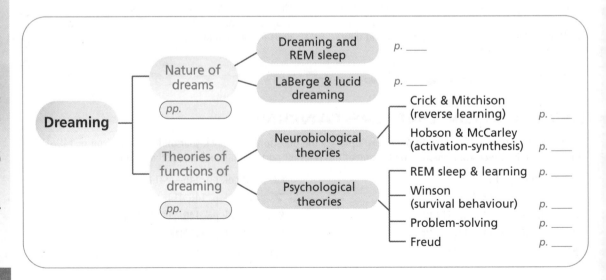

KEEPING TRACK

Use the table below to keep track of your work on this topic and plan your revision. See p. iv of this workbook (Introduction) for guidance on filling it in.

Dreaming		Tick if you ...		
What I need to learn	Where is it?	could make a basic attempt	could make a good attempt	have complete mastery of this
The nature of dreams				
Description of research relating to the nature of dreams				
Evaluation of research relating to the nature of dreams				
Theories of the functions of dreaming				
Description of neurobiological theories of dreaming				
Evaluation of neurobiological theories of dreaming				
Description of psychological theories of dreaming				
Evaluation of psychological theories of dreaming				

THE NATURE OF DREAMS

The first part of this topic considers the nature of dreams, i.e. what they are, what kinds of thing we dream about and when, in our sleep, we are most likely to dream. The work of Oswald (which you also examined in Topic 2) has given us a lot of the information that we know about dreams.

ACTIVITY

Content and types of dreams

1 What are dreams? What do we 'see' or 'experience' when we dream?

2 Does everyone dream? (Refer to Oswald's work with blind people and Mark Solms' work with brain-damaged patients, described on p. 156/424.)

3 What sorts of thing do we dream about?

ACTIVITY

REM sleep and dreaming

What is the relationship between REM sleep and dreaming? Read the text under the heading 'Dreaming and REM sleep' on p. 151/419 and the panel headed 'Dream on, Freud' on p. 156/424. Then answer the following questions.

1 Why is it inaccurate to refer to REM sleep as 'dreaming sleep'?

2 What similarities and differences are there between dreams during REM sleep and those during non-REM sleep?

3 What does the research of Aserinsky and Kleitman tell us about the duration and 'memorability' of dreams?

LaBerge and lucid dreaming

Read the text under this heading on p. 151/419. Then answer the following questions.

1 What is 'lucid dreaming'?

_____

_____

2 How did LaBerge demonstrate its existence?

_____

_____

_____

_____

3 Have you ever experienced lucid dreaming?

_____

_____

_____

Describing the nature of dreams

In the exam, you may be asked specifically about the nature of dreams and research relating to this. Example Exam Question 1 on p. 158/426 is one such question. For the AO1 (descriptive) part of your answer, you could refer to any of the research described on pp. 150–1/418–19 under the heading 'The nature of dreams'. The description of Solms' work in the panel 'Dream on, Freud' (on p. 156/424) also contains some useful information about dreaming and REM sleep that could legitimately be included in your answer.

You might also like to consider the question: do non-human animals dream? Some interesting research using non-human animals is described in the textbook, e.g. Crick and Mitchison's observations regarding the spiny anteater (see p. 152/420) and Winson's work with animals such as rabbits, cats and rats (see p. 154/422).

Using a PC, write 300 words of description that could form the AO1 part of your answer to this question.

THEORIES OF THE FUNCTIONS OF DREAMING

The bulk of this topic is devoted to theories of the functions of dreaming. These divide into two main areas: neurobiological and psychological.

Neurobiological theories

Neurobiological theories try to explain the underlying cognitive function of sleep by focusing on physiological aspects of sleep and dreaming and especially on the activity of the brain. The textbook looks at two such theories, the focus of the next two activities.

Theories of the functions of dreaming

Start by reading from the bottom of p. 151/419 up to the heading 'Crick and Mitchison and reverse learning' on p. 152/420. Also read the short paragraph on p. 153/421 under the heading 'Psychological theories of dreaming'. Then answer the following questions.

1 Why was early research into the functions of dreaming dominated by psychoanalysts such as Freud?

_____

_____

_____

2 What happened to change that?

_____

_____

_____

_____

_____

_____

Crick and Mitchison's reverse-learning model

Read through the Key research panel on p. 152/420. Then check your understanding of their research by making sure you can answer the following questions.

1 What metaphor do Crick and Mitchison use to explain dreaming?

2 What are 'parasitic thoughts' and how does the brain dispose of them?

3 What features of the spiny anteater support their theory?

4 Why did Crick and Mitchison refine their theory to apply only to dreams with bizarre imagery?

Hobson and McCarley's activation–synthesis model

Read through the Key research panel on p. 153/421 and then answer the following questions.

1 Summarize the mechanisms that are involved in the 'activation' part of this model.

_____

_____

_____

2 Where does the 'synthesis' come in?

_____

_____

_____

3 How does the model account for the narrative aspect of dreams?

_____

_____

_____

_____

4 What is the relationship between REM sleep, dreaming and the neurotransmitter acetylecholine?

_____

_____

_____

_____

_____

Describing neurobiological models (AO1)

Write a 150-word summary of each of the two neurobiological models covered in this topic. Use a PC and check the length of each summary by using the 'word count' facility.

You would then need to write 300 words of evaluation. The guidance notes below the question on p. 158/426 suggest one approach, i.e. contrasting neurobiological theories with psychological theories. Another approach would be to comment on how convincing the models are and to highlight any problems with the research. Relevant points are made in several places:

● Crick and Mitchison – see the final paragraph on p. 152/420 beginning 'One problem ...'

● Hobson and McCarley – see the Evaluation panel on p. 153/421

● Hobson and McCarley – see also the paragraph beginning 'Interestingly, ...' in the second column of p. 151/419

● both models – see the general points about dream research on pp. 156–7/424–5.

Answering exam questions on neurobiological theories

The information on the two neurobiological models covered on pp. 152–3/420–1 gives you plenty of material for answering questions such as Example Exam Question 2 on p. 158/426. Taking these two models, you would need to write 150 words of AO1 description on each – the previous two activities will have helped you identify the key points to cover.

Evaluating neurobiological models

Write a 300-word summary of the two neurobiological models covered in this topic. Include as many of the points listed above as you think necessary, but make sure that you relate them closely to the models described. Again, use a PC and check the length of your text by using the 'word count' facility.

PSYCHOLOGICAL THEORIES OF DREAMING

Psychological theories, in contrast to neurobiological theories, focus on the meaning and role of dreams in tasks such as learning, survival strategies and problem-solving.

Dreaming, REM sleep and learning

Several psychologists have investigated the possibility that dreaming may have an important role to play in learning. The results of their research seem to suggest that dreaming – especially during REM sleep – does indeed serve some purpose in this process.

Studies of sleep and learning

Complete the following table to summarize the key points of the research studies into sleep and learning described in the panel at the top of p. 154/422.

Researcher	Procedures	Findings	Conclusions
Karni *et al.* (1994)	Perceptual speed task (identifying background pattern to a letter)		
Stickgold (1998)			
Smith (1999)			

The textbook also considers the role of the hippocampus in helping us to process daily experiences, helping to integrate them with established memories.

Cortical/hippocampal activity during sleep

Read the paragraph starting 'Many investigators ...' at the bottom of p. 153/421 and then complete the diagram below to summarize the key points.

Type of sleep: _____

Hippocampus ⟶ Exchange of neural impulses ⟵ **Cortex**

Type of sleep: _____

Store for: _____
_____

Function of dreaming during REM sleep: _____
_____

Store for: _____
_____

Dreams and survival behaviour

Winson's recent work with non-human animals provides further interesting insights into the possible role of dreams. Read through the text on pp. 154–5/422–3 and then do the following activity.

ACTIVITY

Winson's research into dreams and survival behaviour

1 What is a 'theta rhythm' and when does it occur in non-human animals?

2 What, according to Winson, is the overall purpose of REM sleep?

3 In what ways have humans evolved beyond the behaviours of non-human animals?

4 How does Winson's theory explain:
- the spiny anteater's large forebrain?

- newborn babies' proportionately large amount of REM sleep?

Dreams and problem-solving

Cartwright's (1984) model takes a similar line to that of Winson, but in her work with humans, Cartwright investigated the role of dreams in problem-solving.

ACTIVITY

Cartwright's research into dreams and problem-solving

1 What is Cartwright's basic proposition regarding the role of dreams in humans?

2 What were the key findings of Cartwright's research involving divorced women?

3 According to Cartwright, what effect do strong emotional reactions have on dreams?

Freud and dreams

Freud regarded his work with dreams as a central part of his whole psychodynamic approach. Read through the text about Freud and dreams on pp. 155–6/423–4 and then answer the questions in the next activity.

See also pp. 539/807 and 618–21/886–9 for more discussion of Freud's psychodynamic theory.

ACTIVITY

Freud and dreams

1 What is meant by the following terms?
- Manifest content

- Latent content

- Dream work

- Condensation

- Displacement

- Representability

2 What, according to Freud, is the purpose of dreams?

3 What is the role of the analyst?

4 What did Mark Solms discover in his work with brain-damaged patients that provided some support for Freud's belief in the connection between dreams and unconscious desires?

EXAMPLE EXAM QUESTIONS

In your work on this unit, you have already written a complete answer to Example Exam Question 2 on p. 158/426. Here is another one for you to try.

In your work on this unit, you have already written a complete answer to Example Exam Question 2 on p. 158/426.

ACTIVITY

One for you to try ...

Outline and evaluate two or more psychological theories of dreaming. (24 marks)

Although this question does not specifically ask for theories on the functions of dreaming, these will be the ones you are most likely to use in your answer. The first requirement, of course, is to make sure that you understand what constitutes a psychological theory of dreaming in this context, as opposed to a neurobiological theory. As stated in the textbook, neurobiological models (such as Crick and Mitchison's reverse learning theory) are based on the brain's physiological activity during REM, whereas psychological theories take the dream imagery itself as the issue to be explained. Several types of psychological theory are discussed in the textbook, ranging from Winson's electro-physiological explanation of the relationship between dreams and survival behaviour, through to the full-blown psychoanalytical theories of Freud. You can use any of them to answer questions such as the one above. In this question, it is not a good

idea to try to write about lots of accounts (although the question allows for this) – it's better to focus on just two and provide more detail (AO1) and more commentary (AO2) of your selected theories. This would give you approximately 150 words of AO1 and 150 words of AO2 for each theory. This is not a golden rule, however, and you would be fine offering 200 words of AO1 + 200 of AO2 for one theory and 100 + 100 for the other. The important thing is to balance the AO1 and AO2 components overall in your answer.

If, however, you decided to answer this question with reference to three accounts, you would need to divide your time accordingly. Remember, you have 30 minutes to answer questions in this unit, which is about enough time to write 600 words. Dividing your answer into 'chunks' gives you the following outline plan:

	AO1 (description)		AO2 (commentary)	
Theory 1	5 minutes	100 words	5 minutes	100 words
Theory 2	5 minutes	100 words	5 minutes	100 words
Theory 3	5 minutes	100 words	5 minutes	100 words

Your AO2 commentary might not be so neatly divided, as some of the points you make might refer to more than one of the theories you describe. For example, the points about laboratory-based

research and the subjectivity of dreams (see Evaluation panel, pp. 156–7/424–5) apply generally to much of the research that underpins theories of dreaming.

CHECK YOUR UNDERSTANDING

When you have finished working through this topic, try the questions in 'Check your understanding' on p. 157/425 of the textbook. Check your answers by looking at the relevant parts of the textbook or this workbook, listed below.

1 textbook p. 151/419

2 textbook p. 152/420; workbook p. 63

3 textbook p. 153/421; workbook p. 63

4 textbook p. 154/422

5 textbook pp. 153–4/421–2; workbook p. 64

6 textbook p. 154/422

7 textbook p. 155/423

8 textbook p. 155/423

9 textbook p. 155/423

10 textbook pp. 156–7/424–5

PERCEPTUAL PROCESSES
& Development

PREVIEW

There are three topics in this unit. You should read them alongside the following pages in the Collins *Psychology for A2-level/Psychology* textbook:

Topic	Psychology for A2	Psychology
1 The visual system	pp. 220–27	pp. 488–95
2 Perceptual organization	pp. 227–37	pp. 495–505
3 Perceptual development	pp. 238–48	pp. 506–16

INTRODUCTION

Cognitive Psychology is one of five sections in Module 4 (AQA Specification A), as the diagram below shows. This section is further divided into three sub-sections – 'Perceptual processes and development' is the second of these.

Read the Preview and Introduction on p. 218/486 of the textbook now. This will give you an overview of what's in the unit.

Where this unit fits in to the A-level qualification

Section A:
Social Psychology

Section B:
Physiological Psychology

Module 4

Section C:
Cognitive Psychology

Section D:
Developmental Psychology

Section E:
Comparative Psychology

In the Module 4 exam, there will be a total of 15 questions, three relating to each Section (i.e. one per sub-section). You have to answer **three** questions, from at least **two** sections.

- ATTENTION & PATTERN RECOGNITION
- **PERCEPTUAL PROCESSES & DEVELOPMENT**
- LANGUAGE & THOUGHT

a The visual system
b Perceptual organization
c Perceptual development

Topic 1 >> The visual system

Our eyes are one of our major sense organs, passing visual information about the world around us to our brains. Light is a crucial factor in this process and this topic examines what happens when light enters our eyes. It looks at the structure and function of the visual system. It also explores various aspects of the system whereby we process visual information: sensory adaptation and the processing of contrast, colour and features.

UNDERSTANDING THE SPECIFICATION

Here is what the AQA (A) specification says about this topic. It forms part of A2 Module 4, Section C: Cognitive Psychology.

The first part of this specification entry is probably the most challenging in terms of AO2 content, but you should be able to offer at least some commentary on the structure and functions of the visual system. This might include consequences of the existing structure, reasons why the eye functions in the way it does, consequences of damage, research support, relationship between the structure of the eye and subsequent visual information processing and so on. You will need to be creative to construct a decent AO2 here, but it is possible. The term 'research' in the specification, and in questions

Perceptual processes and development

a. The visual system

Structure and functions of the visual system: the eye, retina and visual pathways. Research into the nature of visual information processing (e.g. sensory adaptation and the processing of contrast, colour and features).

derived from this specification, includes both theoretical explanations and research studies, so both should be covered. You should cover at least two of the examples given below (i.e. sensory adaptation, contrast, etc.), as questions frequently ask for research into two forms of visual information processing. As with all questions in this unit, you must have an equal amount of AO2 commentary to match your AO1 description of research.

TOPIC MAP

The diagram below is a visual 'map' of the content of this topic.

ACTIVITY

Topic map

Look through pp. 220–46/488–514 of the textbook to see where the items shown in the topic map are covered. Note down the relevant page numbers in the spaces left on the topic map.

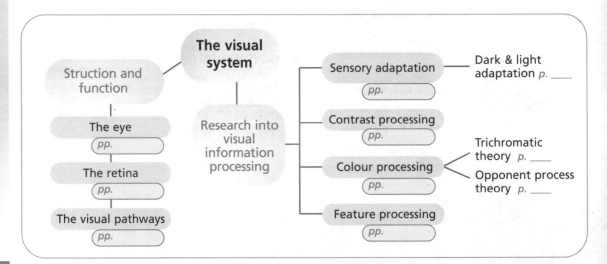

KEEPING TRACK

Use the table below to keep track of your work on this topic and plan your revision. See p. iv of this workbook (Introduction) for guidance on filling it in.

The visual system		Tick if you ...		
What I need to learn	*Where is it?*	*could make a basic attempt*	*could make a good attempt*	*have complete mastery of this*
Structure and function of the visual system				
Description of the structure and function of the eye				
Description of the structure and function of the retina				
Description of the structure and function of the visual pathways				
Commentary on the visual system				
Research into visual information processing				
Description of research into sensory adaptation				
Description of research into contrast processing				
Description of research into colour processing				
Description of research into feature processing				
Evaluation of research into information processing				

THE VISUAL SYSTEM

Pages 220–2/488–90 of the textbook give a detailed account of the physiology of the visual system, consisting of the eye, the retina and visual pathways leading to the brain. The key element in the visual system is light, and the textbook follows the process of 'seeing' from the point at which light, reflected from objects, enters our eyes.

The eye

Figure 8.1/16.1 gives a clear illustration of the different parts of the eye. It is important to understand the function of each of the different parts. Carry out the next activity to summarize these different functions.

ACTIVITY

Functions of parts of the eye

1 Read the information about the structure and functions of the eye on p. 220/488 and then complete the following table.

	Description	Function
Sclera		
Cornea		
Aqueous humour		
Iris		
Lens		

2 The process of 'accommodation' is a vital part of the process of focusing. Note down four key points about this process:

-
-
-
-

The retina

When light reaches the retina, it triggers a set of reactions that end up with the light being converted into a neural response that leaves the eye via the optic nerve.

ACTIVITY

The retina

1 Read the information about the retina on p. 221/489 and then complete the following table.

	Description	Function
Retina		
Fovea		
Photoreceptor cells		
Bipolar neurones		
Ganglion cells		

2 There are two types of photoreceptor cells: cones and rods. In the space below, note down how many there are in each eye, what they do and where they are located.

	Number	Function	Location
Cones			
Rods			

3 What is the 'blind spot'?

HINT

You could use the 'problem' of the blind spot as AO2 commentary in essays about the visual system. If you do so, you should also describe ways in which we solve this problem.

The visual pathways

The optic nerve connects the eyes with the brain, where further processing of the sensory information takes place.

ACTIVITY

The visual pathways

Read the text about visual pathways on p. 222/490 and look at Fig. 4.7/12.7 and relevant text nearby on p. 125/393. Then answer the questions below.

1 What is meant by the following terms?

● Ipsilateral pathway

● Contralateral pathway

● Optic tract

2 What happens in the following parts of the brain?

● Optic chiasma

● Lateral geniculate nucleus (LGN)

● Primary visual cortex

● Visual association cortex

Answering exam questions on the visual system

The information on the structure and functions of the visual system given on pp. 220–2/488–90 gives you plenty of material for answering questions such as Example Exam Questions 1 and 2 on p. 226–7/494–5. In fact, the problem is sifting through all the detailed physiological information to present a succinct summary that covers the main points. The activities above will have helped you to distil the information down to the most important points.

You would also need to write 300 words of evaluation in your answer. The guidance notes below Questions 1 and 2 on pp. 226–7/494–5 contain some useful suggestions. Points you could include in your evaluation are:

- the existence of a blind spot on the retina – how do we cope with that?
- what happens when contralateral visual pathways are broken (e.g. in people with 'split brains')
- the difficulty for the rods–cones system in coping with twilight
- the decline in functions of the visual system with age (e.g. accommodation), creating need for human intervention, such as contact lenses and glasses
- usefulness of the dark and light adaptation system (covered in the next section)
- the effect of 'lateral inhibition' on photoreceptors and how this influences our perception of contrast (see panel at the top of p. 224/492).

RESEARCH INTO VISUAL INFORMATION PROCESSING

The textbook covers four aspects of visual information processing, shown on the topic map on p. 68.

Sensory adaptation

Sensory adaptation is a characteristic of the body's sense systems and applies to the visual system when it has to adjust to a sudden change from light to dark, or vice versa.

Anyone with eyesight will have experienced the principle of dark and light adaptation, outlined on p. 223/491. The physiology behind this process is, however, quite complicated and will need careful reading. The following activity should help you understand it better.

outlined on p. 223/491

ACTIVITY

Dark and light adaptation

Complete the following diagram that summarizes what happens during the process of dark adaptation.

	Bright light	Very dim light	After a few minutes

Photons

Photopigments
○ = bleached
● = unbleached

Lots of photons means that photopigments:
_____
_____

Fewer photons means that the chance of striking unbleached molecules is:
_____

Photopigments regenerate, so that:
_____
_____

Effect is:
_____

Effect is:
_____

Effect is:
_____

Contrast processing

ACTIVITY

Understanding contrast processing

Read the text on pp. 223–4/491–2 about contrast processing and answer the following questions.

1 Define the following terms.
● Brightness
● Visual contrast
● Simultaneous lightness contrast

2 The process of 'lateral inhibition' explains why squares of exactly the same colour and tone can appear more or less bright, depending on the surrounding square (see Fig. 8.4/16.4). In 50 words, summarize what is meant by 'lateral inhibition' and how it works.

A2 Cognitive Psychology

Colour processing

Colour is another important characteristic of human vision. There are two main theories that seek to describe how we process colour: trichromatic theory and opponent process theory.

ACTIVITY

Understanding colour processing

Read the text on pp. 224–5/492–3 about colour processing and then do the following.

1 Define the following terms.
  ● Hue
  ● Saturation

2 Summarize the key points of trichromatic theory and opponent process theory in the space below.

	Trichromatic theory	*Opponent process theory*
Name of researchers:		
Basic proposition of theory:		
Support for theory:		
Problems/challenges for theory:		

3 Explain how it may be possible for the visual system to include elements of both theories?

Feature processing

The pioneering research of Hubel and Wiesel (1959) identified a number of different cells involved in feature processing.

ACTIVITY

Feature processing

Read the text on pp. 225–6/493–4 about feature processing and answer the following questions.

1 How did Hubel and Wiesel identify the different types of cell?

2 What is the function of the following cells?
  ● Simple cells
  ● Complex cells
  ● Hypercomplex cells

3 What types of feature do 'feature detectors' detect?

EXAMPLE EXAM QUESTIONS

In your work on this unit, you have already written a complete 600-word answer to Example Exam Question 2 on p. 227/495. Here is another one for you to try.

One for you to try ...

Describe and evaluate research into two forms of visual information processing (e.g. sensory adaptation and the processing of contrast, colour and features). (24 marks)

Having done all the activities earlier, you are now well prepared to tackle questions on research into visual information processing, such as the one above. This question tells you exactly how many forms of visual information processing you should refer to (i.e. two), which means you can break your answer down in four 'chunks' of 150 words, as shown in the table below (600 words is a reasonable length for a 30-minute essay). You wouldn't have to choose the forms of processing shown, but could base your answer on any two of four different types of visual information processing covered in the textbook.

	AO1 (description)		AO2 (commentary)	
Theory 1: e.g. sensory adaptation	150 words	7.5 minutes	150 words	7.5 minutes
Theory 2: e.g. colour processing	150 words	7.5 minutes	150 words	7.5 minutes

You should be careful to construct your answer so that there are equal amounts of AO1 and AO2. In some cases the AO2 is fairly obvious in the textbook, particularly when related to theories of colour processing (remember that the term 'research' in an exam question allows you to include theories as well as studies in your answer). In other cases, however, as with sensory adaptation, you will need to be more creative in your choice of AO2 commentary. Commentary does not have to be restricted to negative evaluation, but can include almost anything that constitutes a 'comment' on the previously described AO1 material. For example, in relation to sensory adaptation, you might comment that 'sensory adaptation probably has evolutionary significance ...' (p. 223/491) and that the effects of dark adaptation can explain the familiar experience of why driving at night is difficult, as well as why spectators in a cricket match cannot understand why matches are stopped for bad light (because their eyes have adjusted gradually to the changing light conditions).

Here is another question that could be asked:

- **Critically consider research into two or more forms of visual information processing.** (24 marks)

This question varies slightly from the one above. A different injunction has been used ('critically consider' instead of 'describe and evaluate'), but the meaning is the same – you must provide 15 minutes' worth of AO1 and 15 minutes' worth of AO2. This time you are allowed to cover more than two forms of visual processing, but remember the depth–breadth trade-off – the more forms of visual processing you cover, the less detail you can provide for each. Again, it pays to plan your response at the outset and may be useful to divide your answer into 100-word chunks, i.e. 100 words of AO1 and 100 words of AO2 for each of three forms of visual processing.

CHECK YOUR UNDERSTANDING

When you have finished working through this topic, try the questions in 'Check your understanding' on p. 226/494 of the textbook. Check your answers by looking at the relevant parts of the textbook or this workbook, listed below.

1 textbook p. 220/488
2 textbook p. 220/488
3 textbook p. 220/488; workbook p. 69
4 textbook p. 221/489
5 textbook pp. 221–2/489–90

6 textbook pp. 222 & 125/490 & 393
7 textbook pp. 222–3/490–1
8 textbook pp. 223–4/491–2
9 textbook pp. 224–5/492–3
10 textbook p. 225/493

This topic moves on from the physiological aspects covered in Topic 1 to look more closely at the cognitive processes involved in processing sensory information. How do we make something meaningful out of all the stimuli bombarding our senses?

UNDERSTANDING THE SPECIFICATION

Here is what the AQA (A) specification says about this topic. It forms part of A2 Module 4, Section C: Cognitive Psychology.

As with many topics in this specification, there are two distinct components that should be addressed separately, even though there are some cross-over points between the two. The first part is concerned with mainstream theories of visual perception, with two distinct approaches specified. These are the constructivist approach, which emphasizes the fact that information from several sources must be combined to 'construct' our perception of the outside world. Gregory's theory is used as an example of this approach. The other approach, the direct approach, emphasizes that the array of information coming from the senses is sufficient for accurate perception. Gibson's theory is used as an example of this approach.

Perceptual processes and development

b. Perceptual organization

Theories of visual perception, including constructivist theories (e.g. Gregory) and direct theories (e.g. Gibson). Explanations of perceptual organization (e.g. depth, movement, constancies and illusions).

The second part is more concerned with the different aspects that make up perceptual organization. The examples given in the specification include four different aspects of organization. These might be too many to do justice to in an examination answer, so you should be prepared to cover two or perhaps three in detail (not forgetting that you must cover both AO1 and AO2 components of each explanation).

TOPIC MAP

The diagram below gives you an overview of what you are about to study.

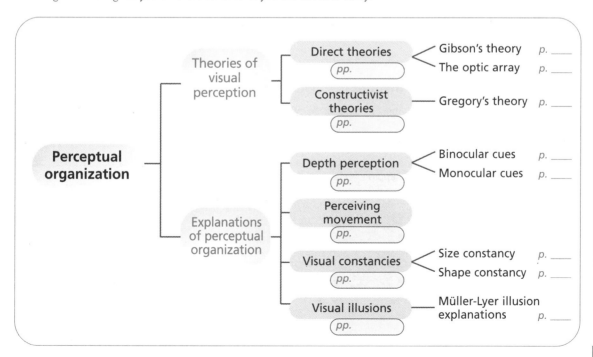

Topic map

Look through pp. 227–36/495–504 of the textbook to see where the items shown in the topic map are covered. Note down the relevant page numbers in the spaces left on the topic map.

KEEPING TRACK

Use the table below to keep track of your work on this topic and plan your revision. See p. iv of this workbook (Introduction) for guidance on filling it in.

Perceptual organization		Tick if you ...		
What I need to learn	*Where is it?*	could make a basic attempt	could make a good attempt	have complete mastery of this
Theories of visual perception				
Description of bottom-up and top-down processing				
Description of direct theories of perception				
Evaluation of direct theories of perception				
Description of constructivist theories of perception				
Evaluation of constructivist theories of perception				
Explanations of perceptual organization				
Description of depth perception				
Description of perceiving movement				
Description of visual constancies				
Description of visual illusions				
Evaluation of explanations of perceptual organization				

THEORIES OF VISUAL PERCEPTION

The first part of this topic outlines the differences between the two main types of theories of visual perception: direct and constructivist theories.

Direct and constructivist theories

Read the text under the heading 'Theories of visual perception' on pp. 227–8/495–6.

1 What is the basis of the bottom-up approach?

2 Why are theories based on this approach also known as 'data-driven'?

3 What is the basis of the top-down approach?

4 Why are theories based on this approach also known as 'concept-driven'?

5 How did Palmer (1975) demonstrate the way the two processes interact?

DIRECT THEORIES OF PERCEPTION

Key research into direct theories of perception was done by J.J. Gibson and this is discussed on pp. 228–30/496–8 of the textbook.

pp. 228–30/496–8

ACTIVITY

Gibsons' theories

Read the text under the heading 'Gibson's theory of direct perception' on pp. 228–9/496–7.

1 What, according to Gibson, is an 'optic array'?

2 Why is movement a crucial part of the process of perception?

3 What did Gibson mean by the term 'invariant information'?

The optic array

The idea of an optic array is central to Gibson's theories. The diagram below illustrates the points made in the four paragraphs on p. 229/497, under the headings 'The optic array' and 'The importance of movement'. It shows how rays of light, structured by objects such as the light and the desk, converge on the observer. When the observer moves, the optic array changes (shown by the brown dotted lines in the diagram below).

Invariant information

Because Gibson believed that light from the objects around us is the starting point for perception, he spent a lot of time investigating the characteristics of objects and the types of information they provide the observer.

ACTIVITY

Invariant information

Read the text under the heading 'Invariant information' on pp. 229–30/497–8.

1 What is texture gradient and how does it aid visual perception?

2 Find a friend or family member who is not studying psychology. Show them each of the three sketches in Fig. 8.8/16.8 on p. 229/497. As you show each one, cover up the other two, so that they are not distracted by them. Ask them to name an object that the sketch might represent.

3 Look at Fig. 8.9/16.9 on p. 229/497. How does this demonstrate the 'horizon ratio'?

4 Define the following terms.
  ● Optic flow patterns

  ● Expanding visual field

  ● Contracting visual field

  ● Motion parallax

5 According to Gibson, what is the particular value of invariant information?

Recognizing objects

Gibson believed that we can recognize objects directly from the information that we perceive. He also assumed that we perceive in order to 'do' – perception is designed for action. From this he developed the notion of 'affordance'. This is quite a subtle concept, so read the paragraph on p. 230/498 under the heading 'Recognizing objects' very carefully, as well as the bullet point 'Affordances' in the Commentary panel below.

ACTIVITY

Recognizing objects

1 What is the link between affordance and behaviour?

_____

_____

2 You see a door. What affordances (i.e. possibilities for action) does the door offer?

_____

_____

_____

3 What criticism do Bruce and Green make of the notion of affordance?

_____

_____

_____

Answering exam questions on direct theories

Exam questions in this area may ask you explicitly about direct theories of perception – see, for example, Example Exam Questions 2 and 4(b) on p. 237/505. The information on Gibson's theory that you have covered so far provides more than enough material for tackling either of these. The question may not specify the type of theory, as in Question 3, and you could use Gibson's direct theory of perception here too.

As so often, the challenge is reducing the information you have to a succinct, but accurate summary.

ACTIVITY

Describing direct theories (AO1)

1 Using a PC, prepare a 300-word description of Gibson's direct theory of perception. This is about as much as you could write in 15 minutes. This would provide an answer to Example Exam Question 2(a) on p. 237/505.

2 Again using a PC, make a copy of the 300-word description, but this time reduce it to a 150-word summary. This is about as much as you could write in 7.5 minutes and would provide an answer to the 'outline' part of Question 4(b) on p. 237/505. As you write this shorter précis, try to identify what the essential points are that you want to include.

As well as AO1 description, you have to provide AO2 evaluation. The Commentary panel on p. 230/498 contains 470 words of 'evaluation', covering both strengths and weaknesses – remember, it is important to include both types of 'criticism' in your evaluation.

AO2 ACTIVITY

Evaluating the ecological theory

1 Using a PC, prepare a 300-word evaluation of Gibson's direct theory of perception, linking it as closely as possible to the 300-word description you wrote in the last activity. This would complete your answer to Question 2 on p. 237/505.

2 Now copy this evaluation and reduce it down to 150 words. This would complete your answer to Question 4(b).

Note that the evaluations you prepared for this activity are only one approach to AO2. As the notes to Question 2 say, another way of evaluating direct theories would be to compare them with alternative approaches, i.e. constructivist theories. You will find out more about these in the next part of this topic.

CONSTRUCTIVIST THEORIES

Constructivist theories have a long pedigree, beginning in the early nineteenth century and continuing to the present day. The work of Richard Gregory is perhaps the most influential in modern times. Read the material in the textbook on pp. 231–2/499–500.

HINT

To find out more about Gregory's experiments, visit his website, which contains some interesting videos of his work: **www.richardgregory.org/index.htm**

EXPLANATIONS OF PERCEPTUAL ORGANIZATION

Depth perception

Read the two paragraphs under this heading on p. 232/500 and then try the following activity.

Various so-called 'depth cues' help us to judge the relative distances of objects. These are described on pp. 232–3/500–1 of the textbook Read the text now and then do the activity on the right.

Perceiving movement

As you might expect from a direct theorist, Gibson explains movement in terms of environmental information. Read the text on perceiving movement on pp. 233–4/501–2 and then try the activity at the top of the next page.

Direct theory explanations of movement cues

1 What are the main elements of Gibson's explanation of movement perception. Summarize them here.

_____

_____

_____

2 How do constructivists explain the perception of movement?

_____

_____

_____

3 What are the strengths and weaknesses of Gibson's explanation?

● Strengths:

_____

_____

_____

● Weaknesses:

_____

_____

_____

Visual constancies

Read through the text on p. 234/502 examining visual constancies and then try the following activity.

Visual constancies

1 Define the following terms:
  ● 'perceptual constancy'
  ● size constancy
  ● shape constancy

2 Complete the following table to summarize different explanations of size and shape constancy.

	Constructivist	Direct theory
Size constancy		
Shape constancy		

Visual illusions

Explaining misperceptions or visual illusions provides theorists with quite a challenge. The textbook describes a number of types of illusion, with examples of each.

Visual illusions

1 Why do you think most of the illusions studied are artificial ones?

2 Can you think of any examples of misperceptions/illusions in everyday life, e.g. mistaking clouds for mountain tops or glancing at fields of plastic sheeting used in farming and seeing a 'lake'.

3 How might different theorists explain these kinds of 'illusions'?

Using diagrams in the exam

It is sometimes a good idea to draw quick sketches in the exam to illustrate your answer. For example, drawing an accurate sketch of the Necker cube (see p. 231/499) or the Müller-Lyer illusions (pp. 235/503 and 236/504) would take very little time. In the latter case, you could use the two versions of the illusion to illustrate the challenge to Gregory's theory outlined in the Commentary panel on p. 236/504 – a good AO2 point!

Above all, though, don't waste time meticulously drawing difficult figures, such as the Penrose triangle.

The Müller-Lyer illusion is an important one to include in an essay on visual illusions, as it has provoked a lot of research and led theorists to different conclusions.

ACTIVITY

Visual illusions

Summarize the key points of the research by Gregory and by Day (1990) to explain the Müller-Lyer illusion.

Researcher	Cues we use	How we process the information
● Gregory		
● Day (1990)		

EXAMPLE EXAM QUESTIONS

In your work on this unit, you have already written complete answers to Example Exam Questions 2 and 4(b) on p. 237/505, as well as planning an answer to Question 1.

ACTIVITY

One for you to try ...

Discuss explanations of perceptual organization (e.g. depth, movement, constancies, illusions).

(24 marks)

Having done all the activities above, you are now well prepared to tackle questions on explanations of perceptual organization, such as Example Exam Question 5 on p. 237/505 (reproduced above). Read this question and the guidance given below it. Note that if you are taking your examination after 2005, the guidance about linking constructivist and direct theories of perception to perceptual organization no longer applies.

In this question, you have a choice as to which types of perception organization you refer to. Four examples are given in the specification and all four are covered in the textbook, but you could limit yourself to just two (as the question simply says 'Discuss explanations'). Your AO1 would involve

describing the explanations of perceptual organization you selected. As far as AO2 is concerned, the guidance on p. 237/505 has several ideas.

As you plan your possible answer to the above question, key questions to consider are these:

1 How many types of perception organization will you cover, and which are they?

2 What form will your AO2 evaluation take?

Before you write a complete answer, draw up an outline plan for your essay (similar to the one on p. 74 of this book) showing the different 'chunks' you could divide your essay into.

CHECK YOUR UNDERSTANDING

When you have finished working through this topic, try the questions in 'Check your understanding' on p. 236/504 of the textbook. Check your answers by looking at the relevant parts of the textbook or this workbook, listed below.

1 textbook p. 228/496
2 textbook p. 229/497
3 textbook p. 229/497
4 textbook p. 230/498
5 textbook p. 231/499; workbook p. 79

6 textbook p. 232–3/500–1
7 textbook p. 233/501
8 textbook p. 234/502
9 textbook p. 235/503
10 textbook pp. 234–6/502–4

When you were born, you already possessed a range of perceptual skills – the ability to see, hear and touch, for example. As we grow older, these skills become more developed and refined – but what is it that determines the way in which they develop? Are these skills innately programmed as aspects of natural physical development? Or are there factors in the environment that shape the way our perceptual skills develop? This topic seeks to answer this question.

UNDERSTANDING THE SPECIFICATION

Here is what the AQA (A) specification says about this topic. It forms part of A2 Module 4, Section C: Cognitive Psychology.

This is a challenging area of the specification to unpack, so it pays to read it carefully. First, you are required to cover explanations of perceptual development. You may choose to concentrate on explanations that illustrate the nature–nurture debate in perception, or you may choose to discuss explanations of the development of specific perceptual abilities (such as depth/distance and visual constancies).

Second, there is a specific requirement to cover the nature–nurture debate in perception. Remember that you will be required to both describe (the AO1 component) and evaluate (the AO2 component) whatever material you choose to illustrate this debate.

> ### Perceptual processes and development
>
> **c. Perceptual development**
>
> Explanations of perceptual development, including the nature–nurture debate in perception. Studies of the development of perceptual abilities (e.g. depth/distance, visual constancies), including infant and cross-cultural studies.

Third, you should cover studies of at least two of the perceptual abilities listed above. As it is theoretically possible for a question to be set exclusively on just one type of perceptual ability, you should cover more than one study on each of your chosen abilities. Note that as the examples given are just that – examples – you cannot be asked a question on any one of these by name. Which you choose to study and, therefore, which you choose for your answer, is very much up to you.

TOPIC MAP

The diagram below gives you an overview of what you are about to study.

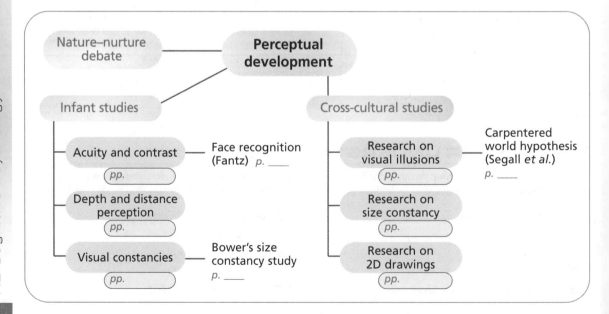

Topic map

Look through pp. 238–46/506–14 of the textbook to see where the items shown in the topic map are covered. Note down the relevant page numbers in the spaces left on the topic map.

KEEPING TRACK

Use the table below to keep track of your work on this topic and plan your revision. See p. iv of this workbook (Introduction) for guidance on filling it in.

Perceptual development		Tick if you ...		
What I need to learn	Where is it?	could make a basic attempt	could make a good attempt	have complete mastery of this
Explanations of perception				
Description of the nature–nurture debate in perception				
Evaluation of the role of innate and environmental factors in perceptual development				
Infant studies				
Description of research into acuity and contrast				
Evaluation of research into acuity and contrast				
Description of research into depth and distance perception				
Evaluation of research into depth and distance perception				
Description of research into visual constancies				
Evaluation of research into visual constancies				
Cross-cultural studies				
Description of research into visual illusions				
Evaluation of research into visual illusions				
Description of research into size constancy				
Evaluation of research into size constancy				
Description of research into two-dimensional drawings				
Evaluation of research into two-dimensional drawings				

THE NATURE–NURTURE DEBATE

An outline of the two sides in the nature–nurture debate is given at the top of p. 238/506. These two contrasting views count as separate 'explanations' of perceptual development, as required in the AQA specification. In any essay focusing on these explanations, you would need to start with a description of the principle of the relevant view.

After this short introduction, the topic looks at six aspects of perceptual development, shown in the blue panels in the topic map on the left. They are grouped under the two headings of 'Infant studies' and 'Cross-cultural studies', as these are the types of research used to investigate those aspects of perceptual development. For each of these six aspects, you will find discussions

of research supporting either the 'nature' or 'nurture' explanation – sometimes both.

HINT

You will learn more about the nature–nurture debate when you study 'Issues and Debates in Psychology' for AQA Module 5. The whole of Topic 4 in Unit 20/28 of the textbook is devoted to this debate and you may find it worthwhile spending a few minutes now reading that – see pp. 599–604/867–72.

INFANT STUDIES

ACTIVITY

Infant studies

Read the text under this heading on p. 238/506 and study Table 8.1/16.1 on p. 239/507.

1 Why is the study of neonates so valuable in investigating whether perceptual skills are innate or learned?

_____

_____

_____

2 The panel in the middle of p. 238/506 lists several difficulties associated with neonate research. Choose a key word or phrase to summarize (and so help you memorize) each one:

- _____
- _____
- _____
- _____
- _____

ACTIVITY

Techniques used in neonate research

This is an ongoing activity that you will need to complete as you work your way through this topic. Table 8.1/16.1 lists eight techniques used by researchers with babies in order to overcome the difficulties described on p. 238/506. As you read the descriptions of research into perceptual development using infants (i.e. up to p. 243/511), identify which techniques the researchers used and note them down in the table below.

Technique	Researcher and area of research
Preferential looking	e.g. Fantz (1980) – Face recognition
Eye-movement monitoring	
Habituation	
Sucking rate	
Conditioning	
Heart and breathing rate	
PET tomography	
VEPs and fMRI	

Acuity and contrast

Read the paragraphs under this heading at the bottom of p. 238/506 and then do the next activity.

ACTIVITY

Acuity and contrast

1 Define 'visual acuity'.

_____

2 What is the level of acuity found in neonates?

_____

3 At what age does it reach the adult level of 20/20?

_____

4 What explanation does Conel (1951) give for its improvement?

_____

_____

5 Does this support the nature or nurture explanation of development?

_____

6 What explanation do Pirchio et al. (1978) give for infants' poor perception of contrast?

_____

_____

7 Does this support the nature or nurture explanation of development?

_____

In exam questions on perceptual development, you may be asked explicitly to discuss research studies, as the specification includes the word 'studies'. Look at Example Exam Questions 2, 3 and 4 on pp. 247–8/515–16. These are all variations on the theme of describing and evaluating research studies. As the notes to Question 3 suggest, using the 'APFCC' method – which you should be familiar with from AS-level pscyhology – is an excellent way of organizing your answers.

ACTIVITY

Fantz's (1961) research into face recognition

In the table below, write a summary of Fantz's research, described on p. 239/507, using trigger phrases, mnemonics or whatever will help you to memorize the important features.

Under 'Criticisms', use the two columns to list separately those arguments that support the nativist ('nature') explanation and those that support the empiricist ('nurture') explanation. You can bring in studies by other researchers that either support or challenge Fantz's findings.

KEY STUDY — textbook p. 239/507

Researchers **Fantz (1961)**	Findings
Title	
Aims	
Procedures	Conclusions
Criticisms – Supporting nature	Criticisms – Supporting nurture

Depth perception

A number of researchers have investigated depth and distance perception in babies, a skill that is essential for making sense of our three-dimensional world.

ACTIVITY

Gibson and Walk's (1960) research into depth perception

Write a summary of Gibson and Walk's research (see p. 240/508), using trigger phrases, mnemonics or whatever will help you to memorize the important features. Follow the format shown above, but write your summary directly into a PC word-processing program.

Again, use the 'Criticisms' to summarize whether the research supports the 'nature' or 'nurture' argument. You can also mention the findings of other research that tried to replicate or adapt Gibson and Walk's studies (summarized in the first two bullet points in the Commentary panel on p. 241/509).

Other research into depth perception

The Commentary panel on p. 241/509 includes several other pieces of research that have given insight into the role of innate and learned factors in depth and distance perception. Complete the following table to summarize the key points. Use the final column to indicate whether the research supports the nature or nurture argument.

Researcher	Key features of research	Findings	Nature or nurture?
Yonas and Owsley (1987)			
Yonas (1981)			
Granrud and Yonas (1985)			

Visual constancies

You learned about size and shape constancy in Topic 2 (see p. 80 of this workbook), and their role in helping us perceive stability in the environment. Researchers have also investigated this in infants.

Bower's (1965) study of size constancy

Read the Key research on p. 242/510, including the Commentary panel at the bottom of the page. Write a summary of Bower's research, following the format shown on p. 85 and writing your summary directly into a PC word-processing program. There is a lot of detail in this panel, so take care to extract only the most significant points. Once again, use the 'Criticisms' to summarize whether the research supports the 'nature' or 'nurture' argument.

Other research into visual constancies

Several other pieces of research into visual constancies are described on pp. 241/509 and 243/511. Using your PC, summarize the key points in the form of a table, using the format shown in the activity at the top of the page.

Summary of research into infant studies

The Commentary panel on p. 243/511 provides a good, general summing-up of the research based on studies of infants. It is a balanced weighing-up of the arguments – with some support for both innate and learned factors – and ends with an appraisal of how we need to consider the interaction between the factors, rather than any presumed opposition. This is a good approach to replicate in any exam answers you write.

Answering an exam question

Look at Example Exam Question 3 on p. 248/516. To answer part (a), you would have to write a total of 300 words: 150 words of AO1 description and 150 words of AO2 evaluation. If faced with this question, which of the studies would you choose to write about? It would be a good idea to select one where you would have plenty of evaluative comments to make – so any of the three studies for which you have done 'APFCC-style' activities would be highly suitable.

Choose one of the infant studies discussed in this topic and, using a PC, write an answer to Question 3(a).

CROSS-CULTURAL STUDIES

The second main group of studies into perceptual development are those that have investigated cultural differences.

ACTIVITY

The value of cross-cultural research

Read the introduction to this area of research at the bottom of p. 243/511 and, on separate paper, do the following.

1 Explain how cross-cultural studies can help researchers distinguish between innate and environmental influences in perceptual development.

2 Briefly summarize the difference between biological and ecological factors in cultural differences.

ACTIVITY

Research into visual illusions

Read from the last paragraph on p. 243/511 to the end of the Commentary panel on p. 244/512. Write a summary of the research by Segall et al.(1963, 1966), following the format shown on p. 85 and writing your summary directly into a PC word-processing program.

Use the 'Criticisms' to summarize whether the research supports the 'nature' or 'nurture' argument. Include the findings of other research which either support or challenge Segall and colleagues' findings, e.g. Pollack (1963).

Research on 2D drawings

Many researchers have focused on the interpretation of two-dimensional drawings in their investigation of cross-cultural differences in perception. The textbook describes several of these, on pp. 245–6/513–14.

ACTIVITY

Research on two dimensional drawings

Read through the text and draw up a table summarizing the findings of the research. Follow the format shown below. Use the final column to indicate whether the research supports the nativist view or the empiricist view.

Researcher	Key features of research	Findings	Nature or nurture?
e.g. Hochberg and Brooks (1962)	Son shielded from pictures for 19 months	Son able to recognize line drawings, despite isolation from images	Nature – recognition of objects in pictures is not learned

Summary of cross-cultural research

The Evaluation panel on p. 246/514 provides a useful evaluation of the research based on cross-cultural studies. In particular, it raises the issue of pictorial art, which illustrates the difficulty of disentangling innate and environmental factors: both seem to be involved in the process of perceptual development.

Evaluating cross-cultural studies

Read the Evaluation panel on p. 246/514 and identify 8 to 10 key points made there. Some points will be general comments on the nature of cross-cultural research; others will provide support for one particular explanation or another.

Answering an exam question

Look again at Example Exam Question 3 on p. 248/516. To answer part (b), you would have to write a further 300 words. If faced with this question, which study would you choose to write about? The work of Segall and colleagues is an obvious choice, but you could also construct an answer based on the work of Deregowski. Again, think carefully about what you might include as AO2 evaluation.

Choose one of the cross-cultural studies discussed in this topic and, using a PC, write an answer to Question 3(b).

EXAMPLE EXAM QUESTIONS

You have already planned and written a complete answer to Example Exam Question 3 on p. 248/516.

Some exam questions pose particular problems. The question below is a prime example. In the specimen answer below, we have tried to take a very structured approach, using material on pp. 238–46/506–14.

Because there is a mass of material that could be used in an answer to this question, you have to be very selective for your eventual 600-word exam answer. We have chosen to use only infant studies and cross-cultural studies to illustrate the nature–nurture debate. This is just one way to answer this question. Try constructing your own answer using different material.

Sample answer

Discuss the nature–nurture debate as it applies to perceptual development.   (24 marks)

The nature view holds that we are born with perceptual abilities that develop with age in a genetically programmed way. The nurture view believes that we are born with only the most basic sensory capacity and that our perceptual abilities develop through experience and by interacting with our environment. If perceptual abilities are inborn, they should be apparent in neonates. Fantz's (1961) studies seemed to show that face recognition was an innate ability. These studies suggested that human babies have an innate preference for human faces over other visual objects. Gibson and Walk (1960) used a 'visual cliff' apparatus to test whether young babies could perceive depth. Most of the babies would not crawl over the deep side of the apparatus, which suggested that depth perception was innate. Research has also suggested that babies as young as 2 months can display both size and shape constancy (Bower 1965, 1966).

This evidence from neonate and infant studies would seem to support the nature argument by suggesting that sophisticated perceptual skills are evident in even the very youngest child. However, there are a number of problems with this type of study that would make such conclusions invalid. In particular, it can be difficult to disentangle the effects of maturation of the visual system from the effects of experience with the visual environment. Some researchers have criticized Fantz's conclusions, saying that the stimuli were artificial and hardly looked like real faces; they simply had more contour evident. Havell (1985) found that there was no difference in preference when babies were shown faces and other stimuli with equal amounts of contour and movement. Critics of Gibson and Walk's study have argued that babies of 6 months could have learned this ability through experience, although Gibson and Walk did also demonstrate the same ability in newborn animals which were independently mobile. Bower's results have proved difficult to replicate and critics have suggested that it is easy to misinterpret babies' behaviour as indicating shape and size constancy where none might exist.

Psychologists have also made use of cross-cultural studies in the nature–nurture debate, as people from different cultures may differ from each other biologically (e.g. in genetic inheritance, diet) and in terms of ecological factors (e.g. local environment, cultural history). Much of the research in this area has centred on the experience of visual illusions. Segall *et al.* (1963) found evidence that people who live in a world which is full of lines and angles (i.e. the 'carpentered world') were more susceptible to the Müller-Lyer illusion than those from non-carpentered environments, indicating that early experience has an influence on later perception. Hudson (1962) showed pictures containing various pictorial depth cues to people in South Africa. He found that non-Western people had difficulty interpreting depth from the cues in the picture. This suggests that being used to seeing pictorial representations of depth, through formal education from an early age, helps people interpret such pictures.

Pollack (1963) suggested that retinal pigmentation, which may be denser in dark-skinned non-Europeans, might be responsible for their reduced susceptibility to the Müller-Lyer illusion. In other words, biological rather than cultural differences might be responsible for the different responses to visual illusions. It is also possible that the difficulties people from other cultures experience with Western art reflect aesthetic rather than perceptual factors. This finding is reinforced by Hudson's later study which showed that African adults and children who had not been exposed to Western culture preferred an unrealistic aerial picture that gave more information about the animal than its perspective. The findings from cross-cultural studies are often ambiguous and difficult to interpret. Early studies were not conducted under controlled conditions and later, more rigorous, studies have been criticized for underestimating perceptual abilities. It is unlikely, therefore, that our perceptual skills can be fully explained by either nature or nurture alone, but through an interaction of innate and environmental factors.

CHECK YOUR UNDERSTANDING

Now try the questions in 'Check your understanding' on p. 247/515 of the textbook. Check your answers by looking at the relevant parts of the textbook or this workbook, listed below.

1 textbook p. 238/506

2 textbook p. 238/506

3 textbook p. 239/507

4 textbook p. 238/506

5 textbook pp. 240–1/508–9

6 workbook p. 86

7 textbook p. 243/511

8 textbook pp. 243–4/511–12

9 workbook p. 87

COGNITIVE
Development

PREVIEW

There are three topics in this unit. You should read them alongside the following pages in the Collins *Psychology for A2-level/Psychology* textbook:

Topic	*Psychology for A2*	*Psychology*
1 Development of thinking	pp. 284–97	pp. 552–65
2 Development of measured intelligence	pp. 298–305	pp. 566–73
3 Development of moral understanding	pp. 306–15	pp. 574–83

INTRODUCTION

Developmental Psychology is one of five sections in Module 4 (AQA Specification A), as the diagram below shows. This section is further divided into three sub-sections – 'Cognitive development' is the first of these.

Read the Preview and Introduction on p. 282/550 of the textbook now. This will give you an overview of what's in the unit.

Where this unit fits in to the A-level qualification

Section A:
Social Psychology

Section B:
Physiological Psychology

In the Module 4 exam, there will be a total of 15 questions, three relating to each Section (i.e. one per sub-section). You have to answer **three** questions, from at least **two** sections.

Module 4

Section C:
Cognitive Psychology

Section D:
Developmental Psychology

Section E:
Comparative Psychology

- **COGNITIVE DEVELOPMENT**
- SOCIAL & PERSONALITY DEVELOPMENT
- ADULTHOOD

a Development of thinking

b Development of measured intelligence

c Development of moral understanding

Cognitive development is the study of how our mental activities develop. Naturally, children have been the focus of much of the research in this area and nowhere more so than in the development of thinking. This topic investigates the work of two great psychologists who devoted their lives to this aspect of research: Piaget and Vygotsky. Both developed highly influential theories that have led to real practical changes in the way children are educated – or rather, encouraged to learn. After a discussion of each psychologist's work, the final section of this topic explores some of the changes in educational practice that have taken place as a result of their work.

UNDERSTANDING THE SPECIFICATION

Here is what the AQA (A) specification says about this topic. It forms part of A2 Module 4, Section D: Developmental Psychology.

Unlike many other areas of the specification, where theories are named only as examples, the two theories given here are prescribed. This means that they can be named in questions, and that you must study them. It is worth studying each theory to an appropriate depth and breadth for a question solely on that theory, and also preparing an outline (and outline evaluation) of each should a question specify both. There is no real need to study more than the two theories given here, although you may choose to study more than these to enrich your

Cognitive development

a. **Development of thinking**

Theories of cognitive development, including Piaget and Vygotsky. Applications of these theories (e.g. to education).

understanding of how theories of cognitive development have been applied to education. Students tend to struggle in this latter part, so you should have sufficient material to answer a question that is solely on applications. A common mistake is to present a discussion of the underlying theory rather than the applications derived from it.

TOPIC MAP

The diagram below is a visual 'map' of the content of this topic.

ACTIVITY

Topic map

Look through pp. 284–96/552–64 of the textbook to see where the items shown in the topic map are covered. Note down the relevant page numbers in the spaces left on the topic map.

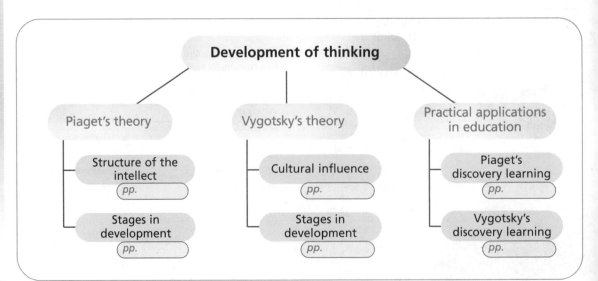

Development of thinking

- Piaget's theory
  - Structure of the intellect
    pp.
  - Stages in development
    pp.
- Vygotsky's theory
  - Cultural influence
    pp.
  - Stages in development
    pp.
- Practical applications in education
  - Piaget's discovery learning
    pp.
  - Vygotsky's discovery learning
    pp.

KEEPING TRACK

Use the table below to keep track of your work on this topic and plan your revision. See p. iv of this workbook (Introduction) for guidance on filling it in.

Development of thinking		Tick if you ...		
What I need to learn	*Where is it?*	could make a basic attempt	could make a good attempt	have complete mastery of this
Piaget's theory of cognitive development				
Description of the structure of the intellect				
Description of the stages of development				
Evaluation of Piaget's theory of cognitive development				
Vygotsky's theory of cognitive development				
Description of the influence of culture				
Description of the process of cultural influence				
Description of stages in the development of thinking				
Evaluation of Vygotsky's theory of cognitive development				
Practical applications in education				
Description of Piaget's discovery learning				
Evaluation of Piaget's approach in education				
Description of Vygotsky's discovery learning				
Evaluation of Vygotsky's approach in education				

PIAGET'S THEORY OF COGNITIVE DEVELOPMENT

Piaget was one of the most influential psychologists of the twentieth century. His theory of cognitive development broke new ground and left a lasting legacy for later researchers. The textbook devotes five pages to his theory. Your challenge – especially when it comes to writing relatively short essays in an exam situation – is to pick out the key points and present them succinctly yet fluently in your essay.

ACTIVITY

The causes of developmental changes

Read through p. 284/552 and up to the first heading on p. 285/553. Then answer the following questions.

1 What led Piaget to conclude that children think differently from adults, and that young children think differently from older ones?

_____

_____

_____

2 In what way does Piaget's theory acknowledge the role of both nature (innate factors) and nurture (environmental factors) in his theory of cognitive development.

_____

_____

_____

3 What did Piaget mean by the following terms?

● Structure

_____

● Schema

_____

● Assimilation

_____

● Accommodation

_____

● Adaptation

_____

● Equilibration

_____

Adaptation

Draw a diagram or flowchart to illustrate the process of 'adaptation', the process whereby schemas become more complex. We have started off the beginning of the process for you:

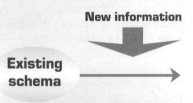

Stages in development

Piaget identified four distinct stages of development, outlined in Table 10.1/18.1.
It is important to understand what causes a change to occur.

The causes of developmental changes

Read through Table 10.1/18.1 and the introductory paragraph to 'Stages of development' on p. 285/553.

1 What two conditions are necessary for a child to reach a new stage of development? Which condition is biologically based and which relates to the environment?

(a) _____

(b) _____

2 In the table below, summarize the four stages of development described in Table 10.1/18.1, using key words or phrases to help you memorize each stage.

Age	Stage	Features
●		
●		
●		
●		

Summarizing Piaget's four stages

Read through the descriptions of Piaget's four stages and the comments on each one given in the Commentary panels (pp. 285–8/553–6). Summarize each stage in a series of key points. In the right-column, note down any evaluative points. For example, for the first stage – the sensorimotor stage – you might write:

Key features	Comments
● Infants construct schemas by combining sensory and motor information.	
● Six sub-stages, including 'circular reactions' (infant repeats actions to learn new schemas)	
● Object permanence develops at around 8 months to 1 year	● Bower (1981) found object permanence in babies of 5 months.

This consists of 40 words – in the exam, you would not have time to write much more than this for each stage. Now work through each of the four stages, picking out the key points in a similar fashion.

Describing Piaget's theory

There is a lot of information about Piaget's theory in the textbook – far more than you could possibly hope to reproduce in the exam. So, as well as understanding the details of Piaget's theory, you need to be able to pick out the most important features. Look at Example Exam Question 1 on p. 297/565. If you were answering this question, you would have about 15 minutes to write a description, i.e. about 300 words, with a further 15 minutes to write an evaluation. Your description should include:

- a brief outline of the basic principles of Piaget's theory (e.g. that children think differently from adults, the role of schemas and the processes of adaptation)
- a short summary of each of the four stages.

ACTIVITY

Preparing summaries for the exam

1 Now write a 300-word summary of Piaget's theory of cognitive development. Do this using your PC, so that you can keep track of the number of words and make changes easily.

For the summary of the four stages, it's a good idea to include points which you know will allow you to make an evaluative (AO2) point later. In the sensorimotor stage, for example, the key feature of object permanence leads to a useful AO2 comment – Bower challenged Piaget's view of the timing of this development.

This activity is quite challenging, so it is worth spending time on it to get it right. This is, in effect, your 12-mark summary of Piaget's theory.

2 Once you have finished your 300-word summary, make a copy of it and reduce it to 150 words! This, too, will prove quite a challenge. In the exam, the description of a theory may be worth only 6 marks (see part (a) of Question 2 on p. 297/565 – that relates to Vygotsky's theory, but a similar question could be set relating to Piaget). This shorter summary is your 6-mark summary of Piaget's theory.

Evaluating Piaget's theory

Looking again at Question 1 on p. 297/565, the 'evaluate' part of the answer is also worth 12 marks. Again, you would have about 15 minutes to write your evaluation, i.e. about 300 words.

Your evaluation could include:

- comments on individual stages in the theory – useful points are contained in the Commentary panels on pp. 285/553, 286/554 and 288/556
- an overall evaluation of Piaget's theory – see the Evaluation panel on pp. 288–9/556–7
- a comparison of Piaget's theory with other theories (e.g. Vygotsky's) – see the Evaluation panel on p. 292/560.

Evaluation involves both positive and negative commentary. The four bullet points in the Evaluation panel on pp. 288–9/556–7 highlight possible challenges to Piaget's claims, but the panel also includes some positive support for Piaget's work. Sara Meadows, in the Expert interview on p. 294/562, also gives an extremely useful assessment of Piaget's work, including its current status and some of its weaknesses. You can use these in your evaluation as well.

Evaluating Piaget's theory

1 Start by drawing up a list of general evaluative (AO2) points relating to Piaget's theory. Do this on your PC, dividing the list into two columns: positive points (support for the theory) and negative points (challenges to the theory).

2 Now write a 300-word evaluation of Piaget's theory of cognitive development. Do this using your PC, so that you can keep track of the number of words and make changes easily.

Some of your evaluative comments will relate specifically to the four stages (see Activity, 'Summarizing Piaget's four stages', p. 92). You could weave these comments into the AO1 description you wrote earlier. If you do this, you could use a different colour for the AO2 material, so that you can see clearly which is which. This would be useful later on when you come to revise for the exam and starting looking back over your work.

This is your 12-mark (15-minute) evaluation of Piaget's theory.

3 Once you have finished your 300-word summary, make a copy of it and reduce it to 150 words. This shorter summary is your 6-mark evaluation of Piaget's theory.

VYGOTSKY'S THEORY OF COGNITIVE DEVELOPMENT

The second major theory discussed in the textbook is that of Vygotsky. Although it shares some common ground with Piaget, there are some clear differences, which we shall examine.

The influence of culture

One of the main differences between Piaget's and Vygotsky's theories is the emphasis given in Vygotsky's theory to culture.

ACTIVITY

The influence of culture

Read through the text from the main heading on p. 289/557 to the end of the Commentary panel on p. 290/558.

1 What did Vygotsky mean by 'culture'?

2 What is the role of 'cultural influence'?

3 Three research studies provide support for Vygotsky's view of culture. Make notes to summarize the key points of each.

The process of cultural influence

Vygotsky stressed the role of teachers or 'mediators' in the learning process. Learning is a social process and knowledge is socially constructed. If you find that you are struggling with this concept, read the first column on p. 293/561, which explains it in practical terms.

EXAM HINT

Using other people's research findings to support the claims of a theory counts as AO2 evaluation in an exam essay – examples here are McNaughton and Leyland's findings regarding the ZPD and Wertsch's studies of self-regulation (see below).

ACTIVITY

Cultural influence and learning

Read through pp. 290–1/558–9 up to the end of the first Commentary panel ('Social and individual planes'). Answer the following questions.

1 What is the zone of proximal development (ZPD)?

2 What is the teacher/mediator's role in helping children reach their potential?

3 How did McNaughton and Leyland's (1990) research demonstrate that the greatest teaching input occurs 'at the edge of the ZPD', as Vygotsky predicted?

4 What is meant by 'semiotic mediation'?

5 How does the learning child move towards self-regulation? Make notes explaining the process.

ACTIVITY

The role of language

Now read from p. 291/559, 'The role of language', to the end of Table 10.4/18.4 on p. 292/560. Answer the following questions.

1 What, in Vygotsky's view, is the role of language in development?

_____

2 What is meant by the following terms and at what ages are they displayed?

	Definition	Age
● Prelinguistic thought		
● Pre-intellectual, social speech		
● Egocentric speech		
● Inner speech		

ACTIVITY

Summarizing Vygotsky's theory

1 Using your PC, write a 300-word description of Vygotsky's theory of cognitive development. This is your 12-mark summary of Vygotsky's theory – you could use it as half of your answer to Example Exam Question 3 on p. 297/565.

Again, it's a good idea to include points which you know will allow you to make an evaluative (AO2) point later.

2 Once you have finished your 300-word summary, make a copy of it and reduce it to 150 words. This shorter summary is your 6-mark summary of Vygotsky's theory. This would be ideal as an answer to part (a) of Question 2 on p. 297/565.

(AO2) ACTIVITY

Evaluating Vygotsky's theory

1 Again using your PC, write a 300-word evaluation of Vygotsky's theory of cognitive development. Again, you can decide whether to weave this into your 300-word description (see the activity on the left) or whether to write a separate 'chunk'.

This is your 12-mark (15-minute) evaluation of Vygotsky's theory.

2 Once you have finished your 300-word summary, make a copy of it and reduce it to 150 words. This shorter summary is your 6-mark evaluation of Vygotsky's theory.

PRACTICAL APPLICATIONS IN EDUCATION

Both Piaget's and Vygotsky's theories have had enormous influence on the practice of education. The final part of this topic examines what these are. Start by reading the first column on p. 293/561 and then try the activity on the right before reading on.

ACTIVITY

Practical applications

1 What, in your own words, is the major difference between Piaget's and Vygotsky's approach, as it applies to the learning context?

2 What is meant by the following terms?
- Discovery learning
- Constructivist approach

Piaget's discovery learning

Read the remainder of p. 293/561, concerning Piaget's discovery learning, and then complete the activities below and right.

(AO2) ACTIVITY

Evaluating Piaget's approach in education

Read the Evaluation panel on p. 293/561 and the Expert interview with Sara Meadows on p. 294/562. Draw up a list of general evaluative (AO2) points you could make relating to the application of Piaget's theory to education. Divide them into positive and negative points.

ACTIVITY

Piaget's discovery learning

The three paragraphs in the second column on p. 293/561 contain three important outcomes for educational practice deriving from Piaget's work. Use the table below to summarize the key point of each, citing the specific aspect of Piaget's theory that led to this outcome.

Outcome	Basis in Piaget's theory
1	
2	
3	

Vygotsky's discovery learning

Read the text under this heading on pp. 295–6/563–4 and then do the following activities.

Read the text under this heading on pp. 295–6/563–4 and then do the following activities.

ACTIVITY

Vygotsky's discovery learning

Page 295/563 mentions three aspects of educational practice where Vygotsky's theory have been influential: scaffolding, collaborative learning and peer tutor. Draw up a table to summarize the key points of each, citing the specific aspect of Vygotsky's theory that led to this outcome.

 ACTIVITY

Evaluating Vygotsky's approach in education

Read the Evaluation panel on p. 296/564. Draw up a list of general evaluative (AO2) points you could make relating to the application of Vygotsky's theory to education. Divide them into positive and negative points.

EXAMPLE EXAM QUESTIONS

In your work on this unit, you have already planned and written a complete answer to Example Exam Question 1 on p. 297/565. The summaries you wrote of Piaget's and Vygotsky's theories will also provide the basis of answers to Questions 2(a), 3 and 4(a).

ACTIVITY

One for you to try ...

Discuss applications of theories of cognitive development (e.g. to education)   **(24 marks)**

The most important requirement of this question is that you discuss *applications* of theories rather than the theories themselves. This is particularly important when discussing Piaget, as it is easy to wander down the stages-of-development path and miss the point completely. Vygotsky's theory, on the other hand, has far more of an educational feel to it anyway, so you are less likely to make that mistake.

There is also a plurality requirement in that you are asked to discuss 'applications' in the plural and (strictly speaking) 'theories' in the plural as well. Appropriate material to help you answer this question can be found on pp. 293–6/561-4. You might choose to structure your answer as follows:

- AO1 – basic principles of Piaget's approach to education, including his views on discovery learning
- AO2 – evaluation of Piaget's approach to education, e.g. his influence on primary education in the UK, the importance of readiness, Sara Meadows's views on the relevance of Piaget's view of cognitive development to modern-day educational practices, etc.
- AO1 – basic principles of Vygotsky's approach to education, including scaffolding, collaborative learning and peer tutoring
- AO2 – evaluation of Vygotsky's approach to education, e.g. individual differences, the role of 'experts', the importance of social influences.

CHECK YOUR UNDERSTANDING

When you have finished working through this topic, try the questions in 'Check your understanding' on p. 296/564 of the textbook. Check your answers by looking at the relevant parts of the textbook or this workbook, listed below.

1 workbook p. 92 (activity)

2 textbook pp. 284–5/552–3

3 textbook pp. 288–9/556–7; workbook p. 93

4 textbook pp. 284–5/552–3

5 textbook p. 289/557

6 textbook p. 289/557

7 textbook p. 290/558

8 textbook pp. 286/554 and 292/560

9 textbook p. 293/561

10 textbook p. 295/563

The nature–nurture debate features highly in discussions of many aspects of psychology. Intelligence is one such area, as researchers have tried to disentangle the various factors – genetic and environmental – that might affect its development. Are we born with a fixed degree of intelligence? Does the way we are brought up affect how intelligent we become? Or is there an element of both genes and environment at work here? We will look at each side of the debate in turn.

UNDERSTANDING THE SPECIFICATION

Here is what the AQA (A) specification says about this topic. It forms part of A2 Module 4, Section D: Developmental Psychology.

The term 'research' in this context means 'theories and/or studies', so either or both of these can contribute to your understanding of this area. What are the factors associated with the development of measured intelligence, and what is 'measured' intelligence? The specification is helpful in telling you what the main 'factors' are (i.e. genetics and environmental factors), and even gives an example of an environmental factor – cultural differences (although there are others). 'Measured' intelligence is simply intelligence as measured by some sort of intelligence test (as distinct from the type of qualitative intelligence

> ### Cognitive development
>
> **b. Development of measured intelligence**
> Research into factors associated with the development of measured intelligence, including the role of genetics and environmental factors (e.g. cultural differences).

we might associate with Piaget's view of the intellect). The word 'including' in the specification entry tells you that you must study both the role of genetics and the role of environmental factors, and be prepared to include both in an answer if requested, or concentrate on only one if that is what the question asks for.

TOPIC MAP

The diagram below gives you an overview of what you are about to study.

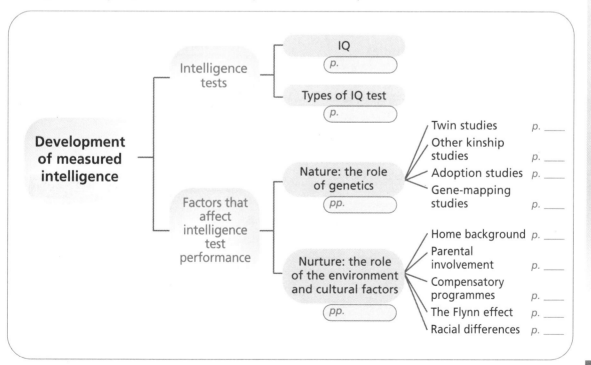

KEEPING TRACK

Use the table below to keep track of your work on this topic and plan your revision. See p. iv of this workbook (Introduction) for guidance on filling it in.

Development of measured intelligence		Tick if you ...		
What I need to learn	*Where is it?*	could make a basic attempt	could make a good attempt	have complete mastery of this
Intelligence tests				
Description of IQ and types of IQ test				
Factors that affect intelligence test performance				
Description of the role of genetics				
Evaluation of the role of genetics				
Description of the role of environmental factors				
Evaluation of the role of environmental factors				
Evaluation of the interdependence of nature and nurture in intelligence test performance				

INTELLIGENCE TESTS

This topic begins by giving the background to the development of intelligence tests, with examples of different kinds of question that might feature in such tests.

FACTORS THAT AFFECT INTELLIGENCE TEST PERFORMANCE

Nature: the role of genetics

The textbook discusses four types of research that psychologists have carried out in order to investigate the role of genetics in the development of intelligence:

- twin studies
- other kinship studies
- adoption studies
- gene-mapping studies.

Twin studies are particularly useful, because they provide the rare opportunity to study people who are genetically identical (or apparently so – possible complications are described in the Commentary panel on p. 299/567).

Read the text under the heading 'Twin studies' on p. 299/567.

ACTIVITY

Shields's (1962) twin study

The focus of this topic is 'research', as that word appears in the relevant part of the AQA specification (see 'Understanding the specification' on p. 97). A typical question might be Example Exam Question 5 on p. 305/573. Your answer to this question could include descriptions and evaluations of specific research studies. Shields's classic twin study would be an excellent piece of research to include. A good way of organizing the information about this study is by using the 'APFCC' method (Aims–Procedures–Findings–Conclusions–Criticisms), which you should be familiar with from AS-level psychology. APF and the first C (conclusions) would be AO1 descriptive material, while the second C (criticisms) would count as AO2.

In the table below, write a summary of Shields's research, using trigger phrases, mnemonics or whatever will help you to memorize the important features. When describing a study in an essay, you may find it helpful to emphasize the findings and conclusions more than the aims and procedures. Alternatively, you could use the aims and conclusions to provide a useful summary of the study.

Under 'Criticisms', use the two columns to list separately points of positive and negative commentary. Positive points could include research support from other studies. Negative points could include criticisms of the research methods or findings from studies by other researchers that challenge Shields's findings – the Commentary panel on p. 299/567 contains several useful AO2 points.

KEY STUDY   textbook p. 299/567

Researchers Shields (1962)	Findings
Title	
Aims	
Procedures	Conclusions
Criticisms – Supporting nature	Criticisms – Supporting nurture

ACTIVITY

Kinship, adoption and gene-mapping studies

Read from the top of p. 300/568 to the first paragraph on p. 301/569. On your PC, draw up a table, using the format shown below, to note down the key points of the research studies discussed in the textbook. Use the columns to summarize the researchers' findings and conclusions that can be drawn. In the final column, note down any evaluative (AO2) comments, e.g. what this tells us about the role of genetic influences in the development of intelligence.

Kinship studies

Researcher	Findings	Conclusions	Genetic influence?
Bouchard and McGue (1981)	IQ correlation, relatives living together:	More closely related	Supports
	0.86 MZ twins – 0.60 DZ twins	individuals are, the	
	0.47 siblings	more similar their IQ	

Answering exam questions on the role of genetics

Look at Example Exam Question 2 on p. 305/573. If you were answering this question, you would have about 15 minutes to write a description of the role of genetics, i.e. about 300 words, with a further 15 minutes to write an evaluation. Your description should include an outline of relevant research, and the findings and conclusions from it.

ACTIVITY

Preparing summaries for the exam

1 Write a 300-word summary, describing research into the role of genetics in the development of measured intelligence. Do this using your PC, so that you can keep track of the number of words and make changes easily.

This will provide you with a 15-minute (or 12-mark) summary of the role of genetics.

2 Once you have finished your 300-word summary, make a copy of it and reduce it to 150 words. This shorter summary is your 6-mark description of the role of genetics. You could use it in an answer to Question 4 on p. 305/573 (if you chose to follow the advice given under the question and divide your answer into four 150-word chunks).

Looking again at Question 2 on p. 305/573, the 'evaluate' part of the answer is also worth 12 marks. Again, you would have about 15 minutes to write your evaluation, i.e. about 300 words. Your evaluation could include:

- comments on the particular research studies you have described – useful points are contained in the Commentary panels on pp. 299/567 and 300/568.

- comments on the difficulty of disentangling nature from nurture – see the Commentary panel on p. 303/571.

 **ACTIVITY**

Evaluating the evidence for a genetic role

1 Now write a 300-word evaluation of the evidence for the role of genetics in the development of measured intelligence. Again, use your PC to write and store your summary.

Some of your evaluative comments will relate specifically to the research studies you outlined in your AO1 summary (see the previous activity). You could weave these comments into the AO1 description you wrote earlier. If you do this, try using a different colour for the AO2 text, so that you can see clearly which is which. This would be useful later on when you come to revise for the exam and start looking back over your work.

This is your 12-mark (15-minute) evaluation of the evidence for the role of genetics and completes your answer to Example Exam Question 2 on p. 305/573.

2 Once you have finished your 300-word summary, make a copy of it and reduce it to 150 words. This shorter summary is your 6-mark evaluation of the evidence for a genetic role.

Nurture: environmental and cultural factors

Read the first paragraph under this heading on p. 301/569. It outlines some of the factors in the environment that might affect the development of intelligence. This part of the topic looks in more detail at five aspects:

- home background
- parental involvement
- compensatory programmes
- the Flynn effect
- racial differences.

ACTIVITY

Research studies into home background, parental involvement and compensatory programmes

Read the text about home background, parental involvement and compensatory programmes on pp. 301–2/569–70. Four important pieces of research are discussed there:

- Sameroff *et al.* (1993) – the Rochester Longitudinal Study
- Caldwell and Bradley (1984) – research into the home environment
- Hart and Risley (1995) – investigation of verbal interactions between parents and children
- Head Start – the enrichment programme carried out in the USA.

Write summaries of these studies. Again, use the APFCC model to organize the information, i.e. summarizing Aims, Procedures, Findings, Conclusions and Criticisms. Use trigger phrases, mnemonics or whatever will help you to memorize the important features. Follow the format shown on p. 99, but write your summary directly into a PC word-processing program.

Under 'Criticisms', use the two columns to separate positive points and negative points, including what the research tells us about the role of environmental factors in the development of intelligence. Here, you should include the points made in the Commentary panels on pp. 301/569 and 302/570.

HINT

Don't try to memorize all ten points listed in Table 10.3/18.3. If you were writing about the Rochester Longitudinal Study in the exam, one or two examples of relevant factors would be enough – you certainly wouldn't have time to list all ten.

ACTIVITY

The Flynn effect

Read the text on p. 302/570 about the Flynn effect and answer the following questions.

1 What is the Flynn effect?

_____

_____

2 What is meant by 'reaction range'?

_____

_____

3 Briefly list three explanations for the Flynn effect. Say whether the explanation supports the genetic or environmental role in the development of intelligence and, in the final column, comment on the plausibility of each explanation.

Explanation	Genetic or environmental?	Plausibility
•		
•		
•		

Unit 10/18 // Cognitive development

101

The question of genetic vs environmental factors in the development of intelligence has particular relevance when it comes to race and measuring intelligence.

Answering exam questions on the role of environmental factors

EXAMPLE EXAM QUESTIONS

In your work on this unit, you have already planned and written complete answers to Example Exam Questions 2 and 4 on p. 305/573.

Note that the AQA specification for exams in 2006 onwards gives 'cultural differences' as an example (rather than saying 'including' as previously).

This means that the wording of Questions 1 and 3 on p. 305/573 will not be possible, as questions cannot be asked specifically about 'cultural differences'. However, you might be set questions on environmental factors, such as the following:

1 Describe and evaluate research (theories **and/or** studies) into the role of environmental factors in the development of intelligence test performance (e.g. cultural differences). (24 marks)

3 (a) Describe research (theories **and/or** studies) into the role of environmental factors in measured intelligence. (12 marks)

(b) To what extent does such research suggest that the development of measured intelligence can be explained by environmental factors? (12 marks)

You have, in effect, already prepared answers to two of these questions – by writing the 300-word summary of the evidence for the role of environmental factors and a 300-word evaluation of the evidence (see central activities on p. 102). This leaves Question 5 on p. 305/573 as the only one unanswered, so we have used some of the material on pp. 298–304/566–72 to construct an answer to this question. Note that we have used the term 'measured intelligence' rather than the previous specification wording 'intelligence test performance' from the textbook. In the answer below, note how the material moves from AO1(blue) to AO2 (brown) in each paragraph, and although there are different proportions of AO1 and AO2 in each, the overall proportions of AO1 and AO2 are the same.

Sample answer

Describe and evaluate research (theories and/or studies) into factors associated with the development of measured intelligence.

(24 marks)

Researchers are able to use twin studies to conduct natural experiments where either genetics or environment is constant or varied. Shields (1962) measured the intelligence of 44 pairs of identical (MZ) twins who had been reared apart and found that the correlation of IQ scores was 0.77. This correlation was very similar to that of MZ twins reared together (0.76). This appears to suggest that environment had very little influence in the development of measured intelligence and that genetic factors were more important. This conclusion was further supported by the fact that correlations between DZ twins reared together were significantly lower at 0.51. Despite this evidence, critics of Shields's study have pointed out that the twins had actually spent a substantial amount of time together, and so had not been truly raised in different environments. However, later, better controlled studies have found similar evidence (e.g. Pederson et al. 1992). A further criticism of twin studies is that assumptions that some of the twins were identical have turned out to be false, invalidating many of the conclusions about this type of research.

Adoption studies allow researchers to compare the IQ correlations of children with both their biological and their adoptive parents. In the Texas adoption project (Horn 1983), children's IQ was shown to be more closely correlated with their biological than their adoptive mother (0.28 compared to 0.15), although the differences were small. When tested again some years later, the correlation with the biological mother had increased, while that with the adopted family had decreased (Plomin et al. 1988). Scarr and McCartney (1983) suggest that genes influence the experiences (i.e. environment) that each individual picks, and that genetically-related individuals tend to select more similar environments than do non-genetically related individuals. These environments then have an effect on the development of their measured intelligence. Research evidence from a transracial adoption study conducted by Scarr and Weinberg (1976) appears to challenge this evidence. However, despite findings that Black American children had IQ scores closer to their White adopted family than their Black biological family at age 7, at age 17, they were more similar to their biological family than their adoptive family. This backs up the argument that genetic influences are ultimately stronger.

The Rochester Longitudinal study demonstrated that a number of important factors in the home contribute to a child's IQ. These include the mother having a history of mental illness and the father being absent from the family. The more factors that a child had, the lower was their measured IQ. Taken together, the ten most significant factors were found to account for almost half the variability in children's IQ scores. However, these data are correlational and it may be that low parental IQ was the cause both of the risk factors (e.g. lack of positive interaction with the child) and of low IQ in the child (because the child had inherited this low IQ from the parent).

Project Head Start was a pre-school intervention programme which tried to boost the measured intelligence level of children from disadvantaged backgrounds. When children who had been involved in this programme entered school, they showed more advanced cognitive and social behaviour than children who were not involved in this programme (Lee et al. 1990). These initial positive effects disappeared in the years following entry, but later research (Lazar and Darlington 1982) showed a 'sleeper effect'. When the children were older, they had higher arithmetic and reading skills and were more likely to go to college. Despite the apparent success of programmes such as Headstart, hereditarians such as Herrnstein and Murray (1994) argue that because IQ has a significant genetic component, then it is a waste of resources to try to educate individuals beyond their potential. However, recent compensatory programmes, such as the Perry Pre-school Project, have clearly demonstrated that environmental enrichment can make a significant difference to the later achievement of underprivileged children.

CHECK YOUR UNDERSTANDING

When you have finished working through this topic, try the questions in 'Check your understanding' on p. 304/572 of the textbook. Check your answers by looking at the relevant parts of the textbook or this workbook, listed below.

1 textbook p. 299/567; workbook p. 99 (activity)
2 textbook p. 299/567
3 textbook p. 300/568
4 textbook p. 300/568
5 textbook pp. 301–2/569–70

6 textbook p. 302/570
7 textbook pp. 299–301/567–9
8 textbook pp. 301–3/569–71
9 textbook p. 303/571
10 textbook pp. 303–4/571–2

In Topic 1 you considered how the way we think changes as we grow older and what the reasons might be for that. Our moral understanding also develops as we grow up. But how do we come to have a sense of what is right and wrong, just and unjust, good and bad? This topic examines various theories that seek to answer this question, including those of Piaget, Kohlberg and Eisenberg. Another question that arises is whether morality is universal. Do all people of all races, cultures and genders have shared moral values, or are there noticeable differences? This topic ends by exploring the question of gender differences and cultural differences.

UNDERSTANDING THE SPECIFICATION

Here is what the AQA (A) specification says about this topic. It forms part of A2 Module 4, Section D: Developmental Psychology.

Sometimes it is hard to decide what category to place a theory in. Is it a theory of moral understanding, pro-social reasoning, or even the development of empathy? Kohlberg's theory is regarded as a theory of moral understanding, while Eisenberg's is a theory of pro-social reasoning. Yet despite these differences in label, there are many similarities in the underlying attributes that are being explained by each theory. As a result, therefore, the specification makes this an 'and/or' instruction, so that you can choose your two theories from moral understanding (i.e. Piaget and Kohlberg), or from a combination of moral understanding and pro-social reasoning (e.g. Kohlberg and Eisenberg). One thing is certain, however: you must cover at least two theories overall. You can study more than two, but this isn't necessary.

Cognitive development

c. Development of moral understanding

Theories of moral understanding/pro-social reasoning (e.g. Kohlberg, Eisenberg), including the influence of gender (e.g. Gilligan) and cultural variations in moral understanding/pro-social reasoning.

The inclusion of 'gender and cultural variations' is not to be ignored, and can be assessed in a number of different ways. It pays, therefore, to prepare each of these as an AO2 response in a parted question (e.g. 'To what extent are there gender variations in ...'), as a complete AO1 + AO2 response ('Discuss gender variations in ...') or even both together in the same format ('Discuss gender and cultural variations in ...').

TOPIC MAP

The diagram below gives you an overview of what you are about to study.

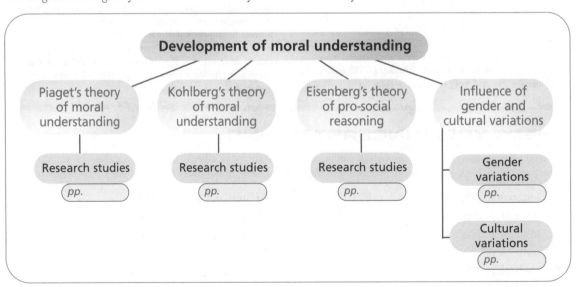

Development of moral understanding

- Piaget's theory of moral understanding
  - Research studies — pp.
- Kohlberg's theory of moral understanding
  - Research studies — pp.
- Eisenberg's theory of pro-social reasoning
  - Research studies — pp.
- Influence of gender and cultural variations
  - Gender variations — pp.
  - Cultural variations — pp.

Topic map

Look through pp. 306–14/574–82 of the textbook to see where the items shown in the topic map are covered. Note down the relevant page numbers in the spaces left on the topic map.

KEEPING TRACK

Use the table below to keep track of your work on this topic and plan your revision. See p. iv of this workbook (Introduction) for guidance on filling it in.

Development of moral understanding		Tick if you ...		
What I need to learn	Where is it?	could make a basic attempt	could make a good attempt	have complete mastery of this
Piaget's theory of moral understanding				
Description of Piaget's theory of moral understanding				
Description of Piaget's research studies				
Evaluation of Piaget's theory of moral understanding				
Kohlberg's theory of moral understanding				
Description of Kohlberg's theory of moral understanding				
Description of Kohlberg's research studies				
Evaluation of Kohlberg's theory of moral understanding				
Eisenberg's theory of pro-social reasoning				
Description of Eisenberg's theory of pro-social reasoning				
Description of Eisenberg's research studies				
Evaluation of Eisenberg's theory of pro-social reasoning				
The influence of gender and cultural variations				
Description of gender variations				
Evaluation of gender variations				
Description of cultural variations				
Evaluation of cultural variations				

PIAGET'S THEORY OF MORAL UNDERSTANDING

In Topic 1, you looked in some detail at Piaget's theory of cognitive development (see pp. 91–3). Piaget extended his theories to include ideas about the development of moral understanding. He identified an equivalent set of stages, through which children pass on their way to full moral reasoning. The table on p. 106 compares the two sets of stages (moral judgement and cognitive development).

Piaget's theory

Read through pp. 306–7/574–5, including the text at the bottom of p. 307/575 under the heading 'Kohlberg's theory ...' In the space below, summarize the key principles of Piaget's theory:

-
-
-
-
-

Piaget's research studies

Piaget's theory

Re-read through the description of Piaget's research studies on p. 306/574. Then complete the 'characteristics' column of the table below, which relates the stages of moral judgement to the equivalent stages of cognitive development.

Comparison of Piaget's stages of moral judgement and stages of cognitive development

Age (approx)	Stage of moral judgement	Characteristics	Equivalent stage of cognitive development
0–5	Pre-moral judgement	●	Pre-operational, egocentric
5–9	Moral realism	● Heteronomous morals (controlled by others)	Intuitive, inability to conserve
		●	
		●	
7+	Moral relativity	● Autonomous morals (controlled by oneself)	Concrete → formal operations
		● Punishment should fit the crime (reciprocity)	
		●	

Note that there is an overlap between the stages. Piaget believed that the age from 7–9 was a period of transition between the two stages and that children in this age range are likely to show evidence of features from both.

 **ACTIVITY**

Research into Piaget's theory of moral development

In exam questions, you can use research findings as effective AO2 evaluation by commenting on whether the research supports the theory or highlights problems with it. Several useful pieces of research are mentioned in the Evaluation panel on p. 307/575. Complete the table below, by noting down the key points of the research studies listed. In the final column, note down how you could use this as AO2 commentary in an essay discussing Piaget's theory of moral development.

Aspect of attraction	Researcher	Key points	How to use as AO2 commentary
Moral stories	Armsby (1971)		
Cross-cultural support	Linaza (1984)		
Peer participation	Kruger (1992)		
Moral rules and social-conventional rules	Turiel (1983)		
Consequences and intentions	Chandler *et al.* (1973)		
	Feldman *et al.* (1976)		

A2 Developmental Psychology

KOHLBERG'S THEORY OF MORAL UNDERSTANDING

Kohlberg's theory builds on Piaget's, but is more complex, seeking to explain the more complex moral reasoning displayed by adolescents and adults. A key part of Kohlberg's theory (as with Piaget's) is the concept of a series of innately determined stages (outlined in Table 10.7/18.7 on p. 308/576).

ACTIVITY

Researching Kohlberg's moral dilemmas

Search on the Internet for examples of Kohlberg's moral dilemmas and the questions that accompanied them. In particular, look for the scenario based on Heinz, faced with the dilemma of having to steal a life-saving drug for his wife, who is dying of cancer. (This case study is mentioned briefly at the bottom of p. 308/576 with an example of a possible response.)

Try typing 'Kohlberg Heinz' into your favourite search engine.

When you have found the dilemmas, work through some of the questions for yourself. You could do this with another student and discuss your answers. Try to work out what stage of reasoning your answers showed. (You may well be able to find a website that will also analyse possible answers for you.)

ACTIVITY

Understanding stages of moral development

The language used to describe Kohlberg's stages of moral development is quite dense and hard to understand. In the space below, complete a shorthand version of Table 10.7/18.7, using more accessible terms that will help you to remember each of the six stages (keep the same headings for the levels). For example, you could characterize Stage 3 as 'Good family/interpersonal relationships'. In the right-hand column, write a shorthand version of the types of moral reasoning displayed at each stage.

Kohlberg's stages of moral development

Level	Stages	Types of moral reasoning displayed
Level 1: Pre-conventional morality	Stage 1:	*Wrong = what is punishable*
		Child obeys as adults have power to punish
	Stage 2:	
Level 2: Conventional morality	Stage 3:	
	Stage 4:	
Level 3: Post-conventional morality	Stage 5:	
	Stage 6:	

Summarizing Kohlberg's theory

In the exam you may be asked to describe and evaluate a theory of moral understanding. If you choose Kohlberg's theory, your description will probably include:

- the basis of the theory – see the bulleted list at the bottom of p. 307/575
- a brief outline of the three levels and six stages
- examples of types of reasoning displayed at different ages – summarized in the penultimate paragraph on p. 308/576 and in Fig. 10.7/18.7.

In describing Kohlberg's theory, you should not spend time describing his research procedures in detail. That is not required here (see 'Understanding the specification' on p. 104) – if it were, the term 'research' would have been used in the specification.

Unit 10/18 // Cognitive development

ACTIVITY

Summarizing Kohlberg's theory

Look at Example Exam Question 1 on p. 315/583. Part (a) requires a description of one theory of moral development. Either Piaget's or Kohlberg's theory would be ideal. Write a 300-word description of Kohlberg's theory, covering the points listed at the bottom of p. 107. There is a lot of information to pack into just 300 words, so spend some time picking out the really important points that need to be included.

Looking again at Question 1 on p. 315/583, part (b) of the answer – the evaluation – is also worth 12 marks. Again, you would have about 15 minutes to write your evaluation, i.e. about 300 words. Your evaluation could include:

● research support for Kohlberg's theory and challenges to it – useful points are contained in the Evaluation panel on p. 309/577, as well as in the last paragraph on p. 308/576

● comments on the methodology of Kohlberg's research – see 'Artificial dilemmas' on p. 309/577

● a discussion of bias in the theory – see 'Gender bias' on p. 309/577 and 'Cultural bias' on p. 310/578

● a comparison of Kohlberg's theory with other theories (e.g. Piaget's).

A02 ACTIVITY

Evaluating Kohlberg's theory

Now write a 300-word evaluation of Kohlberg's theory of moral reasoning. Do this using your PC, so that you can keep track of the number of words and make changes easily.

This would provide an answer to part (b) of Example Exam Question 1 on p. 315/583.

EISENBERG'S THEORY OF PRO-SOCIAL REASONING

Piaget's and Kohlberg's theories focus on issues of right and wrong – 'crime and punishment'. In contrast, Nancy Eisenberg developed a theory of moral development that included a strong emotional element.

ACTIVITY

Eisenberg's theory

Read through pp. 310–11/578–9 and then answer the following questions:

1 What is the role and importance of the following concepts in Eisenberg's theory?

● Empathy
● Role-taking
● Sympathetic distress

2 What is meant by the following observation (p. 311/579): 'There are stable individual differences in pro-social behaviour'?

ACTIVITY

Researching Eisenberg's moral dilemmas

Search on the Internet for examples of Eisenberg's moral dilemmas and the questions that accompanied them. In particular, look for the scenario based on Mary (for girls) or Eric (for boys), where the child might miss a party if they help another child who has hurt themselves. (This case study is mentioned briefly on p. 310/578 with an example of one possible response.) Try typing in 'Eisenberg Mary dilemma' into your favourite search engine.

Evaluating Eisenberg's theory

There are various ways of evaluating a theory such as Eisenberg's. You could, for example, offer both positive and negative commentary. The four bullet points in the Evaluation panel on p. 311/579 include a number of useful evaluative points.

Another approach would be to highlight similarities and differences between Eisenberg's theory and the theories of other psychologists.

Use the next activity to organize the positive and negative points, and to make comparisons between Eisenberg's theory and other theories.

Evaluating Eisenberg's theory

1 Draw up a list of general evaluative (AO2) points relating to Eisenberg's theory. Divide your list into two columns, one for positive points and the other for negative points.

2 On pp. 310–11/578–9, the textbook mentions several similarities between the theories of Piaget and Kohlberg and that of Eisenberg. Make a list outlining the similarities and differences.

THE INFLUENCE OF GENDER AND CULTURAL VARIATIONS

You have already considered some issues relating to gender and culture when evaluating Kohlberg's theory (see textbook, pp. 309/577 and 310/578). Here we focus on those issues more closely.

Gender variations

Read the bullet point 'Gender bias' in the Evaluation panel on p. 309/577, followed by the text about Gender variations on pp. 312–13/580–1. Then try the following activity.

ACTIVITY

Gilligan's research into gender variations

Answer the following questions, making notes on a separate sheet of paper or using a PC.

1 What was Gilligan's main criticism of Kohlberg's theory?

2 What is the main reason for women's stronger sense of interconnectedness?

3 In what ways do Gilligan's stages of moral development differ from those of Kohlberg?

4 What research is there to back up Gilligan's ideas (her own research and other people's)?

5 What research is there that challenges Gilligan's ideas?

Cultural variations

Kohlberg claimed that the principles of moral understanding are universal. This claim has been tested by various researchers who investigated the beliefs of people in various cultures. The results of this research are discussed on pp. 313–14/581–2.

ACTIVITY

Individual vs collectivist cultures

The distinction between individualist and collectivist cultures is discussed in several places in the textbook. Read the first column on p. 57/325 and Table 2.5/10.5 for a reminder of what makes cultures individualistic or collectivist. Then read the text about 'Individualist vs collectivist cultures' on p. 313/581 and the first bullet point in the Commentary panel on p. 314/582 ('Intra-cultural variations'). Create a table, based on the format below, to summarize the findings of the research and conclusions that can be drawn.

Researcher	Cultures studied	Findings/conclusions
Whiting and Whiting (1975)	Kenyan (collectivist) USA (individualist)	100% of Kenyans behaved altruistically; 8% of Americans. Supports view of differences in moral reasoning between cultures.

ACTIVITY

Urban vs rural cultures

You may already have considered urban–rural differences in other contexts (e.g. in Unit 3/11, when examining altruism and bystander behaviour – see p. 92/360). Read the text on p. 313/581 about urban versus rural differences in moral reasoning and create a similar table to the one in the last activity to summarize the relevant research.

Different kinds of moralities

Are moral values universal, i.e. do they apply to every culture? Read the text on 'Different kinds of moralities' on pp. 313–14/581–2 and then make a list of the arguments for and against the view that there are such things as 'universal values'.

EXAMPLE EXAM QUESTIONS

In your work on this unit, you have already planned and written a complete answer to Example Exam Question 1 on p. 315/583.

One for you to try ...

(a) Describe **one** theory of moral understanding/pro-social reasoning. **(12 marks)**

(b) Evaluate the theory of moral understanding/pro-social reasoning you described in part (a) in terms of the influence of gender variations. **(12 marks)**

You have already written an answer to part (a) of this question when you tackled Example Exam Question 1 (as above). However, now you have a completely different task for part (b). You don't need to evaluate the theory in general terms, but specifically in terms of the influence of gender variations. We will outline how you can do this here.

Incidentally, although you can't export a general evaluation (as in Question 1) to a question where a specific evaluation is required (as here), you can export in the other direction. For example, if a question simply asks you to 'evaluate' a theory, it is entirely up to you to decide the form that the evaluation takes. It is just as legitimate to offer an evaluation that focuses totally on gender (or cultural) variations, as it is to provide a broader evaluation that takes into account several different facets of the theory.

Here is an outline answer for part (b):

- Gender bias in Kohlberg's theory, including a statement about how Gilligan explained women's morality as different rather than inferior (see evaluation panel on p. 309/577).

- Evidence that supports Gilligan's claims that Kohlberg ignored the different view that women take towards moral issues. You should remember that this is an evaluation of Kohlberg's theory and that everything you write should be part of an AO2 commentary. Therefore you might say:

  'Gilligan and Attanucci (1988) provided evidence to support this claim, finding that overall, men favoured a justice orientation (Kohlberg's original finding) and women favoured a care orientation (Gilligan's claim).'

- Evaluation of gender variations relevant to this question (see Evaluation panel on p. 312/580 – e.g. limited evidence of gender variations; gender similarities in moral reasoning). Again, you should remember to make these relevant to Kohlberg's theory, so you might say:

  'Despite Kohlberg's claim that women were less morally developed than men, in general, research has found only small gender differences ... etc. Likewise, Gilligan and Attanucci (1988) found that there were large overlaps in the moral reasoning shown by men and women ... etc.'

CHECK YOUR UNDERSTANDING

When you have finished working through this topic, try the questions in 'Check your understanding' on p. 314/582 of the textbook. Check your answers by looking at the relevant parts of the textbook or this workbook, listed below.

1 textbook p. 306/574

2 textbook p. 306/574

3 textbook p. 307/575

4 textbook p. 308/576; workbook p. 107

5 textbook p. 309/577

6 workbook p. 109

7 textbook pp. 310–11/578–9

8 textbook p. 312/580; workbook p. 109

9 textbook p. 312/580; workbook p. 109

10 textbook p. 313/581

SOCIAL & PERSONALITY
Development

PREVIEW

There are three topics in this unit. You should read them alongside the following pages in the Collins *Psychology for A2-level/Psychology* textbook:

Topic	*Psychology for A2*	*Psychology*
1 Personality development	pp. 320–28	pp. 588–96
2 Gender development	pp. 329–36	pp. 597–604
3 Adolescence	pp. 337–48	pp. 605–16

INTRODUCTION

Developmental Psychology is one of five sections in Module 4 (AQA Specification A), as the diagram below shows. This section is further divided into three sub-sections – 'Social and personality development' is the second of these.

Read the Preview and Introduction on p. 318/586 of the textbook now. This will give you an overview of what's in the unit.

Where this unit fits in to the A-level qualification

Section A:
Social Psychology

Section B:
Physiological Psychology

Module 4

Section C:
Cognitive Psychology

Section D:
Developmental Psychology

Section E:
Comparative Psychology

In the Module 4 exam, there will be a total of 15 questions, three relating to each Section (i.e. one per sub-section). You have to answer **three** questions, from at least **two** sections.

- COGNITIVE DEVELOPMENT
- **SOCIAL & PERSONALITY DEVELOPMENT**
- ADULTHOOD

a Personality development

b Gender development

c Adolescence

This topic examines theories that explain how social factors influence personality development. Three major theories are covered. The first is Freud's psychodynamic theory, which emphasizes the role of biological drives and early experiences in determining adult personality traits. The other two theories are so-called social learning theories, which emphasize the importance of social interactions and reinforcement.

UNDERSTANDING THE SPECIFICATION

Here is what the AQA (A) specification says about this topic. It forms part of A2 Module 4, Section D: Developmental Psychology.

The term 'psychodynamic' refers to a wide group of theories that emphasize the overriding influence of instinctive drives and forces, and the importance of developmental experiences in shaping personality. You are not restricted, therefore, to just Freud's psychoanalytic theory, but could include a number of other psychodynamic theories as well, including those of Carl Jung, Alfred Adler, Erik Erikson and many others. It is likely, however, that you will restrict yourself to just the one psychodynamic theory covered in the textbook (Freud). If you do include a second theory from your own study (e.g. Erikson), both theories do not have to be to the same depth. The same applies to the specification entry for social learning theories. There

> ### Social and personality development
>
> **a. Personality development**
>
> Psychodynamic (e.g. Freud, Erikson) and social learning (e.g. Bandura, Mischel) explanations of personality development.

are many more of these, including the theories of Julian Rotter and Martin Seligman. Again, however, you are likely to restrict yourself to just one or possibly both the theories given in the specification (Bandura and Mischel). It is worth noting that many of these theories, Bandura's included, have re-named themselves as 'social-cognitive learning theories'. Such theories are perfectly appropriate here. When studying any of these personality theories, you should endeavour to focus on how they explain the development of personality rather than just a more general account of the theory.

TOPIC MAP

The diagram below is a visual 'map' of the content of this topic.

ACTIVITY

Topic map

Look through pp. 320–7/588–95 of the textbook to see where the items shown in the topic map are covered. Note down the relevant page numbers in the spaces left on the topic map.

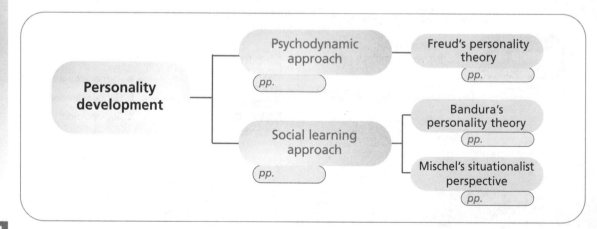

KEEPING TRACK

Use the table below to keep track of your work on this topic and plan your revision. See p. iv of this workbook (Introduction) for guidance on filling it in.

Personality development What I need to learn	Where is it?	Tick if you ...		
		could make a basic attempt	could make a good attempt	have complete mastery of this
The psychodynamic approach				
Description of Freud's personality theory				
Evaluation of Freud's personality theory				
The social learning approach				
Description of learning theory and social learning theory				
Description of Bandura's personality theory				
Evaluation of Bandura's personality theory				
Description of Mischel's situationalist perspective				
Evaluation of Mischel's situationalist perspective				

THE PSYCHODYNAMIC APPROACH

The influence of Sigmund Freud on the study and practice of psychology is hard to overestimate – he is perhaps the one psychologist that everybody has heard of! You should already have learned about his psychodynamic model in your study of abnormality at AS-level. Here, we focus on the aspect of personality development – in particular, the effect that development in childhood has in determining adult personality traits.

ACTIVITY

Freud's personality theory

Read from the top of p. 320/588 up to the heading 'Empirical evidence' on p. 322/590. Then answer the following questions.

1 Why is Freud's theory called a 'psychodynamic' theory?

2 Briefly define the three parts of the personality.
- Id
- Ego
- Superego

3 What is meant by:
- the 'pleasure principle'

- the 'reality principle'?

4 What is the role of the 'libido'?

5 What are 'ego defence mechanisms'?

6 Give three examples of types of defence mechanism and explain how they protect the ego (see also *Psychology for AS-level* Unit 4, p. 131).
-
-
-

7 Outline the process by which early development influences adult personality characteristics.

8 What traits characterize the following adult personality types?
- Oral receptive
- Oral aggressive
- Anal retentive
- Anal expulsive
- Phallic

Freud's stages of psychosexual development

There is a lot of information in Table 11.1/19.1. Summarize it in note form by completing a table using the headings below. This gives you an at-a-glance summary of Freud's stages of psychosexual development – very useful for revision.

Age	Stage	Source of pleasure	Personality structure	Fixations caused by	Adult personality types
0– 18 mths	Oral	Mouth	Id	Breastfeeding: not enough or too much pleasure in	● Oral receptive: trusting, dependent ● Oral aggressive: dominating

Describing Freud's theory

In the exam you might be asked a question such as the following:

● **Describe and evaluate one explanation of personality development (e.g. Freud, Erikson, Bandura, Mischel).** **(24 marks)**

You could answer this question by focusing on any one of the explanations covered in the textbook, but, like many candidates, you might well plump for Freud – there's a lot to say about him and his psychodynamic explanation! In fact, there's rather too much – about 2,000 words in the textbook (*excluding* the Evaluation panel on p. 323/591). In the exam, you would have about 15 minutes to write your description (for AO1),

i.e. about 300 words, with a further 15 minutes to write an (AO2) evaluation.

Your description should include a brief outline of:

● the basic principles of Freud's explanation theory
● the three personality structures (id, ego, superego) and related principles (pleasure, reality)
● the stages of psychosexual development
● the processes involved in personality development (e.g. use of ego defences, fixation)
● the link between early experiences and adult personality types (e.g. the oral, anal and phallic personality types).

The previous activities will have helped you to pick out the most important information for this task.

Summarizing Freud's psychodynamic theory

1 Now write a 300-word summary of Freud's psychodynamic theory of personality development. Do this using your PC, so that you can keep track of the number of words and make changes easily.

Conveying the key points of Freud's theory in only 300 words is a challenge, so it is worth

spending time on it to get it right. You can use this as your 12-mark summary of Freud's theory.

2 Now for an even greater challenge ... In the exam, the description of a theory may be worth only 6 marks (see part (a) of Question 4 on p. 328/596). That allows you only about 150 words, so once you have finished your 300-word summary of Freud's theory, make a copy of it and reduce it to 150 words! This shorter summary will serve as your 6-mark summary of Freud's theory.

Evaluating Freud's theory

Looking again at the possible question shown above, the 'evaluate' part of the answer is also worth 12 marks. Again, you would have about 15 minutes to write your evaluation, i.e. about 300 words. Your evaluation could include:

● research support for and against Freud's theory – some support for it is described on pp. 322–3/590–1 (Myers and Brewin 1994; McGinnies 1949)
● an overall assessment of theoretical merits and the theory's importance and influence

● a discussion of methodological strengths and weaknesses – some weaknesses are described on p. 322/590 (note-taking after the sessions, selective recall) and in the Evaluation panel (limited sample, problems of recollection)
● a comparison with other theoretical explanations – for example, you could mention that Freud's theory has a biological element, in contrast to Bandura's personality theory, or that Freud views personality traits as being fixed, in contrast to Mischel's situationalist perspective.

Evaluation involves both positive and negative 'criticism' – there are potentially a lot of points of both kinds that you could make regarding Freud's theory. Use the next activity to organize the positive and negative points.

 **ACTIVITY**

Evaluating Freud's theory 1

Draw up a list of general evaluative (AO2) points relating to Freud's theory. The Evaluation panel on p. 323/591 will provide several, as will the text under 'Empirical evidence' on 322–3/590–1.

AO2 points **+**	AO2 points **—**
•	•
•	•
•	•
•	•
•	•

ACTIVITY

Evaluating Freud's theory 2

1 Now write a 300-word evaluation of Freud's theory of personality development. Again, use your PC for this task. This is your 12-mark (15-minute) evaluation of Freud's theory.

2 Once you have finished your 300-word summary, make a copy of it and reduce it to 150 words. This shorter summary is your 6-mark evaluation of Freud's theory.

THE SOCIAL LEARNING APPROACH

In your AS-level studies, you should already have learned about behavioural models as they apply to abnormality, including the principles of operant and classical conditioning and social learning. The same principles lie at the basis of the social learning approach to personality development.

ACTIVITY

Bandura's personality theory

Read the information about social learning theory and Bandura's personality theory on pp. 324–5/592–3, up to the Evaluation panel.

1 What is the basic principle of social learning theory?

2 What is meant by the following terms?
- Direct reinforcement
- Vicarious reinforcement

3 What factors make it more or less likely that an observer will imitate the actions of a model?

More likely	Less likely
•	•
•	•
•	•

4 In Bandura's theory, what makes the difference between learning and performance?

continued on next page

Bandura's personality theory continued

5 Summarize the key findings of the following research studies into social modelling:

● Bandura (1965)

_____

_____

_____

_____

● Walters and Thomas (1963)

_____

_____

_____

6 Outline (in no more than 30 words each) what is meant by the following terms.

● Reciprocal determinism

_____

_____

_____

● Self-efficacy

_____

_____

_____

_____

Describing Bandura's theory

It's always a good idea to prepare well in advance of the exam and, as you did with Freud's theory, you should prepare summary descriptions of Bandura's theory. That means both a 300-word (15-minute/12-mark) version and a 150-word (7.5-minute/6-mark) version.

Your description should include a brief outline of:

● the basic principles of social learning theory, as they apply to personality development

● the process whereby behaviours are learned

● the process whereby behaviours are maintained

● the concepts of reciprocal determinism and self-efficacy.

The previous activity should have helped you pick out the most important information for this task.

Summarizing Bandura's personality theory

1 Write a 300-word summary of Bandura's psychodynamic theory of personality development. Do this using your PC, so that you can keep track of the number of words and make changes easily.

2 When you have finished your 300-word summary of Bandura's theory, make a copy of it and reduce it to 150 words. This will be your 6-mark summary.

Evaluating Bandura's theory

When it comes to evaluating Bandura's theory, you can follow the same guidelines as outlined above for evaluating Freud's theory (see pp. 114–15), i.e. include the same range of points (research support, the theory's overall importance/influence, methodological issues and comparisons with other theories) and both positive and negative criticism.

Evaluating Bandura's theory

1 Now write a 300-word evaluation of Bandura's theory of personality development. Again, use your PC for this task. This is your 12-mark (15-minute) evaluation of his theory.

2 Once you have finished your 300-word summary, make a copy of it and reduce it to 150 words. This shorter summary is your 6-mark evaluation of Bandura's theory.

HINT

The research studies by Feltz (1982) and Schunk (1983) could both be used as evaluation of Bandura's concept of self-efficacy.

Mischel's situationalist perspective

Read through the text about Mischel's explanation of personality development on pp. 325–7/593–5 and then answer the following questions.

1 What is the distinctive feature of Mischel's explanation of personality?

_____

2 Why, according to Mischel, do we tend to think personality is consistent? Give two reasons.

● _____

● _____

3 What did Mischel mean by 'behaviour specificity'?

_____

4 Why is Mischel's situationalist perspective an example of a social learning theory approach?

_____

_____

5 What two aspects of behaviour were students rated on in Mischel and Peake's Carleton study?

● _____

● _____

6 In this study, what correlation was found for conscientiousness:

● in the same situation?

_____

● across different situations?

_____

7 What, according to Mischel, are 'person variables' and what is their importance?

_____

_____

_____

Describing Mischel's situationalist perspective

Just as you have prepared summaries of Freud's and Bandura's theories, you should also prepare descriptions of Mischel's theory. That means both a 300-word (15-minute or 12-mark) version and a 150-word (7.5-minute or 6-mark) version. The previous activity should have helped you pick out the most important information for this task.

Summarizing Mischel's personality theory

1 Write a 300-word summary of Mischel's situationalist explanation of personality development. Do this using your PC, so that you can keep track of the number of words and make changes easily.

2 When you have finished your 300-word summary of Mischel's theory, make a copy of it and reduce it to 150 words. This will be your 6-mark summary.

Evaluating Mischel's situationalist perspective

As with the other explanations covered, citing support or challenges from other research studies is one way of evaluating a theory. Two studies – by Epstein (1979) and Fleeson (2001) – have challenged Mischel's findings.

Research challenges to Mischel's theory

Read the text under the heading 'Demonstrating situationalism' on pp. 326–7/594–5 and summarize the key findings and conclusions of the two studies described:

● Epstein (1979)

_____

_____

_____

● Fleeson (2001)

_____

_____

_____

_____

In the evaluation (AO2) part of any essay, you could also use the points in the Evaluation panel on p. 327/595.

A02 ACTIVITY

Evaluating Mischel's explanation

1 Now write a 300-word evaluation of Mischel's theory of personality development. Again, use your PC for this task. This is your 12-mark (15-minute) evaluation of his theory.

2 Once you have finished your 300-word summary, make a copy of it and reduce it to 150 words. This shorter summary is your 6-mark evaluation of Mischel's theory.

EXAMPLE EXAM QUESTIONS

In your work on this unit, you have already prepared shorter and longer summaries of the three theories covered. You could use these summaries as the basis for answers to all four of the Example Exam Questions listed on p. 328/596.

ACTIVITY

One for you to try ...

(a) Outline and evaluate one theory of personality development based on the psychodynamic approach. (12 marks)

(b) Outline and evaluate one theory of personality development based on the social learning approach. (12 marks)

This gives you the chance to practise your skills of précis as discussed earlier. You should be able to produce four 150-word 'chunks' that satisfy each of the four instructions above (i.e. outline one psychodynamic theory, evaluate one psychodynamic theory ... etc.).

When you have done that, ask yourself the following questions:

1 Have you stuck to the word limit for each 'chunk'? (If you haven't, there isn't a problem, provided what you wrote for each chunk didn't take you more than 7.5 minutes).

2 Have you emphasized the development of personality in each of your outlines?

3 Are each of your descriptive points sufficiently detailed and your evaluative points sufficiently elaborated?

4 Is your evaluation effective?

5 Have you wasted time by including material that wasn't really necessary?

6 Check both parts of your answer against the marking criteria on p. 679/947. How many marks would you score?

7 Swap with another person in your class. Repeat stages 1 to 6 above.

8 Compare your answers to stages 1 to 6, and discuss how each answer could be improved.

CHECK YOUR UNDERSTANDING

When you have finished working through this topic, try the questions in 'Check your understanding' on p. 327/595 of the textbook. Check your answers by looking at the relevant parts of the textbook or this workbook, listed below.

1 textbook pp. 320–1/588–9
2 textbook p. 322/590
3 textbook p. 322/590
4 textbook pp. 321–2/589–90
5 textbook pp. 322–3/590–1

6 textbook p. 324/592
7 textbook pp. 324–5/592–3
8 textbook p. 325/593
9 textbook p. 325/593
10 textbook p. 327/595

Topic 2 >> Gender development

Your sex – whether you are a girl or a boy – is determined by biology. Issues of gender, on the other hand, are rather more complex. What makes someone 'masculine' or 'feminine'? What are the influences that teach us to behave in gender-typed ways? Parents? Friends? Peers? Other sources, such as the media? Developmental psychologists are interested in what causes us to develop a sense of gender identity and to fulfil gender roles. Different explanations include those based on social learning theory (already discussed in Topic 1) and cognitive-developmental theories. This topic will examine both types.

UNDERSTANDING THE SPECIFICATION

Here is what the AQA (A) specification says about this topic. It forms part of A2 Module 4, Section D: Developmental Psychology.

By now you should be pretty well expert at unpacking specification entries, but we will go through the process again here. First, you should note that the word 'explanations' is in the plural. This means that you are required to study more than one explanation of the development of gender identity/gender roles. The examples given in the specification entry are just that, examples. You might choose to study one social learning theory and one cognitive-developmental theory, or two completely different theories (such as the psychoanalytic and sociobiological theories).

What does the term gender identity/role mean in this context? Some theories (such as Kohlberg's cognitive-

> ### Social and personality development
>
> **b. Gender development**
>
> Explanations of the development of gender identity/gender roles (e.g. social learning theories, cognitive-developmental theories).

developmental theory) might be thought of as theories of gender identity, whereas others (such as social learning theory) are more theories of gender role. For any questions set on this topic, it really doesn't matter which you choose. This is a friendly instruction, and takes away the worry of whether you are addressing a specific instruction to write about gender identity or gender role (a question which cannot be set).

TOPIC MAP

The diagram below gives you an overview of what you are about to study.

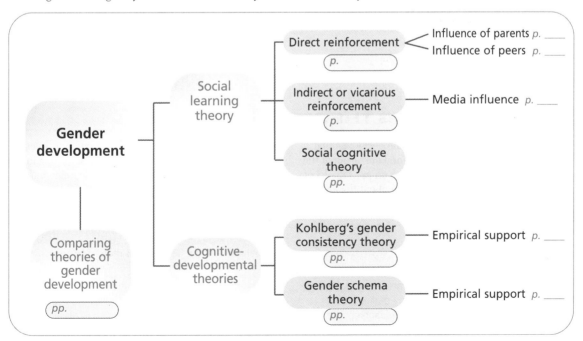

Topic map

Look through pp. 329–35/597–603 of the textbook to see where the items shown in the topic map are covered. Note down the relevant page numbers in the spaces left on the topic map.

KEEPING TRACK

Use the table below to keep track of your work on this topic and plan your revision. See p. iv of this workbook (Introduction) for guidance on filling it in.

Gender development		Tick if you ...		
What I need to learn	Where is it?	could make a basic attempt	could make a good attempt	have complete mastery of this
Social learning theory				
Description of the role of direct reinforcement				
Description of the role of indirect reinforcement				
Description of social cognitive theory				
Evaluation of social learning theory				
Cognitive-developmental theories				
Description of Kohlberg's gender consistency theory				
Evaluation of Kohlberg's gender consistency theory				
Description of gender schema theory				
Evaluation of gender schema theory				
Comparison of theories of gender development				

WHAT IS GENDER?

Understanding gender

Read through the text under the heading 'What is gender?' on p. 329/597. To make sure you are clear about the terms used in this topic, write a short definition of each of the following.

- Sex
- Gender
- Gender identity
- Gender role

SOCIAL LEARNING THEORY

In the last topic you learned about the social learning approach to personality development. Look again at the activity 'Bandura's personality theory' on pp. 115–16 of this workbook, which will remind you about the key concepts underlying this theory. The same principles can be applied to gender development. According to social learning theory, reinforcement of learning may be either direct or indirect.

Direct reinforcement

1 Read about 'Direct reinforcement' on p. 329/597 of the textbook. On a separate sheet of paper or using a PC, make notes briefly outlining how gender-appropriate and gender-inappropriate behaviour might be directly reinforced by (a) parents, (b) peers.

2 Summarize the main points of the research in this area. Draw up a table with the following headings: Research, Findings, Conclusions and Criticisms.

The specification for Gender development specifies 'explanations', not 'research' (see 'Understanding the specification' on p. 119 of this book). This means you would not get credit for lengthy descriptions of research studies, unless the question gave you the option of including research studies in your answer (see, for example, Question 3 on p. 336/604).

ACTIVITY

Indirect reinforcement

A great deal of indirect reinforcement comes from media portrayals of gender and, in particular, gender stereotypes. Read the text about 'Indirect reinforcement' on p. 329–30/597–8 of the textbook.

1 What is meant by a 'stereotype'?

2 What role do stereotypes play in gender development?

3 Under what circumstances are stereotypes more likely to be imitated? (Hint: see question 3 of the activity, 'Bandura's personality theory', on p. 115.)

4 Summarize the main points of the research into media stereotypes. On a separate sheet of paper or using a PC, draw up a table with the following headings: Research, Findings, Conclusions and Criticisms.

ACTIVITY

Social cognitive theory

Read through the text about 'Social cognitive theory' on p. 330/598 and then answer the following questions.

1 Compared to social learning theory, what additional factors does social cognitive theory take account of in gender-identity development?

2 What is meant by the following terms?
  ● Selective reinforcement
  ● Outcome expectancies
  ● Self-regulation

3 Summarize the three sources of influence described in Bussey and Bandura's (1992) social cognitive theory:
  ● **M**
  ● **E**
  ● **D**

4 Summarize the main points of Bussey and Bandura's (1992) research into self-regulation of play by pre-school children. On a separate sheet of paper or using a PC, draw up a table with the following headings: Research, Findings, Conclusions and Criticisms.

Unit 11/19 // Social and personality development

121

Describing and evaluating social learning theory

Look at Example Exam Question 1 on p. 336/604. If you were answering this question, you would have about 15 minutes to outline two explanations, i.e. about 300 words, with a further 15 minutes to evaluate your two explanations. For the purposes of this question, you could count social learning theory and social cognitive theory as either two explanations or as one explanation (i.e. social learning theories overall).

Look at Example Exam Question 1 on p. 336/604.

ACTIVITY

Summarizing social learning theory

1 Write a 150-word summary of social learning theory and a 150-word summary of social cognitive theory. Do this using your PC, so that you can keep track of the number of words and make changes easily.

2 Now write 300 words of evaluation of these theories. Your evaluation could include:

- an overall assessment of the theories' importance or success in explaining gender-role/identity development – relevant points are included in the Evaluation panel on p. 331/599

- descriptions of research into social learning theories and whether research supports or challenges the explanation

- comments on methodological strengths and weaknesses with the research – several points are listed in the Evaluation panel on p. 331/599.

Use the space below to note down points you could include in your evaluation.

AO2 points **+**	AO2 points **−**
●	●
●	●
●	●
●	●

COGNITIVE-DEVELOPMENTAL THEORIES

ACTIVITY

Understanding cognitive-developmental theories

Read the first three paragraphs on p. 332/600 and then answer the following questions. You may also find it useful to read the text on pp. 284–5/552–3 about 'The structure of the intellect' and 'Stages in development', which give a good explanation of the idea of adaptation.

1 What is the basic approach of cognitive-developmental theories?

2 Why is the concept of 'maturation' important?

ACTIVITY

Kohlberg's gender consistency theory

Read the remaining text on p. 332/600 and then answer the following questions.

1 What is meant by the following terms?
- Gender stability

- Gender consistency

- Principle of conservation

2 When, according to Kohlberg, do children learn about gender-appropriate behaviour?

3 Why do children not form stereotypes earlier?

Kohlberg's gender consistency theory

A number of research studies have been carried out that have tested Kohlberg's theory in practice, i.e. with real children. Some have reported results that support his theory; others have disagreed with aspects of it.

Research support for Kohlberg's theory

Under 'Empirical support' on p. 332/600 is a description of Slaby and Frey's research study into how children think about gender identity and gender roles. Their research generally confirmed Kohlberg's theory. In the space below, summarize their key findings and conclusions about each stage of Kohlberg's theory.

Study by Slaby and Frey (1975)

Stage	Findings	Conclusions
1 Gender identity		● Child has a sense of their own gender identity.
2 Gender stability		
3 Gender consistency		

Other studies have reported findings that have either supported or challenged Kohlberg's theory. Several of these are summarized in the Evaluation panel on p. 333/601.

Studies into Kohlberg's theory

Summarize the key points of the research studies into children's development of gender described in the Evaluation panel on p. 333/601. Do this by creating a table, based on the format shown below. In the 'Conclusions' column, say how the study supports or challenges Kohlberg's theory.

Researcher	Procedures	Findings	Conclusions
Emmerlich et al. (1977)	Pre-school children shown drawings with gender-inappropriate hair or dress	Few recognized gender stayed same	Support for K's view of gender constancy at age 7

Gender schema theory

Gender schema theory, proposed by Martin and Halverson, also gives central importance to cognitive processes, but differs from Kohlberg's theory in its view of when children are ready to start learning about gender identity.

ACTIVITY

Gender schema theory

Read the information about 'Gender schema theory' on pp. 333–4/601–2 and then answer the following questions.

1 According to gender schema theory, when does gender development begin, and why?

2 What is meant by the following terms?

- Gender schema
- In-group schema
- Out-group schema

3 Why should children pay more attention to 'in-group schemas'?

4 What is 'confirmatory bias'?

5 How does gender schema theory explain the persistence of gender stereotypes?

As with the other gender-development theories, gender schema theory has been tested in research studies, with some supporting the theory and others disagreeing with aspects of it.

Studies into gender schema theory

Summarize the key points of the research studies relating to gender schema theory (GST), described on p. 333/601 (under 'Empirical support') and in the Evaluation panel on p. 334/602. Again, create a table, based on the format shown below. In the 'Conclusions' column, outline how the study supports or challenges aspects of gender schema theory.

Researcher	Procedures	Findings	Conclusions
Martin et al. (1995)	Kids aged 4–5 shown 'boys' toys + girls' toys'	Kids want to play only with gender-appropriate toy – 'That toy is for boys/girls'	Support for GST's view that kids pay attention to in-group schemas

ACTIVITY

Summarizing cognitive-developmental theories

Look again at Example Exam Question 1 on p. 336/604. You have already prepared summaries of social learning theory and social cognitive theory as potential answers to this question. You could equally well use either or both of the two cognitive-developmental theories discussed above.

1 Write a 150-word summary of Kohlberg's gender consistency theory and a 150-word summary of Martin and Halverson's gender schema theory. Do this using your PC, so that you can keep track of the number of words and make changes easily.

2 Now write 300 words of evaluation of these theories. Your evaluation could include:

- an overall assessment of the theories' importance or success in explaining gender-role/identity development
- descriptions of research into social learning theories and whether research supports or challenges the explanations
- comments on methodological strengths and weaknesses with the research.

There is plenty of evaluative material in the textbook, including the Evaluation panels on pp. 333/601 and 334/602, as well as descriptions of other research studies in the body of the text.

Another excellent approach would be to make comparisons between the two theories you choose to discuss. The next part of this topic focuses on this.

COMPARING THEORIES OF GENDER DEVELOPMENT

The last part of this topic contains a very useful comparison of the different theories of gender development covered in the textbook. Making comparisons is an excellent way of providing evaluative (AO2) material when answering exam questions. For instance, look at Example Exam Questions 1 and 2 on p. 336/604. Both require you to consider more than one theory, and highlighting similarities and differences between them will earn you good marks!

Comparing theories of gender development

Draw up a list of similarities and differences between the three main theories of gender development discussed in this topic, namely:

- Bussey and Bandura's social cognitive theory
- Kohlberg's gender consistency theory
- Martin and Halverson's gender schema theory.

EXAMPLE EXAM QUESTIONS

You have already prepared 300-word summaries of the different theories discussed in this topic (150 words of AO1 + 150 words of AO2). You could use these summaries for questions that allow you to answer with reference to two theories (as, for example, in Questions 1 and 2 on p. 336/604). You also need to be prepared to deal with a question such as the 'One for you to try' below.

ACTIVITY

One for you to try ...

Describe and evaluate one explanation of the development of gender roles and/or gender identity.

(24 marks)

This requires a longer, 600-word discussion of just one explanation. You can choose any of the theories covered in this topic. The way the specification is worded, you will never be asked to discuss just one social learning theory or one cognitive-developmental theory – that is because these are given only as examples in the AQA specification. To prepare yourself for a question such as this (i.e. discussing just one theory), choose the theory you would most like to write about and plan your answer. Remember, you will have time for 300 words of AO1 description and 300 words of AO2 evaluation. On your PC, draw up a list of essential points you would include.

You could use research studies as your AO2 for this question (see 'Exam hint' below), although you must make sure you do more than just describe the findings of each study. Try taking each appropriate research study and doing the following.

- Briefly outline the main findings and conclusions.
- State whether this supports or challenges the assumptions of your chosen explanation.

- Ask yourself 'so what'? Really effective evaluation goes beyond merely identifying a critical point by putting it in context. How does this research enhance or weaken the claims of your chosen explanation?

Alternatively, you could make use of your comparison of different explanations of gender development as AO2. As with the use of research studies discussed above, don't just describe alternative explanations, but actively compare them to your chosen explanation. Try taking each alternative explanation and doing the following.

- Very briefly outline the main assumptions of the alternative explanation(s).
- State in what way(s) this agrees with or differs from your chosen explanation.
- Ask yourself: 'Is it better or worse than my chosen explanation? Why?' How does this comparison enhance or weaken the case for your chosen explanation?'

EXAM HINT

Because the AQA specification changed slightly in 2005, there are some questions that appear in the textbook that would change, given these specification changes. An example in this topic is Question 4 on p. 336/604. As the specification no longer requires you to study research studies related to gender identity/gender role, you cannot be asked to cover these in a question. If you look again at this question, however, how would you evaluate your chosen explanation? You would most probably include some supporting research studies (or even studies that challenge the assumption of this explanation). Therefore, although the requirements of the specification have changed (and hence also the questions that can legitimately be set), your answer would probably still be more or less the same.

CHECK YOUR UNDERSTANDING

When you have finished working through this topic, try the questions in 'Check your understanding' on p. 335/603 of the textbook. Check your answers by looking at the relevant parts of the textbook or this workbook, listed below.

1   textbook p. 330/598
2   textbook p. 330/598
3   textbook p. 330/598
4   textbook p. 332/600
5   textbook p. 332/600

6   textbook p. 332/600
7   textbook p. 333/601
8   textbook p. 333/601
9   textbook p. 333–4/601–2
10 textbook pp. 334–5/602–3; workbook p. 124

Topic 3 >> Adolescence

In this topic you will explore various aspects of adolescence – the period of transition between childhood and adulthood that brings with it all kinds of changes, both biological and psychological. It is a period of major development, as individuals establish their independence and separate identity. You will examine some of the social developments that take place, as well as the shift in relationships that usually accompanies this turbulent period. Or is it so turbulent? Many researchers have explored the notion of conflict in adolescence and you will assess the results of their research. Finally, you will look at cross-cultural research into adolescence and examine how the experience of adolescence differs in different cultures.

UNDERSTANDING THE SPECIFICATION

Here is what the AQA (A) specification says about this topic. It forms part of A2 Module 4, Section D: Developmental Psychology.

The term 'research' has a dual meaning. It can mean research studies but is more commonly used in a catch-all way, i.e. 'Discuss research (theories and/or studies) into...' This gives you the opportunity to incorporate theories of social development in adolescence (e.g. Erikson), as well as studies related to this topic (e.g. Marcia). However, whereas 'theories' cannot be specified, 'studies' can, so it is wise to be prepared for that. For the first part of this topic, you could study adolescent social development generally (e.g. development of autonomy and the development of identity), but you could also receive a question that is specifically on the latter (hence the use of the word 'including' in the specification). For the second part of the topic, the specification states 'parents and peers'.

Social and personality development

c. Adolescence

Research into social development in adolescence, including the formation of identity (e.g. Marcia). Research into relationships with parents and peers during adolescence and cultural differences in adolescent behaviour.

Although you are unlikely to get a question specifically on 'relationships with parents' (or peers), questions that include both aspects must be addressed as such, otherwise you will be guilty of what examiners refer to as 'partial performance' in your answer. Although 'cultural differences in adolescent behaviour' may appear to you just to be tagged on at the end, it is an important topic, and one for which you must have sufficient AO1 and AO2 material.

TOPIC MAP

The diagram below gives you an overview of what you are about to study.

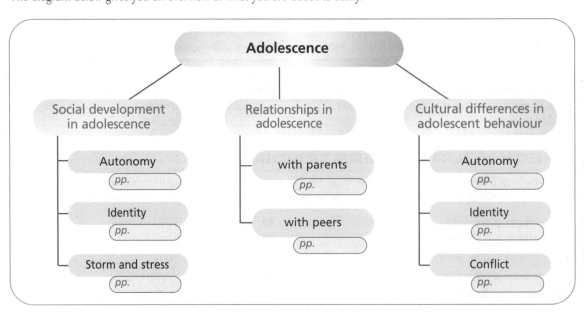

Adolescence

- Social development in adolescence
  - Autonomy — pp.
  - Identity — pp.
  - Storm and stress — pp.
- Relationships in adolescence
  - with parents — pp.
  - with peers — pp.
- Cultural differences in adolescent behaviour
  - Autonomy — pp.
  - Identity — pp.
  - Conflict — pp.

A2 Developmental Psychology

126

Topic map

Look through pp. 337–46/605–14 of the textbook to see where the items shown in the topic map are covered. Note down the relevant page numbers in the spaces left on the topic map.

KEEPING TRACK

Use the table below to keep track of your work on this topic and plan your revision. See p. iv of this workbook (Introduction) for guidance on filling it in.

Adolescence *What I need to learn*	*Where is it?*	*Tick if you ...*		
		could make a basic attempt	*could make a good attempt*	*have complete mastery of this*
Social development in adolescence				
Description of research into the development of autonomy				
Evaluation of research into the development of autonomy				
Description of research into the development of identity				
Evaluation of research into the development of identity				
Description of research into 'storm and stress'				
Evaluation of research into 'storm and stress'				
Relationships in adolescence				
Description of research into relationships with parents				
Evaluation of research into relationships with parents				
Description of research into relationships with peers				
Evaluation of research into relationships with peers				
Cultural differences in adolescent behaviour				
Description of research into cultural differences				
Evaluation of research into cultural differences				

SOCIAL DEVELOPMENT IN ADOLESCENCE

As the first paragraph on p. 337/605 states, adolescence is a time of transition, with both biological and psychological changes taking place. This topic focuses on the latter.

ACTIVITY

Development of autonomy

Read from 'Development of autonomy' on p. 337/605 to the bottom of the page, outlining Blos's ideas about re-individuation and independence. On a separate sheet of paper or using a PC, summarize the main points of Blos's explanation (1967), by concentrating on:

- what psychological developments are taking place
- what conflict exists and with whom.

Note down answers to the following questions.

1 In Blos's explanation, what is the importance of:
   - regression?
   - rebellion?

2 What criticisms of Blos's explanation were made by:
   - Ainsworth *et al.* (1970)
   - Cooper *et al.* (1998)?

Development of identity

Many psychologists have focused on adolescence as a time when individuals forge their own identity.

ACTIVITY

Development of identity

Read the text on p. 338/606, outlining Erikson's ideas about psychosocial development. Summarize the main points of his theory by answering the following questions.

1 What are the main psychological developments taking place?

2 What importance does Erikson give to the idea of conflict?

3 Summarize in note form the four kinds of behaviour related to identity confusion:

- ●
- ●
- ●
- ●

4 What did Erikson mean by a 'psychosocial moratorium'?

5 What is meant by the term 'role sampling'?

6 In what ways could Erikson's theory be described as 'biased'?

James Marcia's (1966) research into adolescent identity (see p. 339/607) is an important study into social development in adolescence. A good way of organizing the information about this study is by using the 'APFCC' method (Aims–Procedures–Findings–Conclusions–Criticisms), which you should be familiar with from AS-level psychology. APF and the first C (conclusions) would be AO1 descriptive material, while the second C (criticisms) would count as AO2.

ACTIVITY

Marcia's research into adolescent identity

In the table below, write a summary of Marcia's research, using trigger phrases, mnemonics or whatever will help you to memorize the important features. The table does not include a space for 'Criticisms', as you will be looking at those in the next activity.

KEY STUDY · textbook p. 339/607

Researchers	Marcia (1966)	Findings
Title		
Aims		
Procedures		Conclusions

Research relating to Marcia's approach

The Evaluation panel on pp. 339–40/607–8 mentions several research studies which you could use as AO2 evaluation of Marcia's research. Complete the table below, by noting down the key points of the research studies listed. In the final column, note down how you could use this as AO2 commentary in an essay discussing Marcia's research.

Researcher	Findings	Conclusions	How to use as AO2 commentary
Meilman (1979)			
Waterman (1985)			
Waterman and Waterman (1975)			
Archer (1982)			

Storm and stress

'Storm and stress' sounds a rather odd term, but it is a translation from the equivalent German phrase '*Sturm und Drang*'. It refers to the experience of turmoil or turbulence that adolescents go through – or do they?

The textbook discusses several pieces of research, from around the world, that investigated whether or not adolescents really do experience turmoil, and if so, possible reasons for it.

Research into storm and stress

Read the text under the heading 'Storm and stress' on p. 340/608 to the end of the Evaluation panel on p. 342/610. Summarize the findings of all the research studies discussed using the headings shown below.

Researcher	Working with	Findings	Conclusions	Criticisms
Csíkszentmihalyi and Larson (1984)	75 US students	Frequent and drastic mood swings	● Adolescence is time of turmoil ● Result of conflict with society's rules/values	● Limited sample ● Western bias

Explaining adolescent turmoil: focal theory

1 How does Coleman (1974) seek to explain the conflicting findings about adolescent turmoil?

2 What practical applications does this theory have?

Adolescent turmoil – a Western phenomenon?

Consider the following question: 'Is adolescent turmoil (or 'storm and stress') a phenomenon of Western cultures?

On your PC, draw up a list of arguments for and against this proposition, citing relevant research evidence.

RELATIONSHIPS IN ADOLESCENCE

Adolescence is seen as a period when significant relationships with people outside the family begin to form, especially with people of the same age ('peers'). Family relationships change, too. This part of the topic examines the relationships adolescents have with parents and with peers, and how this affects their social development.

Relationships with parents

Read through the text about relationships with parents, on pp. 342–3/610–11 of the textbook. Summarize the main points discussed, in tabular form, using your PC if possible. In particular, note down what are the key features of the adolescent–parent relationship and how this relationship affects the adolescent's development. In the right-hand column, list relevant research.

Create one table for the points in the main body of the text and a separate one for the points in the Evaluation panel.

Key features of relationship with parents	How parental relationships affect adolescent's development	Relevant research
Autonomy – time of growing independence from parents	Connectedness & secure attachment promote healthy development	Apter (1990) – study of 65 mother/daughters – most girls felt closest to mother

Relationships with friends assume a greater significance during adolescence. Researchers have focused on what role these relationships serve and how they assist in adolescents' development.

Relationships with peers

Read through the text about relationships with peers, on pp. 343–4/611–12 of the textbook. Summarize in tabular form the main points discussed.

Create one table for the points in the main body of the text and a separate one for the points in the Evaluation panel. Do this on your PC if possible.

Key features of relationships with peers	How relationships with peers help adolescent's development	Relevant research
Peer relationships are egalitarian (unlike parent-child relationships)	Help adolescents form balanced relationships	Piaget (1932)

Answering exam questions on relationships

The last two activities should have helped you prepare for exam questions on relationships in adolescence. Relationships may form the focus of whole questions (such as Example Exam Question 2 on p. 347/615) or of parts of questions (as in Question 3 on p. 347/615).

Answering exam questions on relationships with parents and peers

Imagine you are planning your response to Question 2 on p. 347/615. Read the guidance notes under the question and then think about how you would answer this question. You would have to decide:

1 whether to make theories or studies the focus of your AO1 description

2 which types of relationships to cover – parents, peers, or both?

3 what points of criticism/evaluation to make.

If you decide to include relationships both with parents and with peers, then you could divide your response into four 150-word chunks:

	AO1 (description)		AO2 (commentary)	
Relationships with parents	150 words	7.5 minutes	150 words	7.5 minutes
Relationships with peers	150 words	7.5 minutes	150 words	7.5 minutes

Using your PC, draw up a list of the key points (and research studies) you will include for each 'chunk'. Then write your complete answer to the question.

CULTURAL DIFFERENCES IN ADOLESCENT BEHAVIOUR

Researchers have found that young people growing up in different cultures have very different experiences of adolescence or the transition from childhood to adulthood. The textbook explores some of these differences.

Summarizing research studies

Read from the bottom of p. 344/612 to the top of the second column on p. 345/613, stopping at the heading 'Ethnic minorities'. This text includes various examples of research that have uncovered cultural issues that affect young people growing up in different cultures. Summarize the key points in the form of a table, such as the one below.

Researcher	Cultures studied	Findings/conclusions
Jensen (1999)	Various (review of research)	More difficulties for adolescents in individualist societies, i.e. in need to search for individual identity and autonomy

Adolescents in ethnic minorities

Read the text on 'Ethnic minorities' on p. 345/613 and then answer the following questions.

1 What special difficulties do young people from ethnic minorities face in establishing their identity?

2 What ways of dealing with these problems does Berry (1997) identify?

3 What, according to research, is the most successful approach?

The final paragraph on p. 345/613 gives a final appraisal of the notion whether or not adolescence is a time of conflict. The clear answer is that it is not a universal experience, being more apparent in Western cultures than in other, collectivist cultures.

Culture has a historical dimension, too, as outlined on p. 346/614.

Evaluating cultural differences

Read the Evaluation panel on p. 346/614 and then, in no more than 120 words, write an answer to the following question: 'What does cross-cultural research tell us about adolescence and social development?'

EXAMPLE EXAM QUESTIONS

In your work on this unit, you have already planned and written a complete answer to Example Exam Question 2 on p. 347/615. One of the more challenging questions on p. 347/615 is Question 4, where you are required to present both AO1 and AO2 material related to cultural differences in adolescent behaviour. We have used the information on pp. 344–6/612–4 to answer this question. Note that, as well as using material from the Evaluation panel on p. 346/614, we have also modified some of the material elsewhere in this section to make it into AO2 commentary. Remember, nearly all material can be used as AO2 provided you build it into a sustained critical commentary.

Sample answer

Critically consider research (theories and/or studies) into cultural differences in adolescent behaviour.

(24 marks)

Jensen's review of research on adolescence in different cultures concluded that some of the difficulties associated with adolescence might come from the emphasis placed on individual needs and independence in individualist societies. In collectivist societies such as Japan, on the other hand, dependence is more highly valued and is seen as an important part of becoming an adult. Gilani (1995) compared Asian and White British families, particularly in terms of family relationships with teenage daughters. In Asian families, more than in White families, the wishes of the parents came first, with girls being expected to conform to family values rather than becoming independent.

The concept of 'identity' may also be unique to individualist societies. In Western cultures, group identities help to make up an individual's identity. In Chinese culture, in contrast, the individual's identity is sacrificed for a group identity and successful development is related to interdependence between group and individual identity. In contemporary Western culture, adolescents have many choices to help them build up their individual adult identity; these choices are not available in non-industrialized, more rural communities. Tupuola (1993) found that in Samoa, adult roles are decided by the wider community and a child becomes an adult when they are regarded as mature – there is no concept of adolescence. In fact, the transition from child to adult in many non-industrialized rural communities is marked by 'rites of passage', which make it clear that the child is now an adult. In contrast, in Western cultures, the transitional period between childhood and adulthood is a stage where the individual is no longer allowed to be a child, but is not yet given the status of an adult. This may cause confusion for both adults and adolescents.

Identity formation may be particularly difficult for adolescents from minority ethnic groups, as it may be the first time that they have been consciously aware of their ethnicity. Berry (1997) suggested that there are four routes that can be taken by members of ethnic minorities. These include assimilation (the adolescent identifies with the dominant culture and rejects their ethnic origins) and integration (they identify with both dominant and ethnic cultures). Research has generally found that integration is associated with better adjustment (White and Burke 1987). However, young people from minority ethnic groups may still face problems because of the lack of suitable role models, and because minority ethnic groups are often portrayed negatively. As a result, some adolescents may distance themselves from their ethnic origins and so delay their identity achievement. However, the differences evident in adolescent development may reflect historical rather than cultural differences. Shaffer (1993) claimed that adolescence was an 'invention' of the twentieth century that appeared when it became illegal to employ children, creating a separate 'adolescent peer culture'.

Cross-cultural research is important because it shows us how much social context affects adolescent development. Cultural values, such as individualism or collectivism, have a major impact on adolescent development. This cultural influence is not surprising since adolescents are learning how to become members of their society. However, in the past, studies of people in non-Western cultures were conducted by Western psychologists, who may not have understood local people. They may have recorded biased observations based on their pre-existing expectations about that particular culture. This situation has improved, as more research is now done by psychologists who are members of the society being studied and so are better able to understand the population they are studying. Despite this, however, there are always sampling issues for any research, with psychologists not always having access to a wide cross-section of members of the society being studied. Also, psychologists may use tests and other measurement techniques that have been developed for Western participants. These techniques may not be appropriate for members of different cultures and may make any conclusions drawn from their use invalid.

CHECK YOUR UNDERSTANDING

When you have finished working through this topic, try the questions in 'Check your understanding' on p. 346/614 of the textbook. Check your answers by looking at the relevant parts of the textbook or this workbook, listed below.

1 textbook p. 337/605 (Commentary) and 342/610

2 textbook p. 338/606

3 textbook p. 338/606

4 textbook p. 339/607

5 textbook p. 339/607

6 textbook p. 341/609

7 textbook pp. 342–3/610–11

8 textbook p. 343/611

9 textbook p. 345/613

10 textbook pp. 345–6/613–4

EVOLUTIONARY EXPLANATIONS OF
Human Behaviour

INTRODUCTION

Comparative Psychology is one of five sections in Module 4 (AQA Specification A), as the diagram below shows. This section is further divided into three sub-sections – 'Evolutionary explanations of human behaviour' is the third of these.

Read the Preview and Introduction on p. 432/700 of the textbook now. This will give you an overview of what's in the unit.

Where this unit fits in to the A-level qualification

Section A:
Social Psychology

Section B:
Physiological Psychology

Module 4

Section C:
Cognitive Psychology

Section D:
Developmental Psychology

Section E:
Comparative Psychology

In the Module 4 exam, there will be a total of 15 questions, three from each Section (i.e. one per sub-section). You have to answer **three** questions, from at least **two** sections.

- DETERMINANTS OF ANIMAL BEHAVIOUR
- ANIMAL COGNITION
- **EVOLUTIONARY EXPLANATIONS OF HUMAN BEHAVIOUR**

a Human reproductive behaviour

b Evolutionary explanations of mental disorders

c Evolution of intelligence

Topic 1 >> Human reproductive behaviour

According to Darwin and other 'evolutionists' who followed him, modern human sexual behaviour is a product of evolutionary forces that operated at the time of our ancestors millions of years ago. This topic examines these forces and the effects they have had, both on the way humans behave and how they look today. The second part of the topic explores the differences in the investment that mothers and fathers make in their offspring. Why is there such a difference? And how does it affect mating behaviour and the mating systems of different cultures?

UNDERSTANDING THE SPECIFICATION

Here is what the AQA (A) specification says about this topic. It forms part of A2 Module 4, Section E: Comparative Psychology.

Sexual selection refers to the view that competition for mates between individuals of the same sex affects the evolution of certain traits that give some individuals an advantage over others. These characteristics then become passed down from generation to generation, with those who possess these characteristics being reproductively more successful than those who don't, or don't to the same degree. This part of the specification is all about knowing what these characteristics are, and how they might impact on modern reproductive behaviour. There is no prescribed 'list' that you have to learn, and the textbook provides

> ### Evolutionary explanations of human behaviour
>
> **a. Human reproductive behaviour**
>
> The relationship between sexual selection and human reproductive behaviour including evolutionary explanations of parental investment (e.g. sex differences, parent–offspring conflict).

you with plenty of choice from which to construct your answer to a question on this relationship. The second part of this topic specifically requires you to cover evolutionary explanations of parental investment (who invests more in offspring). The use of the plural 'explanations' refers more to different types of parental investment (male investment, female investment, parent–offspring conflict, etc.) than it does to different evolutionary theories.

TOPIC MAP

The diagram below is a visual 'map' of the content of this topic.

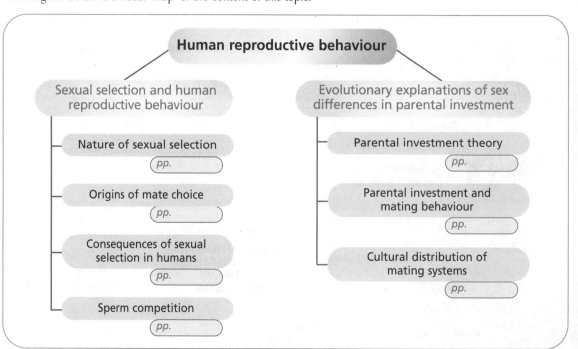

Human reproductive behaviour

Sexual selection and human reproductive behaviour
- Nature of sexual selection
  - pp.
- Origins of mate choice
  - pp.
- Consequences of sexual selection in humans
  - pp.
- Sperm competition
  - pp.

Evolutionary explanations of sex differences in parental investment
- Parental investment theory
  - pp.
- Parental investment and mating behaviour
  - pp.
- Cultural distribution of mating systems
  - pp.

Topic map

Look through pp. 434–40/702–8 of the textbook to see where the items shown in the topic map are covered. Note down the relevant page numbers in the spaces left on the topic map.

KEEPING TRACK

Use the table below to keep track of your work on this topic and plan your revision. See p. iv of this workbook (Introduction) for guidance on filling it in.

Human reproductive behaviour		Tick if you ...		
What I need to learn	*Where is it?*	*could make a basic attempt*	*could make a good attempt*	*have complete mastery of this*
Sexual selection and human reproductive behaviour				
Description of the nature of sexual selection				
Description of the origins of mate choice				
Description of the consequences of sexual selection in humans				
Evaluation of evolutionary influences on human morphology				
Description of sperm competition				
Evaluation of sperm competition				
Evolutionary explanations of parental investment				
Description of parental investment theory				
Description of sex differences in mating behaviour				
Description of cultural distribution of mating systems				
Evaluation of evolutionary explanations of sex differences in parental investment				

SEXUAL SELECTION AND HUMAN REPRODUCTIVE BEHAVIOUR

Read the definitions of 'Natural selection' and 'Sexual selection' in the Key concepts panel on p. 433/701. Then read the panel on 'Natural selection' underneath and continue reading p. 434/702 up to and including the first paragraph on p. 435/703.

Understanding sexual selection

1 What is meant by 'sexual selection'. Give a short description (no more than 25 words!).

_____

_____

2 How does sexual selection explain the following traits?
- The relative hairlessness of humans

_____

- Male preference for an hourglass figure in women

_____

3 Why does the process of sexual selection lead to the exaggeration of certain traits?

_____

_____

Natural selection and sexual selection

The section on natural selection at the start of this topic is included to help you appreciate the different pressures in natural and sexual selection. In the exam, you would not have time to discuss natural selection in this way – you would need to focus on sexual selection. Similarly, the case of the peacock's tail is an excellent illustration of the different pressures, but you should not waste time in the exam going into this one (non-human) example in detail.

Intersexual and intrasexual selection

It is important to understand the difference between intersexual and intrasexual selection. In practice, it is sometimes hard to distinguish between the effects of each type. For example, in the case of the peacock's tail, did this evolve so that males could out-compete other males to gain access to females (intra)? Or did it evolve because females tended to choose males with the gaudiest displays (inter)?

Intersexual and intrasexual selection

1 Define the following terms and give an example of each. As you read through the rest of the topic, add further examples of each type of selection.

	Definition	Example
● Intersexual selection		
● Intrasexual selection		

2 Why should polygyny (see hint below) lead to intrasexual selection?

Polygyny: Strictly, this term refers to males having more than one *female* partner. The equivalent term for females having more than one male partner is **polyandry**.

The origins of mate choice

This part of the topic discusses some of the reasons why humans' choice of mates has evolved in the way it has. It also considers several of the criteria that humans (and non-humans) use when making their choice of mate.

EEA: For a definition of this, see the Key concepts panel on p. 433/701.

Origins of mate choice

Read through the paragraph on p. 435/703 under the heading 'The origins of mate choice' and then answer the following questions.

1 What is the fundamental principle of mate choice, according to evolutionary explanations?

2 How and when did mate preferences originate?

Criteria for selection

Read through the paragraphs summarizing selection for indicators, provisioning and mental characteristics on p. 435/703. For each of the three criteria, note down the key points in the table below, noting down the names of relevant researchers:

Criterion	Key points	Relevant researchers
Indicators	We look for indicators of viability (→ survival) and fertility (→ reproduction) in mates	
Provisioning		
Mental characteristics		

The consequences of sexual selection in humans

According to evolutionary explanations, we humans look the way we do partly because of the pressures of sexual selection. The textbook looks at its effect on two aspects of our appearance: faces and sexual organs.

The consequences of sexual selection in humans

Read the text about 'The consequences of sexual selection in humans' from the bottom of p. 435/703 to the end of the Evaluation panel on p. 436/704. Draw up a table, using the same format as the one above, to summarize the key points. The two criteria to summarize are 'Facial features' and 'Sex organs'.

Criterion	Key points	Relevant research
Facial features	Facial features advertise 'good genes'	

Writing an exam question

One of the skills of writing good exam answers is to fit a lot into a little! You have only half an hour to answer a complete question. For example, if you were writing about the consequences of sexual selection in humans, you would have to summarize all the text you have just read in far fewer words. To practise this skill, do the following.

1 Write a 150-word summary *describing* how sexual selection has shaped our bodies.

2 Then write a 150-word summary *evaluating* this explanation.

There is no shortage of material (nearly 900 words in the textbook), so you need to choose carefully what you will include in each part of your 'answer'. Use your PC to write your answer, so that you can make changes easily and keep track of your word count.

You could use this summary as part of your answer to Example Exam Questions 1 and 2 on p. 441/709.

Sperm competition

Read the text about 'Sperm competition' on pp. 436–7/704–5 and then answer the following questions.

1 What is meant by sperm competition?

_____

_____

2 In evolutionary terms, what is the consequence of sperm competition?

_____

_____

3 Complete the following table, summarizing the observations and explanations of relative differences in testicle size in primates.

	Testicle size	Explanation	Relevant research
Chimpanzees			
Human beings			
Gorillas			

3 How do Harvey and May (1989) explain differences in testicle size between different human ethnic groups?

_____

_____

_____

_____

_____

Research with non-human animals

Another useful AO2 evaluative point to make regarding research in this area is the reliance on studies using non-human animals. You might question how easy it is to generalize from such research to humans.

SEX DIFFERENCES IN PARENTAL INVESTMENT

The next part of the topic looks at parental investment, i.e. the behaviour of parents in caring for offspring. It concentrates on the differences that exist between the sexes in this regard. It also looks at how these differences affect mating behaviour, and at cultural differences in mating systems.

Parental investment theory

Read from the heading 'Parental investment theory' on p. 437/705 to the end of the first paragraph on p. 438/706. Then answer the following questions.

1 What is meant by 'parental investment'?

_____

_____

2 Why do males and females not invest equally?

_____

_____

3 What is the consequence of this unequal investment?

_____

_____

4 Summarize the key concerns of males and females in terms of investment in offspring.
- Females:

_____

_____

_____

_____

- Males:

_____

_____

_____

_____

ACTIVITY

Parental investment and mating behaviour

Read about 'Parental investment and mating behaviour' on p. 438/706 and answer the following questions.

1 How do sex differences in parental investment suggest that:

- women should be disposed towards monogamy

_____

_____

- men should be disposed towards polygyny?

_____

_____

_____

2 Given these differences, why do you think most Western societies give most approval to monogamous relationships?

_____

_____

_____

_____

3 Explain what Clutton-Brock and Vincent (1991) meant by a 'reproductive bottleneck':

_____

_____

_____

_____

ACTIVITY

Cultural distribution of mating systems

Read about 'Cultural distribution of mating systems' on pp. 438–9/706–7 and answer the following questions.

1 What type of mating system is preferred in traditional, non-Western or pre-Westernized cultures?

_____

2 Why is a high degree of polygyny generally unsustainable in societies based on foraging?

_____

3 Why is polyandry not the favoured mating system:

- for women _____
- for men? _____

 ACTIVITY

Evaluating sex differences in parental investment

The Evaluation panel on p. 439/707 and Key research on p. 438/706 mention a number of research studies that throw interesting light on the parental investment theory. In the space below, summarize the findings and conclusions of each study mentioned. In the final column, suggest how you could use each study in an exam essay to make an AO2 evaluative point.

Research	Findings	Conclusions	How to use as AO2 point
Andersson et al. (1999)			
Buss et al. (1992)			
Harris (2003)			

EXAMPLE EXAM QUESTIONS

In your work on this unit, you have practised summarizing information to make it suitable for answering exam questions (see activity, bottom of p. 137). Here is another question for you to try.

ACTIVITY

One for you to try ...

Discuss the relationship between sexual selection and human reproductive behaviour.   **(24 marks)**

When first encountering a very general question such as this, most students breathe a sigh of relief, but very soon find out that wide-open questions such as this create their own problems. Even if you were to restrict your choice of material to the content on pp. 434–7/702–5, there is still far more there than you could ever hope to include in an exam answer. There is no need to include all of this, but just a sample that you think represents the relationship between sexual selection and human reproductive behaviour (hint: don't waste too much

time describing what sexual selection is, but get straight to how it influences reproductive behaviour). You should try to put together 300 words that do just that, perhaps in three 100-word paragraphs that cover three aspects of sexual selection as it relates to human reproductive behaviour.

For the AO2 component of your answer, have a go at the activity below, and then add the resulting AO2 material (also 300 words worth) to your AO1 material for this question.

Expert interview

The Expert interview with Lance Workman on p. 440/708 of the textbook gives a fascinating insight into current evolutionary thinking about human reproductive behaviour. In the interview, Lance Workman responds to three common challenges made to evolutionary explanations. This offers a rich source of AO2 evaluative material for exam essays!

For example, in almost any essay, you could introduce the potential challenge: 'This evolutionary perspective has been criticized by those who claim that the

emphasis on inherited features makes us "prisoners" of our genes ...' (see also Nicolson's claim mentioned in the Evaluation panel on p. 437/705).

You could then follow this up with the evolutionists' counter-claim – that genes interact with input from the environment – as outlined in Lance Workman's response to the first question. You could reference this counter-claim as 'Workman (2004)'.

Think about how else you could use Lance Workman's comments as AO2 material in exam essays. Note down some ideas here:

_____

_____

_____

_____

_____

_____

_____

CHECK YOUR UNDERSTANDING

When you have finished working through this topic, try the questions in 'Check your understanding' on p. 439/707 of the textbook. Check your answers by looking at the relevant parts of the textbook or this workbook, listed below.

1 textbook p. 433–4/701–2; workbook p. 135 (activity)

2 textbook p. 435/703; workbook p. 137 (activity)

3 textbook p. 436/704

4 textbook p. 436/704

5 textbook p. 437/705

6 textbook pp. 437–8/705–6

7 textbook pp. 438–9/706–7

8 workbook p. 136 (see Hint); also check in a dictionary

Topic 2 >> Evolutionary explanations of mental disorders

At first sight it would appear that mental disorders such as depression, schizophrenia or phobias serve no useful purpose at all. They make the life of the sufferer difficult, even unbearable at times. According to evolutionary explanations, however, these disorders may once have served a useful function for our ancestors. This topic examines possible explanations of three types of disorder: depression, anxiety disorders (including phobias and obsessive–compulsive disorder) and schizophrenia.

UNDERSTANDING THE SPECIFICATION

Here is what the AQA (A) specification says about this topic. It forms part of A2 Module 4, Section E: Comparative Psychology.

In an exam question, if you were asked to 'discuss two evolutionary explanations of human mental disorders', you might interpret this as meaning that you have to use two different evolutionary explanations for each of the mental disorders being discussed. This is not what the question setter requires, so they would tend to ask this question in a slightly different way, i.e. 'Discuss the explanation of two mental disorders from an evolutionary perspective'. This lets you know the true requirement of the question, i.e. explaining two disorders (e.g. depression and anxiety disorders) from an evolutionary perspective. You should be careful with your interpretation of 'including' and 'e.g.' here. You can be asked for depression and anxiety

> ### Evolutionary explanations of human behaviour
>
> **b. Evolutionary explanations of mental disorders**
>
> Evolutionary explanations of human mental disorders including depression (e.g. unipolar and bipolar depression) and anxiety disorders (e.g. phobias and obsessive–compulsive disorder).

disorders (because they are specified) but you can't be asked for unipolar and bipolar depression, or phobias and obsessive–compulsive disorder. These are just examples that you might choose to answer a question on depression or anxiety disorders. You could, in response to a question asking you to discuss two disorders, choose to write about two types of depression, or two types of anxiety disorder. Make sure you don't explain these disorders from a clinical perspective rather than an evolutionary perspective.

TOPIC MAP

The diagram below gives you an overview of what you are about to study.

Topic map

Look through pp. 441–7/709–15 of the textbook to see where the items shown in the topic map are covered. Note down the relevant page numbers in the spaces left on the topic map.

ACTIVITY

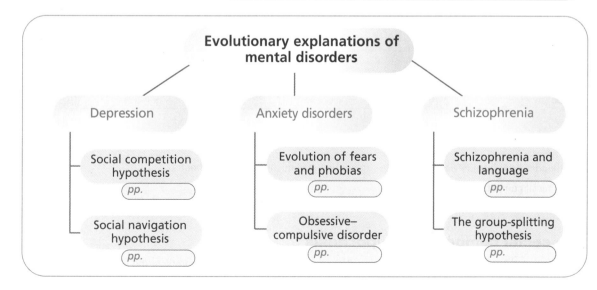

Evolutionary explanations of mental disorders

Depression
- Social competition hypothesis — pp.
- Social navigation hypothesis — pp.

Anxiety disorders
- Evolution of fears and phobias — pp.
- Obsessive–compulsive disorder — pp.

Schizophrenia
- Schizophrenia and language — pp.
- The group-splitting hypothesis — pp.

KEEPING TRACK

Use the table below to keep track of your work on this topic and plan your revision. See p. iv of this workbook (Introduction) for guidance on filling it in.

Evolutionary explanations of mental disorders		Tick if you ...		
What I need to learn	*Where is it?*	*could make a basic attempt*	*could make a good attempt*	*have complete mastery of this*
Depression				
Description of the social competition hypothesis				
Evaluation of the social competition hypothesis				
Description of the social navigation hypothesis				
Evaluation of the social navigation hypothesis				
Anxiety disorders				
Description of the evolution of fears and phobias				
Evaluation of the evolution of fears and phobias				
Description of obsessive–compulsive disorder				
Evaluation of obsessive–compulsive disorder				
Schizophrenia				
Description of schizophrenia and language				
Evaluation of schizophrenia and language				
Description of the group-splitting hypothesis				
Evaluation of the group-splitting hypothesis				

DEPRESSION

Depression is a serious mental disorder that affects large numbers of people, but according to evolutionary explanations, it may once have served a useful – or adaptive – purpose.

ACTIVITY

Evidence for depression as an adaptive response

Read the first column on p. 442/710 under the heading 'Depression'. What three factors could evolutionists cite as evidence for their assertion that depression may have evolved as an adaptive response?

Reason	Research
1	
2	
3	

Two theories have been devised recently to explain how this might have come about:

- the social competition hypothesis
- the social navigation hypothesis.

The social competition hypothesis

Read the text about 'The social competition hypothesis' on p. 442/710 and then complete the following activity.

The social competition hypothesis

1 The social competition hypothesis proposes that depression is an adaptive response for the loser in any social competition. In the table below, summarize the three effects of depression proposed by Price *et al.* (1994) and why these might be adaptive.

Effect of depression	Why this is adaptive
● Loser stops competing	
●	
●	

2 In what kind of situations would a depressive response be adaptive:

(a) in the EEA

(b) in modern society

3 Give two examples of situations where a depressive response is not adaptive:

●

●

The social navigation hypothesis

The social navigation hypothesis focuses on the problem-solving aspect of depression, and in particular on two complementary aspects: social rumination and social motivation.

The social navigation hypothesis

Read from the bottom of p. 442/710 to the end of p. 443/711 and, on a separate sheet of paper, answer the following questions.

Social rumination

1 What is meant by 'social rumination'?

2 What adaptive purpose does it serve?

3 What is 'anhedonia' and how does that contribute to the effect?

4 To what are people with depression likely to attribute their failures?

5 Why might this be an adaptive response?

6 What evidence in favour of this view was collected by Hartlage *et al.* (1993)?

Social motivation

1 What is meant by 'social motivation'?

2 What does the text mean when it describes depression as an 'honest display'?

3 Is depression always an 'honest display'? Can you think of circumstances where it might be a dishonest signal? (Hint: read the text under 'Deception in communication' on p. 418/686.)

4 What is meant by 'fitness extortion' and how might this be adaptive?

5 Attempted suicide is perhaps the most extreme form of 'fitness extortion'. What are the 'payoffs' and 'risks' in this situation for the person with depression and those around them?

6 Why, according to Watson and Andrews (2002), is anti-depressant medication *on its own* not a suitable way of treating depression?

Answering exam questions on depression

Looking back at 'Understanding the specification' on p. 141, you will see that 'depression' is specified as one of the mental disorders that you can be tested on (the word 'including' tells you that). That means you could be asked a question specifically about evolutionary explanations of depression – see, for instance, Example Exam Question 3 on p. 449/717, where the entire question relates to depression. You have 30 minutes to answer the whole question – enough time to write about 600 words. This means 300 words of AO1 description and 300 words of AO2 evaluation.

Summarizing evolutionary explanations of depression

Do the following tasks:

1 Prepare a 300-word summary *describing* evolutionary explanations of depression.

2 Write a 300-word summary *evaluating* these explanations.

There is no shortage of material in the textbook, so you need to choose carefully what you will include and what can be left out. Use your PC to write your answer, so that you can make changes easily and keep track of your word count.

Now look at Example Exam Question 2 on p. 449/717. Here, only half of your answer should be explicitly about depression. So, when planning your answer, you would think of your answer in terms of four 'chunks', as shown below:

	AO1 (description)		AO2 (commentary)	
1 Depression	150 words	7.5 minutes	150 words	7.5 minutes
2 Anxiety	150 words	7.5 minutes	150 words	7.5 minutes

Reducing your summaries

1 Make a copy of your 300-word description of evolutionary explanations of depression. Reduce it to just 150 words, taking great care to choose the most relevant material.

2 Likewise, make a copy of your 300-word evaluation of these explanations and reduce that to 150 words.

ANXIETY DISORDERS

Anxious? Apprehensive? Nervous? We all know what it's like to feel like this. Exams, for example, create plenty of anxiety. That tends to be short lived, however – anxiety vanishes as soon as the exam is over. For some people, however, anxiety takes on a much greater, even overwhelming dimension. Phobias are one example of this. Another is obsessive–compulsive disorder.

Anxiety disorders

Read from the top of p. 444/712 up to the heading 'The evolution of fears and phobias'. Then consider the following questions. If possible, discuss your answers with other students studying psychology.

1 What is the difference between a fear and a phobia?

2 Table 15.1/23.1 illustrates how fears might be evolved responses that had an adaptive purpose for our ancestors. Think of other fears that people have. How would you explain them in terms of evolutionary processes? For example:

(a) fear of water (hydrophobia)

(b) fear of fire (pyrophobia)

(c) fear of cats (ailurophobia or felinophobia).

3 The textbook also outlines the possible social dimension of biological fears, e.g. why a child might cry when confronted with an unknown adult. Think of another social situation which causes anxiety, e.g. entering a room full of strangers. Can you explain that as an evolved response? If so, what was its adaptive origin?

The evolution of fears and phobias

Read about 'The evolution of fears and phobias' on pp. 444–5/712–13 and then do the following.

1 Outline Seligman's (1970) theory of biological preparedness.

_____

_____

2 What assumption does the theory make regarding the types of objects that humans fear?

_____

_____

3 Cook and Mineka's (1989) research study with monkeys provided support for this theory. Summarize the main findings and conclusions of the research here. In the right-hand column, note down any criticisms (i.e. positive and negative evaluation).

Findings	_Conclusions_	_Criticisms_

4 The Evaluation panel on p. 445/713 gives four examples of clear cultural differences in responses to one common object of phobias – spiders. List the main points of each example here.

Researcher	_Finding_
● Davey (1994)	
●	
●	
●	

Obsessive–compulsive disorder

Read the text on 'Obsessive–compulsive disorder (OCD)' on pp. 445–6/713–14. Make notes on the explanations described, using the following tasks to organize your notes.

1 Summarize the main points of Abed and de Pauw's evolutionary explanation of OCD. In particular, note down:
  - what is meant by the 'modular mind'
  - how obsessional phenomena (e.g. compulsive behaviours) arise
  - what is meant by IRSGS
  - why this system might have been adaptive

2 Why does the universality of obsessions and compulsive rituals support the biological explanation?

3 Why do gender differences also lend support to this theory?

Answering exam questions on anxiety disorders

Like 'depression', 'anxiety disorders' are specified as one of the mental disorders that you can be tested on (the word 'including' tells you that). That means you could be asked a question specifically about evolutionary explanations of anxiety disorders – see, for instance, Example Exam Questions 2(b) and 4 on p. 449/717. In Question 4, the entire question is about anxiety disorders, whereas in Question 2(b), anxiety disorders will take up only half of your answer. For this reason, you need to be able to write précis of different lengths – a 600-word answer for Question 4, but only 300 words for Question 2(b) (see the outline answer plan for this question on p. 144). The next activity on p. 146 will help you prepare your summaries.

EXAM HINT

2006 AQA Specification

Re the guidance notes to Example Exam Question 4 on p. 449/717: The 2006 AQA specification does now give examples of anxiety disorders – 'e.g. phobias and obsessive–compulsive disorders' – both of which you have covered in this topic.

Summarizing evolutionary explanations of anxiety disorders

Do the following tasks.

1 Prepare a 300-word summary *describing* evolutionary explanations of anxiety disorders (AO1).

2 Write a 300-word summary *evaluating* these explanations (AO2).

3 Make a copy of the 300-word description you wrote for part 1. Reduce it down to just 150 words, taking great care to choose the most relevant material.

4 Likewise, make a copy of your 300-word evaluation and reduce that down to 150 words.

There is no shortage of material in the textbook, so choose carefully what you will include and what you will leave out. Use your PC to write your answer, so that you can make changes easily and keep track of your word count.

SCHIZOPHRENIA

The evidence for a genetic component in the development of schizophrenia is strong, implying that evolutionary biological factors play an important part.

Genetic component in schizophrenia

Read the paragraph under the heading 'Schizophrenia' on p. 446/714 and then read pp. 488–9/756–7 of the textbook, 'Genetic explanation for schizophrenia'. Note down four research findings that point to a genetic explanation of schizophrenia.

1 _____

2 _____

3 _____

4 _____

Schizophrenia and language

Crow (2002) proposes that the origins of schizophrenia can be found by examining its connection with language.

Schizophrenia and language

Read the text under this heading on pp. 446–7/714–15. Use the questions below to summarize the key points of Crow's argument.

1 Support for the link between schizophrenia and language has come from research into two aspects of the brain's activity. Summarize the key findings and conclusions of each:

- Zaidel (1999) – brain symmetry

  _____

- Francks *et al.* (2003) – handedness

  _____

  _____

2 What is meant by the term 'punctuated equilibria'?

  _____

  _____

3 Challenges to Crow's theory have come from several quarters. What are the main arguments of:

- Polimeni and Reiss (2003)

  _____

  _____

- Savage-Rumbaugh and Fields (2000)

  _____

  _____

- Deacon (1997)

  _____

  _____

The group-splitting hypothesis

Stevens and Price (2000) view schizophrenia as an evolutionarily advantageous condition, i.e. behaviour with an adaptive origin.

ACTIVITY

The group-splitting hypothesis

Read the text under this heading on p. 447/715 and answer the following questions.

1 What, according to Stevens and Price, was the adaptive function of schizophrenia?

2 What features of the disorder would have made it adaptive?

3 What alternative explanations are offered by:

- Polimeni and Reiss (2002)
- Nesse (1999)?

EXAMPLE EXAM QUESTIONS

In your work on this unit, you have already planned and written summaries of depression and anxiety disorders which would serve as the basis for answers to Example Exam Question 2, 3 and 4 on p. 449/717.

You could also use the same summaries to answer Example Exam Question 1 on p. 448/716, although you could also bring schizophrenia into your answer here. Here is another one for you to try.

ACTIVITY

One for you to try ...

'All human mental disorders may be explained as inappropriate expressions of what was adaptive behaviour for our ancestors.'

Discuss the explanation of one or more human mental disorders from an evolutionary perspective.

(24 marks)

Questions such as this appear more challenging simply because they have a quotation. Quotations are there to help you by suggesting ideas that you might pursue in your answer. In this case it refers to the fact that many mental disorders have ultimate causes that were adaptive for our ancestors, but their expression nowadays may no longer serve the same adaptive function. Interpreting this quotation is in itself worth marks, so don't ignore it. There is no penalty for not referring to the quotation unless you are specifically instructed to do so. The question that accompanies this quotation is essentially the same as Question 1 on p. 448/716. However, here you are given the choice of whether to restrict your answer to just one mental disorder, or to include more than one. The choice is very much up to you. Don't feel pressurized into writing about more than one explanation if you feel you can get sufficient depth and breadth into your answer without the second (or even third) disorder.

You might like to try answering this question using just one mental disorder. Even then it takes a fair bit of selective pruning in order to keep your word limit down. If you have time, you could plan an answer on the evolutionary explanation of depression, then one on the evolutionary explanation of anxiety disorders (or even just one type of anxiety disorder) and then finally one on the evolutionary explanation of schizophrenia. Hard work but good revision!

CHECK YOUR UNDERSTANDING

When you have finished working through this topic, try the questions in 'Check your understanding' on p. 448/716 of the textbook. Check your answers by looking at the relevant parts of the textbook or this workbook, listed below.

1 textbook p. 441/709

2 textbook p. 442/710

3 textbook p. 442–3/710–11

4 textbook p. 443/711

5 textbook p. 444/712

6 textbook p. 445/713

7 textbook pp. 445–6/713–14

8 textbook p. 446/714

9 textbook p. 446–7/714–15

10 textbook p. 447/715

Intelligence is clearly one characteristic that confers advantages to the animal (human or non-human) that possesses it. Intelligent animals that can come up with solutions to problems of, say, finding food are more likely to survive and reproduce than those that can't. As humans, we are justly proud of the intelligence that our advanced brain gives us, but how did it come to evolve to its current state? This topic examines evolutionary factors that may have been involved, including the relationship between brain size and intelligence.

UNDERSTANDING THE SPECIFICATION

Here is what the AQA (A) specification says about this topic. It forms part of A2 Module 4, Section E: Comparative Psychology.

It is vital that you fully appreciate what is meant by 'evolutionary factors' in this context. This is not an invitation to write about the nature–nurture argument and intelligence, or the contribution of genetics and/or environment to the development of measured intelligence. In the ancestral environment, early humans faced many challenges which made it essential to develop characteristics that we now refer to as 'intelligence'. This topic examines what they might have been. The specification gives two examples, one focusing on the environmental demands faced by our ancestors (e.g. finding food and the development of tools) and one focusing more on the demands of living in close proximity to other humans. A question on this part of the specification would invite you to consider how these factors might have resulted in the evolution

> ### Evolutionary explanations of human behaviour
>
> **c. Evolution of intelligence**
>
> Evolutionary factors in the development of human intelligence (e.g. ecological demands, social complexity). The relationship between brain size and intelligence (e.g. the adaptive value of large brains, comparative studies across species).

of human intelligence. The textbook covers quite a few factors, ranging from foraging demands to meat-sharing.

The second part of this specification entry requires you to study the link between brain size and intelligence. This is an invitation to consider why and how brains got bigger, and how this was related to the development of intelligence among our ancestors. Two avenues of research are suggested for you, the adaptive value of large brains (why large brains would help us fare better) and comparative studies across species (whether large brains equal greater intelligence in all species).

TOPIC MAP

The diagram below gives you an overview of what you are about to study.

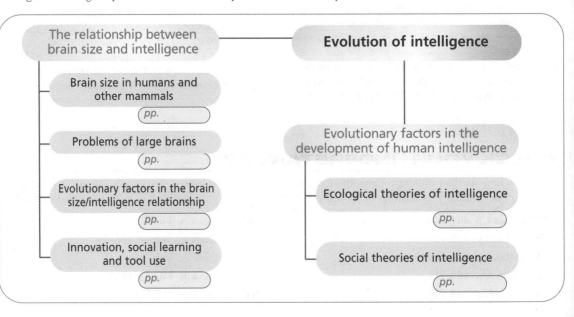

A2 Comparative Psychology

Topic map

Look through pp. 449–54/717–22 of the textbook to see where the items shown in the topic map are covered. Note down the relevant page numbers in the spaces left on the topic map.

KEEPING TRACK

Use the table below to keep track of your work on this topic and plan your revision. See p. iv of this workbook (Introduction) for guidance on filling it in.

Evolution of intelligence		Tick if you ...		
What I need to learn	*Where is it?*	could make a basic attempt	could make a good attempt	have complete mastery of this
The relationship between brain size and intelligence				
Description of brain size in humans and other mammals				
Description of the problems of large brains				
Description of evolutionary factors in the brain size/intelligence relationship				
Description of innovation, social learning and tool use				
Evaluation of the brain size/intelligence relationship				
Evolutionary factors in the development of human intelligence				
Description of ecological theories of intelligence				
Evaluation of ecological theories of intelligence				
Description of social theories of intelligence				
Evaluation of social theories of intelligence				

THE RELATIONSHIP BETWEEN BRAIN SIZE AND INTELLIGENCE

Brain size seems an obvious measure of intelligence – the brain is, after all, the place where all our thinking, problem-solving and other mental activities take place. But we have to be very careful about how we relate brain size to intelligence.

ACTIVITY

Brain size in humans and other mammals

Read the textbook from the start of Topic 3 on p. 449/717 to the top of the second column on p. 450/718. Also, read the first bullet point in the Evaluation panel on p. 451/719, discussing the limitations of the EQ.

1 Why is brain size alone an unreliable measure of intelligence? _____

_____

2 Fill in the missing words: EQ = e _____ q _____ = $\dfrac{\text{Actual brain mass}}{\text{_____}}$

3 What is indicated by an EQ of:
  ● more than 1?
  ● less than 1?

continued on next page

Brain size in humans and other mammals continued

4 Note down, in numerical order, the EQs of all the mammals currently living that are mentioned on pp. 449–50/717–18.

_____

_____

_____

_____

6 What does the textbook mean when it says: 'Human infants are born, effectively, 12 months premature'?

_____

_____

_____

_____

5 What two problems did the increase in brain size pose for humans and how have these been solved by evolutionary processes?

Problem 1 _____

Solution _____

Problem 2 _____

Solution _____

7 Summarize three limitations of the notion of EQ.

● _____

● _____

● _____

Evolutionary factors in the brain size/intelligence relationship

The human brain is expensive to maintain, in terms of the body's resources it uses up. From an adaptationist viewpoint, the brain would not have evolved to this situation unless it contributed substantially to evolutionary fitness. Explanations of why this evolution took place include:

● the need to respond to severe climate change
● the primate life style
● selective pressures of hunting.

Evolutionary factors in the brain size/intelligence relationship

Continue reading from this heading up to the heading 'Racial differences' on p. 451/719. In the space below, outline the main factors or pressures that would have led to the evolution of the brain, given the following needs:

● The need to respond to severe climate change

_____

_____

● The primate life style

_____

_____

● The need to hunt

_____

_____

This part of the topic discusses the question of gender differences in brain size. Do men and women have different-sized brains, and, if so, what does that tell us, if anything at all, about their relative intelligence?

AO2 **ACTIVITY**

The 'man-as-hunter' hypothesis

The 'man-as-hunter' hypothesis is, not surprisingly, a fairly controversial one, as it gives prime importance to apparently 'male' activities in the evolution of the human brain.

1 What are the main arguments supporting the 'man-as-hunter' hypothesis? List them here, with the names of relevant researchers.

- _____
- _____
- _____

2 What are the counter-arguments? See, for example, the Evaluation panel on p. 451/719. You may also find it useful to search for more information on the Internet.

- _____
- _____
- _____

AO2 **ACTIVITY**

Racial differences – the 'out-of-Africa' hypothesis

The 'out-of-Africa' hypothesis is equally controversial, as it can be used by racists to make arguments about racial superiority.

1 What are the main arguments supporting the 'out-of-Africa' hypothesis. List them here, with the names of relevant researchers.

- _____
- _____
- _____

2 What are the counter-arguments? See, for example, the Evaluation panel on p. 451/719.

- _____
- _____
- _____

ACTIVITY

Innovation, social learning and tool use

Read the text under this heading on p. 451/719 and the two bullet points in the panel at the top of p. 452/720.

1 Primates have been found to have unusually large brains, with humans largest of all. Why, according to Reader and Laland, do our unique linguistic abilities *not* account for this?

_____
_____
_____

2 What, in their view, might be more important factors in determining primates' brain size, and what research has shown this?

_____
_____
_____

Answering exam questions on brain size and intelligence

Example Exam Questions 1 and 2 on p. 455/723 are examples of the type of question you might be set on this subject. Read the questions and the guidance notes beneath them. They suggest choosing six main points which you can outline (in 50 words each) and then evaluate (in another 50 words). If you wanted to make fewer points in more detail, you could limit yourself to five (60 words of AO1 + 60 words of AO2 each).

ACTIVITY

Answering an exam question

Plan your answer to Example Exam Question 2 on p. 455/723. Decide how many main points you plan to include and divide your answer into an appropriate number of 'chunks'. On separate paper, or using a PC, note down the points you want to include and the corresponding points of evaluation. Divide your points into two lists: descriptive points (AO1) and evaluative points (AO2).

When you are satisfied with your plan, write it up into a complete essay. Use a PC, so that you can check your word counts and make any changes easily.

EVOLUTIONARY FACTORS IN THE DEVELOPMENT OF HUMAN INTELLIGENCE

In searching for clues about what factors might have contributed to the development of human intelligence, researchers have focused on two areas:

- ecological factors – the ever-changing demands of the environment
- social factors – the demands of living in complex social groups.

Ecological theories of intelligence

ACTIVITY

Foraging and tool use

Read the text under this heading on p. 452/720, up to the end of the Evaluation box on p. 453/721. Then answer the following questions.

1 What demands did the hunting-and-foraging life style put on our ancestors' intelligence?

2 Why was being a fruit-eater a more demanding activity than dining on leaves?

3 Why should opening nuts or extracting termites demand a higher intelligence than more straightforward forms of foraging?

4 What distinction do Parker and Gibson (1979) make about different types of extractive foraging?

5 And what conclusion does this lead Parker and Gibson to make about the link between tool use and intelligence?

6 According to Horrobin (1998), what steps in the process of evolution have led to increased incidences of mental disorder?

Social theories of intelligence

The textbook considers two so-called 'social theories of intelligence'.
These are covered in the next two activities.

ACTIVITY

Machiavellian intelligence hypothesis

Read the text under this heading on pp. 453–4/721–2, including the first two bullet points in the Evaluation panel on p. 454/722.

1 What is the Machiavellian intelligence hypothesis?

_____
_____
_____

2 How does grooming behaviour illustrate this?

_____
_____
_____

3 How did Robin Dunbar test the link between use of social strategies and intelligence?

_____
_____
_____

4 What were Dunbar's findings and what conclusions did he draw from them?

_____
_____
_____
_____

5 According to Harcourt (1992), what is unique about the types of alliances formed by primates?

_____
_____
_____

6 What other type of behaviour is unique to primates and illustrates the link between social living and intelligence? Give an example of this type of behaviour.

_____
_____
_____
_____

ACTIVITY

Meat-sharing

Read the text under this heading on p. 454/722, including the final two points in the Evaluation panel.

1 What is Stanford's hypothesis regarding the link between meat and intelligence?

_____
_____

2 Why does meat-sharing demand advanced cognitive abilities?

_____
_____

3 What observations support Stanford's hypothesis?

_____
_____

4 What points of criticism might you make about Stanford's research?

_____
_____
_____

5 How does Hill and Kaplan's (1988) research answer one of those criticisms?

_____
_____
_____

6 What alternative hypothesis for meat-sharing does Wrangham (1975) suggest?

_____
_____
_____

EXAMPLE EXAM QUESTIONS

In your work on this unit, you have already planned and written a complete answer to Example Exam Question 2 on p. 455/723. In the sample answer below, we use some of the material on pp. 449–52/717–20 to answer Example Exam Question 1.

Unit 15/23 // Evolutionary explanations of human behaviour

Discuss the relationship between brain size and intelligence.   (24 marks)

One way of investigating the relationship between brain size and intelligence is to examine brain sizes in different species. Jerison (1973) suggested that an accurate idea of the intelligence of different species could be gained by comparing the actual brain size of species with the brain size that we might expect for that body mass. The degree to which the actual brain size exceeds the expected brain size gives us the encephalization quotient (EQ) for that species. Using this method, humans have the highest EQ of any animal (7), whereas dolphins score 4.5 and primates about 2.3.

The notion of an EQ offers a more meaningful explanation of intelligence than simply comparing absolute brain size across species, but it has proved difficult to establish a strong correlation between EQ and intelligence. One problem is that animals vary greatly in their body and brain weights at different times of the year and at different times of life, which makes it hard to estimate an accurate brain-to-body ratio. Also, some animals have a low EQ, but are not necessarily unintelligent. For example, foliovores, who need an extensive digestive tract to break down cellulose, might be said to have large bodies for their brain size rather than small brains for their body size.

Anthropologists believe that the primate life style acted as a selective pressure that led to the development of larger brains. Early humans had to develop cognitive skills to help them find fruit, or hunt and trap animals. These complex skills would have required the evolution of new brain regions or the development of more cells in existing regions. The 'man-as-hunter' hypothesis (Washburn and Lancaster 1968) suggests that the differing roles of men and women during human evolution may have contributed to the different development of their brains. This may explain why males tend to be better at visuo-spatial and navigation tasks and why male brains are consistently found to be heavier than female brains. Ankney (1995) claims that selection for hunting abilities would have led to relatively larger brains in men to process spatial information. As well as gender differences, racial differences have also been used as evidence of a brain size/intelligence relationship.

Beals et al. (1984) discovered that the cranial volume of East Asians was bigger than that of Europeans, with that of Africans being lower still. Rushton (1995) suggests that this can be explained by the fact that the further north our ancestors migrated, the more they encountered cognitively demanding problems, such as finding food and shelter in long winters, resulting in the development of greater adaptive intelligence.

The 'man-as-hunter' hypothesis has largely neglected the role of the female in the evolutionary process. However, anthropological evidence from many traditional societies has shown that food gathering by females was more nutritionally important for these groups (Zihlmann and Tanner 1978). There are also problems with suggesting racial differences in brain size based on estimates of cranial capacity. These estimates may have different validity for men and women. For example, Willerman et al. (1992) found a significant correlation between brain size and head perimeter for women, but not for men, and Reed and Jensen (1993) found a difference of only 1 cm^3 between a high-IQ group and a low-IQ group. There are also many other possible explanations for differences in intelligence that have nothing to do with brain size. Among East Asians, for example, intelligence is culturally valued, which could explain why this group typically displays higher intelligence levels than other racial groups.

A more recent approach to the brain size/intelligence relationship has been to examine evidence for innovation, social learning and tool use in different species. These behaviours are seen as a measure of the behavioural flexibility of species, and an ecologically valid measure of a species' intelligence. Reader and Laland (2002) found that the frequency of all three behaviours was significantly correlated with brain size in 116 primate species. This finding challenges the view that large brains arose mainly because of the unique problems faced during human evolution. It also suggests that intellectual developments unique to human beings, such as language, may have played a smaller part in the development of intelligence than was previously believed.

CHECK YOUR UNDERSTANDING

When you have finished working through this topic, try the questions in 'Check your understanding' on p. 455/723 of the textbook. Check your answers by looking at the relevant parts of the textbook or this workbook, listed below.

1   textbook p. 449/717; workbook p. 149
2   textbook p. 450/718; workbook p. 150
3   textbook pp. 450–1/718–19
4   textbook p. 451/719
5   textbook pp. 451–2/719–20
6   textbook p. 452/720
7   textbook p. 453/721
8   textbook pp. 453–4/721–2
9   textbook p. 454/722
10 textbook p. 454/722

Psychopathology

PREVIEW

There are three topics in this unit. You should read them alongside the following pages in the Collins *Psychology for A2-level/Psychology* textbook:

Topic		Psychology for A2	Psychology
1	Schizophrenia	pp. 486–97	pp. 754–65
2	Depression	pp. 498–508	pp. 766–76
3	Anxiety disorders	pp. 508–18	pp. 776–86

INTRODUCTION

Individual Differences is one of three sections in Module 5 (AQA Specification A), as the diagram below shows. This section is further divided into three sub-sections – 'Psychopathology' is the second of these.

Read the Preview and Introduction on p. 484/752 of the textbook now. This will give you an overview of what's in the unit.

Where this unit fits in to the A-level qualification

Module 5

- Section A: **Individual Differences**
- Section B: Perspectives (Issues & Debates)
- Section C: Perspectives (Approaches)

- ISSUES IN THE CLASSIFICATION & DIAGNOSIS OF PSYCHOLOGICAL ABNORMALITY
- **PSYCHOPATHOLOGY**
- TREATING MENTAL DISORDERS

- **a** Schizophrenia
- **b** Depression
- **c** Anxiety disorders

In Section A of the Module 5 exam, you are offered a choice of three questions, one from each section. You have to answer **one** of these three questions.

This topic concentrates on schizophrenia, one of the most serious of mental disorders. You will find out about the clinical characteristics of this disorder – or more accurately, set of disorders, since there are a number of sub-types of schizophrenia characterized by different symptoms. Psychologists have sought to explain schizophrenia in different ways. Biological approaches focus on the physiological causes, such as genetics, biochemical imbalances and neuroanatomical explanations, while psychological explanations are more concerned with aspects such as family relationships and cognitive malfunctioning.

UNDERSTANDING THE SPECIFICATION

This topic forms part of A2 Module 5, Section A: Individual Differences.

The first sentence in this entry (see right) specifies the 'clinical characteristics of schizophrenia'. What does it mean by this? It can legitimately be interpreted as meaning the different types and *sub-types* of schizophrenia (e.g. acute/chronic, hebephrenic/ catatonic) or the *symptoms* of schizophrenia (e.g. thought control, delusions, hallucinations). You could mix and match these, although the limited time available to answer a question on clinical characteristics will probably restrict you to one or other approach. Note that you are only expected to be able to *describe* these characteristics, not evaluate them.

Far more substantial are the explanations of schizophrenia. It is important that you cover at least two biological (e.g. genetics and biochemical explanations such as the dopamine hypothesis) and at

> ### Psychopathology
> #### a. Schizophrenia
> Clinical characteristics of schizophrenia. Biological (e.g. genetics, biochemistry) and psychological (e.g. social and family relationships) explanations of schizophrenia, including the evidence on which they are based.

least two psychological (e.g. social/familial and cognitive) explanations. The last part of this entry ('including the evidence on which they are based') is easy to miss, but it does mean that you might have both to describe and evaluate this evidence. It is more likely, though, that you would be asked to use this evidence as evaluation of the preceding explanations. It is always better to be safe than sorry, however, and be prepared for all eventualities.

TOPIC MAP

The diagram below is a visual 'map' of the content of this topic.

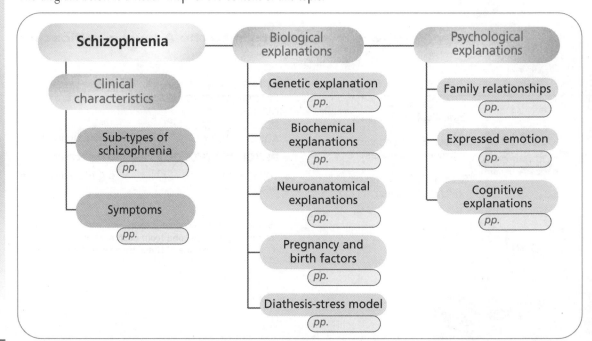

Topic map

Look through pp. 486–96/754–64 of the textbook to see where the items shown in the topic map are covered. Note down the relevant page numbers in the spaces left on the topic map.

KEEPING TRACK

Use the table below to keep track of your work on this topic and plan your revision. See p. iv of this workbook (Introduction) for guidance on filling it in.

Schizophrenia		Tick if you ...		
What I need to learn	*Where is it?*	*could make a basic attempt*	*could make a good attempt*	*have complete mastery of this*
Clinical characteristics of schizophrenia				
Description of the symptoms of schizophrenia				
Description of the sub-types of schizophrenia				
Biological explanations of schizophrenia				
Description of the genetic explanation				
Evaluation of the genetic explanation				
Description of the biochemical explanation				
Evaluation of the biochemical explanation				
Description of neuroanatomical explanations				
Evaluation of neuroanatomical explanations				
Description of pregnancy and birth factors as explanations				
Evaluation of pregnancy and birth factors as explanations				
Description of the diathesis-stress model explanation				
Psychological explanations of schizophrenia				
Description of family relationships explanation				
Description of expressed emotion explanation				
Evaluation of family relationships and expressed emotion				
Description of cognitive explanations				
Evaluation of cognitive explanations				

CLINICAL CHARACTERISTICS OF SCHIZOPHRENIA

Start your work on this topic by reading the text under the heading 'What is schizophrenia?' on p. 486/754. This gives a good introduction to what we currently understand by this label and stresses the difficulties that researchers have faced because of the lack of agreement about what schizophrenia actually is. Having said that, there is agreement about many of the characteristics of the disorder and these are outlined on p. 487/755.

Sub-types and characteristics of schizophrenia

Read through the text under the heading 'Clinical characteristics' on p. 486/754 to the end of p. 487/755.

1 What two types of schizophrenia are in ICD-10, but not in DSM-IV?

2 Which sub-type is labelled differently in DSM-IV?

continued on next page

Sub-types and characteristics of schizophrenia continued

3 Complete the table below to give examples of positive and negative symptoms of schizophrenia, and the sub-types of schizophrenia of which they are characteristic:

	Examples of symptom	Sub-type of schizophrenia
Positive		
Negative		

4 What is meant by 'flattened affect' or 'flat affect'

_____

_____

_____

When an exam question asks about the clinical characteristics of schizophrenia, it will always be asking for *AO1 description*; you will not be asked to *evaluate* the clinical characteristics.

Outlining clinical characteristics

Example Exam Question 4(a) on p. 497/765 illustrates the type of question that might be asked about clinical characteristics of schizophrenia. Read the guidance notes underneath the question and, using your PC, write an answer to part (a).

Limit yourself to 120 words, as suggested in the guidance notes, or as many words as you could write in about 6.5 minutes (the time you would have for this part of the question in the exam).

BIOLOGICAL EXPLANATIONS OF SCHIZOPHRENIA

Genetic explanation for schizophrenia

Pages 488–9/756–7 of the textbook outline the genetic explanation for schizophrenia, focusing mainly on the evidence for a genetic link found in various types of study. It is also important to understand (and be able to outline in an exam answer) the genetic principles involved. The Expert interview with Paul Harrison on p. 496/764 gives an excellent summary of current thinking about the causes of schizophrenia, including recent genetic discoveries.

Genetic explanations for schizophrenia

Read through pp. 488–9/756–7 of the textbook and the Expert interview on p. 496/764. Then answer the following questions.

1 Outline briefly the process whereby genes might lead to schizophrenia. _____

_____

_____

2 What is mean by:

(a) a first-degree relative

_____

(b) a second-degree relative

_____

3 According to Zimbardo *et al.* (1995), which two categories of relatives carry by far the highest lifetime risk of developing schizophrenia?

_____

_____

4 What is the lifetime risk of developing schizophrenia in the general population?

_____

_____

Research evidence of a genetic link in schizophrenia

Several research studies into genetic links in schizophrenia are described on pp. 488–9/756–7. Complete the following table, summarizing the key features of these studies and their main findings.

Researcher	Key features of research	Findings
Family studies		
Kety et al. (1962) (Copenhagen High-Risk Study)	● 207 offspring (aged 10-18) of schiz. mothers – 104 non-schiz. ● studies in 1962, 1974, 1989	● 35% diagnosis of schizophrenia in high-risk group ● 6.9% in low-risk group
Erlennmeyer-Kimling et al. (1997)		
Twin studies		
Gottesman and Shields (1982)		
Fischer (1971)		
Cardno et al. (1999)		
Adoption studies		
Tienari et al. (1987) (Finnish Adoption Study)		

Problems with research into genetic explanations

The textbook mentions at least four problems with research studies into schizophrenia – either methodological or to do with the types of conclusions that can be drawn from the studies. Highlighting such problems can be a good way of providing AO2 evaluation in exam essays. Note down what these problems are and how they might limit the usefulness of the studies.

Problems	How they might limit usefulness
●	
●	
●	

Biochemical explanations of schizophrenia

Researchers have also investigated the brain to search for structural or biochemical abnormalities that might give us clues about the causes of schizophrenia.

Biochemical explanations of schizophrenia

Read about biochemical explanations on p. 490/758 and then answer the following questions.

1 Summarize the current thinking about the link between the neurotransmitter dopamine and schizophrenia. Comment in particular on the nature of any link.

continued on next page

Biochemical explanations of schizophrenia continued

2 What are the effects of the following drugs on people with schizophrenic symptoms?

● phenothiazine

● L-dopa

● amphetamines

3 What were the findings of researchers based on post-mortems of patients with schizophrenia and on PET scans with living patients?

Researcher	Findings
●	
●	
●	

4 Why is it important to choose drugs carefully when treating different sub-types of schizophrenia?

Neuroanatomical explanations

MRI and, more recently, fMRI have given researchers the opportunity to investigate the living brain. See Unit 4/12, pp. 113–14/381–2 for a summary of these imaging techniques.

Neuroanatomical explanations

Read about neuroanatomical explanations on pp. 490–1/758–9 and then answer the following questions.

1 The findings of several research studies are described on pp. 480–1/758–9. Summarize the main points in the table below:

Researcher	Findings
● Brown *et al.* (1986)	● Decreased brain weight and enlarged ventricals
●	
●	
●	
●	
●	

2 Different conclusions can be drawn from the fact that structural abnormalities have been found more in people with negative symptoms, rather than positive ones. What are these conclusions?

3 The textbook mentions two main problems with studies of brain imaging carried out so far. What are they?

●

●

4 How might a prospective study shed light on the direction of causality of schizophrenia (i.e. whether structural abnormalities cause schizophrenia, or vice versa)?

5 What are the problems involved in carrying out such research?

Pregnancy and birth factors

Read the text about pregnancy and birth factors on pp. 491–2/759–60 and then, on separate paper, or using a PC, summarize the key points by doing the following.

1 Summarize the steps whereby an unborn baby exposed to a particular virus might develop schizophrenia in later life.

2 What research evidence points to a possible link between Influenza A and schizophrenia?

3 Outline three possible problems with Torrey and colleagues' explanation of the cause of schizophrenia.

4 Summarize the key arguments for and against the possibility that birth complications might be a cause of schizophrenia.

Diathesis-stress model

Read the text about the diathesis-stress model on p. 492/760 and then answer the following questions.

1 How does the diathesis-stress model combine both biological and environmental factors in explaining the onset of schizophrenia?

2 What were the main findings of the following studies suggesting that environmental factors helped precipitate schizophrenia:

● Finnish Adoption Study

● Israeli High Risk Study

3 Why do the findings of the Finnish Adoption Study suggest that environmental factors cannot be the only cause of schizophrenia?

Answering exam questions on biological explanations of schizophrenia

In the exam you could be asked a question specifically about biological explanations of schizophrenia – see, for instance, Example Exam Question 2 on p. 497/765. You have 40 minutes to answer this question – enough time to write about 800 words. This means 400 words of AO1 description (for 15 marks) and 400 words of AO2 evaluation (also for 15 marks).

If you chose to answer the question with reference to two explanations only, you would think of your answer in terms of four 'chunks', as shown below.

AQA Unit 5: time and marks

Remember: in AQA Unit 5, questions are worth 30 marks and you have 40 minutes to answer them. In AQA Unit 4, questions are worth 24 marks and you have 30 minutes to answer them.

	AO1 (description)			AO2 (commentary)		
(a) Explanation 1	200 words	10 mins	7.5 marks	200 words	10 mins	7.5 marks
(b) Explanation 2	200 words	10 mins	7.5 marks	200 words	10 mins	7.5 marks

Alternatively, you could include three explanations in your answer, in which case you would divide your essay into six chunks, each worth 5 marks.

Remember that your AO2 can be wide ranging, and might include research evidence that supports or challenges the particular biological explanation you have been describing, or perhaps even link these explanations to issues and debates. For example, the dopamine hypothesis might be considered reductionist because it ignores other, more social and cognitive influences on schizophrenia.

Summarizing biological explanations of depression

1 If you were writing a 'six-chunk' essay (i.e. discussing three biological explanations), work out:

- how many words would be in each chunk
- how long you should spend on each chunk.

2 For each of the biological explanations of schizophrenia discussed on pp. 488–92/756–60:

(a) write a 200-word description (AO1) and a 200-word evaluation (AO2)

(b) write a 135-word description (AO1) and a 135-word evaluation (AO2).

The summaries you prepare for 2(a) will be your 10-minute/7.5-mark version of the explanations, while those you prepare for 2(b) will be the 6.5-minute/5-mark versions.

PSYCHOLOGICAL EXPLANATIONS OF SCHIZOPHRENIA

It is now generally accepted that there is a clear biological involvement in schizophrenia, but many researchers have also focused on psychological factors in trying to explain aspects of the disorder.

Family relationships

1 What is meant by the following terms and who coined them?

	Meaning	Researcher
● Schizophrenogenic		
● Double-bind hypothesis		
● Marital schism		

2 Outline the methodological problems with family relationship studies of schizophrenia.

Expressed emotion

On separate paper, do the following.

1 Summarize what is meant by 'expressed emotion'.

2 Draw up a table to summarize information about Vaughn and Leff's (1976) study of relapse rates among discharged patients. Use the following four headings: Findings, Conclusion, Application of research and Criticisms (to include both positive and negative points).

Cognitive explanations of schizophrenia

Disturbed thought patterns are a characteristic of schizophrenia. Researchers have sought to establish whether these are a cause or consequence of the disorder. Read the information about cognitive explanations on pp. 494–5/762–3.

Hemsley's and Frith's models

Two so-called 'neuropsychological' theories have been developed by Hemsley (1993) and Frith (1992). Read the description of the studies and the comments on them in the Evaluation panel on pp. 494–5/762–3, and then, for each study, note down:

1 the basic proposition of the model

2 the biological mechanisms involved

3 what 'malfunctions' or breakdowns exist in these mechanisms

4 evidence or research support for the model

5 possible criticisms of the model.

Genetic links

Several research studies into genetic links are described on pp. 494–5/762–3:

- Park *et al.* (1995)
- Faraone *et al.* (1999)
- Cannon *et al.* (1994)

Summarize the main findings of these studies. Write your notes in the form of a table, using the headings: Findings, Conclusions and Criticisms (noting down both positive and negative criticisms of these studies).

Answering exam questions on psychological explanations of schizophrenia

In the exam you may be asked specifically about psychological explanations of schizophrenia – see, for instance, Example Exam Question 3 on p. 497/765. You have 40 minutes to answer this question – enough time to write about 800 words, i.e. 400 words of AO1 description (for 15 marks) and 400 words of AO2 evaluation (also for 15 marks).

As discussed earlier in this topic, you could limit yourself to just two explanations, in which case you could divide your answer into four 'chunks' of 200 words (2 × 200-word descriptions for AO1 and 2 × 200-word evaluations for AO2). See the top of p. 162 for ideas about what to include for AO2.

Alternatively, you could include three explanations in your answer, in which case you would divide your essay into six chunks of about 135 words each.

Summarizing psychological explanations of schizophrenia

For each of the psychological explanations of schizophrenia discussed on pp. 493–5/761–3:

(a) write a 200-word description (AO1) and a 200-word evaluation (AO2)

(b) write a 135-word description (AO1) and a 135-word evaluation (AO2).

The summaries you prepare for (a) will be your 10-minute/7.5-mark version of the explanations, while those you prepare for (b) will be the 6.5-minute/5-mark versions.

EXAMPLE EXAM QUESTIONS

In your work on this unit, you have already planned and written summaries of the various explanations of schizophrenia. These would serve as the basis for answers to Example Exam Questions 2 and 3 on p. 497/765.

You could also draw on your summaries to provide answers to Questions 1 and 4(b), although these broader questions give you the opportunity to combine biological and psychological explanations. If you do this,

your AO2 would be need to be carefully constructed to highlight similarities and differences between the different theories. You might also choose to weigh up the relative contributions of each type of theory to our understanding of the causes of schizophrenia.

We have used the material on pp. 486–96/754–64 to answer the question below. Note the careful division of material, with part (a) all AO1, and part (b) two-fifths AO1 and three-fifths AO2.

(a) Outline **two** clinical characteristics of schizophrenia. **(5 marks)**

(b) Discuss **two or more** explanations of schizophrenia. **(25 marks)**

(a) DSM identifies five different sub-types of schizophrenia. These are paranoid schizophrenia, where delusions and/or hallucinations are the predominant characteristic; disorganized schizophrenia, marked by disorganized behaviour, incoherence of speech and flattened affect; catatonic schizophrenia, characterized by psychomotor abnormality and negativism; undifferentiated schizophrenia, a general category for individuals with insufficient or too many symptoms to fit the other sub-types; and residual schizophrenia, where the criteria for schizophrenia have been met in the past, but are not met at the present time.

(b) The dopamine hypothesis explains schizophrenia as a product of excess dopamine activity in the brain. Antipsychotic drugs, which reduce the symptoms of schizophrenia, work by inhibiting dopamine activity. Similarly, L-dopa, a dopamine-releasing drug which is used in the treatment of Parkinson's Disease, can induce symptoms resembling acute schizophrenia in non-psychotic people. Post-mortems have discovered a specific increase of dopamine in the left amygdala (Falkai *et al.* 1988) and increased dopamine receptor density in the caudate nuclei of schizophrenics, while PET scans of live brains of schizophrenics have also revealed greater dopamine receptor density compared to non-schizophrenics.

Research tends to support some form of the dopamine hypothesis. Excess dopamine activity has been demonstrated in some people with schizophrenia, particularly those with positive symptoms. Antipsychotic drugs alleviate the positive symptoms of schizophrenia, although they are not as effective with the negative symptoms. This suggests that not all schizophrenia can be explained in terms of excess dopamine activity. These inconclusive findings might merely reflect the different sub-types of schizophrenia (Type I and Type II), with Type I receptive to antipsychotic drugs, but not Type II. Cause and effect is another problem for the dopamine hypothesis. Post-mortems and PET scans cannot reveal whether increased activity in the dopaminergic system causes schizophrenia or whether the disorder itself somehow increases dopamine activity.

Some research has suggested that viral infections, particularly the virus Influenza A, might be involved in the development of schizophrenia (Torrey *et al.* 1996). Influenza A is most common in the winter, and so might explain the high proportion of winter births in those diagnosed with schizophrenia. If the mother is infected during pregnancy, particularly in the second third of pregnancy, then the fetus is exposed to the virus at the time when there is accelerated growth in the cerebral cortex. It is claimed that either the viral infection enters the brain and gestates until it is activated by the hormonal changes in puberty, or that there is a gradual degeneration of the brain which eventually becomes severe enough for the symptoms of schizophrenia to emerge.

There are a number of problems for the viral infection theory. First, studies such as those carried out by Torrey *et al.* were based on correlational data only, and do not tell us anything about the causal relationship between viral infections such as Influenza A and schizophrenia. The data used in this study were also based on the diagnostic criteria for DSM-II, a much earlier version of the DSM, and one which included a broader diagnostic range for schizophrenia than in DSM-III, which is used now. Torrey *et al.* do not claim that viral infection causes schizophrenia directly, but that it only occurs in those who are genetically predisposed to develop schizophrenia. However, there would then be 100% concordance for MZ twins as they share both the same genes and the same early environment in the womb.

Cognitive psychologists suggest that disturbed thought processes actually cause schizophrenia rather than being the consequence of it. They think that schizophrenics have defective attentional systems, as the mechanisms that operate in the brains of normal people to filter incoming information do not function in people with schizophrenia. They cannot filter information selectively and so let in too much irrelevant information. As they are bombarded by external stimuli which they cannot interpret properly, they experience the world differently to non-schizophrenics.

Despite the claims that these cognitive disturbances are the cause of schizophrenia, cognitive theories are actually only describing some of the symptoms of the disorder in cognitive terms. However, even if they cannot fully explain schizophrenia, they may help to explain the origins of particular symptoms such as hallucinations and delusions. Another problem for this explanation is that brain injuries such as strokes can also cause cognitive impairments, but these hardly ever develop into a mental disorder such as schizophrenia. In order to deal with these problems, Hemsley (1993) has tried to link the cognitive impairments of schizophrenia with an underlying part of the brain such as the hippocampus. Although there is little evidence from human studies for this link, animal studies have provided some support for this idea.

CHECK YOUR UNDERSTANDING

When you have finished working through this topic, try the questions in 'Check your understanding' on p. 495/763 of the textbook. Check your answers by looking at the relevant parts of the textbook or this workbook, listed below.

1 textbook p. 486/754

2 textbook p. 486–7/754–5

3 textbook p. 487/755

4 textbook p. 488/756

5 textbook p. 489/757

6 textbook p. 490/758

7 textbook p. 492/760

8 textbook p. 493/761

9 textbook p. 494–5/762–3

10 whole topic, but especially textbook p. 496/764

This topic concentrates on depression and, in particular, on unipolar depression (as opposed to bipolar (or manic) depression. It starts by considering various types of depression and the clinical characteristics of depression. As with schizophrenia, psychologists have sought to explain depression with both biologically based and psychologically based theories. This topic explores both types.

UNDERSTANDING THE SPECIFICATION

Here is what the AQA (A) specification says about this topic. It forms part of A2 Module 5, Section A: Individual Differences.

The first sentence in this specification entry invites you to describe the clinical characteristics of depression. Again this can be interpreted in different ways. You could describe the different categories of depression (e.g. reactive and endogenous depression) or give the DSM classificatory sub-types of depression (i.e. major depressive disorder and dysthymic disorder). Alternatively you could outline the symptoms of depression (e.g. general symptoms as in Table 17.1/25.1 on p. 498/766, or the DSM diagnostic criteria for depression). Note that the specification entry gives the examples of bipolar and unipolar disorder, but you would not be asked specifically for either of these.

> ### Psychopathology
>
> **b. Depression**
>
> Clinical characteristics of depression (e.g. bipolar disorder, unipolar disorder). Biological (e.g. genetics, biochemistry) and psychological (e.g. learned helplessness) explanations of depression, including the evidence on which they are based.

In order for your answer to be synoptic, questions will always involve at least two separate explanations, so be prepared! As with the previous topic on schizophrenia, you do need to cover the 'the evidence on which these explanations are based' as both AO1 and AO2.

TOPIC MAP

The diagram below gives you an overview of what you are about to study.

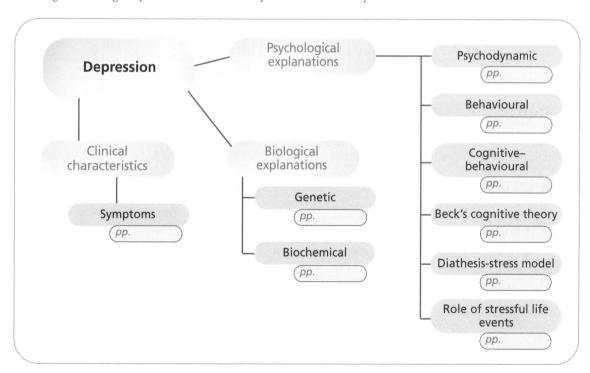

Topic map

Look through pp. 498–506/766–74 of the textbook to see where the items shown in the topic map are covered. Note down the relevant page numbers in the spaces left on the topic map.

KEEPING TRACK

Use the table below to keep track of your work on this topic and plan your revision. See p. iv of this workbook (Introduction) for guidance on filling it in.

Depression		Tick if you ...		
What I need to learn	*Where is it?*	*could make a basic attempt*	*could make a good attempt*	*have complete mastery of this*
Clinical characteristics of depression				
Description of the types and symptoms of depression				
Biological explanations of depression				
Description of the genetic explanation for depression				
Evaluation of the genetic explanation for depression				
Description of the biochemical explanation for depression				
Evaluation of the biochemical explanation for depression				
Psychological explanations of depression				
Description of psychodynamic explanations of depression				
Evaluation of psychodynamic explanations of depression				
Description of behavioural explanations of depression				
Evaluation of behavioural explanations of depression				
Description of cognitive–behavioural explanations for depression				
Evaluation of cognitive–behavioural explanations for depression				
Description of Beck's cognitive theory of depression				
Evaluation of Beck's cognitive theory of depression				
Description of the role of stressful life events in depression				
Evaluation of the role of stressful life events in depression				

CLINICAL CHARACTERISTICS OF DEPRESSION

Start your work on this topic by reading the text under the heading 'What is depression?' and 'Clinical characteristics' on p. 498/766. This gives a good introduction to this most common of psychological abnormalities.

Types and characteristics of depression

1 What is meant by the following terms:
- affective disorder
- unipolar depression
- bipolar depression
- endogenous depression
- reactive depression

2 What are the two types of depressive disorder listed in DSM-IV?

3 When does the onset of depression usually occur?

4 Does depression affect men or women more? (Be careful how you answer this!)

Outlining clinical characteristics

Example Exam Question 4(a) on p. 508/776 illustrates the type of question that might be asked about clinical characteristics of depression. Read the guidance notes underneath the question and, using your PC, write an answer to this part (a). Limit yourself to 120 to 135 words, which is about 5 marks' worth, i.e. as much as you could write in about 6.5 minutes.

When an exam question asks about the clinical characteristics of depression, it will always be asking for *AO1 description*; you will not be asked to *evaluate* the clinical characteristics.

BIOLOGICAL EXPLANATIONS OF DEPRESSION

Biological factors

The textbook lists five factors that suggest the involvement of biological factors in depression. Think of a key word or phrase to help you memorize each of these. For example, for the second point, you could pick 'Universal'. Create an acronym out of the first letters of your key words.

Genetic explanation for depression

The fact that depression seems to run in families implies a clear genetic component (although, of course, families tend to share the same environment, so environmental factors have to be considered too). As with schizophrenia, three types of study have helped researchers establish the degree of that link: family studies, twin studies and adoption studies.

Research evidence of a genetic link in depression

Complete the following table, summarizing the main findings of family, twin and adoption studies into depression.

Researcher	Key features of research	Findings
Family studies		
Gershon (1990)		
Twin studies		
McGuffin *et al.* (1996)		
Bierut *et al.* (1999)		
Adoption studies		
Wender *et al.* (1986)		

Genetic explanations for depression

Read about genetic explanations on p. 499/767 of the textbook, including the Evaluation panel, and answer the following questions.

1 Outline briefly the process whereby genes might lead to depression.

2 How certain can we be that genes contribute to depression?

Biochemical explanations of depression

Researchers have also investigated the brain to search for structural or biochemical abnormalities that might give us clues about the causes of depression.

ACTIVITY

The role of neurotransmitters

Neurotransmitters are thought to be important in helping regulate drives such as appetite and in the control of emotion. Read about the role of neurotransmitters on pp. 499–500/767–8 and in the Evaluation panel on p. 501/769. Then summarize the key points made in the textbook relating to the following neurotransmitters.

Neurotransmitter	Key point
1 noradrenaline	● Tricyclics (effective in treating depression) increase noradrenergic function
	● Cooper (1988) – post-mortems of depressed patients ...
2 serotonin	● Drug Prozac ...
3 dopamine	

ACTIVITY

The role of hormones

Hormone imbalances have also been suggested as an explanation for depression. Read the relevant text on p. 500/768 and the Evaluation panel on p. 501/769, and summarize the key points made about the following hormones:

1 cortisol

2 oestrogen

3 progesterone.

Seasonal affective disorder (SAD)

Winter depression is the most common seasonal depressive disorder. Read the text on p. 500/768 and on p. 137/405 (Unit 5/12 on biological rhythms) and complete the activity on p. 48 of this workbook (if you haven't already done so).

Answering exam questions on biological explanations of depression

In the exam you could be asked a question specifically about biological explanations of depression – see, for instance, Example Exam Questions 1 and 2 on p. 507/775. You have 40 minutes to answer one question – enough time to write about 800 words, i.e. 400 words of AO1 description (for 15 marks) and 400 words of AO2 evaluation (also for 15 marks).

If you chose to answer Question 2, you could limit yourself to just two explanations, in which case you could divide your answer into four 'chunks' of 200 words (2 × 200-word descriptions for AO1 and 2 × 200-word evaluations for AO2). Alternatively, you could include three explanations in your answer, in which case you would divide your essay into six chunks of about 135 words each, each worth 5 marks.

You could count the role of neurotransmitters, the role of hormones and SAD as separate 'explanations'. Alternatively, you could lump them together and treat them as one 'biological' explanation, with the role of genetics as the other explanation. For Question 2, it would be a good idea to include the role of genetics, as part (b) of the question (the AO2 part) requires you to bring in research studies. Here you could comment on the findings of family, twin and adoption studies.

Summarizing biological explanations of depression

For each of the biological explanations of depression discussed on pp. 499–501/767–9:

(a) write a 200-word description (AO1) and a 200-word evaluation (AO2)

(b) write a 135-word description (AO1) and a 135-word evaluation (AO2).

For this activity, treat the role of neurotransmitters, the role of hormones and SAD as separate explanations.

The summaries you prepare for (a) will be your 10-minute/7.5-mark version of the explanations, while those you prepare for (b) will be the 6.5-minute/5-mark versions.

PSYCHOLOGICAL EXPLANATIONS OF DEPRESSION

The lack of clear-cut evidence for structural brain abnormalities in people with depression has led many researchers to concentrate on psychological explanations.

Psychodynamic explanations of depression

Two main psychodynamic explanations of depression are described on p. 501/769: Freud's psychoanalytic approach and Bowlby's 'attachment and separation' theory. You can read more about Freud's theory in Unit 11/19, pp. 320–3/588–91, while Bowlby's theory is discussed in *Psychology for AS-level* Unit 2, pp. 53–6.

Psychodynamic explanations

Complete the following table, summarizing the main points of Freud's and Bowlby's explanations. In the right-hand column, note down potential criticisms (positive and negative) of these studies (that can include research support/challenges – see p. 502/770).

	Key points	Criticisms
Freud		
Bowlby (1973)		

Behavioural explanations of depression

Behavioural explanations

Draw up a similar table to that in the last activity, this time summarizing the two main behavioural theories of depression described on p. 502/770:

- Lewinsohn's (1974) learning theory

- Seligman's (1974) theory of 'learned helplessness'.

Again, include the key points of the theory, as well as any positive and negative evaluative points (including research support/challenges).

Cognitive–behavioural explanations of depression

A criticism of Seligman's behavioural explanation was that it did not take account of cognitive processes. Abramson *et al.*'s (1978) 'hopelessness theory of depression' addresses this criticism.

Cognitive–behavioural explanations

Read the description of the 'hopelessness theory of depression' on pp. 502–3/770–1 and then summarize the following aspects of the explanation:

1 the basic proposition of the theory

2 the three dimensions of judgement that people use to explain failures

3 what is meant by a 'maladaptive attributional style'

4 evidence or research support for the model

5 possible criticisms of the model.

Beck's cognitive theory of depression

Beck's theory concentrates on the negative thought processes displayed by people prone to depression. Read the description of Beck's cognitive theory of depression on pp. 503–5/771–3 and then summarize the following aspects of the explanation, under the following headings.

1 *Cognitive triad* – Draw a diagram illustrating Beck's 'cognitive triad', using a triangle for each of the three aspects of negativity. Include examples of negative thoughts people might have about each aspect, e.g. 'I am worthless'.

2 *Negative self-schemas* – Summarize what is meant by 'negative self-schemas' and outline how they arise.

3 *Cognitive distortions* – Note down what is meant by a 'cognitive distortion' and for each of the five types of cognitive distortion listed, think of a different example from the one given in the textbook.

4 *Personality types* – Describe the role of different personality types in responding to events that trigger depressive episodes.

5 *Criticisms* – Summarize possible criticisms of the model, dividing your list into two parts: positive points/support for the theory and negative points/challenges to the theory.

Stressful life events as triggering factors

A number of researchers have investigated the possibility that stressful life events can act as triggers setting off depressive episodes. Several important studies are described on pp. 505–6/773–4.

Stressful life events as triggering factors

Read the descriptions of the studies by Brown and Harris (1978), Parker *et al.* (1998), Brown and Harris (1993), Bifulco *et al.* (1998) and Veijola *et al.* (1998), described on pp. 505–6/773–4. Summarize the key points about the studies, including findings and conclusions, in the form of a table, using the format shown below.

Study	People studied	Findings	Conclusions
Brown and Harris (1978)	Housewives in Camberwell	• Precipitating factors for depression = – severe life events – long-term difficulties	Life events can trigger depressive episodes

Answering exam questions on psychological explanations of depression

In the exam you may be asked specifically about psychological explanations of depression – see, for instance, Example Exam Question 3 on p. 507/775. As outlined in the guidance notes underneath the question, you must discuss at least two explanations, but you can limit yourself to just two explanations, if you wish. In this case you could divide your answer into four 'chunks' of 200 words (2 × 200-word descriptions for AO1 and 2 × 200-word evaluations for AO2).

Alternatively, you could include more explanations in your answer. For example:

- If you decide to cover three explanations, you would divide your essay into six chunks of about 135 words each (with 6.5 minutes per chunk).

- If you go for four explanations, you would need eight chunks of about 100 words each (with 5 minutes per chunk).

Summarizing psychological explanations of depression

For each of the psychological explanations of depression discussed on pp. 501–6/769–74:

(a) write a 200-word description (AO1) and a 200-word evaluation (AO2)

(b) write a 135-word description (AO1) and a 135-word evaluation (AO2).

The summaries you prepare for (a) will be your 10-minute/7.5-mark version of the explanations, while those you prepare for (b) will be the 6.5-minute/5-mark versions.

If you hope to cover several explanations in a possible answer, you could reduce these summaries to just 100 words each. Be careful, though, as exam questions may not give you a choice about how many explanations to include. Look at Exam Question 5 on p. 508/776, for example: here, you must only discuss two explanations, one biological and one psychological, so you would need to roll out your 200-word summaries.

EXAMPLE EXAM QUESTIONS

In your work on this unit, you have already planned and written summaries of the various explanations of depression. These would serve as the basis for answers to Example Exam Questions 2 and 3 on p. 507/775.

You could also draw on your summaries to provide answers to all the other questions on pp. 507–8/775–6. Question 4(b) is a broader question giving you the opportunity to combine biological and psychological explanations, something you have to do in Question 5. Here, your AO2 would be need to be carefully constructed to highlight similarities and differences between the different theories. You might also choose to weigh up the relative contributions of each type of theory to our understanding of the causes of depression.

One for you to try ...

Compare and contrast one biological explanation of depression and one psychological explanation of depression.
(30 marks)

The most straightforward way of answering a 'compare and contrast' question such as this is for your AO1 (perhaps the first two paragraphs) to be an outline of one biological and one psychological explanation of depression. The next two paragraphs could be points of similarity between the two explanations (the 'compare' bit) and points of difference (the 'contrast' bit). You should perhaps choose explanations where comparing and contrasting is likely to be fruitful. Your answer may look a little like this:

- *Paragraph 1:* Outline of a biological explanation of depression (e.g. biochemical influences)
- *Paragraph 2:* Outline of a psychological explanation of depression (e.g. cognitive)
- *Paragraph 3:* Comparing the two explanations (e.g. both have problems of establishing causation; neither can explain depression on its own; but as part of an integrative model, both have strong research support; both have led to effective therapies for depression)
- *Paragraph 4:* Contrasting the two explanations (e.g. biochemical explanations stress the influence of specific biological factors which can be tested through drug therapy whereas cognitive explanations stress the influence of more global distortions of thinking that contribute to the experience of depression; in the biochemical explanation, depression may be caused by changes in physiology [e.g. in old age] whereas in cognitive explanations depression may be a consequence of life experiences [e.g. parental rejection]; biochemical explanations are *reductionist* whereas cognitive explanations are more *holistic*).

CHECK YOUR UNDERSTANDING

When you have finished working through this topic, try the questions in 'Check your understanding' on p. 507/775 of the textbook. Check your answers by looking at the relevant parts of the textbook or this workbook, listed below.

1 textbook p. 498/766

2 textbook p. 498/766

3 textbook p. 499/767

4 textbook pp. 499–500/767–8

5 textbook pp. 499/767 and 501/769

6 textbook p. 501/769

7 textbook pp. 502–3/770–1

8 textbook pp. 503–5/771–3

9 textbook pp. 505–6/773–4

10 textbook pp. 501–6/769–4

This topic covers two types of anxiety disorder: phobias – irrational fears of objects and situations – and obsessive–compulsive disorder, where an individual is plagued by uncontrollable thoughts and performs seemingly senseless rituals. As with other mental disorders, psychologists have searched for both biological explanations and psychological ones. By now, you may not be surprised to learn that no one type of explanation is likely to be sufficient to explain these serious disorders; instead, it is more productive to look at how different factors interact.

UNDERSTANDING THE SPECIFICATION

Here is what the AQA (A) specification says about this topic. It forms part of A2 Module 5, Section A: Individual Differences.

As with the entries on schizophrenia and depression, there are different ways to describe the 'clinical characteristics' of your chosen disorder. You could describe different forms or sub-types of your chosen disorder, or describe the symptoms of that disorder. Although three different types of disorder are mentioned as examples in the specification entry, you only need cover one of these. This is an important point, as there is absolutely no point in covering more than one (except perhaps for interest). In an exam, the synoptic element of any question will not be to cover more than one type of anxiety disorder, but more than one explanation of one disorder. Remember also that it is your choice which disorder you choose to illustrate the category 'anxiety disorders'. However,

Psychopathology

c. Anxiety disorders

Clinical characteristics of any **one** anxiety disorder (e.g. post-traumatic stress disorder, phobic disorders, obsessive–compulsive disorder). Biological (e.g. genetics, biochemistry) and psychological (e.g. conditioning) explanations of the chosen disorder, including the evidence on which they are based.

having settled on one (we have included phobias and obsessive–compulsive disorder in the textbook), you should cover at least two biological explanations of that disorder and at least two psychological explanations of the same disorder. Again, don't forget to study the evidence on which these explanations are based.

TOPIC MAP

The diagram below gives you an overview of what you are about to study.

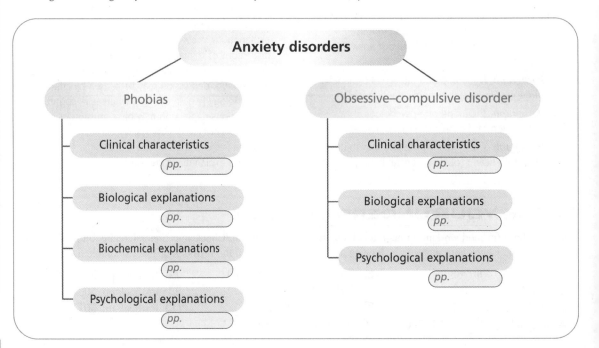

Anxiety disorders

Phobias
- Clinical characteristics
  pp.
- Biological explanations
  pp.
- Biochemical explanations
  pp.
- Psychological explanations
  pp.

Obsessive–compulsive disorder
- Clinical characteristics
  pp.
- Biological explanations
  pp.
- Psychological explanations
  pp.

Topic map

Look through pp. 508–16/776–84 of the textbook to see where the items shown in the topic map are covered. Note down the relevant page numbers in the spaces left on the topic map.

KEEPING TRACK

Use the table below to keep track of your work on this topic and plan your revision. See p. iv of this workbook (Introduction) for guidance on filling it in.

Anxiety disorders		Tick if you ...		
What I need to learn	Where is it?	could make a basic attempt	could make a good attempt	have complete mastery of this
Phobias				
Description of the clinical characteristics of phobias				
Description of biological explanations of phobias				
Evaluation of biological explanations of phobias				
Description of biochemical explanations of phobias				
Evaluation of biochemical explanations of phobias				
Description of psychological explanations of phobias				
Evaluation of psychological explanations of phobias				
Obsessive–compulsive disorder (OCD)				
Description of the clinical characteristics of OCD				
Description of biological explanations of OCD				
Evaluation of biological explanations of OCD				
Description of psychological explanations of OCD				
Evaluation of psychological explanations of OCD				

PHOBIAS

Start your work on this topic by reading from the start of Topic 3 on p. 508/776 to the end of p. 509/777. As well as a general introduction to anxiety disorders, it gives a good description of what constitutes a phobia and the three main categories of phobia.

Types and characteristics of phobias

1 What is a phobia?

2 Summarize the clinical characteristics of the three main categories of phobia:

Category	Clinical characteristics
● Specific (simple) phobias	
● Social phobia	
● Agoraphobia	

3 What distinguishes so-called 'simple' phobias from social phobia or agoraphobia?

Outlining clinical characteristics

Example Question 1(a) on p. 517/785 illustrates the type of question that might be asked about clinical characteristics of anxiety disorders. Read the guidance notes underneath the question and, using your PC, write an answer to this part (a). Limit yourself to 120 to 135 words, which is about 5 marks' worth, i.e. as much as you could write in about 6.5 minutes.

Note that this question asks for 'two or more' clinical characteristics. This one of those occasions where more is better, and you can either describe the different types of phobias (e.g. specific, social and agoraphobia) or the different sub-types of specific phobias (e.g. animal, situational).

BIOLOGICAL EXPLANATIONS OF PHOBIAS

Genetic explanations of phobias

As the textbook explains on p. 510/778, fear and anxiety are part of the genetic make-up of human beings. However, studies into phobias have not provided the clear-cut evidence of the kinds of genetic links that exist in other mental disorders such as schizophrenia.

Research evidence of a genetic link in phobic anxiety disorders

Read about biological explanations of phobias on p. 510/778 and then complete the following table, summarizing the main findings of family and twin studies into phobias.

Researcher	Phobia studied	Findings
Family studies		
Solyom *et al.* (1974)		• 45% of phobic patients had family history of psychiatric disorder • 30% had mothers with phobias • 19% of controls had family history
Noyes *et al.* (1986)	• agoraphobia • panic disorder	
Fryer *et al.* (1990)		
Reich and Yates (1988)	• social phobia	
Twin studies		
Slater and Shields (1969)		
Torgersen (1983)		
Kendler *et al.* (1992)	• agoraphobia • specific phobias	

AO2 ACTIVITY

Evaluating genetic explanations

Research into genetic explanations of phobias has not proved conclusive. On separate paper, draw up two lists, one listing support for genetic explanations and one listing challenges (which can include inconclusiveness of research or problems with it). You could include these points in the AO2 part of any essay you write about genetic explanations of phobias.

Biochemical explanations of phobias

Researchers have also searched for a link between biochemical imbalances and phobias.

ACTIVITY

Biochemical explanations

Read about biochemical explanations on pp. 510–11/778–9. Then answer the following questions.

1 What is GABA and what function does it serve?

2 What has research found regarding GABA activity in people with anxiety disorders?

3 How do benzodiazepines work?

Answering exam questions on biological explanations of phobias

In the exam you could be asked a question specifically about biological explanations of anxiety disorders – see, for instance, Example Exam Questions 1(b), 3 and 4 on p. 517–18/785–6.

ACTIVITY

Planning exam answers for AQA Unit 5

Look at Example Exam Question 1(b). Part (b) is worth 25 marks: of this, 10 marks would be description (AO1) and 15 marks would be evaluation (AO2).

1 Why is there this division of marks for part (b)?

2 When planning your response to (b), how many minutes and words would you have for AO1 and AO2? (Remember that you have 40 minutes for your complete answer, enough time for about 800 words.)

	Minutes	Words
● Description (AO1)		
● Evaluation (AO2)		

Check your answers with those given on p. 178.

ACTIVITY

Practice exam question

Practise writing a complete answer to Example Exam Question 2(b) on p. 517/785. Your first task will be to calculate the word count and division of AO1/AO2 that you will need for this part of the question.

For this question, genetic and biochemical explanations of phobias would count as your two explanations. Describing the explanations would count as your AO1. To evaluate them, you could bring in research studies (of which there are plenty for genetic explanations), but read the guidance notes under Question 1 on p. 517/785 carefully for advice about using studies, rather than describing them.

You will find that you need to search out more information on the biochemical explanations of phobias in order to construct a complete answer. This is a very worthwhile exercise as it lets you decide what is worthy of inclusion. You might try the following website for some relevant information on the biochemistry of agoraphobia.

www.medicinenet.com/agoraphobia/article.htm

PSYCHOLOGICAL EXPLANATIONS OF PHOBIAS

Phobias have generated a great deal of theorizing by psychologists looking for psychological explanations. Several of these are covered in the textbook.

Psychodynamic explanations of phobias

ACTIVITY

Two main psychodynamic explanations are described on p. 511/779: Freud's psychoanalytic approach and Bowlby's 'attachment and separation' theory. You can read more about Freud's theory in Unit 11/19, pp. 320–3/588–91, while Bowlby's theory is discussed in *Psychology for AS-level* Unit 2, pp. 53–6.

Draw up a table, similar to the one shown on p. 169 to summarize the main points of Freud's and Bowlby's explanations of phobias. Include a column where you can note down potential criticisms (positive and negative) of these studies.

ACTIVITY

Behavioural explanations of phobias

Read the description of the 'hopelessness theory of phobias' on pp. 511–12/779–80 and then summarize the following aspects of the explanation:

1 the basic proposition of the theory

2 the role of classical and operant conditioning

3 evidence or research support for the model

4 possible criticisms of the model.

ACTIVITY

Preparedness theory

The concept of preparedness was first discussed in Unit 15/23, which considered evolutionary explanations of human behaviour (see pp. 444–5/712–13 of the textbook).

Read the description of the 'preparedness theory' on pp. 512–13/780–1 and look at the activity on p. 145 of this workbook. Complete that activity, if you haven't already done so. Then do the following.

1 On separate paper, or on your PC, summarize the findings of the research by Ohman *et al.* (1976). Do this in the form of a table, with three columns headed: Findings, Conclusions and Criticisms (which should include both positive and negative points).

2 Then draw up two lists of key points, one listing support for preparedness theory and one listing challenges to it. You can include points from the Evaluation panel on p. 445/713 of the textbook.

ACTIVITY

Other psychological explanations

The textbook goes on to discuss three further psychological explanations of phobias. Read about social learning theory, cognitive–behavioural explanations and the diathesis-stress model on pp. 513–14/781–2. For each explanation, summarize the following aspects:

1 the basic proposition of the theory

2 evidence or research support for the model

3 possible criticisms of the model.

Answering exam questions on psychological explanations of phobias

In the exam you may be asked specifically about psychological explanations of phobias or you may be able to bring them in to questions that don't specify any particular type of explanation (as in Example Exam Question 5 on p. 518/786). As discussed earlier, the key to answering questions successfully is to have a clear idea of the main points of the explanations that you plan to discuss, both in terms of description (AO1) and evaluation (AO2).

Summarizing psychological explanations of phobias

For each of the psychological explanations of phobias discussed on pp. 511–14/779–82:

(a) write a 200-word description (AO1) and a 200-word evaluation (AO2)

(b) write a 135-word description (AO1) and a 135-word evaluation (AO2).

The summaries you prepare for (a) will be your 10-minute/7.5-mark version of the explanations, while those you prepare for (b) will be the 6.5-minute/5-mark versions.

If you hope to cover several explanations in a possible answer, you could reduce these summaries to just 100 words each. Be careful, though, as exam questions may not give you a choice about how many explanations to include.

OBSESSIVE–COMPULSIVE DISORDER (OCD)

The second anxiety disorder covered in this topic is obsessive–compulsive disorder (OCD). Read the paragraphs at the bottom of p. 514/782 and the description of clinical characteristics on p. 515/783.

Outlining clinical characteristics of OCD

Look again at Example Exam Question 1(a) on p. 517/785. You have already written an answer to this based on phobias. You could equally well answer it with reference to OCD. In describing two characteristics of OCD, an obvious choice would be to focus on the two aspects of the disorder indicated in the name: obsessiveness and compulsiveness. You could then bring in some of the typical types of obsessions and compulsions described on p. 515/783.

Read the guidance notes underneath the question and, using your PC, write an answer to this part (a). Limit yourself to 120 to 135 words, which is about 5 marks' worth, i.e. as much as you could write in about 6.5 minutes.

Biological explanations of OCD

Three types of biological explanation of OCD are discussed on pp. 515–16/783–4. Read the paragraph about 'Genetic explanations' and then summarize the key points by doing the following.

1 Outline the biological mechanisms involved in the triggering of OCD.

2 Summarize the evidence or research support for the model provided by:
- Carey and Gottesman (1981)
- Hoaker and Schnurr (1980).

3 Note down possible criticisms of this explanation (see the Evaluation panel).

4 Prepare similar summaries of the biochemical and neuroanatomical explanations of OCD discussed on p. 515/783.

Psychological explanations of OCD

Three psychological explanations of OCD are discussed on p. 516/784 – the psychodynamic, behavioural and cognitive–behavioural explanations. For each explanation, summarize:

1 the basic proposition of the theory

2 evidence or research support for the model

3 possible criticisms of the model.

EXAMPLE EXAM QUESTIONS

In your work on this unit, you have already planned and written summaries of the various explanations of phobias. These would serve as the basis for answers to several of the Example Exam Questions on pp. 517–18/785–6. You might also like to prepare similar summaries for the biological and psychological explanations of OCD, described on pp. 515–16/783–4. Your teacher will probably have decided for you which anxiety disorder you will cover, so spend your time mastering that one.

One for you to try ...

'The strength of biological explanations is the increasing research evidence now available in relation to anxiety disorders.'

With reference to the quotation, discuss biological explanations of one anxiety disorder. (30 marks)

This question needs to be read carefully. So what exactly is required? First, there is a quotation. Do you need to take this into consideration? Some questions say 'With reference to issues such as those in the quotation…', or make no reference to the quotation in the question. In those cases you can safely ignore it, *although* it is there to help and guide you in constructing your answer. In this question, however, it says 'With reference to the quotation …' which means that you cannot ignore it, and must pay some attention to it in your answer.

Second, you are asked to discuss 'biological explanations'. This tells you two things – that you must cover *more than one* explanation, and that they must be *biological* rather than psychological in nature. You can use psychological explanations as part of your AO2 commentary, but these should be carefully built into a critical commentary rather than just being presented as alternative description.

Finally, you are asked for just one type of anxiety disorder, so don't use more than one. What counts as one anxiety disorder? You could use phobias as one type of anxiety disorder, and cover some or all the different types of phobia in your answer, or (and equally legitimately), just focus on one type of phobia (e.g. agoraphobia). What follows is a sample plan for your answer to this question. Remember that this is a 40-minute answer, so if you follow the four-paragraph rule, the paragraphs will be closer to 200 words than 150 words. Note that 'biochemical' explanations also count as 'biological'. You will need to use the Internet to expand your description of biochemical explanations and your evaluation of each of the two biological explanations. For example,

www.freud.org.uk/phobia.html has the following to say about genetic explanations of phobias:

> 'Genetic explanations are also limited in scope, unable to explain the multitude of phobias that actually exist. Further, since we succeed in passing on our genes if we respond to danger in an appropriate way, it is difficult to see how the genetic argument can account for the curious incapacity that overwhelms the person with a phobia when faced with the object of their fear.'

You might also look up the link between neurotransmitters such as serotonin and phobias. If SSRIs (selective serotonin reuptake inhibitors) are used in the treatment of phobias, what does this tell you about the underling biochemical nature of the disorder?

An outline of the answer could be as follows.

- Genetic explanations of phobic anxiety disorders (e.g. family history studies and twin studies) including reference to research studies that inform these explanations.

- Evaluation of genetic explanations of phobic anxiety disorders, making particular reference to the research evidence that has been used to support genetic explanations.

- Biochemical explanations of phobic anxiety disorders including reference to research studies that inform these explanations.

- Evaluation of biochemical explanations of phobic anxiety disorders, making particular reference to the research evidence that has been used to support biochemical explanations.

CHECK YOUR UNDERSTANDING

When you have finished working through this topic, try the questions in 'Check your understanding' on p. 517/785 of the textbook. Check your answers by looking at the relevant parts of the textbook or this workbook, listed below.

1 textbook p. 508/776

2 textbook pp. 508–9/776–7

3 textbook p. 509/777

4 textbook p. 510/778

5 textbook pp. 510–11/778–9

6 textbook p. 511/779

7 'learned helplessness' should read 'preparedness' – textbook pp. 512–13/780–1

8 textbook p. 515/783

9 textbook pp. 515–16/783–4

10 textbook pp. 511–14/779–82 and 516/784

ANSWERS TO ACTIVITIES

Planning exam answers for AQA Unit 5, p. 175

1 Exam questions in AQA Unit 5 are divided equally between AO1 and AO2 skills (15 marks each). Part (a) of Question 1, worth 5 marks, is AO1 description, which leaves 10 marks of AO1 for part (b), with the remaining 15 marks all AO2.

2 ● *Description* (AO1): 13.5 minutes approx = 265–270 words

   ● *Evaluation* (AO2): 20 minutes = 400 words

TREATING
Mental disorders

INTRODUCTION

Individual Differences is one of three sections in Module 5 (AQA Specification A), as the diagram below shows. This section is further divided into three sub-sections – 'Treating mental disorders' is the third of these.

Read the Preview and Introduction on p. 520/788 of the textbook now. This will give you an overview of what's in the unit.

Where this unit fits in to the A-level qualification

Module 5

Section A: **Individual Differences**

Section B: Perspectives (Issues & Debates)

Section C: Perspectives (Approaches)

- ISSUES IN THE CLASSIFICATION & DIAGNOSIS OF PSYCHOLOGICAL ABNORMALITY
- PSYCHOPATHOLOGY
- **TREATING MENTAL DISORDERS**

a Biological (somatic) therapies

b Behavioural therapies

c Alternatives to biological and behavioural therapies

In Section A of the Module 5 exam, you are offered a choice of three questions, one from each section. You have to answer **one** of these three questions.

Those who support the use of biological therapies focus on the biological causes of mental disorders and attempt to treat the disorder by dealing with biochemical imbalances. Three types of biological therapy are discussed in this topic: chemotherapy (the use of drugs), electroconvulsive therapy (ECT) and psychosurgery. This topic looks at each therapy in turn, examining its use, followed by an evaluation of its effectiveness and appropriateness.

UNDERSTANDING THE SPECIFICATION

Here is what the AQA (A) specification says about this topic. It forms part of A2 Module 5, Section A: Individual Differences.

You have already met the biological (medical) model of abnormality in your AS studies, and may well know something about the way that this model translates its assumptions about the causes of abnormality to its treatment. You should cover at least two such therapies in your revision. Why? Because for your answer to be *synoptic* (a requirement of this unit), you need to show familiarity with at least two different therapies – and also because the question will ask you to cover at least two! Although there are three types of biological therapy mentioned in the specification, you would not be asked to cover all three in an answer. The word 'including' tells you you must, however, cover all three in your revision, as a question could be

> ### Treating mental disorders
>
> **a. Biological (somatic) therapies**
>
> Biological therapies including chemotherapy, ECT, and psychosurgery. Issues surrounding the use of such therapies (e.g. appropriateness and effectiveness).

specifically asked on any one of these. You cannot be asked specifically to comment on the appropriateness and effectiveness of these therapies, but just on the 'issues' surrounding their use. We have translated those issues as appropriateness and effectiveness in the textbook, but there are many others you could include as well, such as cultural bias, ethics and so on.

TOPIC MAP

The diagram below is a visual 'map' of the content of this topic.

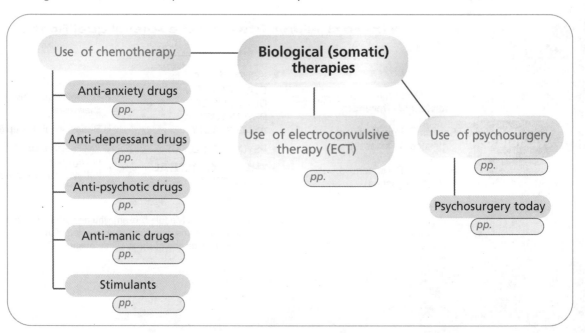

- Use of chemotherapy
  - Anti-anxiety drugs
    - *pp.*
  - Anti-depressant drugs
    - *pp.*
  - Anti-psychotic drugs
    - *pp.*
  - Anti-manic drugs
    - *pp.*
  - Stimulants
    - *pp.*
- **Biological (somatic) therapies**
  - Use of electroconvulsive therapy (ECT)
    - *pp.*
  - Use of psychosurgery
    - *pp.*
    - Psychosurgery today
      - *pp.*

ACTIVITY

Topic map

Look through pp. 523–9/791–7 of the textbook to see where the items shown in the topic map are covered. Note down the relevant page numbers in the spaces left on the topic map.

KEEPING TRACK

Use the table below to keep track of your work on this topic and plan your revision. See p. iv of this workbook (Introduction) for guidance on filling it in.

Biological (somatic) therapies		Tick if you ...		
What I need to learn	*Where is it?*	*could make a basic attempt*	*could make a good attempt*	*have complete mastery of this*
Use of chemotherapy				
Description of the use of anti-anxiety drugs				
Evaluation of the use of anti-anxiety drugs				
Description of the use of anti-depressant drugs				
Evaluation of the use of anti-depressant drugs				
Description of the use of anti-psychotic drugs				
Evaluation of the use of anti-psychotic drugs				
Description of the use of anti-manic drugs				
Evaluation of the use of anti-manic drugs				
Description of the use of stimulants				
Evaluation of the use of stimulants				
Overall evaluation of the use of drugs				
Use of electroconvulsive therapy				
Description of the use of ECT				
Evaluation of the use of ECT				
Use of psychosurgery				
Description of the use of psychosurgery				
Evaluation of the use of psychosurgery				

IMPORTANT GENERAL ISSUES

On p. 522/790 of the textbook you will find a discussion of several important issues relevant to all the types of therapy discussed in this unit.

A02 ACTIVITY

Important general issues in the use of therapy for mental disorders

Read through the text on p. 522/790 of the textbook and summarize in note form each of the issues discussed. For each issue, note down:

- the key points
- problems relating to the issue
- examples of types of patients that might be affected

- examples of therapies most concerned.
- ways of solving problems.

For example, the first issue – of operational definitions – could be summarized as shown at the top of p. 182.

Issue	Operational definitions	Examples of patients affected:

Issue   *Operational definitions*

Key points relating to this issue:

- *Operational definition = concrete measure of an abstract concept*
- *Researchers rely on diagnostic manuals (e.g. DSM, ICD)*

Problems:

- *Unreliable definitions in manuals*
- *Patients included in research not comparable*

Examples of patients affected:

- *Schizophrenics, who may display widely differing symptoms*

Examples of therapies concerned:

- *Drug treatments may alleviate different types of symptom*

Ways of solving problems:

- *Strict ODs must be used when recruiting samples*

USE OF CHEMOTHERAPY

Pages 523–6/791–4 look in turn at five types of drugs used to treat mental disorders. For each type of drug, the textbook includes information about:

- what the drug is
- how the drug works
- the sorts of mental disorder the drug is mainly used to treat
- the positive and negative aspects of using this drug ('evaluation').

A C T I V I T Y

Use of anti-anxiety drugs

Read from the start of Topic 1 to the bottom of p. 523/791. Complete the following form to summarize the main points relating to anti-anxiety drugs.

In the 'Evaluation' column, include the details of any research that has supported or challenged the effectiveness of these drugs.

Type of drug	**Anti-anxiety drugs**	How it works

Type of drug   **Anti-anxiety drugs**

Brief description

Types of mental disorder treated

How it works

- *Sedatives – inhibit nervous system*
  - *– muscle relaxation and overall calming effect*

Evaluation +

- *Overdose not fatal (unlike opioids, prescribed before)*
- *Effective in reducing symptoms of anxiety & panic*
- *Gelernter et al. (1991)*

Evaluation −

- *Can create dependence – often for years*

A C T I V I T Y

Use of other types of drugs

Read from the top of p. 524/792 to the end of the Commentary panel at the top of p. 526/794, describing the use of the remaining four types of drugs. For each type, create a table similar to the one above and summarize the main points. The easiest way to do this is to create a table on your PC, like the one above. You can then copy this and complete one table per type of drug.

Evaluating the use of drugs

As well as evaluating specific types of drugs (as you did in the last two activities), there are also more general criticisms you can make relating to chemotherapy.

Several points are made in the Evaluation panel on p. 526/794, but you could also bring in one or more of the general points made on p. 522/790 ('Important general issues ...').

ACTIVITY

Evaluating the use of drugs

The Evaluation panel on p. 526/794 outlines six aspects of chemotherapy that you could use in the evaluation part of any exam essay. Note down the key points made under each heading below.

Aspects of chemotherapy	Key points
Use of drugs to control	● ●
Dangers of the right to refuse	● ●
Dangers of inaccurate prescription	● ●
Treating the symptoms, not the cause	● ●
Costs versus benefits	● ●
Combining drugs and psychological treatment	● ●

EXAM HINT

The six points listed in the Evaluation panel highlight problems or dangers with chemotherapy. In exam answers, there is a danger of being too critical; you would need to balance negative criticism with positive aspects.

Answering exam questions on chemotherapy

In the exam you could be asked a question specifically about the three biochemical therapies named in the AQA specification (see 'Understanding the specification' on p. 180) – this is the case in Example Exam Questions 2 and 4 on p. 530/798. On the other hand, a question may refer in general terms to 'biological therapies'; in this instance you can take chemotherapy as one of your chosen therapies. Questions 1 and 3 on pp. 529/797 and 530/798 are examples of these types of more general question.

However the question is phrased, you will have 40 minutes to answer it – enough time to write about 800 words. This means 400 words of AO1 description (for 15 marks) and 400 words of AO2 evaluation (also for 15 marks). Taking Question 2, for example, you would think of your answer in terms of four 'chunks', as shown below:

EXAM HINT

Marks and minutes

Remember: in AQA Unit 5, questions are worth 30 marks and you have 40 minutes to answer them. In AQA Unit 4, questions are worth 24 marks and you have 30 minutes to answer them.

Use of	AO1 (description)			AO2 (commentary)		
(a) Chemotherapy	200 words	10 mins	7.5 marks	200 words	10 mins	7.5 marks
(b) ECT	200 words	10 mins	7.5 marks	200 words	10 mins	7.5 marks

Question 4 on p. 530/798 is divided into three parts, and so you would divide your essay into six chunks of about 135 words each, each worth 5 marks and taking about 6.5 minutes to write.

Summarizing the use of chemotherapy

Using a PC, prepare the following summaries of the main points discussed on pp. 523–7/791–5 regarding the use of chemotherapy:

(a) write a 200-word description (AO1) and a 200-word evaluation (AO2)

(b) write a 135-word description (AO1) and a 135-word evaluation (AO2).

You have more than enough material for these summaries. In fact, the challenge will be to reduce over 3000 words of material to a fraction of that length! Think carefully about what you will include.

You may not have time or space to cover every type of drug in detail. What do you need to leave out?

The summaries you prepare for (a) will be your 10-minute/7.5-mark version of chemotherapy – they could form the basis of part of your answers to Example Exam Questions 1, 2 or 3 on pp. 529–30/797–8.

The summaries you prepare for (b) will be the 6.5-minute/5-mark versions and would be suitable as the basis for your answer to Question 4(a). You could also use them for Questions 1 and 3, if you chose to include three types of biological therapy.

USE OF ELECTROCONVULSIVE THERAPY (ECT)

ECT is a controversial therapy, regarded by many as crude and brutal, but seen by others as a valuable, not to say indispensable, option for treatment. Read the description of the use of ECT on p. 527/795, followed by the Evaluation panel on pp. 527–8/795–6.

EXAM HINT

ECT

Although interesting, the historical information in the first column on p. 527/795 of the textbook is not as relevant (in terms of answering exam questions) as the information about modern methods and uses, so in any essay, choose carefully the best material to include.

Use of ECT

Complete the following table to summarize the main points relating to the use and effectiveness of ECT.

In the 'Evaluation' column, include the key points covered in the Evaluation panel on pp. 527–8/795–6.

Type of therapy	**Electroconvulsive therapy**	How it works
Brief description		
Types of mental disorder treated		

Evaluation **+**	Evaluation **−**
●	●
●	●
●	●
●	●
●	●
●	●

Summarizing the use of ECT

Using a PC, prepare the following summaries of the main points discussed on pp. 527–8/795–6 regarding the use of ECT:

(a) write a 200-word description (AO1) and a 200-word evaluation (AO2) and a

(b) write a 135-word description (AO1) and a 135-word evaluation (AO2).

The summaries you prepare for (a) will be your 10-minute/7.5-mark version of ECT – they could form the basis of half your answer to Example Exam

Question 2, which specifically asks you to outline and evaluate ECT. You can also use these summaries to answer more general questions, such as Questions 1 and 3 on pp. 529/797 and 530/798.

The summaries you prepare for (b) will be the 6.5-minute/5-mark versions and would be suitable as the basis for your answer to Question 4(b). You could also use these summaries for Questions 1 and 3, if you chose to include three types of biological therapy.

USE OF PSYCHOSURGERY

Psychosurgery is perhaps even more controversial than ECT as a therapy, because it inflicts permanent damage on the brain. As with ECT, however, psychosurgery has its supporters, who regard it as an important, if 'last-resort', option. Read the description of the use of psychosurgery and the Evaluation panel on pp. 528–9/796–7.

Psychosurgery

Again, if you choose to describe psychosurgery in an exam answer, focus on the modern techniques and applications, rather than historical ones that may not reflect current uses of the therapy.

Use of psychosurgery

Complete the following table to summarize the main points relating to the use and effectiveness of psychosurgery.

In the 'Evaluation' column, include the key points covered in the Evaluation panel on pp. 528–9/796–7.

Type of therapy	**Psychosurgery**	How it works
Brief description		
Types of mental disorder treated		

Evaluation **+**	Evaluation **−**
●	●
●	●
●	●
●	●
●	●
●	●

Summarizing the use of psychosurgery

Using a PC, prepare the following summaries of the main points discussed on pp. 528–9/796–7 regarding the use of psychosurgery:

(a) write a 200-word description (AO1) and a 200-word evaluation (AO2)

(b) write a 135-word description (AO1) and a 135-word evaluation (AO2).

The summaries you prepare for (a) will be your 10-minute/7.5-mark version of psychosurgery. You could use these summaries as part of your answer to

general questions, such as Questions 1 and 3 on pp. 529/797 and 530/798.

The summaries you prepare for (b) will be the 6.5-minute/5-mark versions and would be suitable as the basis for an answer to Question 4(c), which asks you to outline and evaluate psychosurgery (not 'psychotherapy', as in some editions of the textbook).

You could also use these summaries for Questions 1 and 3, if you chose to include three types of biological therapy.

EXAMPLE EXAM QUESTIONS

In your work on this unit, you have already written summaries of all three biological therapies discussed in the textbook – chemotherapy, ECT and psychosurgery.

In various combinations, these summaries would give you enough material to write answers to all the Example Exam Questions on pp. 529–30/797–8.

One for you to try ...

'Biological therapies, such as chemotherapy, ECT and psychosurgery, have both strengths and limitations.'
With reference to the quotation, discuss biological (somatic) therapies. **(30 marks)**

Note that this question, unlike Question 3 on p. 530/798 in the textbook, *does* require you to address the quotation. However, it *does not* require you to cover all three of the therapies mentioned there (note the use of the phrase 'such as' in the quotation). If you do not address the quotation, a partial performance penalty will be applied to your AO2 mark because your answer lacks effectiveness. You would probably address both strengths and limitations, but there is no explicit instruction to do that. Your response may look something like this.

- The nature of anti-anxiety, anti-depressant and anti-psychotic drugs. How they work and why they are used.

- Research on the effectiveness of each of these drugs, e.g. Lecrubier *et al.* (1997) on BZs, Prien (1988) on anti-depressants and APA (1997) on phenothiazines. Other issues concerning appropriateness (e.g. anti-psychotics enable many

to live a reasonably normal life in the community).

- ECT – how and why it is used. Possible mechanisms of ECT.

- Effectiveness of ECT – e.g. two-thirds of patients improve with ECT (Sackeim 1988); ECT is effective in 80 per cent of people who had not responded to medication (Mukherjee *et al.* 1994). Other issues about the use of ECT, e.g. claims of memory loss and studies challenging this (e.g. Devanand *et al.* 1994).

- Psychosurgery – the nature and reasons for use of the pre-frontal lobotomy and the cingulotomy.

- Effectiveness of psychosurgery – e.g. Beck and Cowley (1990) argue that the procedure can be beneficial in a number of disorders. Issues about its use, e.g. claims that it was used to silence political activists and control difficult mental patients in institutions (Comer 1995).

CHECK YOUR UNDERSTANDING

When you have finished working through this topic, try the questions in 'Check your understanding' on p. 529/797 of the textbook. Check your answers by looking at the relevant parts of the textbook or this workbook, listed below.

1 textbook p. 523/791

2 textbook p. 523/791

3 textbook p. 523/791

4 textbook p. 523/791

5 textbook p. 524/792

6 textbook pp. 524–5/792–3

7 textbook pp. 526–7/794–5

8 workbook p. 185 (activity)

9 workbook p. 186 (activity)

10 textbook pp. 522–9/790–7 (see Evaluation and Commentary panels)

Behavioural therapies are based on the notion that some mental disorders involved 'learned behaviour' and that that behaviour can be 'unlearned'. This topic looks first at therapies based on classical conditioning, followed by those based on operant conditioning. As in the last topic, you will look at each therapy in turn, examining its use, followed by an evaluation of its effectiveness and appropriateness.

UNDERSTANDING THE SPECIFICATION

Here is what the AQA (A) specification says about this topic. It forms part of A2 Module 5, Section A: Individual Differences.

You have already met the behavioural model of abnormality in your AS studies, and so will be familiar with the main idea behind behavioural therapies, which is that abnormal behaviours are learned, so that behavioural therapies concentrate on 'unlearning' these behaviours and replacing them with more desirable ones. Questions can (and will, on occasion) ask for named types of therapy as identified in the specification, i.e. those based on classical and operant conditioning. As you could be asked a question just on therapies based on classical conditioning (or just therapies based on operant conditioning), you must study at least two examples of each. The specification gives you one example of each, but there are others in

Treating mental disorders

b. Behavioural therapies

Behavioural therapies, including those based on classical (e.g. flooding) and operant (e.g. token economies) conditioning. Issues surrounding the use of such therapies (e.g. appropriateness and effectiveness).

the textbook. For example, as well as flooding, therapies based on classical conditioning also include systematic desensitization and aversion therapy.

The comments made in the previous topic regarding the issues surrounding the use of therapies also apply here.

TOPIC MAP

The diagram below gives you an overview of what you are about to study.

ACTIVITY

Topic map

Look through pp. 530–3/798–801 of the textbook to see where the items shown in the topic map are covered. Note down the relevant page numbers in the spaces left on the topic map.

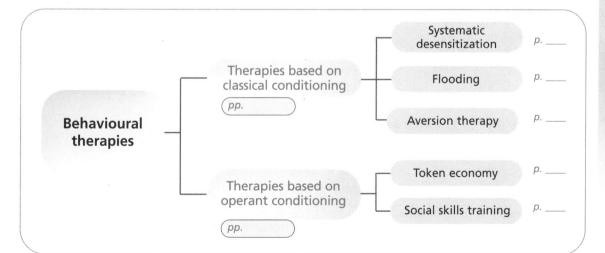

Behavioural therapies

- Therapies based on classical conditioning
  pp.
  - Systematic desensitization   p. ___
  - Flooding   p. ___
  - Aversion therapy   p. ___

- Therapies based on operant conditioning
  pp.
  - Token economy   p. ___
  - Social skills training   p. ___

KEEPING TRACK

Use the table below to keep track of your work on this topic and plan your revision. See p. iv of this workbook (Introduction) for guidance on filling it in.

Behavioural therapies *What I need to learn*	*Where is it?*	could make a basic attempt	could make a good attempt	have complete mastery of this
Use of therapies based on classical conditioning				
Description of systematic desensitization				
Description of flooding				
Description of aversion therapy				
Evaluation of therapies based on classical conditioning				
Use of therapies based on operant conditioning				
Description of token economy				
Description of social skills training				
Evaluation of therapies based on operant conditioning				

BEHAVIOURAL THERAPIES

ACTIVITY

Behavioural therapies

Read from the start of Topic 2 to the bottom of p. 530/798 and then answer the following questions.

1 What is the basic principle of behavioural therapy?

_____

_____

_____

2 What part does 'functional analysis' play in the therapy?

_____

_____

_____

THERAPIES BASED ON CLASSICAL CONDITIONING

You should have a clear idea of the principles of classical conditioning from your AS-level studies (see *Psychology for AS-level* Unit 2, p. 52, and Unit 4, pp. 133–5). It is also covered at A2 level in Unit 13/21 (see pp. 388–91/656–9).

ACTIVITY

Therapies based on classical conditioning

Read the descriptions of the three therapies based on classical conditioning described on p. 531/799 (systematic desensitization, flooding and aversion therapy). Complete the following form to summarize the main points relating to these three therapies.

Type of therapy	**Systematic desensitization**	How it works
Brief description		
Types of mental disorder treated		

Type of therapy	Flooding	How it works
Brief description		
Types of mental disorder treated		

Type of therapy	Aversion therapy	How it works
Brief description		
Types of mental disorder treated		

Understanding terminology

1 Without looking at the textbook, describe what is meant by the following terms?

- Visualization
- *In vitro*
- *In vivo*
- Implosion therapy
- Habituation
- Covert sensitization

2 What are the ethical risks involved in using *in vivo* techniques?

Summarizing techniques based on classical conditioning

Using a PC, prepare two summary descriptions of behavioural therapies based on classical conditioning. The first summary should be 200 words long and the second 135 words long.

The first summary is your 10-minute/7.5-mark description, which you could use as part of your

answers to Example Exam Questions 1 and 3 on p. 534/802, where it would provide half the necessary AO1 material.

The second summary is your 6.5-minute/5-mark version. This would be suitable as the basis for an answer to Question 4(a) on p. 535/803.

Evaluating techniques based on classical conditioning

The Evaluation panel on p. 532/800 discusses several aspects of therapies based on classical conditioning, including their effectiveness and appropriateness, as well as ethical issues.

Evaluating techniques based on classical conditioning

Read through the Evaluation panel on p. 532/800 and summarize the key points in the table below.

	Support for the therapies	Challenge for the therapies
Effectiveness		
Appropriateness		
Ethical issues		

Evaluating behavioural therapies based on classical conditioning

Using a PC, prepare a 200-word summary evaluating behavioural therapies based on classical conditioning. You could use this, for example, as part of your answer to Example Exam Question 3 on p. 534/802, where it would provide half the necessary AO2 material.

THERAPIES BASED ON OPERANT CONDITIONING

You also looked at operant conditioning in your AS-level studies (see *Psychology for AS-level* Unit 2, p. 52, and Unit 4, pp. 134–5). It is also covered at A2 level in Unit 13/21 (see pp. 392–5/660–3). Refresh yourself about the principles of operant conditioning now if you need to.

ACTIVITY

Therapies based on operant conditioning

Read the descriptions of the two therapies based on operant conditioning described on pp. 532–3/800–1 (token economy and social skills training). Complete the following form to summarize the main points relating to these two therapies.

Type of therapy	**Token economy**	How it works
Brief description		
Types of mental disorder treated		

Type of therapy	**Social skills training**	How it works
Brief description		
Types of mental disorder treated		

ACTIVITY

Summarizing techniques based on operant conditioning

Using a PC, prepare two summary descriptions of behavioural therapies based on operant conditioning. The first summary should be 200 words long and the second 135 words long.

The first summary is your 10-minute/7.5-mark description, which you could use as part of your

answers to Example Exam Questions 1 and 3 on p. 534/802, where it would provide half the necessary AO1 material.

The second summary is your 6.5-minute/5-mark version. This would be suitable as the basis for an answer to Question 4(b) on p. 535/803.

Evaluating techniques based on operant conditioning

The Evaluation panel on p. 533/801 discusses several aspects of therapies based on operant conditioning, including their effectiveness and appropriateness, as well as ethical issues.

ACTIVITY

Evaluating techniques based on operant conditioning

Read through the Evaluation panel on p. 533/801 and summarize the key points in the form of a table, using the same format as the AO2 activity at the top of p. 190.

ACTIVITY

Evaluating behavioural therapies based on operant conditioning

Using a PC, prepare a 200-word summary evaluating behavioural therapies based on operant conditioning. You could use this, for example, as part of your

answer to Example Exam Question 3(b) on p. 534/802, where it would provide half the necessary AO2 material.

EXAMPLE EXAM QUESTIONS

In your work on this unit, you have already written summaries of biological therapies based on classical conditioning and operant conditioning, which would provide the basis of answers to Example Exam Questions 1, 3 and 4 on pp. 534–5/802–3.

A frequent problem with questions on therapies is that candidates spend too much time on the approach rather than the therapy. Understanding the processes of classical and operant conditioning is obviously important for helping you understand the therapies

derived from these principles, but, in an exam question, there is no credit for an outline of the basic principles except insofar as they do explain how the therapy functions. For example, it would be creditworthy to talk about how token economies involve the use of reinforcers to increase the probability of new behaviours.

In the sample answer on p. 192, we use material from pp. 530–3/798–801 to answer the question given.

Discuss issues surrounding the use of behavioural therapies (e.g. flooding, token economies). (30 marks)

Behavioural therapies based on classical conditioning are more appropriate for certain disorders than others. They are especially effective in treating disorders such as phobias and post-traumatic stress disorder. McGrath (1990) found that systematic desensitization was effective for around 75% of people with specific phobias, while Barlow and Lehman (1996) reported that graded exposure was especially effective for specific phobias. One of the most difficult phobias to treat is agoraphobia. Craske and Barlow (1993) found that systematic desensitization helped approximately 70% of cases. Despite this success, these therapies are not regarded as suitable for psychotic disorders such as schizophrenia. Even in the treatment of agoraphobia, improvements are only partial – relapses occur in 50% of cases. Some studies have reported spectacular success using systematic desensitization to treat a specific phobia (over 90% success rate four years after treatment), but it is doubtful that the recovery rate could be explained solely in terms of the one session of systematic desensitization. Despite this, behavioural therapies are widely used in the NHS, as they are relatively quick, usually taking just a few months, in contrast to psychodynamic therapies that can last for several years.

Evidence suggests that not all behavioural therapies are equally effective. For example, *in vivo* techniques, where the patient works through the feared item in real life, are found to be more effective for specific phobias than *in vitro* techniques (through imagined imagery). Behaviour therapies are sometimes used in conjunction with other therapies. A number of studies (e.g. Burke *et al.* 1997), comparing different types of therapy, found systematic desensitization to be equally effective for phobias when administered alone, or when used in combination with other treatments. However, Beurs *et al.* (1995) found that systematic desensitization combined with medication was the most effective treatment for panic disorder with agoraphobia. When agreeing to a particular therapy, patients, and even therapists, cannot always anticipate what may occur during the course of therapy. Even with *in vitro* rather than *in vivo* techniques, dangerous consequences may occur, such as hyperventilation, raised blood pressure or even heart attacks. Psychoanalytic theorists claim that treating phobias using behaviour therapies is inappropriate, because the phobia is only a signal from the unconscious that something is wrong. If the phobia is removed, they claim, a new phobia will simply emerge because the treatment does not resolve the underlying conflict.

Therapies based on operant conditioning depend on monitoring behaviour over a number of situations, so they are not as suitable for therapy sessions as techniques based on classical conditioning. They are, however, used in situations such as schools, mental hospitals and prisons, where this constant monitoring is possible. Token economies have, for example, been used extensively in psychiatric institutions with psychotic patients, and found to be very effective in reducing inappropriate behaviour. However, critics say that these programmes do not offer a cure for mental disorders, but simply try to make patients 'fit' better into their social world. It has also been claimed that the success of token economies has more to do with the closer interaction between patient and nurse, which suggests that it is the extra attention that is therapeutic rather than the technique. An indirect advantage of this technique is that nursing staff can become more involved in and committed to treatment.

The success of a token economy programme may be measured in how far it guides a patient toward a target behaviour. For example, chronic psychiatric patients often have no motivation to maintain personal hygiene. Through the token economy, they can gain rewards which can eventually be replaced by others acting in a more sympathetic way towards them. Whenever goals are imposed by others (even when the goal is believed to be for the patient's own good), then desirable behaviour is bound to be influenced by personal or institutional bias. A major criticism of this approach is that, in order to make the token economy work, penalties are often imposed. A strict token economy regime may, therefore, violate basic human rights by imposing restrictions on food, privacy and freedom of movement. One of the saddest consequences of token economy programmes is that some people become dependent on the regime and find it very difficult to think for themselves when they are returned back to the community after a long period in institutional care.

CHECK YOUR UNDERSTANDING

When you have finished working through this topic, try the questions in 'Check your understanding' on p. 534/802 of the textbook. Check your answers by looking at the relevant parts of the textbook or this workbook, listed below.

1 textbook p. 530/798
2 textbook p. 531/799
3 textbook p. 531/799
4 textbook p. 532/800
5 textbook pp. 532–3/800–1
6 workbook p. 190 (activity)
7 textbook pp. 532–3/800–1
8 textbook p. 533/801
9 textbook pp. 532–3/800–1
10 workbook pp. 190 & 191 (AO2 activities)

In this topic you will explore alternatives to the biological and behavioural therapies that you looked at in Topics 1 and 2. Two main alternatives are considered. Cognitive–behavioural therapies are based on the idea that thoughts (cognitions) can influence behaviour, so therapies include a strong cognitive element. Psychodynamic therapies, derived from the work of Freud, attempt to uncover unconscious anxieties and conflicts in order to disable their power over behaviour.

UNDERSTANDING THE SPECIFICATION

There are two therapies mentioned in the specification entry for this topic (see right), but you only need to cover one of them (i.e. psychodynamic or cognitive–behavioural) in your revision. Obviously, we have covered both in the textbook and in this workbook, because we don't know which one you have chosen. Whichever one you choose, you must cover at least two types of that approach. So, for example, if you have chosen to study therapies derived from the psychodynamic model of abnormality, you should study psychoanalysis *and* psychodrama. If you have chosen to study therapies derived from the cognitive–behavioural model, you should at least study rational-emotive therapy and stress inoculation therapy. Note that the more contemporary description of rational-emotive therapy is 'rational-emotive behaviour therapy (REBT)', but they are essentially the same thing. Some of the comments you might make

> ### Treating mental disorders
>
> c. **Alternatives to biological and behavioural therapies**
>
> Therapies derived from *either* the psychodynamic (e.g. psychoanalysis, psychodrama) *or* cognitive–behavioural (e.g. rational-emotive therapy, stress inoculation therapy) models of abnormality. Issues surrounding the use of such therapies (e.g. appropriateness and effectiveness).

when describing (or evaluating) these therapies would be general to the whole approach (i.e. psychodynamic or cognitive–behavioural). This is perfectly acceptable. The same comments in Topic 1 concerning issues apply here as well.

TOPIC MAP

The diagram below gives you an overview of what you are about to study.

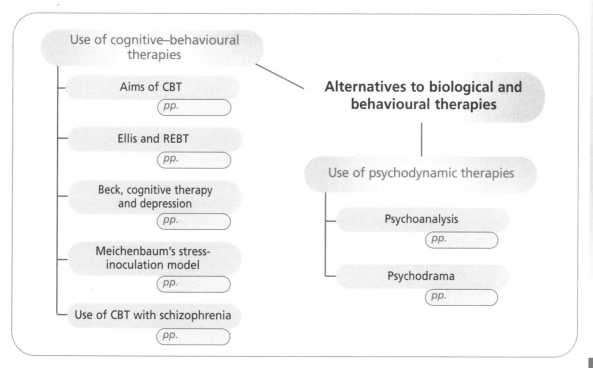

Topic map

Look through pp. 535–42/803–10 of the textbook to see where the items shown in the topic map are covered. Note down the relevant page numbers in the spaces left on the topic map.

KEEPING TRACK

Use the table below to keep track of your work on this topic and plan your revision. See p. iv of this workbook (Introduction) for guidance on filling it in.

Alternatives to biological and behavioural therapies		Tick if you ...		
What I need to learn	*Where is it?*	*could make a basic attempt*	*could make a good attempt*	*have complete mastery of this*
Use of cognitive–behavioural therapies				
Description of aims of CBT				
Description of Ellis's rational-emotive-behaviour therapy				
Evaluation of Ellis's rational-emotive-behaviour therapy				
Description of Beck's cognitive therapy				
Description of Meichenbaum's stress-inoculation therapy				
Description of use of CBT with schizophrenia				
Evaluation of cognitive–behavioural therapies				
Use of psychodynamic therapies				
Description of the use of psychoanalysis				
Evaluation of the use of psychoanalysis				
Description of the use of psychodrama				
Evaluation of the use of psychodrama				

COGNITIVE–BEHAVIOURAL THERAPIES

Cognitive–behavioural therapies

Read from the start of Topic 3 to the bottom of p. 535/803 and then answer the following questions.

1 What is the basic principle of cognitive–behavioural therapy?

_____

_____

_____

2 In your own words, what is the role of the cognitive and behavioural elements in therapy sessions?
- role of cognitive element

_____

- role of behavioural element

_____

_____

_____

ELLIS AND REBT

Albert Ellis is one of the most important names in the development of cognitive–behavioural therapies. Read about his work on p. 536/804 of the textbook and look at Fig. 18.1/26.1 on p. 535/803. Then complete the following activity.

Read about his work on p. 536/804 of the textbook and look at Fig. 18.1/26.1 on p. 535/803.

ACTIVITY

Ellis and REBT

1 What, in Ellis' ABC model, is meant by an 'activating event'?

_____

_____

2 The first three letters of REBT indicate the important role Beck saw for those aspects of human thinking and behaviour. Complete the table below to summarize the role played by each aspect in his therapy:

Aspect	Role:
R stands for	_____
E stands for	_____
B stands for	_____

3 The Commentary panel mentions three pieces of research that assessed the effectiveness of REBT. Summarize the findings of that research here.

● Haaga and Davison (1989)

_____

● Engels *et al.* (1993)

_____

● Haaga and Davison (1993)

_____

OTHER FORMS OF CBT

On pp. 536–7/804–5, other forms of CBT are described, including the therapies devised by Beck and Meichenbaum.

On pp. 536–7/804–5, other forms of CBT are described

ACTIVITY

Beck's and Meichenbaum's therapies

Read the text about Beck's and Meichenbaum's models on pp. 536–7/804–5 and then complete the forms below to summarize the main features of each.

Read the text about Beck's and Meichenbaum's models on pp. 536–7/804–5

Type of therapy	**Beck's cognitive therapy**
Types of mental disorder treated	

Summary of therapy

_____

_____

_____

_____

Type of therapy	Meichenbaum's stress-inoculation therapy
Beliefs that underpin the model	
Stages involved in the model	
1	
2	
3	
Types of mental disorder treated	

ACTIVITY

Summarizing cognitive–behavioural therapies

Look at Example Exam Question 1 on p. 543/811 and read the guidance notes underneath the question. To answer part (a), you would use half your allotted time, that is about 20 minutes or enough time to write about 400 words. You have to restrict yourself to just one type of therapy (e.g. Ellis's REBT or Meichenbaum's stress-inoculation therapy).

Using a PC, prepare a 400-word description of each of these two types of therapy. Either one would be suitable for use as your answer to part (a). Then make copies of your summaries and reduce each one to just

200 words. These shorter summaries would be suitable for questions that asked you to describe **two (or more)** therapies – for example:

(a) Describe **two or more** therapies derived from a cognitive–behavioural model of abnormality.

(15 marks)

(Note that the above question could not be asked in an exam, as you have a choice of cognitive–behavioural or psychodynamic therapies, but it is good practice to prepare an answer to this type of question *if* this is the type of therapy you have chosen]

Appropriateness and effectiveness of CBT

The textbook includes a lot of useful information about how CBT is used and how effective it is, including :

- its use with schizophrenia – see p. 536/804
- the Key research panel on p. 537/805
- the Evaluation panels on pp. 536/804 & 538/806.

The Evaluation panel on p. 538/806 includes a good assessment of the overall strengths and appeal of CBT (first three bullet points) as well as mentioning some of the problems with evaluating CBT. It also looks at the use of CBT in treating particular types of mental disorder.

A02 ACTIVITY

Effectiveness of CBT for specific types of mental disorder

Read through the text listed above and then complete the following table, summarizing the main points about how effective CBT is for treating different types of mental disorder.

Use	Support for CBT	Challenge for CBT
with people with depression	• Hollon et al. (1992) – CBT more effective than drugs • Evans et al. (1992) –	
with people with phobias		
with people with schizophrenia		

ACTIVITY

Effectiveness of CBT in combination with other therapies

The textbook also discusses the use of CBT in combination with other therapies, including systematic desensitization (graded exposure) and drug therapy. Read the Key research panel on p. 537/805 and the panel at the bottom of p. 538/806. Then, in 150 words, answer the following question.

● Does the use of CBT in combination with other therapies improve the outcome for those with the mental disorder? Use research evidence to support your answer.

PSYCHODYNAMIC THERAPIES

Psychodynamic therapies are based on the psychodynamic approach developed by Sigmund Freud. You have probably already spent some time reading about Freud's theories (see, for example, Unit 5/13, p. 65, and Unit 11/19, p. 113, of this workbook) and may like to review them quickly.

ACTIVITY

Summarizing techniques based on psychoanalysis

Complete the form below to summarize the main features of therapies based on psychoanalysis, described on pp. 539/807 of the textbook.

Type of therapy **Psychoanalysis**	Techniques used
Principles of the therapy	● Free association
	● Word association
	● Dream analysis
Types of mental disorder treated	● Transference
	● Projective tests

ACTIVITY

Summarizing psychoanalysis

Look again at Example Exam Question 1 on p. 543/811. You could answer this using psychoanalysis as the 'one therapy' indicated in the question. Using a PC, prepare a 400-word description of psychoanalysis, basing your answer on the notes you made for the previous activity.

Then make a copy of your summary and reduce it to just 200 words. This shorter summary would be suitable for questions that asked you to describe **two (or more)** therapies.

Evaluating psychoanalysis

Psychoanalysis is a therapy that tends to polarize opinion. Those who support it believe it to be invaluable for treating many types of mental disorder; those who challenge it regard it as a waste of time and quite a lot of money. Some people even argue that psychoanalysis can be positively damaging, especially when it comes to the issue of inducing false memories (see the panel on 'False memory syndrome (FMS)' at the bottom of p. 540/808).

ACTIVITY

Evaluating psychoanalysis

Read from the start of the Evaluation panel on p. 539/807 to the end of the second Key research panel on p. 541/809. These pages include a great deal of material that will enable you to evaluate psychoanalysis, especially in terms of its effectiveness and appropriateness.

Summarize the key points in the form of a table similar to the one in the AO2 activity on p. 191, highlighting both support for the therapies and challenges to it. Group the points under the headings 'Effectiveness', 'Appropriateness' and 'Ethical issues'. Use a word processing program to create this table.

ACTIVITY

Writing a summary evaluation

Using a PC, prepare a 400-word summary evaluating psychoanalysis, including a discussion of its effectiveness and appropriateness, as well as ethical issues it raises. This summary could form the answer to an exam question such as Example Exam Question 1(b) on p. 543/811.

PSYCHODRAMA

Psychodrama is a group therapy technique that enables individuals to work through anxieties by acting them out in a safe and supportive environment.

ACTIVITY

Summarizing psychodrama

Read the description of psychodrama on pp. 541–2/809–10 of the textbook and then summarize the main features of this therapy in the table below, including the different roles played by members of the group.

Type of therapy Psychodrama	Roles played by members of the group
Principles of the therapy	● Director
	● Protagonist
	● Auxiliary egos
Types of mental disorder treated	● Double
	● Audience

ACTIVITY

Summarizing psychodrama for the exam

Look again at Example Exam Question 1 on p. 543/811. You could answer this using psychodrama as the 'one therapy' indicated in the question. Using a PC, prepare a 400-word description of psychodrama, basing your answer on the notes you made for the previous activity.

Then make a copy of your summary and reduce it to just 200 words. This shorter summary would be suitable for questions that asked you to describe **two (or more)** therapies.

Evaluating psychodrama

The Evaluation panel on p. 542/810 discusses several aspects of psychodrama, including its effectiveness and appropriateness.

A2 Individual Differences

ACTIVITY

Evaluating psychodrama

1 Read through the Evaluation panel on p. 542/810 and summarize the key points in the form of a table. Use the format shown in the activity at the top of p. 190.

2 Psychoanalysis and psychodrama are both therapies based on Freud's psychodynamic theory, but they take very different approaches when it comes to putting the theory into practice. Draw up a list of similarities and differences between the two types of therapy.

EXAM HINT

If an exam question asks you to discuss two or more therapies, an excellent way of providing AO2 evaluation is by comparing them, i.e. describing the similarities and differences between them or pointing out how one therapy deals with problems encountered with the other. Some exam questions may ask you specifically to 'compare and contrast' two therapies – see, for instance, Example Exam Question 4 on p. 544/812.

EXAMPLE EXAM QUESTIONS

You have already written 400-word and/or 200-word descriptions and evaluations of the therapies discussed. These would provide you with the basis for answers to Example Exam Question 1 on p. 543/811.

ACTIVITY

One for you to try ...

Discuss issues surrounding the use of one or more therapies derived from either the psychodynamic or cognitive–behavioural model of abnormality.

(30 marks)

It is important to disentangle exactly what is required in this question. You need to consider how you would satisfy the requirement to be synoptic in your response to it. Being synoptic means that you must discuss at least two issues (such as appropriateness and effectiveness) in your answer, although you are not obliged to cover more than one therapy derived from your chosen approach. The question also specifies that you should choose therapies derived from *either* the psychodynamic *or* cognitive–behavioural model of abnormality, so you would not write about both in your answer, unless you were contrasting them as part of an issue of effectiveness.

In this context, a comparison would count as AO2 commentary.

Read the instructions for this question (Example Exam Question 2) on p. 543/811 of the textbook, and then look again at the sample answer in the previous topic. Your task here is to construct an equivalent answer to the question. In the previous topic, the start of each paragraph was the AO1 description of an issue, and the latter part of each paragraph was the AO2 commentary on that issue. Use the material on pp. 535–8/803–6 (for the cognitive–behavioural approach) or pp. 539–42/807–10 (for the psychodynamic approach) for your answer.

CHECK YOUR UNDERSTANDING

When you have finished working through this topic, try the questions in 'Check your understanding' on p. 543/811 of the textbook. Check your answers by looking at the relevant parts of the textbook or this workbook, listed below.

1 textbook pp. 535–6/803–4

2 textbook pp. 535–6/803–4

3 workbook p. 196

4 textbook p. 538/806; workbook p. 197

5 textbook p. 539/807

6 textbook p. 539/807

7 textbook pp. 541–2/809–10

8 workbook p. 199 (AO2 activity)

9 workbook pp. 196 & 197 (AO2 activities)

10 workbook pp. 198 & 199 (AO2 activities)

Unit 18/26 // Treating mental disorders

199

ISSUES IN
Psychology

PREVIEW

There are four topics in this unit. You should read them alongside the following pages in the Collins *Psychology for A2-level/Psychology* textbook:

Topic	Psychology for A2	Psychology
1 Gender bias	pp. 547–53	pp. 815–21
2 Cultural bias	pp. 553–58	pp. 821–26
3 Ethical issues with human participants	pp. 558–68	pp. 826–36
4 The use of non-human animals	pp. 569–77	pp. 837–45

INTRODUCTION

'Issues and debates' is the second of three sections in Module 5 (AQA Specification A), as the diagram below shows. This section is further divided into two sub-sections – 'Issues' is the first of these.

Read the Preview and Introduction on p. 546/814 of the textbook now. This will give you an overview of what's in the unit.

Where this unit fits in to the A-level qualification

Section A:
Individual Differences

Module 5 — Section B: **Perspectives (Issues & Debates)** — • **ISSUES**
• DEBATES

— a Gender bias
b Cultural bias
c Ethical issues with human participants
d The use of non-human animals

Section C: Perspectives (Approaches)

In Section B of the Module 5 exam, you are offered a choice of four questions, two from the 'Issues' section and two from the 'Debates' section. You have to answer **one** of these four questions.

This unit looks at four major issues that are of importance to psychologists. Much of published psychological research is carried out by, and on, members of Western cultures, and more often than not on males rather than females. This has led to the claim that much of what we know about human behaviour is both culturally biased and gender biased. The consideration of ethical issues is also a very important part of psychological research, and applies as much to animals as it does to humans. This unit takes you 'behind the scenes' of psychology, and encourages you to be more critical of psychological research in general.

UNDERSTANDING THE SPECIFICATION

Here is what the AQA (A) specification says about this unit. It forms part of A2 Module 5, Section B: Issues and Debates.

To answer questions on gender bias, you will need to *define* what it is, and offer at least two different types of gender bias (e.g. alpha and beta bias). The specification requires you to be able to locate gender bias in psychological theories (e.g. Kohlberg and Freud) and psychological research. You can use alternative theories (such as Gilligan's) as commentary on gender-biased theories.

The same applies to cultural bias, in that you should be able to explain different types (e.g. ethnocentrism and the imposed etic) as AO1, and then discuss how these impact on at least two theories and at least two areas of research.

There are three things to stress about ethical issues.

1 There is a requirement to discuss *issues* rather than ethical *guidelines*.

2 Socially sensitive research is a special area of ethics, and should not be ignored.

3 Finally, you will be required to offer AO2 commentary on these ethical issues rather than just describe them.

The final area covers *how* and *why* animals are used in research, the legislation and rules that control this research, and the arguments that surround animal

research. It is important to note that you should cover both scientific *and* ethical arguments, and be able to offer AO1 and AO2 on *both*.

Section B – Issues and debates

a. Issues

Gender bias in psychological theory and research (e.g. alpha/beta bias, androcentrism).

Cultural bias in psychological theory and research (e.g. ethnocentrism, historical bias, the imposed etic).

Ethical issues involved in psychological investigations using human participants, including the ethics of socially sensitive research.

The use of non-human animals in psychological investigations, including constraints on their use and arguments (both ethical and scientific) for and against their use.

UNIT MAP

The diagram at the top of p. 202 is a visual 'map' of the content of this unit, giving you an overview of what you are about to study.

ACTIVITY

Unit map

Look through pp. 547–75/815–43 of the textbook to see where the items shown in the unit map are covered. Note down the relevant page numbers in the spaces provided.

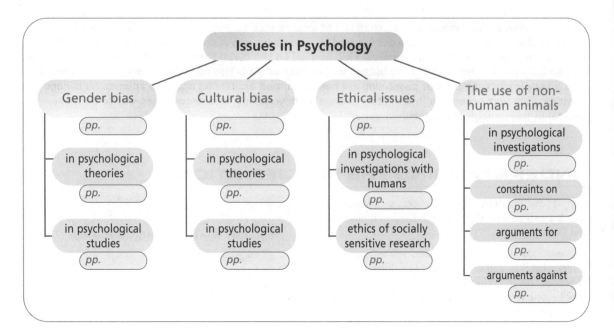

KEEPING TRACK

Use the table below to keep track of your work on this topic and plan your revision. See p. iv of this workbook (Introduction) for guidance on filling it in.

Issues in Psychology		Tick if you ...		
What I need to learn	*Where is it?*	*could make a basic attempt*	*could make a good attempt*	*have complete mastery of this*
Gender bias				
Description of gender bias in psychological theories				
Evaluation of gender bias in psychological theories				
Description of gender bias in psychological research				
Evaluation of gender bias in psychological research				
Cultural bias				
Description of cultural bias in psychological theories				
Evaluation of cultural bias in psychological theories				
Description of cultural bias in psychological studies				
Evaluation of cultural bias in psychological studies				
Ethical issues				
Description of ethical issues involved in psychological investigations using humans				
Evaluation of ethical issues involved in psychological investigations using humans				
Description of the ethics of socially sensitive research				
Evaluation of the ethics of socially sensitive research				
Use of non-human animals in research				
Description of the use of non-human animals in research				
Evaluation of the use of non-human animals in research				
Description of constraints on the use of animals				
Evaluation of constraints on the use of animals				
Description of arguments for the use of animals				
Evaluation of arguments for the use of animals				
Description of arguments against the use of animals				
Evaluation of arguments against the use of animals				

Gender bias is a significant issue in psychological research, not least because the discipline – like so many others – has been dominated by men (and usually White, middle-class, American men). Likewise the research carried out by psychologists has often been done using male participants only. That raises all sorts of questions about the value of the research. Identifying, and seeking to overcome, gender bias is now recognized as a duty of all psychologists. This topic looks at what forms gender bias can take and how it can distort psychological theories and research.

WHAT IS GENDER BIAS?

Start by reading the whole of p. 548/816 of the textbook. This gives an overview of gender bias and the different forms it can take – in particular, alpha bias and beta bias.

ACTIVITY

Different types of gender bias

On pp. 548–9/816–17 of the textbook, several types of gender bias are described. In the space below, summarize each of the types of gender bias listed.

1 Alpha bias

2 Beta bias

3 Androcentrism

4 Estrocentrism

Exam questions may ask you to describe one, two or more examples or types of gender bias – as in Example Exam Questions 1 and 4 on pp. 552/820 and 553/821. You can pick whichever of these four types of bias you want to. Note that the specification lists 'alpha/beta bias' and 'androcentrism' as examples, but not estrocentrism (an example of gender bias in the specification, perhaps?). Even so, you could legitimately take estrocentrism as your answer to part (a) of Question 4 on p. 553/821.

The text in the Commentary panel at the bottom of p. 548/816 looks at two important factors that put gender bias into context:

● *feminist psychology* – outlining ways in which the androcentric bias of much of psychology has been challenged

● *real differences* – exploring whether there are real gender differences between men and women.

You can use this material as AO2 commentary by offering feminist psychology as an alternative – or, if you prefer, an *antidote* – to androcentric psychology. If alpha-biased theories assume real differences between men and women, and beta-biased ignore any differences, commentary could focus on whether such differences really do exist.

HINT

Types of gender bias

You will notice that there is an overlap between different types of gender bias.

● Alpha- and beta-biased theories describe the **basis** of bias (whether exaggerating or minimizing differences).

● Androcentrism and estrocentrism describe the **direction** of the bias (whether towards men or women).

In the exam, however, they all count as different types of gender bias.

GENDER BIAS IN PSYCHOLOGICAL THEORIES

In the exam, you may be asked specifically about gender bias in psychological theories, as in Example Exam Questions 1 and 2 on p. 552/820. When answering questions such as these, you could use any two or more of the five examples of biased theories described on p. 549/817:

Alpha bias
- Freud's psychodynamic theory
- Gilligan's theory of moral development

Beta bias
- Bem's theory of psychological androgyny
- Minuchin's family systems theory
- Kohlberg's theory of moral development.

Describing gender bias in psychological theories

Taking Example Question 2 on p. 552/820, you would need to write 400 words of description for your AO1.

But be careful! You need to describe the *bias* in the theories, not the theories themselves.

You would also need to decide *how many* examples to include: the more you include, the less detail you can provide (this is called the 'depth-breadth' trade-off). As 'detail' is an important criterion for AO1, it's best to avoid introducing too many examples, as this restricts your opportunities for detail. The same point applies to the AO2 part of your essay where 'elaboration' is one of the criteria (see pp. 670–1/938–9). It is difficult to elaborate AO2 points if you are trying to cover, say, four theories.

The following activity will help you gather more 'detail' about the gender bias in three of the theories.

ACTIVITY

Describing alpha- and beta-biased theories

1 Read the text on Freud's psychodynamic theory in Unit 11/19, pp. 320–3/588–91. Note down any points that could be used to illustrate gender bias in his theory. Look in particular at the description of the development of young boys and girls at the bottom of p. 320/588 and the points in the Evaluation panel on p. 323/591.

_____

_____

2 Read the text on Gilligan's theory of moral development in Unit 10/18, pp. 312/580. Note down any points that could be used to illustrate gender bias in her theory.

_____

_____

3 Read the text on Kohlberg's theory of moral development in Unit 10/18, pp. 307–10/575–8. Again, note down any points that could be used to illustrate gender bias in Kohlberg's theory.

_____

_____

_____

_____

ACTIVITY

Describing gender bias in psychological theories

Now write 400 words describing gender bias in Freud's psychodynamic theory and one other psychological theory.

Evaluating gender bias in psychological theories

Again, exam questions in this area are likely to ask you to evaluate theories in terms of their gender bias, i.e. you need to evaluate the *bias*, rather than the theories themselves. The kinds of aspects to consider here are:

- Is the theory actually biased in the way that has been claimed?
- What light has been thrown on the theories by other research?

- What are the effects of the bias, if any? Has it had positive or negative consequences?

The Evaluation panels on pp. 549/817 and 550/818 make several useful points which you can bring into the commentary, or AO2, part of your essay. The text on 'Feminist psychology' in the Commentary panel on p. 548/816 also makes several telling points that you could make when evaluating androcentric theories.

ACTIVITY

Evaluating gender bias in Freud's theory

1 What points could you make and elaborate regarding the feminist response to his theory?

_____

_____

_____

_____

_____

_____

2 Use the Internet to find out more about Freud's ideas about 'penis envy' and 'hysteria' – ideas that have been heavily criticized by feminist psychologists for pathologizing female behaviour. Note down relevant points that you could use in your evaluation of Freud's theory.

_____

_____

_____

_____

_____

_____

ACTIVITY

Evaluating gender bias in psychological theories

Write 400 words evaluating gender bias in Freud's psychodynamic theory and the other psychological theory you described earlier (see activity below left). If you add this evaluation to the description you have already written, that provides a complete answer to Example Exam Question 2 on p. 552/820.

GENDER BIAS IN PSYCHOLOGICAL STUDIES

Gender bias may be present at all stages of the research process, as outlined on pp. 550–1/818–19.

ACTIVITY

Bias in the research process

The textbook lists six ways in which bias can be evident in the research process (see bullet list, pp. 550–1/818–19). Some of these produce alpha bias, while others produce beta bias. Decide what sort of bias each aspect produces and complete the table below.

Aspect	Type of bias produced	How bias is produced
Question formation	●	●
Research design	●	●
Research methods	●	●
Selection of participants	●	●
Inappropriate conclusions	●	●
Publication bias	●	●

Grouping the different aspects of research design in this way can be useful for answering questions such as the one shown below:

● Outline **two or more different types of gender bias in psychology.(15 marks)**

With a broad question such as this, you could write about different types of bias in the research process, and alpha bias and beta bias would count as your two types. Alternatively, you could refer to bias in theories (as discussed earlier) and/or studies (discussed below).

Alpha-biased and beta-biased studies

On p. 551/819, several examples are given of studies that displayed either an alpha bias or a beta bias.

ACTIVITY

Alpha-biased and beta-biased studies

Draw up a table, using the headings shown below, to summarize the main points of any psychological studies that exhibit bias. Use the examples given in the textbook on p. 551/819, but include any others. For example, you could look through Topic 1 of Unit 15/23, pp. 433–40/701–8, which considers evolutionary explanations of human reproductive behaviour – an area often accused of alpha bias.

Research	How the research displays bias	Effect of the bias
e.g. Zimbardo (1973)		

Evaluating gender bias in psychological studies

When it comes to evaluating gender bias in studies, you can make many of the same points as for evaluating gender bias in theories. For example, the points made in the Evaluation panels on p. 548/816 and 550/818 can be rephrased to apply to psychological studies.

A02 ACTIVITY

Evaluating gender bias in psychological studies

In the space below, summarize the main points you would make in an essay evaluating gender bias in psychological studies. Include any points that refer to the specific studies you listed in the last activity. Think, too, about how you might elaborate each point (see pp. 669–1/937–9).

Point	Elaboration

Answering exam questions on gender bias in psychological studies

Looking at the wording of the specification, it would be legitimate for the examiner to set a question that asked explicitly about gender bias in psychological research. For example:

● **Discuss two or more examples of gender bias in psychological research.** (30marks)

You could tackle this in a number of ways, depending on what you take as your examples. The question says 'two or more examples'. That means you could choose from any of the following:

1 alpha bias in the research process
2 beta bias in the research process

3 alpha-biased studies
4 beta-biased studies.

Or you could group these points into larger sets, e.g. alpha bias (1 + 3 above) and beta bias (2 + 4), or bias in the research process (1 + 2) and bias in specific studies (3 + 4). In making your choice, think about which aspects give you the best chance to write effective AO2 material.

Planning your answer

Write an outline answer to the question above. Remember that for Module 5 questions, you have 40 minutes to write your answer, with a maximum of 30 marks. That's enough time for about 800 words, or 400 words of AO1 and 400 words of AO2. You can then divide your response into an appropriate number of 'chunks' – for example:

	AO1 (description)	AO2 (commentary)
Example 1: Alpha bias in research	200 words	200 words
Example 2: Beta bias in research	200 words	200 words

EXAMPLE EXAM QUESTIONS

In your work on this unit, you have already looked in detail at two possible exam questions (Example Exam Question 2, p. 552/820 and the one for which you planned an outline answer in the last activity).

One for you to try ...

(a) Describe one **example of gender bias in psychology.** (5 marks)
(b) Describe and evaluate two or more **psychological theories in terms of their gender bias.** (25 marks)

As you are reminded in the advice on this question on p. 553/821 of the textbook, there are 10 marks for AO1 and 15 for AO2 in part (b) of this question. Note that there is an error in the textbook, as part (b) should say 'Describe and evaluate' rather than just 'evaluate'. You might structure your response to this question in the following way (note: each of these bullet points represents approximately 120 words):

Part (a)

● AO1 – description of one example of gender bias (e.g. alpha bias)

Part (b)

● AO1 – description of the gender bias of alpha-biased theories (e.g. Freud and androcentrism, Gilligan and estrocentrism)

● AO2 – evaluation of alpha-biased theories (e.g. Williams 1987, Hare-Mustin and Maracek 1988, positive consequences of alpha bias)

● AO1 – description of the gender bias of beta-biased theories (e.g. Bem on androgyny, Kohlberg on moral development)

● AO2 – evaluation of beta-biased theories (e.g. positive and negative consequences of beta bias)

● AO2 commentary – feminist psychology as an alternative to androcentric psychology; commentary on whether differences between males and females are real or imagined.

CHECK YOUR UNDERSTANDING

When you have finished working through this topic, try the questions in 'Check your understanding' on p. 552/820 of the textbook. Check your answers by looking at the relevant parts of the textbook, listed below.

1 beta bias, see textbook p. 548/816
2 textbook p. 549/817

3 textbook p. 550/818
4 textbook p. 550/818

5 textbook pp. 550–1/818–19

Topic 2 >> Cultural bias

As the introduction to this unit says on p. 546/814, the history of psychology is largely a record of American, undergraduate, male behaviour. The dominance of one culture – American or Western – raises questions about the value of research and whether conclusions drawn apply to people of other cultures. It also raises questions about research methods and whether those methods used by psychologists in one culture can be used in other cultures to investigate the same thing. This topic looks at what forms cultural bias can take, how it can distort psychological theories and research, and how psychologists try to counteract it.

WHAT IS CULTURAL BIAS?

Start by reading the description of cultural bias on p. 553/821 of the textbook. This gives an overview of cultural bias and the different forms it can take. Then answer the questions in the following activity.

ACTIVITY

Different types of cultural bias

1 What is ethnocentrism?

_____

_____

_____

2 Why is eurocentrism the most dominant form of ethnocentric bias?

_____

_____

_____

3 What is the link between eurocentrism and individualism?

_____

_____

_____

4 Why is the etic approach biased?

_____

_____

_____

5 What is meant by 'historical bias'?

_____

_____

_____

ACTIVITY

Tackling cultural bias

The Commentary panel describes two ways of countering cultural bias. What does this mean in practical terms? If you were a psychologist planning research, how might you:

1 take a culturally relativist approach?

_____

_____

_____

2 take an emic perspective?

_____

_____

_____

_____

ACTIVITY

Explaining the issue of cultural bias

Look at Example Exam Question 3 on p. 558/826. Part (a) is a short, 5-mark part asking for a brief explanation of why cultural bias is important. Using your PC, write about 135 words of explanation. You might, for example, outline different types of cultural bias, explain what the notion of cultural bias means in psychology or perhaps consider why psychologists need to take notice of any potential cultural bias.

Exam questions may ask you to describe one, two or more examples or types of cultural bias – as in Example Exam Questions 2 and 3 on pp. 558/826. Note that the specification lists ethnocentrism, historical bias and the imposed etic as examples, but not individualist bias, but you could choose any of these types of bias.

The text in the Commentary panel at the top of p. 554/822 looks at ways of combating cultural bias and some of the dangers inherent in doing this.

CULTURAL BIAS IN PSYCHOLOGICAL THEORIES

In the exam, you may be asked specifically about cultural bias in psychological theories, as in Example Exam Questions 2 and 3 on p. 558/826. When answering questions such as these, you could use any two or more of the four examples of biased theories described on p. 554–6/822–4:

1 *beta bias* – Kohlberg's theory of moral development
2 *ethnocentrism* – economic theories of relationships
3 *etic approach* – use of Western diagnostic manuals to diagnose mental illness
4 *historical bias* – Freud's psychodynamic theory.

Describing cultural bias in psychological theories

Taking Example Question 2, you would need to write 400 words of description for your AO1. But remember, you need to describe the *bias* in the theories, not the theories themselves. You should also bear in mind the comments on p. 204 about the 'depth–breadth' trade-off – that is, deciding how many examples to include and how much detail to give.

The following activity will help you gather more 'detail' about cultural bias in four of the theories.

ACTIVITY

Describing culturally-biased theories

Read the descriptions of examples of cultural bias on pp. 554–6/822–4 of the textbook, as well as the following pages in other units. Note down any points that could be used to illustrate cultural bias in the theories discussed. Limit yourself here to describing the cultural bias.

1 Unit 10/18, pp. 307–10/575–8 – Kohlberg's theory of moral development:

_____
_____
_____

2 Unit 2/10, pp. 45–8/313–6 – economic theories of relationships. In particular, note the comments in the Evaluation panel on p. 47/315:

_____
_____
_____

3 Unit 16/24, p. 465/733 – use of Western diagnostic manuals to diagnose mental illness and cultural bias in the diagnosis of mental disorders:

_____
_____
_____

4 Unit 11/19, pp. 320–3/588–91 – Freud's psychodynamic theory. Look in particular at the 'Limitations' in the Evaluation panel on p. 323/591:

_____
_____
_____
_____

Evaluating cultural bias in psychological theories

Again, exam questions in this area are likely to ask you to evaluate theories in terms of their cultural bias, i.e. you need to evaluate the bias, rather than the theories themselves. The kinds of aspects to consider here are:

- Is the theory actually biased in the way that has been claimed?

- What light has been thrown on the theories by other research?
- What are the effects of the bias, if any? Has it had positive or negative consequences?
- In what ways could the bias be counteracted?

The Commentary and Evaluation panels on pp. 554–6/822–4 make several useful points which you can bring into the AO2 part of your essay.

(AO2) ACTIVITY

Evaluating cultural bias in psychological theories

In the space below, summarize any evaluative points you could make about the four examples of cultural bias in psychological theories that you described in the last activity.

1 Kohlberg's theory of moral development: _____

_____

_____

_____

2 Economic theories of relationships: _____

_____

_____

3 Use of Western diagnostic manuals to diagnose mental illness and cultural bias in the diagnosis of mental disorders: _____

_____

_____

_____

4 Freud's psychodynamic theory: _____

_____

_____

Finally, note down any other general evaluative points you could make about cultural bias in psychological theories. See, for example, the two points in the Evaluation panel at the top of p. 556/824.

_____

_____

_____

_____

Answering exam questions on cultural bias in psychological theories

Look at Example Exam Question 2 on p. 558/826. You have 40 minutes to answer this question – enough time to write about 800 words, i.e. 400 words of AO1 description (for 15 marks) and 400 words of AO2 evaluation (also for 15 marks).

When answering this question, you could limit yourself to just two examples of cultural bias, in which case you could divide your answer into four 'chunks' of 200 words (2 × 200-word descriptions for AO1 and 2 × 200-word evaluations for AO2). Alternatively, you could include three examples in your answer, in which case you would divide your essay into six chunks of about 135 words each, each worth 5 marks.

Whatever you decide, it would be a good idea to choose examples where you have plenty to say, not only in terms of description, but also of an evaluative nature.

ACTIVITY

Summarizing cultural bias in psychological theories

For each of the examples of cultural bias you have considered:

(a) write a 200-word description (AO1) and a 200-word evaluation (AO2)

(b) write a 135-word description (AO1) and a 135-word evaluation (AO2).

The summaries you prepare for (a) will be your 10-minute/7.5-mark version of the explanations, while those you prepare for (b) will be the 6.5-minute/5 mark-versions.

CULTURAL BIAS IN PSYCHOLOGICAL STUDIES

In the previous topic, you considered how gender bias might be present at all stages of the research process, as outlined on pp. 550–1/818–9. Cultural bias can also be introduced at any or all of these stages.

ACTIVITY

Cultural bias in the research process

How might cultural bias be introduced into the research process in any of the various stages? Work through the list below (taken from the textbook, pp. 550–1/818–9) and describe how cultural bias could arise at each stage.

Aspect	How cultural bias might arise
Question formation	
Research design	
Research methods	
Selection of participants	
Inappropriate conclusions	
Publication bias	

On p. 556/824, the textbook examines three aspects of bias in the research:

- cross-cultural research
- biases in sampling
- imposed etics.

ACTIVITY

Bias in cross-cultural research

1 Why do psychologists carry out cross-cultural research?

2 On p. 556/824, the textbook lists three problems with cross-cultural research. Summarize the main points made using the following headings. Add any other problems you can think of.

Problems in cross-cultural research	How this problem might affect the research	Ways of solving this problem
• Translation		
• Manipulation of variables		
• Participants		

Bias in sampling

On p. 556/824, the textbook cites two studies that found bias in sampling. Summarize those findings in the space below:

- Smith and Bond (1993)
  _____
  _____

- Sears (1985)
  _____
  _____

What is the result of such bias?
_____
_____
_____
_____

Imposed etics

On p. 556/824, research into the Strange Situation is given as an example of an imposed etic. You probably read about this technique in your AS-level studies. Look at *Psychology for AS-level* Unit 2, pp. 46–51, and in particular on the text describing cross-cultural variations in attachment (p. 48) and Takahashi's study (p. 50).

Explain why using the Strange Situation with Japanese infants was an example of an imposed etic.
_____
_____
_____
_____
_____
_____

Evaluating cultural bias in psychological studies

When it comes to evaluating cultural bias in studies, you can make many of the same points as for evaluating cultural bias in theories. For example, the points made in the Commentary panel at the top of p. 554/822 and the Evaluation panel on pp. 555–6/823–4 can be rephrased to apply to psychological studies.

Evaluating cultural bias in psychological studies

In the space below, summarize the main points you would make in an essay evaluating cultural bias in psychological studies. Your evaluation can include ways of countering cultural bias, and the three points in the Commentary panel on p. 557/825 would all be relevant here.

Think, too, about how you might elaborate each point (see pp. 669–71/937–9).

Point	Elaboration

EXAMPLE EXAM QUESTIONS

In your work on this unit, you have already prepared summaries of the examples of cultural bias that would serve as the basis for answers to Example Exam Questions 2 and 3 on p. 558/826.

In the sample answer on p. 213, we use the material from the textbook (pp. 553–7/821–5) to answer the question given. This is Example Exam Question 1 on p. 557/825. Read the advice on answering this question before you read the sample answer.

'Many psychological theories are based on research with "Western" participants, but accepted as explanations of human behaviour. We probably haven't begun to understand the effects that such generalizations have had on modern life.'

Discuss cultural bias in psychology, with reference to the issues raised by the quotation above. (30 marks)

Cross-cultural research in psychology is conducted to test universal theories by repeating the same tests in different cultural contexts. Examples include replications of Milgram's obedience studies, which found that the percentage obedience ranged from 16% for female students in Australia (Kilham and Mann 1974) to 92% in Holland (Meeus and Raaijmakers 1986). These differences may be attributed to differences in the cultural contexts, but it is also possible that they are due to a lack of equivalence of procedures in these different cultures. For example, Smith and Bond (1998) suggest that, while participants in these studies may be taken from similar social groups, they may have quite different social backgrounds and experiences *within* those groups. This would make conclusions about the universality of a particular behaviour less valid.

Cultural bias is clearly seen in a study of introductory psychology textbooks by Smith and Bond (1993), who found that in one American textbook, 94% of the studies referred to were American. Sears (1985) reported that 82% of research studies used undergraduates as participants and, in half the studies sampled, the participants were psychology students. As a result, and as suggested by the quotation, psychological research is unrepresentative on a global scale, but is also unrepresentative *within* Western culture. One way to overcome this problem is to encourage research which uses participants from other cultures. This may lead to a different source of bias, if the researcher uses methods developed by Western psychologists for use in Western cultures. By using such methods, the researcher is assuming that they will have the same meaning in both cultures. This is unlikely to be true, and means that any such comparisons are invalid.

Berry (1969) suggested that one way to overcome this imposed etic was to observe participants in their natural environment. Researchers could learn about culturally specific traditions before the studies are carried out. This would enable them to take a viewpoint more appropriate to that home culture, thus making any conclusions more valid. The growth of psychology and psychological research in different cultures means that we will become more enlightened about how people in different cultures behave, rather than imposing our own Western ideas onto culturally specific behaviour. The growth of such indigenous psychologies is supported by the observation that there are now more social psychologists working in Asia than in Europe.

Any theory based on research conducted with one cultural group that is then presented as a theory of all human behaviour is beta-biased, because it ignores or minimizes cultural differences. For example, Kohlberg proposed that developmental changes in moral reasoning are driven by biological changes in cognitive maturity which must, therefore, be universal. In social psychology, 'economic' theories of relationships, such as social exchange theory, are mainly based on US students, and probably only apply to North American individuals in short-term relationships, a very specific sub-culture. Mental illness is diagnosed using classification systems (such as DSM) developed in Western cultures. These systems are used regardless of the cultural background of individuals being assessed. Misapplying norms from one culture to another may explain why African-Caribbean immigrants in the UK are seven times more likely than White people to be diagnosed as schizophrenic (Cochrane and Sashidharan 1995).

Despite claims that Kohlberg's theory is beta-biased, there is evidence that his proposed stages of moral reasoning are, in fact, universal. For example, Snarey *et al.* (1985) examined 44 different studies conducted in 26 countries and discovered that all found that same progression from Stages 1 to 4 at about the same ages as Kohlberg found in the US. The fact that the highest stages of Kohlberg's theory occur mainly in more developed, industrialized societies (Snarey and Keljo 1991), can be explained by the fact that the complexity of urban societies demands greater moral sophistication, posing more conflicts for individuals, leading to further moral development. This research, therefore, does not suggest that one group is superior, but that there are differences that can be attributed to cultural background.

The 'economic' theories of relationships suffer from an ethnocentric bias because they are written from one cultural perspective, and imply that it is psychologically healthier to have choice in relationships. They also imply that it is more desirable to have the option of being able to assert individual rights rather than following duty and tradition. However, it does not follow that an ethnocentric position must necessarily be one of superiority or inferiority. Other forms of bias, such as Afrocentrism (centred on individuals of Black African descent), provide alternative perspectives which remind us that biases often go unrecognized. There are other explanations of cultural differences in the diagnosis of mental illness that do not constitute cultural bias. For example, it may be that immigrants and minority group members experience higher levels of stress from living in a hostile majority culture.

CHECK YOUR UNDERSTANDING

When you have finished working through this topic, try the questions in 'Check your understanding' on p. 557/825 of the textbook. Check your answers by looking at the relevant parts of the textbook, listed below.

1 textbook p. 553/821   **3** textbook p. 554–5/822–3   **5** textbook p. 556/824

2 textbook p. 553/821   **4** textbook p. 556/824

You should already be familiar from your AS-level studies with some of the ethical issues that affect psychologists, especially with regard to ethical issues in social influence research. Remember Milgram's obedience studies, where participants thought they were giving electric shocks to another human being? Or Zimbardo's prison simulation study, which had to be stopped early because of the brutal behaviour of the 'guards' and the distress experienced by the 'prisoners'? This topic explores ethical issues as they affect human participants in a wide range of psychological contexts. It also explores the ethics of socially sensitive research, such as research into sexual orientation, racial differences, gender-related abilities and mental illness.

ETHICS AND MORALITY

The first few paragraphs of this topic give a good introduction to the importance of ethics in psychology, as well as explaining the difference between ethics and morality.

ACTIVITY

Ethics and morality

Read from the start of Topic 3 on p. 558/826 up to the heading 'Deception' on p. 559/827.
Then answer the following questions.

1 In your own words, what is the difference between 'ethics' and 'morality'?

2 What is the role of ethics in the professional areas such as law and medicine?

3 On p. 559/827, the textbook lists three elements necessary for ethics to have a role. From your knowledge of the work of professional psychologists, how do they meet these requirements of:

(a) acquiring specialized knowledge?

(b) working to standards of competence?

(c) following well-defined sets of practices?

If you don't know the answers to these questions, look up the website of professional bodies such as the British Psychological Society or the Association for Psychological Therapies.

EXAM HINT

In the exam, you shouldn't spend any time outlining what ethics are in general or the difference between ethics and morality. This is because questions about ethics are likely to ask you to focus on ethical *issues* (deception, consent, etc.), rather than discuss ethics in general.

Questions will not ask you to discuss ethical *guidelines*, so you should be clear as to the difference between the ethical issues faced by psychologists (required here) and their attempts to resolve them (not required here, although you *could* make use of them in your AO2 commentary).

ETHICAL ISSUES: DECEPTION, INFORMED CONSENT, PRIVACY AND HARM

Pages 559/827 to 561/829 focus on four particular ethical issues that often arise in psychological research:

- deception
- informed consent
- privacy
- psychological and physical harm.

ACTIVITY

Deception

Read the discussion of the issue of deception on p. 559/827, including the Commentary panel. Then answer the following questions:

1 What is deception?

_____

_____

What is meant by:

(a) active deception? _____

(b) passive deception? _____

2 What are the main issues for psychological researchers relating to the issue of deception?

- _____
- _____
- _____

3 What negative consequences may arise when participants are deceived?

- _____
- _____
- _____

4 What are the possible ways of resolving this issue?

- _____
- _____
- _____

5 What alternatives are there to deception?

- _____
- _____
- _____

ACTIVITY

Other ethical issues

Read the discussion of the three other ethical issues (informed consent, privacy, and psychological and physical harm) on p. 559–61/827–9, including the Commentary panel on p. 560/828 and the Evaluation panel on p. 561/829.

Then, for each of the three issues discussed, summarize the main points relating to that issue under the following headings (i.e. using the same five questions as in the previous activity):

1 Definition

2 Main issues for psychological researchers relating to the issue

3 Negative consequences that may arise for participants

4 Possible ways of resolving this issue/minimizing the negative effects

5 Alternatives

 ACTIVITY

Ways of dealing with ethical issues

The Evaluation panel on p. 561/829 lists several ways of dealing with ethical issues, but also highlights problems with these approaches.

	Advantages	Disadvantages
1 Carrying out a cost–benefit analysis		
2 Gaining prior general/ presumptive consent		
3 Debriefing		
4 Ethical guidelines		
5 Sanctions from ethical committees		

ETHICAL ISSUES IN PSYCHOLOGICAL INVESTIGATIONS WITH HUMAN PARTICIPANTS

Milgram's obedience research

Stanley Milgram's studies investigating obedience provide a clear example of research that raises huge ethical issues. His work was discussed in some detail in AS-level studies of social influence. Read the text on pp. 561–3/829–31 on ethical issues in Milgram's research, as well as *Psychology for AS-level* Unit 5, pp. 171–5 and 182–6. Then try the following activities.

ACTIVITY

Milgram and deception

1 What deception was involved in Milgram's research?

2 What negative consequences arose or might have arisen because of Milgram's use of deception?

3 What alternatives could Milgram have considered to deception (see *Psychology for AS-level* Unit 5, p. 183)?

4 How appropriate would these alternatives have been?

5 Was Milgram justified in deceiving participants? Summarize the arguments for and against Milgram's use of deception.

Arguments for
-
-
-

Arguments against
-
-
-

Milgram and harm

1 What harm was, or might have been, caused to Milgram's participants?

2 How did Milgram justify continuing his experiments, despite the obvious distress to some participants?

3 What alternatives could Milgram have considered to his experiments that would have avoided any risk of harm?

4 How appropriate would these alternatives have been?

5 Were Milgram's participants harmed, in either the short term or the long term? Summarize the arguments supporting or criticizing Milgram's research with regard to the risk of harm.

Arguments for
-
-
-

Arguments against
-
-
-

A02 ACTIVITY

The importance of Milgram's research

One of the arguments supporting Milgram's research is that it proved to be of immense importance in helping us to understanding human behaviour and the reasons why we obey others. As in all aspects of Milgram's research, this claim has received both great support and intense criticism. If you are studying psychology in a group or class, discuss the arguments for and against the claim that Milgram's work is both important and significant (see in particular the Evaluation panel on pp. 562–3/830–1 and *Psychology for AS-level* Unit 5 pp. 174 and 184–6). If you are not studying in a group, note down on separate paper the key points for and against.

Other investigations

Tables 19.1/27.1 and 19.2/27.2 on pp. 563–4/831–2 summarize details of seven psychological studies and the ethical issues raised by the research. Two of the studies were from AS-level studies and the remaining five from A2 study areas.

ACTIVITY

Examining ethical issues in psychological research

Choose four of the psychological investigations from Tables 19.1/27.1 and 19.2/27.2 to explore further with regard to ethical issues. Read the relevant pages in the textbook referred to and search for more information on the Internet. For each of the investigations, summarize the ethical issues raised using the following questions to prompt you. Note down the key points on separate paper or using your PC.

1 What ethical issues did the investigation raise?

2 What negative consequences arose or might have arisen relating to these issues?

3 What alternative ways of approaching the research could the researchers have considered?

4 How appropriate would these alternatives have been?

5 Was the research justified, given the ethical issues it raised?

Tackling exam questions about ethical issues in psychological investigations

The notes you made in the last activity, as well as those about Milgram's obedience study, will be useful for tackling exam questions such as Example Exam Questions 1 and 2 on p. 568/836. Taking Question 2, you would need to write 400 words of AO1 description for part (a) and 400 words of AO2 evaluation for part (b). But remember, you need to describe and evaluate the *ethical issues* relating to the research, not the research studies themselves.

Determining what is AO1 and what AO2 is not always that easy when answering questions in this area, although examiners will always look to divide material that brings you the highest marks. For example, in the activity at the bottom of p. 217, question 1 would be AO1, question 2 is probably AO1 but could be AO2,

question 3 could be AO1 but is probably AO2, while questions 4 and 5 would be AO2.

When answering Example Exam Question 2 on p. 568/836, you could limit yourself to just two psychological investigations, but beware of just doing Milgram and Zimbardo – they both fall into the category of social influence research and it would be more 'synoptic' to include examples from different areas of psychology. If you limit yourself to two investigations, you could divide your answer into four 'chunks' of 200 words (2 × 200-word descriptions for AO1 and 2 × 200-word evaluations for AO2). Alternatively, you could include three examples in your answer, in which case you would divide your essay into six chunks of about 135 words each, each worth 5 marks.

SOCIALLY SENSITIVE RESEARCH

Issues in socially sensitive research

Research has a social aspect and, in some areas of psychology, this social aspect imposes particular responsibilities on researchers. Read the text from the bottom of p. 564/832 up to the heading 'Gay and lesbian relationships' on p. 565/833, as well as the first question-and-answer in the Expert interview with Joan Sieber on p. 567/835. Then answer the following questions.

1 What do we mean by 'socially sensitive research'? Summarize the features that would make an area of research socially sensitive.

_____

_____

_____

2 What particular ethical issues arise in socially sensitive research? Complete the table below summarizing the issues raised. In the second column, note down the potential dangers to individual participants and to groups, while in the third column, think of what responsibilities that places on researchers.

Ethical issue	Dangers to participants/groups	Responsibilities on researchers
Privacy	• Information which individual wants kept private is divulged to others • Social policies developed that threaten privacy of groups, e.g. compulsory drug-testing	• Must respect participants' privacy • Must have watertight procedures for maintaining confidentiality, e.g. in record-keeping
Confidentiality		
Methodology		
Justice and equitable treatment		
Scientific freedom		

The textbook includes many examples of areas of research that are socially sensitive – some on p. 565/833 and more in the Expert interview on p. 567/835.

The textbook includes many examples of areas of research that are socially sensitive – some on p. 565/833 and more in the Expert interview on p. 567/835.

ACTIVITY

Examples of socially sensitive research

On pp. 565–6/833–4, three examples of socially sensitive research are discussed and commented upon, i.e. research into:

- gay and lesbian relationships (see also Unit 2/10, pp. 60–2/328–30)
- race and intelligence (see also Unit 10/18, pp. 303–4/571–2)
- eating disorders (see also *Psychology for AS-level* Unit 4, pp. 139–50).

Read the relevant sections of the textbook that describe research into these areas (listed above). For each issue, draw up a list of key points covering the following areas:

1 ethical issues raised by research into that area

2 risks to individuals being studied (e.g. the individual gay man or lesbian)

3 implications for the wider social group (all gay men and lesbians)

4 responsibilities placed on researchers undertaking the research

5 ways of overcoming problems or meeting difficulties

6 other important observations to make about the research.

Use separate paper for your notes or write them directly into a word-processing program on your PC. If there are any areas that you are particularly interested in, you might like to research them further.

ACTIVITY

More examples of socially sensitive research

In the Expert interview on p. 567/835, Joan Sieber mentions several examples of social sensitive research and ways in which researchers responded to the situations. Draw up a table to note down the key points, following the format shown below.

Example of socially sensitive research	Risks to individuals groups	Responsibilities on researchers
• Domestic violence	• Abuser may react to news of research with violence (to researcher or subject)	

ACTIVITY

Research on the front line

1 In the Expert interview on p. 567/835, Joan Sieber says that 'socially sensitive research is not for the faint of heart'. What does she mean by this? Give examples from the textbook.

_____

_____

_____

_____

2 Joan Sieber also says that 'to shy away from socially sensitive research topics is to fail to study socially important issues'. Why is it important to undertake research into these 'difficult' areas, despite the risks?

_____

_____

_____

_____

_____

Research into genetics

One of the areas of research that has proved controversial – or 'socially sensitive' – in recent years is genetics. Gene mapping projects have uncovered genes linked to conditions such as restricted growth disorders. That raises the possibility of couples choosing to abort fetuses found to have a restricted growth disorder. Understandably, people with restricted growth disorders – and many others – view this development with alarm. Similarly, scientists have investigated whether there is a gene linked to homosexuality, again raising the possibility of parents choosing the sexuality of their children.

Carry out research into the ethics of genetics, using the Internet as your starting point. As you gather information, consider the following questions.

● What ethical issues are raised by genetic research?

● How are researchers and others trying to tackle these issues?

● What questions do these issues raise about whether such research is justified?

EXAMPLE EXAM QUESTIONS

In your work on this unit, you have already planned a response to Example Exam Question 2 on p. 568/836. Questions on socially sensitive research are, however, just as likely as questions on ethical issues, so you may like to have a go at the question below.

One for you to try ...

Discuss issues relating to the ethics of socially sensitive research. (30 marks)

In exam conditions many candidates, when faced with this question, simply focus on ethical issues and ignore the fact that this is a completely different question to the 'ethics question'. What you must avoid is a general discussion of ethical issues – it is creditworthy to include material on socially sensitive research in an essay on ethical issues, but it is not creditworthy to include material on ethical issues generally in an essay on socially sensitive research, except if it has been made relevant. If you cannot avoid basing your answer around Milgram and Zimbardo, then at least make some attempt to explain why this is socially sensitive research. There is plenty of alternative material for this question, so you might follow the following format (each paragraph would be approximately 120 words):

● AO1 – the nature of socially sensitive research (pp. 564–5/832–3, and question 1 in the Expert Interview on p. 567/835)

● AO1 – examples of socially sensitive research (Expert Interview, question 2) and the ethical issues in socially sensitive research (p. 565/833)

● AO1 – sensitive research in specific areas (e.g. gay and lesbian relationships, intelligence and race, eating disorders) and the ethical issues raised (p. 565/833)

● AO2 – commentary on general issues in socially sensitive research (see second AO2 panel on p. 566/834)

● AO2 – commentary on specific areas of socially sensitive research (see first AO2 panel on p. 566/834)

● AO2 – responding to the issues of socially sensitive research or simply avoiding it? (Expert interview, questions 3 and 4)

CHECK YOUR UNDERSTANDING

When you have finished working through this topic, try the questions in 'Check your understanding' on p. 568/836 of the textbook. Check your answers by looking at the relevant parts of the textbook, listed below.

1 textbook pp. 559–60/827–8

2 textbook p. 561/829

3 textbook pp. 561–2/829–30

4 textbook p. 563/831

5 textbook pp. 564–5/832–3 and 567/835

Topic 4 >> The use of non-human animals

In your studies, both at AS and A2, you will have read about some of the many psychological investigations that have taken place involving animals. Research involving animals has yielded some extremely important information about human and animal behaviour, but has also fuelled much controversy. Some of the best-known and most important experiments (such as Harlow and Harlow's study of attachment in infant monkeys) would not be allowed today for ethical reasons. In this topic, you will consider some of the psychological studies that have used animals, before moving on to look at constraints that exist on how non-human animals are used in research. The final part of the topic examines the arguments for and against the use of non-human animals in psychological research, looking in turn at ethical and scientific arguments.

USE OF NON-HUMAN ANIMALS IN PSYCHOLOGICAL INVESTIGATIONS

The first part of this topic gives a sample of psychological investigations involving non-human animals. Read from the start of the topic to the end of the Evaluation panel on p. 570/838.

ACTIVITY

Non-human animals and laboratory experiments

Answer the following questions relating to the two laboratory experiments mentioned.

1 Re-read the description of the Harlows' experiment into the formation of attachment in infant monkeys in *Psychology for AS-level* Unit 2, p. 53. What aspects of this experiment raise ethical concerns?

_____

_____

_____

2 Read the description of the use of Skinner's box in Unit 13/21, p. 392/660. What aspects of this research raise ethical concerns?

_____

_____

_____

ACTIVITY

Non-human animals and field experiments

Field experiments may appear less intrusive because they take place in an animal's natural environment, but the manipulation of variables can be drastic and cause dangerous disruption to the animals' habitat/way of life.

1 Read the description of the Seyfarth and Cheney's experiment into animal communication among vervet monkeys in Unit 14/22, p. 421/689. In what way could the research disrupt the monkeys' existence?

_____

_____

_____

2 Read the description of the Andersson's field experiment investigating tail length and mating success in long-tailed widow birds in *Psychology for AS-level* Unit 6, p. 199. In what way could the research affect the existence or population of long-tailed widow birds?

_____

_____

_____

Non-human animals and naturalistic observations

Naturalistic observations appear to raise the least ethical concerns about the treatment of animals, as no attempt is made to influence the behaviour being observed, but there may still be dangers involved. Suggest what these dangers might be. (Hint: look back at *Psychology for AS-level* Unit 6, pp. 205–6 for some ideas.)

_____

_____

_____

CONSTRAINTS ON THE USE OF NON-HUMAN ANIMALS IN RESEARCH

The use of non-human animals in psychological research is constrained in various ways. The textbook covers three aspects:

1 legal constraints

2 codes of conduct

3 the use of criteria for assessing research.

Read from the middle of p. 570/838 to the bottom of p. 572/840 and then carry out the following activities.

ACTIVITY

Statutory constraints on the use of animals

1 What is the main law regulating the use of animals in research?

_____

_____

2 What is the role of the Home Office in applying the law?

_____

_____

_____

3 What are the sanctions for someone failing to follow these legal guidelines?

_____

_____

_____

4 What are the sanctions for someone failing to follow the BPS Code of Conduct?

_____

_____

5 Read the Guidelines given in Table 19.3/27.3 on p. 571/839. These date from 1986, long after the Harlows' experiments with monkeys. Which of the guidelines would these experiments breach?

_____

_____

_____

ACTIVITY

The BPS Code of Conduct

The BPS Code of Conduct covers many of the same areas as the Animals Act 1986. Compare the list on pp. 570–1/838–9 with the points in Table 19.3/27.3. In the space below, summarize the areas of overlap and difference.

The BPS Code of Conduct and the Animals Act 1986

Areas of overlap	Areas of difference

Bateson's decision cube, illustrated on p. 571/839 in Fig. 19.1/27.1, provides an excellent, summary model for testing whether a research project is acceptable, based on the interaction of three criteria.

ACTIVITY

Bateson's decision cube in practice

1 Give an example of a research project that you think would meet the criteria for acceptability, using Bateson's decision cube. This could be an actual research study you have read about or you could think of one for yourself (or in discussion). Why is it acceptable?

_____

_____

_____

2 Give an example of a research project that you would reject using these criteria. Give your reasons for rejecting the project.

_____

_____

_____

_____

3 Read the panel on 'Alzheimer's disease' on p. 572/840. Do you think research into brain function in order to find a cure for Alzheimer's is acceptable, when using:

(a) rats?

_____

(b) monkeys?

_____

_____

Bateson's decision cube

In the exam, you shouldn't waste time trying to sketch Bateson's decision cube. A sketch may help you to revise its principles prior to the exam, but you should go for a written description in the exam itself.

Describing the constraints on the use of non-human animals in research

Look at Example Exam Question 3 on p. 577/845. You would have 40 minutes to answer this question – enough time to write about 800 words, i.e. 400 words of AO1 description (for 15 marks) and 400 words of AO2 evaluation (also for 15 marks).

For your AO1, you could include the role of all three types of constraint considered in this topic, i.e. the role of legislation, codes of conduct and the criteria for assessing research on animals. You could restrict yourself to just two, if you felt you had plenty to say about each (and would need to write roughly 200 words on each). Alternatively you could group legislation and the BPS Code of Conduct together, given the overlap in the areas they cover.

ACTIVITY

Summarizing constraints on the use of non-human animals

For each of the three types of constraint on the use of non-human animals you have considered:

(a) write a 200-word description (AO1)

(b) reduce this to a 135-word description (AO1).

The summaries you prepare for (a) will be your 10-minute/7.5-mark version of the various constraints, while those you prepare for (b) will be the 6.5-minute/5-mark versions.

Evaluating the constraints on the use of non-human animals in research

In the exam, you may need to evaluate the various constraints on the use of non-human animals. The guidance notes to Question 3 on p. 577/845 outline ways of doing this, including:

● considering the success of such constraints

● looking at alternatives

● problems imposing constraints

● advantages or disadvantages.

Evaluating the use of legislation

On separate paper or using a PC, summarize the key points you would make if you needed to evaluate the use of legislation. Answer the following questions.

1 How effective are the legal constraints in force (see the Evaluation panel on p. 570/838)?

2 What problems can you think of in enforcing the law relating to use of animals in research?

3 What alternatives might there be to legal constraints (e.g. voluntary codes of conduct)?

4 Summarize the benefits of using legislation to protect animals.

5 Summarize any other problems not already mentioned.

Evaluating the BPS Code of Conduct

Answer the following questions to help you evaluate the BPS Code of Conduct relating to the use of non-human animals. You might find it useful to read *Psychology for AS-level* Unit 5, pp. 187–9 about ethical guidelines. It refers to research with human participants, but does raise many general issues about the use of guidelines that apply in the context of non-human animals.

1 What problems can you think of in using or enforcing the BPS Code of Conduct?

2 How effective do you think it is, compared to alternatives (e.g. legal constraints)?

3 What are the benefits of using a professional Code of Conduct?

Evaluating Bateson's decision cube

In the space below, summarize some of the issues involved in making judgements using each of the three criteria in Bateson's decision cube. This should include difficulties involved or factors you have to take into account.

Issues involved in making this judgement

1 Evaluating quality of the research

2 Measuring animal suffering

3 Establishing certainty of benefit

Answering exam questions: constraints on the use of non-human animals

Look again at Question 3 on p. 577/845. Now plan how you would approach the AO2 or evaluation part of the essay. What points you make would obviously depend on what you described in the first part of the essay.

Evaluating constraints on the use of non-human animals

For each of the three types of constraint on the use of non-human animals you have considered:

(a) write a 200-word evaluation (AO2)

(b) reduce this to a 135-word evaluation (AO2).

The summaries you prepare for (a) will be your 10-minute/7.5-mark evaluations of the various constraints, while those you prepare for (b) will be the 6.5-minute/5-mark versions.

EXAM HINT

Comparing the use or effectiveness of the various constraints would also be a good approach. For example, you could compare the sanctions or punishments imposed on those breaking the law or contravening the BPS Code of Conduct. Similarly, you could make a comment about the relative effectiveness of each, or could point out similarities in the problems involved in creating, agreeing, using or updating the various constraints.

ARGUMENTS FOR AND AGAINST THE USE OF NON-HUMAN ANIMALS

The last three pages of this topic (pp. 573–5/841–3) examine the arguments for and against the use of non-human animals in research. Pages 573–4/841–2 present the arguments *for* the use of animals in a clear, succinct form, dividing them into ethical and scientific arguments. The Commentary panels then offer the opposing view to each numbered point.

You should find it easy to use this material in answering exam questions, such as Example Exam Question 4 on p. 577/845. The arguments for would be your AO1 material, while the counterarguments would form the basis of your AO2. Include as a fifth scientific argument the text under that heading at the bottom of p. 575/843.

ACTIVITY

Summarizing the arguments for and against

Draw up a checklist of arguments for and against the use of non-human animals, based on the material on pp. 573–4/841–2.

Ethical arguments for	Ethical arguments against
●	
●	
●	
●	
●	

Scientific arguments for	Scientific arguments against
●	
●	
●	
●	
●	

You could use much of the same material to answer a question such as the following:

● **Discuss the case against the use of non-human animals in psychological research.**

(30 marks)

Here, however, the arguments against the use of non-human animals would be your AO1 description, while the arguments for would be your AO2. For this question, you might also take as your starting point the uncompromising views of campaigners for animal rights such as Peter Singer and Tom Regan.

ACTIVITY

Ethical arguments against the use of animals

Read the two panels at the top of p. 575/843, describing the views of Regan and Singer. Again, draw up a checklist of the key points of each, together with possible counterarguments, in the space below.

Regan's view of animal rights	Counterarguments
●	
●	
●	

Singer's utilitarian view	Counterarguments
●	
●	
●	

EXAMPLE EXAM QUESTIONS

In your work on this unit, you have already planned a response to Example Exam Question 3 on p. 577/845. To answer the question that follows, we have used the material on pp. 569–75/837–43. Before looking at the sample answer, read the advice on answering this question on p. 576/844 of the textbook.

Sample answer

Critically consider the use of non-human animals in psychological investigations. (30 marks)

Animals have been used in many different areas of psychological investigation. Harlow and Harlow (1962) isolated young monkeys from their mothers, raising them with surrogate wire mothers in order to test whether contact comfort or feeding was more important for the development of attachment. The most significant ethical issue raised in this study was the lasting effects on all of the monkeys. They became maladjusted as adults and made poor parents. Ethical issues are not restricted to laboratory studies of animals. Seyfarth and Cheney (1992) recorded the use of different alarm calls in vervet monkeys. They tested the monkeys' understanding of these alarm calls by using playback in the absence of real predators. The ethical issue in this study concerns the possibility that the monkeys might have become accustomed to the calls heard in the study so that they no longer responded appropriately when a real predator came along, thus putting themselves at risk.

Laboratory experiments involving animals do not always involve harm to the animals concerned. In fact, field experiments such as Seyfarth and Cheney's can cause as much harm as laboratory experiments because they alter the natural environment of the animal in some way. This may then place animals in stressful situations (as in the use of dummy predators) or make them reliant on extra feeding which is then withdrawn when the study is over. It is important to weigh up any harm to non-human participants against the benefits for humans. The Harlows' research has made a significant contribution to our understanding of attachment behaviour, as before this research, no one believed that comfort alone might be of such importance.

Animal research is regulated by legislation, the Animals (Scientific Procedures) Act, which governs what type of research project is allowed, as well as the type of procedures that are permissible. The BPS has also produced a code of conduct to guide animal researchers. A recent House of Lords committee emphasized the importance of the 'three Rs' in animal research: researchers should aim to refine their experimental procedures, reduce the number of animals used, and eventually replace the use of animals by other methods. Bateson (1986) suggested that when deciding whether to carry out a piece of animal research, we should weigh up three factors – the quality of the research, the certainty of benefit, and any suffering of the animals concerned. A study that has high quality, high certainty of benefit and low suffering would be allowed, whereas one of low quality, low certainty of benefit and high suffering would not.

Legislation about the use of animals in research has been reasonably effective, as the number of experiments involving non-human animals has halved in the UK since the 1970s. More recently, though, this decline has slowed down, which has led to the recommendations concerning the three Rs. The effectiveness of Bateson's decision model depends on an accurate evaluation of quality, benefit and level of animal suffering. Assessing the quality of research may be relatively straightforward, but assessing the other two criteria may be problematic. Different species react differently to stress, and their reactions may be very different to those that cause human beings to act in an avoidant manner. The potential benefits of research are also difficult to judge. The aims of research should certainly go beyond mere curiosity. Most critics might accept certainty of medical benefit, but the benefits of psychological research are not usually that clear.

Ethical arguments for the use of animals in psychological research include the fact that this sort of research can ease human suffering and so we are morally obliged to carry it out. We may also argue that animal research is covered by strict legislation, giving animals protection during the research procedures. Scientific arguments include the fact that using animals offers us the opportunity for greater control and objectivity. Also, we may use animals when it is impossible to carry out research on humans (e.g. in deprivation research). Ethical arguments against animal research include Regan's claim that animals have the right not to be treated as 'renewable resources', and have the right to be treated with respect and not to be harmed. To treat animals differently to humans in this respect, would be to be guilty of 'speciesism' (Singer 1975).

Although there are many claims about the 'usefulness' of animal research, these contributions have often been achieved at great cost to the animals concerned, in terms of suffering. As the potential suffering of animals is so difficult to predict, it becomes hard to judge the cost–benefit relationship accurately. The argument that we may use animals in situations when research with humans is impossible an example of speciesism. Singer argues that we have no moral basis for elevating the interests of one species over another. However, in defence of the use of animals in research, the British Association for the Advancement of Science statement claims that continued research involving animals is essential for the conquest of many unsolved conditions, including developmental, neurological and psychiatric conditions.

CHECK YOUR UNDERSTANDING

When you have finished working through this topic, try the questions in 'Check your understanding' on p. 576/844 of the textbook. Check your answers by looking at the relevant parts of the textbook, listed below.

1 textbook p. 570/838

2 textbook p. 571/839

3 textbook pp. 573–4/841–2; workbook p. 225

4 textbook p. 575/843

5 textbook p. 575/843

DEBATES IN
Psychology

PREVIEW

There are four topics in this unit. You should read them alongside the following pages in the Collins *Psychology for A2-level/Psychology* textbook:

Topic	Psychology for A2	Psychology
1 Free will and determinism	pp. 582–89	pp. 850–57
2 Reductionism	pp. 589–93	pp. 857–61
3 Psychology as a science	pp. 593–99	pp. 861–67
4 Nature and nurture	pp. 599–605	pp. 867–73

INTRODUCTION

'Issues and debates' is the second of three sections in Module 5 (AQA Specification A), as the diagram below shows. This section is further divided into two sub-sections – 'Debates' is the second of these.

Read the Preview and Introduction on p. 580/848 of the textbook now. This will give you an overview of what's in the unit.

Where this unit fits in to the A-level qualification

Section A:
Individual Differences

Module 5 — Section B: **Perspectives (Issues & Debates)** — • ISSUES
• **DEBATES** —
a Free will and determinism
b Reductionism
c Psychology as a science
d Nature and nurture

Section C: Perspectives (Approaches)

In Section B of the Module 5 exam, you are offered a choice of four questions, two from the 'Issues' section and two from the 'Debates' section. You have to answer **one** of these four questions.

There are many 'debates' within psychology, but the ones in this unit have a special place in the development of psychology as a discipline because they are fundamental to how we perceive human behaviour, and how we believe it is best studied and explained. Do we have free will or is our behaviour determined by forces outside our control? Can we, or indeed should we, adopt the methods of the physical sciences when studying human behaviour? Together with the debates on reductionism and nature–nurture, these make up the topics in this unit. You will address each of the debates in turn, and see how they impact on psychological theories and research.

UNDERSTANDING THE SPECIFICATION

Here is what the AQA (A) specification says about this unit. It forms part of A2 Module 5, Section B: Issues and Debates.

There are four distinct 'debates' mentioned in the specification. Most students do *either* issues *or* debates, although your teacher may have decided that you will cover both. There will be two questions on separate debates in the examination, so you will have a choice. Does this mean you can leave one out when revising? Theoretically yes, although that does limit your choices. Can you leave two out? That would be too much of a gamble, as the two you leave out may well be the two that turn up in the exam (you just *know* that would happen!).

There are a number of 'sub-topics' within each debate, so pay special attention to the way that we have treated these within the four topics in this unit. Some of these sub-topics, such as definitions of terms, would only ever be asked as AO1 questions, but most would have an AO2 component as well. Don't restrict yourself to just the material in Unit 20/28 of the textbook when answering these questions, but use the *whole* textbook to gather material. Questions do not just ask you to describe a theory or a research study, but require you to discuss that theory **within the context of the debate in question**. This is most important.

Section B – Issues and debates

b. Debates

Free will and determinism, including definitions of these terms, arguments for and against their existence. The debate in relation to psychological theory and research (e.g. Freud's and Skinner's theories).

Reductionism, including reductionism as a form of explanation, examples of reductionism in psychological theory and research (e.g. physiological, machine, experimental), and arguments for and against reductionist explanations.

Psychology as science, including definitions/varieties of science, arguments for and against the claim that Psychology is a science (e.g. Kuhn's concept of a paradigm, objectivity, and the use of the experimental method).

Nature–Nurture, including definitions of the terms, assumptions made about nature and nurture in psychological theory and research (e.g. Piaget's theory and sociobiology), and different views regarding their relationship (e.g. gene–environment interaction).

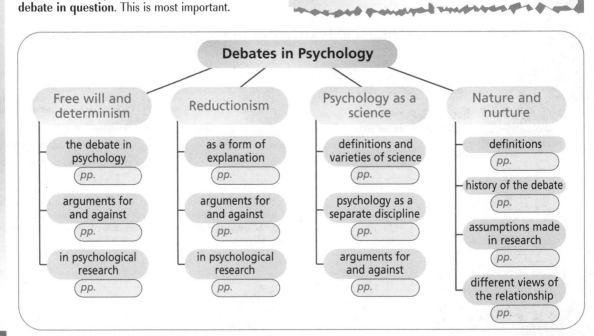

Debates in Psychology

Free will and determinism
- the debate in psychology
  pp.
- arguments for and against
  pp.
- in psychological research
  pp.

Reductionism
- as a form of explanation
  pp.
- arguments for and against
  pp.
- in psychological research
  pp.

Psychology as a science
- definitions and varieties of science
  pp.
- psychology as a separate discipline
  pp.
- arguments for and against
  pp.

Nature and nurture
- definitions
  pp.
- history of the debate
  pp.
- assumptions made in research
  pp.
- different views of the relationship
  pp.

UNIT MAP

The diagram on p. 228 gives you an overview of what you are about to study.

Unit map

Look through pp. 582–604/850–72 of the textbook to see where the items shown in the unit map are covered. Note down the relevant page numbers in the spaces left on the unit map.

KEEPING TRACK

Use the table below to keep track of your work on this unit and plan your revision. See p. iv of this workbook (Introduction) for guidance on filling it in.

Debates in Psychology		Tick if you ...		
What I need to learn	Where is it?	could make a basic attempt	could make a good attempt	have complete mastery of this
Free will and determinism				
Definitions of free will and determinism				
Arguments for and against the existence of free will				
Evaluation of arguments for and against free will				
Arguments for and against the existence of determinism				
Evaluation of arguments for and against determinism				
Descriptions of the free will and determinism debate in psychological theory and research				
Evaluation of the free will and determinism debate in psychological theory and research				
Reductionism				
Description of reductionism as a form of explanation				
Description of arguments for and against reductionist explanations				
Evaluation of arguments for and against reductionist explanations				
Description of reductionism in psychological theory and research				
Evaluation of reductionism in psychological theory and research				
Psychology as a science				
Definitions of science				
Description of the characteristics and varieties of science				
Description of the development of psychology as a separate discipline				
Description of arguments for and against the claim that psychology is a science				
Evaluation of these arguments				
Nature–nurture				
Definitions of nature and nurture				
Description of the history of the nature–nurture debate				
Description of assumptions made about nature and nurture in psychological theory and research				
Evaluation of these assumptions				
Description of different views regarding the relationship between nature and nurture				
Evaluation of these different views				

Topic 1 >> Free will and determinism

Are we free to make our own decisions and choices in this life? Or are our actions actually determined by factors beyond our control – by our genetic make-up or by the influences in the world about us? Or is there an element of both in the way we are and the way we behave? The debate between those who support the notion of free will and those who support determinism is an important one, as many psychological theories are based wholly on one position or the other, as you will read in this topic. This topic examines arguments in favour of, and against, both free will and determinism, followed by an exploration of various psychological theories and where they stand on the debate.

THE FREE WILL/DETERMINISM DEBATE IN PSYCHOLOGY

Start by reading the text and commentary on p. 582/850, which outlines the main points in the free will/determinism debate.

ACTIVITY

What are free will and determinism?

1 Note down the key features of:
- free will
- determinism

2 Why should scientific psychology be incompatible with a notion of free will?

3 The textbook mentions several types of determinism. What is meant by the following terms?
- Environmental determinism
- Biological determinism
- Soft determinism
- Liberal determinism

ACTIVITY

Describing free will and determinism

In the exam you may be asked to describe what is meant by 'free will' and/or 'determinism'. Example Exam Question 1 on p. 588/856 does exactly this in part (a). Your brief description is worth 5 marks, or one sixth of the total marks available. That means you would spend about 6.5 minutes answering the question – enough time to write about 135 words. Using a PC, write a 135-word response to part (a).

EXAM HINT

If the exam question doesn't ask you to explain what is mean by free will and determinism, then don't waste time doing that!

ARGUMENTS FOR AND AGAINST FREE WILL AND DETERMINISM

The next three pages of this topic (pp. 583–5/851–3) examine the arguments for and against free will and determinism. Each sub-section present the arguments in a clear, succinct form, the numbered points matching the counter-arguments given in the Commentary panels. You should find it easy to use this material to answer exam questions, such as Example Exam Question 4 on p. 589/857. The arguments for determinism would be your AO1 material, together with any relevant arguments against free will. Arguments against determinism would be your AO2 material (plus any relevant arguments for free will).

The next four activities, on pp. 231–2, will help you to summarize and revise the arguments for and against free will and determinism.

Arguments for and against free will

Draw up a checklist of arguments for and against the notion of free will, based on the material on pp. 583–4/851–2.

Arguments for free will	Counterargument
●	●
●	●

Arguments against free will	Counterargument
●	●
●	●

Free will

1 Do you feel that you have freedom to make choices about what you do and how you behave?

2 How would someone growing up in poverty in a developing country answer the same question?

In what ways could they exercise their free will?

If you haven't already done so, try the activity at the top of p. 582/850.

Arguments for and against determinism

Draw up a checklist of arguments for and against the notion of determinism, based on the material on pp. 584–5/852–3.

Arguments for determinism	Counterargument
●	●
●	●
●	●

Arguments against determinism	Counterargument
●	●
●	●

ACTIVITY

Determinism and DNA

Read the panel entitled 'The DNA made me do it, M'lud ...' on p. 585/853.

1 Summarize the main points of the Danish study by van Dusen *et al.* (1983) under the following headings.

- Procedures

_____

- Findings

_____

_____

- Conclusions

_____

_____

2 What criticisms can you make of this research study's conclusions?

- _____
- _____
- _____

Answering exam questions on free will and determinism

Having completed the activities above, you are well prepared to tackle questions about the free will vs determinism debate, such as Example Exam Question 4 on p. 589/857. This question focuses on the determinism side of the debate, but you can bring in relevant points about free will either as AO1 or as AO2. For example, in arguing that science has been successful in investigating human behaviour and uncovering cause-and-effect relationships (an argument for determinism), you can also point out that free will is inconsistent with science, because it suggests that humans are free to make any choice regardless of past events or actions.

ACTIVITY

Example Exam Question 4

Using a PC, write an answer to Example Exam Question 4 on p. 589/857, following the guidelines given below the question and above. Weaving arguments (AO1) and counterarguments (AO2) together (as suggested in the textbook) is a very good way of linking the material together in an effective way, rather than simply describing all your arguments *for* determinism and then describing all your arguments *against* determinism.

Your answer should be about 800 words long, divided evenly between AO1 and AO2. Use the word count facility in your word processing program to keep track of the length of your essay.

FREE WILL AND DETERMINISM IN PSYCHOLOGICAL THEORY AND RESEARCH

Looking at the AQA specification for this subject area, you need to be able to discuss the free will/determinism debate in the context of psychological theories and research (see 'Understanding the specification' on p. 228). On pp. 586–8/854–6, four different theories are discussed, each of which can be brought into essays about this debate.

The psychodynamic approach

Freud's psychodynamic approach is essentially a determinist approach. The next activity will help you identify what it is, according to Freud, that determines human behaviour and what input Freud's theory has in the free will/determinism debate.

Freud's psychodynamic approach and determinism

Read the text about the psychodynamic approach on p. 586/854, together with the description of Freud's theories in Unit 11/19, pp. 320–3/588–91 and in Unit 21/29, pp. 618–21/886–9.

1 What is meant by 'psychic determinism'?

2 Why is this an example of biological determinism?

3 Give two examples from Freud's theory of how adult behaviour might be determined.

-
-

4 What aspects of Freud's theory can be used to support the notion of determinism and what aspects can be used to challenge it? Summarize the main points in the space below.

Arguments for determinism	Arguments against determinism

The behaviourist approach

Behaviourists also take a determinist view, seeing behaviour (and that includes personality characteristics) as being conditioned by factors in the environment, which are largely beyond our control. Behaviourists include Skinner and Bandura, whose work is described in several places in the textbook.

The behaviourist approach and determinism

Read the text about the behaviourist approach on pp. 586–7/854–5, together with the descriptions of the behavioural approach in Unit 21/29, pp. 622–4/890–2, of social learning theory in Unit 11/19, pp. 324–7/592–5, and of therapies based on behavioural approaches in Unit 18/26, pp. 530–3/798–91.

1 Why do the principles of classical and operant conditioning support a determinist view of human behaviour?

2 Give two examples from the behaviourist approach of how adult behaviour might be determined.

-
-

3 How, according to Bandura, are our personality traits also determined by factors beyond our control?

4 What aspects of the behaviourist approach can be used to support the notion of determinism and what aspects can be used to challenge it? Summarize the main points in the space below.

Arguments for determinism	Arguments against determinism

The cognitive approach

The cognitive approach includes elements of both determinism and free will. This approach is outlined on p. 587/855, and a fuller explanation is given in Unit 21 on pp. 626–8/894–6.

ACTIVITY

The cognitive approach, free will and determinism

Read the text about the cognitive approach on p. 587/855 and pp. 626–8/894–6.

1　What aspects of the cognitive approach support the notion of free will?

_____

_____

2　What aspects of this approach are more determinist?

_____

_____

_____

The humanist approach and free will

The humanist approach exemplifies free will, assuming that we are free to make choices about our lives – in how we are and how we behave.

ACTIVITY

The humanist approach and determinism

Read the text about the humanist approach on pp. 587–8/855–6, together with the descriptions of Maslow's hierarchy of needs in Unit 6/14 on pp. 173–4/441–2 and Jahoda's ideas about 'ideal mental health' in *Psychology for AS-level* Unit 4, pp. 119–20.

1　What aspects of the humanist approach support the notion of free will?

_____

_____

_____

2　According to Maslow, what is the role of free will in helping us to achieve 'self-actualization'?

_____

_____

3　Jahoda identified six 'criteria for optimal living' that she believed promoted psychological health and well-being. What is the role of free will in meeting these criteria (see *Psychology for AS-level* Unit 4, pp. 119–20)?

_____

_____

_____

4　Give one strength and one weakness of humanism with regard to its status as an approach based on free will.

● Strength: _____

● Weakness: _____

EXAMPLE EXAM QUESTIONS

In your work on this unit, you have already written a complete answer to Example Exam Question 4 on p. 589/857 and to part (a) of Question 1 on p. 588/856. In the sample answer opposite, we use the material from the textbook (pp. 582–8/850–6) to answer the question shown. The quotation does not have to be addressed when answering this question (because of the phrase 'issues such as those raised'), but it is there to remind you that material related to determinism can be made relevant to this essay. Arguments *against* determinism can be adapted so that they become arguments *for* free will, and some of the arguments *for* determinism can be turned into arguments *against* free will.

'On balance most psychologists accept determinism, even those who are sympathetic to the idea of free will.'

Discuss arguments for free will in psychological theories, with reference to issues such as those raised in the quotation.

(30 marks)

A psychological argument for free will is that people have the subjective sense of free will. Most people feel that they possess free will and are able, at any time, to make free choices. The ethical argument is that in order to expect moral responsibility, one must accept the concept of free will. If an individual's behaviour is determined by forces beyond the individual's control, then they cannot be held responsible for their actions. If we want to make an attribution of personal responsibility in law, then we must view humans as capable of free choice. By the same argument, the responsibility for an individual's behaviour may be reduced if there are extenuating circumstances.

Despite the fact that people feel they have free will, it does not mean that this is the case. Skinner claimed that free will was actually an illusion – we think we are free, but that is because we are not aware of how our behaviour is determined by reinforcement. Freud also claimed that most of the causes of our behaviour are largely hidden from us and are unconscious. A problem with the ethical argument for free will is that it may be possible to behave in a moral fashion without having moral responsibility. Behaviourists suggest that moral behaviour is learned largely through punishment or the threat of punishment, and so there is no need for a sense of individual responsibility.

If actions are merely the product of past experience or biological programming, then the consequence would be that we have no free will and therefore cannot be held responsible for our behaviours. While some studies (e.g. van Dusen et al. 1983) have suggested a link between biology and crime, others fail to demonstrate an association between the two. Those who argue that crime has a genetic component, instead of being a product of free will, are more likely to argue that people deemed genetically unfit or dangerous should be contained and controlled. Therefore, the question of whether criminal behaviour is a product of biology (and, therefore, potentially predictable) or free will becomes largely a matter of faith than proof.

The concept of free will is rejected in behaviourist theory. Behaviourists believe that human behaviour is a product of the reinforcement provided by the environment. Skinner (1971) suggested that most

human beings somehow believe that we are both free to choose and are yet controlled at the same time, but for behaviourists the position is clearer: we have no freedom to choose our actions. The view that changes in behaviour are mainly a consequence of reinforcement may be acceptable when explaining the behaviour of many non-human animals, but such a claim is difficult to reconcile with the complexity of human behaviour, which has multiple determinants. Bandura has explained how both free will and determinism may influence behaviour in his notion of reciprocal determinism, where individuals are controlled by their environment, but also in control of it. As the individual acts, this changes the environment, thus affecting subsequent behaviour.

Humanistic psychologists believe that human beings are free to plan their own actions. People are seen as struggling to grow and to make difficult decisions that will affect their lives (Rogers 1974). As a result of these decisions, each of us becomes unique and responsible for our own behaviour. Self-actualization is one of the key concepts of the humanistic approach, the idea that we have many different potentials, which we constantly strive to fulfil. Jahoda's view of ideal mental health is that mental health problems occur when we are prevented from fulfilling our true potential. Maslow (1964) also stressed the importance of free will. He agreed that human behaviour is driven by biological needs, but argued that once these have been satisfied, other motives, particularly self-actualization, become important.

Support for the humanistic concept of free will comes from the success of humanistic therapies. Humanistic psychologists see the individual as very powerful in determining their own destiny. This is in contrast to the more deterministic theories, such as Freud's theory and the biological approach, which focus on our lack of power over ourselves. Despite this, however, with the basic concept behind the theory being free will, it is difficult to assess the effectiveness of this technique. Free will may be a less important concept in collectivist societies, which are more concerned with interdependence and group needs, than independence and self-actualization.

CHECK YOUR UNDERSTANDING

When you have finished working through this topic, try the questions in 'Check your understanding' on p. 588/856 of the textbook. Check your answers by looking at the relevant parts of the textbook or this workbook, listed below.

1 textbook p. 582/850

2 textbook p. 582/850

3 textbook p. 583/851

4 textbook p. 584/852

5 textbook p. 582/850

Put simply (which is what reductionism is all about), reductionism is the tendency or desire to put things simply. So half of that first sentence could be cut ... which means calling for Occam's Razor. In this topic, you'll find out what reductionism is (and Occam's Razor) and what the arguments are for and against taking a reductionist approach. The topic also looks at reductionism in three psychological theories/approaches: physiological, evolutionary and environmental.

REDUCTIONISM AS A FORM OF EXPLANATION

Read the first three paragraphs of Topic 2 on p. 589/857. These explain what is meant by 'reductionism' and the different forms it can take in psychology.

ACTIVITY

What is reductionism?

What is meant by the following terms:

1 reduction in explanations

2 methodological reductionism

3 theoretical reductionism

Reductionism is a well-known logical principle that underlies all scientific modelling and theory-building. It is sometimes more picturesquely called applying 'Occam's Razor', named after mediaeval philosopher William of Occam (or Ockham). His principle states that we should not make more assumptions than the minimum needed. Occam's razor helps us to 'shave away' assumptions or ideas that are not needed to explain something.

ACTIVITY

Applying Occam's Razor

Look at the two dots below. Take a pen and draw a line to join them together. Then take your pen and join them together again using a different path. Then experiment joining them with lines that take different paths again – e.g. curved, angular or spiral.

Which of the lines you drew illustrates the use of Occam's Razor?

If you think about it, there is an infinite number of ways of joining these two dots together, some fairly simple, some amazingly complex. Following the principle of reductionism (using Occam's Razor), you would take the simple straight line route. The principle may seem obvious, but it can lead to some fairly significant conclusions. For example, atheists use Occam's razor to argue that God does not exist for the reason that God is an unnecessary hypothesis. The world can be 'explained' without resorting to metaphysical ideas of a divine superbeing.

ARGUMENTS FOR AND AGAINST REDUCTIONISM

The arguments for and against reductionism are examined on pp. 589–91/857–9. As with the previous topic, the arguments are presented in a clear, succinct form, the numbered points matching the counter-arguments given in the Commentary panels.

ACTIVITY

Arguments for reductionism

Reductionism as a scientific approach

1 Why is reductionism appropriate for scientific research?

2 Give an example of reductionism in practice in psychological research (e.g. where a straightforward cause-and-effect relationship is investigated).

3 Why is reductionism less appropriate for some areas of psychological research?

4 Give an example where a reductionist approach is less appropriate.

Levels of explanation

1 Think of an example of human or animal behaviour and try to explain it using Rose's idea of different levels of explanation. For example, how would you explain eating disorders:
- in physiological terms?
- in psychological terms?
- in social terms?

Which of these do you think is most appropriate for explaining eating disorders?

2 Think of other human behaviours (e.g. altruistic behaviour, forgetting or dreaming) and try to explain them, using the same multi-level approach. Again, what do you think is the most appropriate level of explanation?

3 Why is it difficult to link the different levels of explanation?

Arguments against reductionism

Erroneous explanations of behaviour

1 What is the danger of simplifying key variables in psychological experiments?

2 Think back to your studies of memory at AS-level (see *Psychology for AS-level* Unit 1). Give an example of a study where simplified variables were used.

Inappropriate for psychology

1 What is the argument against reductionism put by humanists such as Rogers and Maslow?

2 What do they mean by the term 'emergence'?

3 Why does the relatively modest success achieved by drug therapies support a holistic view?

Appropriate for only certain kinds of question

1 What kinds of question are suitable for reductionist explanations?

2 Which of the following areas of study do you think would be suitable for reductionist explanations and which might require higher-level explanations (e.g. a holistic approach).
- Eating disorders
- Optic pathways
- Hunger
- Visual illusions
- Speech development

3 What is meant by the phrase: 'Higher-level explanations lack predictive power'?

REDUCTIONISM IN PSYCHOLOGICAL THEORY AND RESEARCH

One of the arguments for reductionism is that reductionist theories have been successful in explaining psychological processes and behaviour. On pp. 591–2/859–60, two reductionist approaches are discussed.

Physiological reductionism

Read the text and Evaluation panel on p. 591/859 discussing physiological reductionism. Those psychologists that support this approach look for biological or structural explanations of behaviour. The example of schizophrenia is discussed. This is a good example to reflect on, because a lot of research has been carried out searching for biological explanations, but the lack of success in pinpointing the causes of this disorder highlights the complexity of the problem.

Physiological reductionism and schizophrenia

Read about the various biological explanations of schizophrenia discussed in Unit 17/25 on pp. 488–92/756–60 of the textbook.

1 List three examples of research that has looked for biological causes of schizophrenia.

_____

_____

_____

_____

2 How successful has this research been in establishing the causes of the disorder?

_____

_____

_____

3 What is thought to be the psychological role in the onset and development of schizophrenia (read the Expert interview with Paul Harrison on p. 496/764)?

_____

_____

_____

4 Summarize what the example of schizophrenia tells us about the strengths and weaknesses of physiological reductionism:

Strengths	_Weaknesses_

Evolutionary reductionism

Read the text and Evaluation panel on p. 592/860 discussing evolutionary reductionism. To understand the background to Darwin's theory, (re-)read Unit 13/21, pp. 380–2/648–50, where Darwin's ideas about natural selection are discussed.

Evolutionary reductionism

1 Why is Darwin's evolutionary theory reductionist?

_____

_____

2 Why, according to evolutionary theory, is it permissible to study simpler species (such as fruit flies) in order to understand more about more complex species (such as human beings)?

_____

_____

3 Summarize two criticisms of evolutionary reductionism.

- _____
- _____

Environmental reductionism

Another form of reductionism, not discussed in the textbook, is environmental reductionism, which comes from a behavioural approach. If you have read about behaviourism, you may have reached the conclusion that people are constantly being controlled by forces outside their control – in the words of John Watson, given the right environment, anybody can be made into anything. The application of behaviourist principles in behaviour-modification programmes can have considerable success, e.g. in training severely disturbed adults and those with severe learning difficulties to earn a living in the community (see Unit 18/26, pp. 532–3/800–1). But is it all as simple as it sounds? Can we reduce everything to environmental influences in the way that behaviourists suggest?

Evaluation
environmental reductionism

- *Biological constraints on learning* – Of particular importance is the finding that all organisms appear to be biologically prepared to learn some responses more easily than others. Conditioning procedures that capitalize on these inborn tendencies are more likely to be successful than those which do not. When two psychologists attempted to train animals to carry out actions for which they were not biologically prepared (i.e. the behaviour had no specific relevance in their evolutionary past and therefore they had no inborn tendency to learn it), they soon encountered problems (Breland and Breland 1961). In one example, a pig was trained to drop large wooden coins into a 'piggy bank'. The animal was then reinforced for its performance by being given food. The Brelands found that, after a while, the pig started to drop the 'coins' on the ground and push them along with its snout. As this delayed the onset of the reinforcer (which was given when the animal deposited the coin in the piggy bank), it posed a problem for a simple conditioning explanation. Breland and Breland explained this behaviour as 'instinctive drift', a reversion to an instinctive behaviour more usually associated with

gaining food. In this case, the pig was reverting to its rooting instinct where it uses its snout to uncover edible roots.

- *Behaviourist explanations are oversimplifications* – Restricting ourselves to the study of only one influence at a time may make sense in the context of a laboratory science, but we may miss the complexity of influences on any one behaviour. These influences interact in complicated ways and it can be frustratingly difficult to ascertain which, if any, of them really is causing the behaviour in question.

- *Applying behaviourist explanations to the real world* – In a world dominated by either reinforcement or punishment, it might appear that the only way to motivate people is with the 'carrot and the stick'. Kohn (1993) argues that this sort of 'pop behaviourism' distracts us from asking whether the behaviour being reinforced is worthwhile in the first place. Skinner never believed that life should be reduced to the mindless use of extrinsic reinforcers that were merely 'bribes in disguise' – 'Too rarely are people reinforced for creativity, risk, participation, taking gambles. Too rarely are they given an opportunity to take pride in the products of their work, or to exercise initiative in their choice of pleasures.' (Skinner 1987)

ACTIVITY

Environmental reductionism

Read the Evaluation panel on p. 533/801 of the textbook. This includes both positive and negative criticism of behavioural therapies such as token economy and social skills training. What do these criticisms tell us about the strengths and weaknesses of environmental reductionism? Make a list of strengths and weaknesses.

EXAMPLE EXAM QUESTIONS

You have already written a complete answer to Example Exam Question 1 on p. 593/861. In the sample answer on the next page, we use material from this topic, and from pp. 589–92/857–60 of the textbook, to answer the question shown.

'Some psychologists believe that reductionism has led to major advances in psychology whereas others see reductionism as a threat to a true understanding of human behaviour.'

With reference to the issues raised in the quotation, discuss reductionism in psychological research (theories and/or studies).

(30 marks)

Reductionism creates the possibility of a fully scientific psychology, where we might be able to understand completely the causes of behaviour, and predict our world with more certainty. Rose (1997) has distinguished between different levels of explanation, each of which has a valid contribution to make. The lowest level is the molecular level (physics), then the level of an individual's physiology, with the highest level being the behaviour of groups and societies (sociology and anthropology). We can explain any particular behaviour at all these different levels. For example, a mental illness such as schizophrenia can be explained in physiological terms (e.g. the action of neurotransmitters) or even in terms of social systems (e.g. family relationships).

Because human beings are biological organisms, it should be possible, in theory, to reduce even complex behaviours into their constituent neurophysiological components. For example, researchers interested in the causes of schizophrenia have found evidence that excess activity of the neurotransmitter dopamine is a characteristic of the disorder. Evidence for the importance of dopamine in schizophrenia comes from the discovery that anti-psychotic drugs which reduce dopamine activity in the brain also reduce the symptoms of the disorder. The discovery of a neurophysiological basis for schizophrenia has led to the hope that the disorder could be eradicated by controlling the brain chemistry of schizophrenics by administering anti-psychotic drugs. This would effectively de-emphasize the importance of 'higher' environmental factors in the development of the disorder.

Despite the potential advantages of a reductionist approach, reductionist goals may be inappropriate for psychology. Humanistic psychologists, such as Rogers and Maslow, claim that higher-level descriptions and understandings cannot be derived from lower-level ones. A disadvantage of higher-level explanations, however, is that they lack predictive power. It is difficult to test cause-and-effect predictions unless we reduce complex behaviours to simpler ones. Complex behavioural systems may not behave predictably, e.g. as a simple summation of the underlying physiological parts. For example, Laing (1965) claimed that it was entirely inappropriate to see schizophrenia as a complex physical–chemical system that had gone wrong, and that the disorder only makes sense when studied at the level of an individual's experience of it. As a result, rather than being considered a major advance in psychology, reductionism has obscured our understanding of disorders such as schizophrenia.

Most theorists agree that schizophrenia is probably caused by a combination of factors. Genetic and biological factors may establish a predisposition to develop the disorder, psychological factors may trigger its expression, and sociocultural factors, such as societal labelling, may help to maintain or worsen the symptoms. Examples such as schizophrenia show us that complex phenomena cannot easily be explained by reference to an underlying physiological imbalance. To argue that brain chemicals cause schizophrenia is to neglect all other potential influences in the course of this disorder. It may be, as argued by Laing, that some higher-level factor, such as family stress, is the cause of the disorder, which then creates the physiological imbalance.

Darwin's theory of evolution offers a reductionist explanation based on the principles of natural selection. Together with the principles of genetics, this provided a way of explaining how species change and how such variety is possible within the natural world. Behaviours that can be shown to have arisen from genetic factors must have had some survival value to our ancestors. It is possible that many human behaviours have also evolved because of their survival value, or perhaps their ability to increase an individual's opportunities for passing on their genes. Believing in the idea of evolutionary continuity, behaviourists choose to study simpler species as a way of understanding the behaviour of more complex, human behaviour.

Darwin's view stresses that it is our biology that affects the way we experience the world, but the opposite may also be true. There are many studies that have shown how a stimulating environment can change the structure of an animal's brain (neural plasticity). For example, a study of people playing computer games found that an efficient brain (in terms of glucose metabolism rate) was the result of superior game play rather than the cause of it. Some critics of genetic reductionism have argued that we tend to overestimate the power of genes in human behaviour. Tavris and Wade (1995) claim that words like 'control' and 'determine' imply an inevitability of genetic influence that may not actually exist.

CHECK YOUR UNDERSTANDING

When you have finished working through this topic, try the questions in 'Check your understanding' on p. 592/860 of the textbook. Check your answers by looking at the relevant parts of the textbook or this workbook, listed below.

1 textbook p. 589/857

2 textbook p. 589–90/857–8

3 textbook p. 590/858

4 textbook p. 591/859

5 textbook p. 592/860

Topic 3 >> Psychology as a science

The question of whether psychology is a science is one that greatly exercises the minds of psychologists and non-psychologists alike. It is a relevant question, because the way it is answered influences the way psychology is perceived – and valued – by people in society as a whole. This topic explores what 'science' actually means and what its various characteristics are. It also looks at how science can be divided into different sub-types. The topic also covers the development of psychology as a discipline separate from other sciences, before finally weighing up the arguments for and against recognizing psychology as a science.

DEFINITIONS AND VARIETIES OF SCIENCE

ACTIVITY

How do you know what you know?

Consider various things you know: such as knowing that your friend is a good friend, knowing that you can (or can't) ride a bicycle, knowing that snow is cold to touch.

1 How did you come to gain knowledge about the world?

2 Can you be certain that your knowledge is true, or do you believe it to be true?

3 How can you decide whether or not something is true?

The characteristics of science

Read from the start of Topic 3 on p. 593/861 to the end of the Commentary panel on p. 594/862. Here the textbook explains what is mean by 'science' and what its main characteristics are.

ACTIVITY

Characteristics of science

1 What is meant by 'empirical investigation'?

2 In what ways does science go beyond empirical observation?

3 Summarize the four main characteristics of science outlined by Slife and Williams (1995).
-
-
-
-

Varieties of science

Read the text under this heading on pp. 594–5/862–3, including the Commentary panel.

ACTIVITY

Varieties of science

Summarize the key points that the textbook makes about the following six 'varieties' of science.

1 Science as knowledge

2 Science as method

3 'Hard' sciences

4 'Soft' sciences

5 Induction involves reasoning from the _____ to the _____

6 Deduction involves reasoning from the _____ to the _____

The Commentary panel on p. 595/863 includes a description of Thomas Kuhn's ideas about the evolution of science – or rather the progress of science through revolution, rather than evolution.

ACTIVITY

Kuhn and the paradigm shift

1 What criticisms did Kuhn make of the 'logical' view of science?

2 What evidence supports his view?

3 What, according to Kuhn, is a 'paradigm'?

4 What is meant by the term 'zeitgeist'?

5 And what is a 'paradigm shift'?

ACTIVITY

Describing science

In the exam, you may be asked to describe what is meant by 'science'. Example Exam Question 2 on p. 599/867 does exactly this in part (a). Your brief description is worth 5 marks, so you should spend about 6.5 minutes on it, producing about 130 words. Using a PC, write a 130-word response to part (a).

EXAM HINT

If the exam question doesn't ask you to explain what is mean by 'science', then don't spend time doing that.

DEVELOPMENT OF PSYCHOLOGY AS A SEPARATE DISCIPLINE

ACTIVITY

Development of psychology as a separate discipline

The text at the bottom of p. 595/863 describes some of the key developments in psychology that distinguished it as a separate discipline. Using separate paper, draw up a timeline, i.e. a chronological list of the important developments.

Include all the researchers and movements listed on p. 595/863. Include any others you think are significant, such as Darwin and his theory of evolution, Freud and his psychodynamic theory, or Rogers and his person-centred approach. Include any other events you consider significant, such as the development of the EEG and brain scanning, that for the first time allowed researchers to investigate brain activity without using invasive methods (see Unit 4/12, pp. 112–14/380–2).

Next to any event, researcher or theory you include, note down any remarks that you could use as commentary or evaluation, such as:

- why they were important in helping psychology develop as a separate discipline
- whether there is agreement or disagreement about their importance
- whether they fell out of favour or were superseded by other developments.

The notes in the Commentary panel at the top of p. 596/864 will start you off, but you should be able to come up with lots of comments of your own, based on your previous studies.

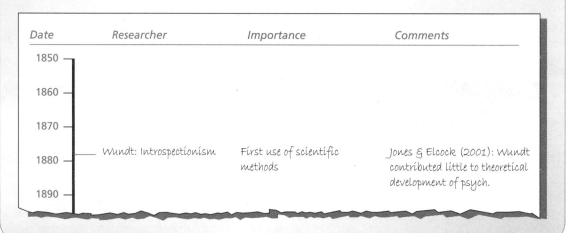

Date	Researcher	Importance	Comments
1850			
1860			
1870			
1880	Wundt: Introspectionism	First use of scientific methods	Jones & Elcock (2001): Wundt contributed little to theoretical development of psych.
1890			

ACTIVITY

Searching the Internet

Using your favourite search engine, do an Internet search for ideas about key events, personalities and theories in the development of psychology as a separate discipline. Depending on the key words you choose, you are likely to uncover a lot of information, so it will be important to be highly selective!

EXAM HINT

2006 AQA Specification

The development of psychology as a separate discipline is not now specified in the AQA 2006 Specification. This means that in exams from 2006 onwards, you will **not** be asked specific questions about this, so a question such as Example Exam Question 2 on p. 599/867 could not be set. However, if you are using this book for the 2005 exam, you should be prepared to answer any question on the development of psychology as a separate discipline. Try the next activity.

Describing psychology as a separate discipline

Look at Example Exam Question 2 on p. 599/867. Part (b) asks you to outline the development of psychology as a separate discipline. This part of the question is all AO1 (shown by the use of the term 'outline'). Your description is worth 10 marks, so you should spend about 13 minutes on it, producing about 270 words. Using a PC, write a 270-word response to part (b), highlighting the key developments, as recorded on your timeline.

ARGUMENTS FOR AND AGAINST PSYCHOLOGY AS A SCIENCE

The arguments for and against psychology as a science are examined on pp. 596–7/864–5. As in the previous topics, the arguments are numbered, with the counterarguments given in the Commentary panels.

Arguments for and against psychology as a science

Complete the table below, to summarize arguments for and against the view that psychology is a science, based on the material on pp. 596–7/864–5.

Arguments for psychology as a science	Counterargument
1	**1** Low validity of psychology's methods
2	**2**

Arguments against psychology as a science	Counterargument
1	**1**
2	**2**
3	**3**
4	**4** Paradigms in psychology

Psychologists' scientific methods

If you are writing an essay about the arguments for and against psychology as a science, it will be very useful if you can give examples – on either side of the argument. Think back to some of the investigations you have learned about during your AS and A2 psychology studies and note down examples of the following.

1 Three examples of well-controlled laboratory experiments:

- _____
- _____
- _____

2 Two experiments with high internal validity:

- _____
- _____

Two experiments with low internal validity:

- _____
- _____

3 Two experiments with high external validity:

- _____
- _____

Two experiments with low external validity:

- _____
- _____

4 Two experiments with a high level of objectivity:

- _____
- _____

Two experiments with a low level of objectivity:

- _____
- _____

Alternative views on the science–psychology relationship

The final part of this topic, on p. 598/866, raises the question of whether psychology should be considered to be a science, given the broad scope of the matters with which it concerns itself (from the workings of individual cells to the behaviour of complex individuals and societies).

A science of human behaviour?

Slife and Williams (1995) make the case for alternative approaches to psychology. Explain what is meant by each of the terms given below and outline its importance for psychology.

1 Empirical validation: _____

_____

2 Qualitative methods: _____

_____

_____

3 Methodological pluralism: _____

_____

Answering exam questions on arguments for and against psychology as a science

You should now be well prepared to tackle questions on the debate about whether psychology is a science, such as Example Exam Questions 3 and 4 on p. 599/867. Question 3, for example, focuses on the 'pro' side of the debate. Here you can use the arguments _for_ on p. 596/864 as AO1, but you can also bring in the counterarguments to arguments _against_ psychology as a science (given in the Commentary on p. 597/865). For example, the point that 'psychology has had dominant paradigms through its history' (in column 2 of the Commentary) is a clear argument _for_ psychology as a science, and you can present it as such.

You have 40 minutes to answer this question – enough time to write about 800 words. This means 400 words of AO1 description (for 15 marks) and 400 words of AO2 evaluation (also for 15 marks). One approach would be to present your AO1 point (e.g. psychology uses scientific methods), followed by the counterargument (for AO2). Then you can present a second point with the counterargument, and so on.

If you choose to answer the question with reference to four points in favour of psychology as a science, followed by counterarguments, you would think of your answer in terms of eight 'chunks', as follows:

	AO1 (argument for)		AO2 (counterargument)	
(a) Argument 1	100 words	5 mins	100 words	5 mins
(b) Argument 2	100 words	5 mins	100 words	5 mins
(a) Argument 3	100 words	5 mins	100 words	5 mins
(b) Argument 4	100 words	5 mins	100 words	5 mins

ACTIVITY

Planning an essay answer

Plan your answer to Example Exam Question 3 on p. 599/867. Decide how many arguments you will present, and hence how many chunks you will divide your essay into and how long each chunk will be. Using a PC, draw up a skeleton answer to the question, noting down the key points you will include in each chunk.

EXAMPLE EXAM QUESTIONS

In your work on this topic, you have already written answers to parts (a) and (b) of Example Exam Question 2 on p. 599/867 and planned an answer to Question 3.

ACTIVITY

One for you to try ...

(a) **Describe arguments** against **the claim that psychology is a science.** (15 marks)

(b) **Evaluate the arguments** against **the claim that psychology is a science that you presented in part (a).** (15 marks)

Questions may sometimes appear convoluted, like part (b) above. It is phrased in this way to avoid the problem of markers having to credit material in part (b) when part (a) has been irrelevant. For example, without this form of wording, you could write about something completely irrelevant in part (a), get zero marks for that, but then legitimately pick up marks for evaluating your irrelevant arguments in part (b)! The wording here prevents that. Read the advice on answering this question on p. 599/867, and read the material in this topic and on pp. 596–8/864–6 before attempting your response. You might structure your response as follows (each paragraph approximately 120 words):

Part (a)

- Science is deterministic and reductionist, which may not be the most appropriate route for psychology (e.g. the problem of free will, and attempts to apply reductionist principles in psychology).
- Objectivity is not possible, e.g. the problem of observer bias.

- Psychology does not have a paradigm. Kuhn argued that when data emerges which are inconsistent with an established theory that is part of a dominant paradigm (e.g. psychoanalysis), the theory is not abandoned or revised (as would happen in the physical sciences), but reasons are found to dismiss the data as coming from an unreliable source.

Part (b)

- Science is not necessarily deterministic and there are problems with a reductionist approach.
- Objectivity is not possible in any science, i.e. true objectivity can only be an ideal for scientific research.
- Counterarguments to paradigms in psychology – lack of a single paradigm; psychology has experienced major paradigms and paradigm shifts (e.g. the behaviourist paradigm dominated from 1930 to 1960, until the new cognitive paradigm led to a paradigm shift); evolution rather than revolution of scientific knowledge).

CHECK YOUR UNDERSTANDING

When you have finished working through this topic, try the questions in 'Check your understanding' on p. 598/866 of the textbook. Check your answers by looking at the relevant parts of the textbook or this workbook, listed below.

1 workbook p. 243

2 textbook p. 595/863

3 textbook pp. 594–5/862–3

4 textbook p. 596/864

5 textbook p. 595/863

'.. a born devil, on whose nature nurture can never stick ...'

This is how Shakespeare describes Caliban, a character in his play *The Tempest*, written in 1611. This 'nature–nurture' idea was borrowed by Sir Francis Galton in the late nineteenth century to describe the debate between those who regarded biological factors (nature) as the main determining factors in human make-up and those who considered the environment (nurture) as more important. Over a century – and vast amounts of research – later, the debate is still far from clear cut. This topic examines this debate, with particular reference to psychological research that supports one side or the other, or indeed views the two aspects as complementary.

DEFINITIONS OF NATURE AND NURTURE

ACTIVITY

Nature and nurture

Read the text from the bottom of p. 599/867 to halfway down p. 600/868. Then complete the following table to summarize the differing viewpoints of those on either side of the nature–nurture debate.

	Nature	Nurture
1 What influences aspects of our physical and mental being:	●	●
	●	●
2 Name given to people who support this argument:	●	●
	●	●

ACTIVITY

Nature and nurture in psychology

Try the activity on p. 600/868 of the textbook, using the space below to draw up your lists. This activity will be useful for noting down examples which you can use to illustrate your answer to questions such as Example Exam Question 1(a) on p. 605/873.

Nature	Nurture	Nature and nurture
●	●	●
●	●	●
●	●	●
●	●	●
●	●	●

Describing the nature–nurture debate

In the exam you may be asked to give a brief outline of the nature–nurture debate, as in Example Exam Questions 1(a) and 2(a) on p. 605/873. In each case, the description is worth 5 marks, so you should spend no more than 6.5 minutes on it, producing about 135 words. Using a PC, write a 135-word outline of what is meant by the nature–nurture debate.

If the exam question doesn't ask you to give an outline of what is meant by the nature–nurture debate, then don't waste time writing one.

THE HISTORY OF THE NATURE–NURTURE DEBATE

Philosophical views

The early history of psychology lies in the discipline of philosophy and the nature–nurture debate has a long history in that particular science.

Philosophical views

Read the paragraphs under this heading on p. 600/868. What were the views of the following philosophers?

- Plato

- René Descartes

- John Locke

Learning and instinct

Behaviourism vs ethology

The textbook describes the tension between the conflicting views of behaviourists, dominant in the USA in the middle of the 20th century, and ethologists, who favoured an evolutionary approach. Complete the table below to outline the position each took and also the challenges to their position.

	Their position on nature vs nurture	Challenge to their position
Behaviourists		
Ethologists		

2006 AQA Specification

The history of the nature–nurture debate is not now specified in the AQA 2006 Specification. This means that in exams from 2006 onwards, you will **not** be asked specific questions about the history of the debate, so questions such as Example Exam Questions 3(a) and 4 on p. 605/873 could not be set. However, if you are using this book for the 2005 exam, you should be prepared to answer such questions. Try the next activity.

ACTIVITY

Searching the Internet

Using your favourite search engine, do an Internet search to uncover more about the history of the nature–nurture debate. Make notes on key personalities and theories that influenced the way psychologists approached the question of whether nature or nurture was more influential.

ACTIVITY

Describing the history of the nature–nurture debate

Look at Example Exam Question 3(a) on p. 605/873. This part of the question is all AO1 (shown by the use of the term 'outline'). Your description is worth 15 marks, so you should spend about 20 minutes on it, producing about 400 words. Using a PC, write a 400-word outline of the history of the nature–nurture debate.

ASSUMPTIONS MADE ABOUT NATURE AND NURTURE IN PSYCHOLOGICAL RESEARCH

Nature

On p. 601/869 the textbook focuses on the evolutionary approach as an example of the nature approach in psychology. Read up to the end of the Commentary panel and then do the following activity.

 **AO2** ACTIVITY

Assumptions of the nature argument

Two examples of theories based on the nature argument are Bowlby's theory of attachment (see *Psychology for AS-level* Unit 2, pp. 53–6) and Selye's General Adaptation Syndrome (see *Psychology for AS-level* Unit 3, pp. 78–81). Read about these theories and summarize key assumptions of each that illustrate the nature argument.

Think, too, about the role of environmental factors in each theory. See, for example, the Commentary panel on p. 601/869 and the comments about human stress responses in a modern environment (*Psychology for AS-level* Unit 3, pp. 80–1).

Think of a third example of a psychological theory based on the nature argument. What are the key assumptions of that theory? In what ways do environmental factors challenge or complement this theory?

1 Bowlby's theory of attachment
- Assumptions made: _____

- Role of environmental factors: _____

2 Selye's General Adaptation Syndrome
- Assumptions made: _____

- Role of environmental factors: _____

3 _____
- Assumptions made: _____

- Role of environmental factors: _____

Nurture

On pp. 601–2/869–70, the textbook focuses on the behaviourist approach as an example of the nurture approach in psychology, and in particular social learning theory. Read up to the end of the Commentary panel at the top of p. 602/870 and then do the following activity.

Assumptions of the nurture argument

Two examples of theories based on the nurture argument are Bandura's explanation of aggression (see Unit 3/11, pp. 72–4/340–2) and social learning theories of gender development (see Unit 11/19, pp. 329–31/597–9). Read about these theories and summarize key assumptions of each that illustrate the nurture argument.

Think, too, about the role of biological or innate factors in this theory and how they might offer a challenge to it. See, for example, the Evaluation panels on p. 74/342 and 331/599.

Think of a third example of a psychological theory based on the nurture argument. What are the key assumptions of that theory? In what ways do biological factors challenge or complement this theory?

1 Bandura's explanation of aggression
  ● Assumptions made: _____

  ● Role of biological factors: _____

2 Social learning theories of gender development
  ● Assumptions made: _____

  ● Role of biological factors: _____
  _____

3 _____
  ● Assumptions made: _____

  ● Role of biological factors: _____
  _____

Nature and nurture, and psychological research

Exam questions in this subject area may require you to discuss examples of psychological research. It is important, therefore, to have at your fingertips examples of research that illustrate different sides of the nature–nurture debate or the tension between them. On pp. 602–3/870–1, three examples are considered:

  ● perception
  ● Piaget's theory of cognitive development
  ● intelligence.

Read about these examples and then try the following activities.

Nature, nurture and perception

The whole of Topic 3 of Unit 8/16 (pp. 238–46/506–14) is devoted to an area where the nature–nurture debate is of great relevance: perceptual development. You may already have worked through that topic in this workbook (pp. 82–88). If so, you will have plenty of material to use in weighing up the roles of nature and nurture. For example, the activities on pp. 85–7 ask you to consider various pieces of research and decide whether they support a nativist or empiricist view.

Read through Topic 3 of Unit 8/16 and pages 82–88 of this workbook. On separate paper, note down the details of research you could use to illustrate different aspects of the nature–nurture debate. You could do this in the form of a table, as below. The example of Fantz' research into face recognition is included.

Research	Research finding/conclusion	Relevance to nature–nurture debate	Comments
Fantz (1961)	Human babies possess an innate preference for human faces over other stimuli	Supports nativist viewpoint	● Other research failed to support this ● Support from Walton et al. (1992)

Piaget and Vygotsky

Read about Piaget's theory of cognitive development, Unit 10/18, pp. 284–9/552–7. Summarize key assumptions that illustrate aspects of the nature–nurture debate.

Then read about Vygotsky's theory of cognitive development, Unit 10/18, pp. 289–92/557–60. Summarize key assumptions that illustrate aspects of the nature–nurture debate.

Nature, nurture and intelligence

Much of Topic 2 of Unit 10/18 (pp. 299–304/567–72), about the development of measured intelligence, looks at the subject from the perspective of nature and nurture. You may already have worked through that topic in this workbook (pp. 97–103). If so, you will have plenty of material to use in essays specifically about nature and nurture.

Read through Topic 2 of Unit 10/18 and the equivalent topic in this workbook (see pp. 97–103). On a separate sheet of paper, note down the details of research you could use to illustrate different aspects of the nature–nurture debate. Again, you could do this in tabular form, as for the activity on perception at the bottom of p. 251.

EXAM HINT

The Evaluation panel on p. 603/871 describes two methodological problems relating to research into environmental factors:

- how to define or measure 'the environment' – and hence manipulate variables

- differences in research into animal behaviour and human behaviour.

DIFFERENT VIEWS REGARDING THE RELATIONSHIP BETWEEN NATURE AND NURTURE

The final part of this topic looks at various aspects of the relationship between nature and nurture, and in particular at how genes and the environment interact.

ACTIVITY

Views of the relationship between nature and nurture

Summarize the key points given in the textbook on pp. 603–4/871–2 under the headings shown below. Examples are given in the text to illustrate the relationships. Note down these examples in the final column or think of examples of your own, e.g. how do individuals achieve sporting prowess?

	Key points	Examples
● Gene–environment interactions		
– passive relationship		
– evocative relationship		
– active relationship		
● Reaction range		
● Nature via nurture		

EXAMPLE EXAM QUESTIONS

In your work on this topic, you have already written answers to Example Exam Questions 1(a), 2(a) and 3(a) on p. 605/873. Here is another one for you to try.

ACTIVITY

One for you to try ...

(a) What is meant by the terms 'nature' and 'nurture'? **(5 marks)**

(b) Discuss **two** areas of psychological research (theories and/or studies) in terms of the assumptions they make about nature and nurture. **(25 marks)**

Before attempting this question, you should read pp. 599–603/867–71 of the textbook and search the Internet to boost your understanding of this area. For example, see the following website for a discussion on Piaget and nature–nurture:

www.accessexcellence.org/LC/SER/BE/whatc.html

Note that as the first part of this question is only worth 5 marks, it should only occupy one-sixth of the total time and space of your answer.

In part (b), 10 marks are available for AO1 and 15 for AO2. You should bear that in mind when structuring your response. In the three AO1 paragraphs for part (b), you would be simply offering a brief overview of the main positions in this area.

Finally, remember not to just describe and evaluate your chosen psychological research, but to concentrate on its position in the nature–nurture debate.

You might structure your answer in the following way.

Part (a)
- Definitions of nature and nurture (see p. 600/868)

Part (b)
- AO1 – Nature–nurture and perception (see also pp. 238–46/506–14)
- AO1 – Nature–nurture and cognitive development (Piaget and Vygotsky) (see also pp. 284–92/552–60)
- AO1 – Nature–nurture and intelligence (see also pp. 299–304/567–72)
- AO2 – Nature–nurture and perception (see p. 603/871 and pp. 238–46/506–14)
- AO2 – Nature–nurture and cognitive development (see p. 603/871 and pp. 284–92/552–60)
- AO2 – Nature–nurture and intelligence (see p. 603/871 and pp. 299–304/567–72)

CHECK YOUR UNDERSTANDING

When you have finished working through this topic, try the questions in 'Check your understanding' on p. 604/872 of the textbook. Check your answers by looking at the relevant parts of the textbook or this workbook, listed below.

1 textbook p. 600/868; workbook p. 248
2 textbook pp. 600–1/868–9
3 textbook pp. 601–2/869–70
4 textbook p. 602/870
5 textbook pp. 603–4/871–2

APPROACHES IN
Psychology

PREVIEW

There are five topics in this unit. You should read them alongside the following pages in the Collins *Psychology for A2-level/Psychology* textbook:

Topic		*Psychology for A2*	*Psychology*
1	The physiological approach	pp. 610–14	pp. 878–82
2	The evolutionary approach	pp. 614–18	pp. 882–86
3	The psychodynamic approach	pp. 618–22	pp. 886–90
4	The behavioural approach	pp. 622–25	pp. 890–93
5	The cognitive approach	pp. 626–28	pp. 894–96

INTRODUCTION

'Approaches' is the third and final section of Module 5 (AQA Specification A), as shown in the diagram below.

Read the Preview and Introduction on p. 608/876 of the textbook now. This will give you an overview of what's in the unit.

Where this unit fits in to the A-level qualification

Section A:
Individual Differences

Module 5

Section B: Perspectives
(Issues & Debates)

Section C: **Perspectives
(Approaches)**

a biological/medical, behavioural, psychodynamic and cognitive approaches

b other psychological approaches, not named in the specification, such as social constructionism, Humanistic Psychology, Evolutionary Psychology, etc.

c approaches deriving from other, related disciplines, such as Sociology, Biology and Philosophy (for example, symbolic interactionism and functionalism)

In Section C of the Module 5 exam, you are given two pieces of stimulus material, outlining a novel situation or psychological phenomenon. You have to choose one of them and then answer four questions about the stimulus material. The form of the four questions will always be the same (p. 255).

There are almost as many different approaches within psychology as there are psychologists, although some approaches are more central and therefore more influential in the subject's development. In this final unit, we look at the main assumptions and methods of five of these – the physiological, evolutionary, psychodynamic, behavioural and cognitive approaches – and show how each of these approaches can be applied to an understanding of novel behaviours.

UNDERSTANDING THE SPECIFICATION

Here is what the AQA (A) specification says about this unit. It forms Section C, Approaches, of A2 Module 5.

Perspectives

Section C – Approaches

Candidates will be required to apply their knowledge and understanding of any **two** theoretical/methodological approaches to a novel situation or psychological phenomenon presented in the stimulus material given in the examination questions. These approaches might be selected from:

(a) biological/medical, behavioural, psychodynamic and cognitive (as specified in AS/A2 Individual Differences);

(b) other psychological approaches, not named in the specification, such as social constructionism, Humanistic Psychology, Evolutionary Psychology, etc;

(c) those deriving from other, related disciplines, such as Sociology, Biology and Philosophy (for example, symbolic interactionism and functionalism). [These may overlap with samples from (b)]

This part of Perspectives will be assessed through a *stimulus material* question. While the stimulus material will change from examination to examination, the basic form of the questions will remain the same. They will be as follows:

(a) Describe how the subject presented in the stimulus material might be explained by **two** different approaches. *(6 marks + 6 marks)* **AO1**

(b) Assess **one** of these explanations of the subject presented in the stimulus material in terms of its strengths and limitations. *(6 marks)* **AO2**

(c) How might the subject presented in the stimulus material be investigated by **one** of these approaches? *(6 marks)* **AO2**

(d) Evaluate the use of this method of investigating the subject material presented in the stimulus material. *(6 marks)* **AO2**

There will be **two** stimulus material questions, of which candidates must answer **one**.

The specification has three 'groups' of acceptable approaches, although it is most likely that your responses will come almost exclusively from the first two groups. These include the five approaches that we have covered in this unit. Some approaches can be divided into 'sub-approaches', each counting as a separate approach for the purposes of the Approaches question. For example, the 'biological' approach could be divided into the physiological and evolutionary approaches, the psychodynamic into Freudian and Eriksonian, and so on.

The stimulus material will either be a *general* scenario (e.g. why do people play the lottery?) or an *individual* one (e.g. why does someone steal for their friends?).

You are required to address four questions:

(a) How can this behaviour be explained from *two* different approaches?

(b) Assess *one* of these explanations.

(c) How might *one* of these explanations of the behaviour be investigated?

(d) Evaluate this method of investigating the behaviour.

It is important to make your explanations and investigations *plausible*, and to keep your answers rooted firmly within the context of the stimulus material at all times.

UNIT MAP

The diagram on the right gives you an overview of what you are about to study.

ACTIVITY

Unit map

Look through pp. 610–28/878–96 of the textbook to see where the items shown in the unit map are covered. Note down the relevant page numbers in the spaces provided.

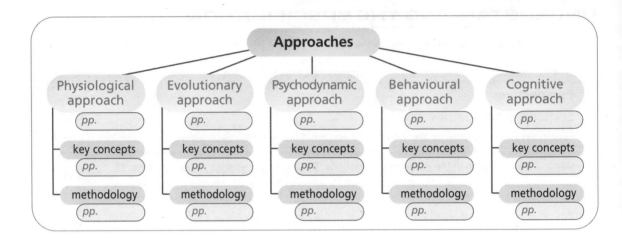

KEEPING TRACK

Use the table below to keep track of your work on this topic and plan your revision. See p. iv of this workbook (Introduction) for guidance on filling it in.

Approaches		Tick if you ...		
What I need to learn	*Where is it?*	*could make a basic attempt*	*could make a good attempt*	*have complete mastery of this*
The physiological approach				
Description of key concepts of the physiological approach				
Evaluation of key concepts of the physiological approach				
Description of methodology used by the physiological approach				
Evaluation of methodology used by the physiological approach				
The evolutionary approach				
Description of key concepts of the evolutionary approach				
Evaluation of key concepts of the evolutionary approach				
Description of methodology used by the evolutionary approach				
Evaluation of methodology used by the evolutionary approach				
The psychodynamic approach				
Description of key concepts of the psychodynamic approach				
Evaluation of key concepts of the psychodynamic approach				
Description of methodology used by the psychodynamic approach				
Evaluation of methodology used by the psychodynamic approach				
The behavioural approach				
Description of key concepts of the behavioural approach				
Evaluation of key concepts of the behavioural approach				
Description of methodology used by the behavioural approach				
Evaluation of methodology used by the behavioural approach				
The cognitive approach				
Description of key concepts of the cognitive approach				
Evaluation of key concepts of the cognitive approach				
Description of methodology used by the cognitive approach				
Evaluation of methodology used by the cognitive approach				

Topic 1 >> The physiological approach

As the Introduction on p. 608/876 of the textbook outlines, the physiological approach is one of the traditional approaches used by psychologists. It focuses on how we are made, looking at behaviour in terms of its biological causes.

In this topic, you will look at the key assumptions and concepts of the physiological approach, assessing them in terms of their strengths and weaknesses. You will also look at typical methods used by those favouring this approach – in particular, at methods of investigating the brain, again assessing these in terms of their strengths and weaknesses.

THE PHYSIOLOGICAL METAPHOR

ACTIVITY

The physiological metaphor

Read from the start of Topic 1 up to the heading 'Key concepts ...' on p. 610/878 of the textbook.

1 What is the main assumption of the physiological approach?

_____

_____

2 What implications does this have for the study of human behaviour?

_____

_____

_____

KEY CONCEPTS OF THE PHYSIOLOGICAL APPROACH

When you see the exam paper for AQA Unit 5 and turn to the Approaches question, you will know exactly what questions you are going to be asked. Turn to the Example Exam Question on p. 629/897 and read the text at the top of the page. As it states, the question parts are the same for every exam.

Part (a) will always ask you to describe how two approaches might try to explain the behaviour outlined in the stimulus material. To do this, you need to know what concepts underlie the approaches you choose. For the physiological approach, the key concepts are outlined in the textbook on pp. 610–11/878–9, divided according to the two major systems of the body – the CNS and the ANS.

EXAM HINT

AQA Specification

The exam wording of the questions for the Approaches question is shown in 'Understanding the specification' on p. 255 of this workbook.

Central nervous system (CNS)

Read the information under this heading on pp. 610–11/878–9 and then try the following three activities.

ACTIVITY

Brain organization

1 Summarize the key features of the two hemispheres:

Left hemisphere	Right hemisphere
●	●
●	●

2 How would you describe yourself: as a left-brained person or a right-brained person?

Areas of the brain

1 Complete the following table to summarize the key details about areas of the brain and their functions. You may need to look back to Unit 4/12 (pp. 116–30/384–98) to gather some of the information.

Area of the brain	Brief description	Function
Cortex	● Thin layer of grey matter covering surface of brain	●
Motor cortex	●	●
Pre-frontal cortex	●	●
Limbic system	●	●
Hypothalamus	●	●

2 At the top of p. 611/879, the textbook explains how many aspects of human behaviour can be explained in terms of localized areas of the brain. The study by Maguire *et al.* (2000) into the hippocampi of taxi drivers is one example. Find two other examples of studies investigating areas of the brain and what conclusions they reached about its control over human behaviour. (Hint: Unit 4/12 is a good place to start.)

Study	Area of brain studied	Conclusion
1	●	●
2	●	●

Neurotransmitters

1 What is a 'neurotransmitter'?

2 Some important neurotransmitters are listed below. For each, describe their influence in regulating human behaviour. You may have to search through the textbook for more information than on p. 611/879. (Hint: use the index!)

Neurotransmitter	Role in regulating human behaviour
● Endorphins	
● Serotonin	
● Dopamine	
● Noradrenaline	

Autonomic nervous system (ANS)

You should already be familiar with the workings of the ANS from your AS-level studies. The ANS is a crucial network in the body's response to stress – see *Psychology for AS-level* Unit 3, pp. 78–81. Now read the information about the ANS on p. 611/879 of the textbook and try the following activity.

The ANS

1 Think of two situations in which bodily functions would be controlled by:
- the parasympathetic state
- the sympathetic state.

2 What is a hormone and how does it work?

3 Some important hormones are listed below. For each, describe how they can affect human behaviour. Again, use the textbook's index for more information.

Hormone	Effect on human behaviour
Melatonin	
Testosterone	
Oxytocin	
Oestrogen	

4 What are pheromones and how do they influence human behaviour?

Answering part (a) of the exam question

The text on pp. 610–11/878–9 provides a good understanding of the physical processes that are involved in human behaviour. In the exam you have to apply your understanding to the question, and in particular to explaining the behaviour described in the stimulus material. A good way to do this is by asking yourself questions such as the following.

- *Human behaviours* – What human behaviours are described in the stimulus material? Think not just in general terms (e.g. 'celebrating festivals' in Example Exam Question on p. 629/897), but also in specific terms (e.g. becoming excited, drinking alcohol, laughing, dancing).

- *Physical processes* – What physical processes are involved in these behaviours?

- *Body systems* – How could these behaviours be explained in terms of the two main body systems (CNS and ANS)?

- *Neurotransmitters and hormones* – What particular neurotransmitters or hormones might play important roles?

Explaining behaviour in physiological terms

Look again at the stimulus material Example Exam Question on p. 629/897. Think about how you might answer part (a), taking the physiological approach. Ask yourself each of the four questions above and, on a separate sheet of paper, jot down some ideas in response to them.

Taking the example of celebrating festivals in the Example Exam Question on p. 629/897, this often involves a great deal of bodily stimulation and arousal (through excitement, singing, dancing, drinking alcohol) and researchers taking a physiological approach would certainly be keen to explore that aspect.

You might also observe that many cultures celebrate festivals in winter, at the darkest time of year, and that these festivals often involve lots of bright lights.

Think of Christmas with its fairy lights and candles. Or Guy Fawkes' night, with its bonfires and fireworks. A physiological explanation might focus on the connection between light and the suppression of the hormone melatonin, and the latter's role in seasonal depression (see, for example, the text on SAD in Unit 5/13, p. 137/405). Are some festivals a communal response to seasonal depression, caused by light deprivation?

Answering part (b) of the exam question

The second part of the Approaches question will ask you to assess one of your explanations in terms of its strengths and weaknesses – see part (b) of the question on p. 629/897 (for exams up to 2005) or on p. 255 of this workbook (for exams from 2006 onwards). The Evaluation panel on p. 612/880 discusses the physiological approach in just these terms.

(A02) ACTIVITY

Assessing the physiological explanation

Each of the bulleted items in the Evaluation panel on p. 612/880 can be interpreted as either a strength or a weakness. Complete the table below to identify how each can be either a strength or a weakness, or both.

	Strength	Weakness
1 Determinist	Determinist approach assumes cause-effect relationships – good for scientific investigation	Implies we have no free will
2 Reductionist		
3 Mind–body division		
4 Individual and cultural differences		
5 Applications		

The analysis from the last activity provides a very useful template for part (b) of the Approaches question. Use the two columns to analyse the strengths and weaknesses of the physiological explanation of the behaviour(s) described. For example, in assessing the explanation as a reductionist approach, you could ask:

1 What aspects of the chosen behaviour seem to be at a level suitable for a physiological explanation?

2 What aspects of the chosen behaviour seem to be unsuitable for a physiological explanation?

(A02) ACTIVITY

Explaining celebrations in reductionist terms

Answer the two questions above in terms of celebrating festivals.

1 What aspects of celebrations seem to be at a level suitable for a physiological explanation?

2 What aspects of celebrations seem to be unsuitable for a physiological explanation?

METHODOLOGY USED BY THE PHYSIOLOGICAL APPROACH

Read the introductory paragraph to this section on p. 612/880. The physiological approach, being reductionist and determinist, implies a preference for experimental methods and, indeed, experiments are one common approach used by those investigating the physiological aspects of behaviour. Experiments are covered in the textbook in Topics 2 and 4 of this unit.

Case studies are another favoured approach – these are considered in Topic 3.

The brain is the focus of investigations – not surprisingly, given that organ's primary role in controlling all aspects of our functioning. The textbook focuses on the two ways of investigating the brain: invasive and non-invasive techniques.

ACTIVITY

Invasive and non-invasive techniques

Read about invasive and non-invasive techniques for studying the brain on pp. 612–13/880–1. Summarize the main features of the techniques described. In the final column, give an example of a situation where this has been used or might be used today.

Technique	Main features	Example of use
Invasive techniques		
● Electrical stimulation		
● Chemical stimulation		
● Ablation/lesioning		
Non-invasive techniques		
● EEG		
● fMRI		
● PET		

Answering part (c) of the Approaches question

In part (c) of the Approaches question, you have to think about how someone taking a physiological approach would investigate the behaviour described in the stimulus material.

1 What methodology might this approach favour?

2 Which of the types of method would be suitable for investigating the behaviour described? Experiment? Case study? Invasive or non-invasive methods of investigating the brain?

3 What practical steps might that involve (e.g. choosing a sample, operationalizing variables)?

ACTIVITY

Investigating celebratory behaviour taking a physiological approach

Look at the stimulus material Example Exam Question on p. 629/897. Think about how you might answer part (c), taking the physiological approach. Ask yourself each of the three questions on the left and jot down some ideas in response to them. This is quite a hard question, as the behaviour described in the stimulus material (celebrating festivals) is not one that obviously lends itself to physiological investigation. Be imaginative (but not implausible – such as sending someone off to a party attached to an EEG monitor!).

Answering part (d) of the exam question

The final part of the Approaches question – part (d) – will ask you to evaluate the methods you suggested in part (c) for investigating the behaviour described in the stimulus material. By thinking ahead when you are answering part (c), you can pick a method that has both clear strengths and weaknesses when it comes to investigating the behaviour described.

The Evaluation panel on p. 613/881 discusses the strengths and weaknesses of techniques for investigating the brain.

ACTIVITY

Evaluating techniques of investigating the brain

Read through the Evaluation panel on p. 613/881 and pick out the strengths and weaknesses of the various invasive and non-invasive techniques. Draw up a table with two columns, listing the strengths in one column and weaknesses in another.

The evaluation activities on pp. 268 and 273 will also be useful, if you decide to opt for an experimental or case-study-based method of investigating the behaviour in the stimulus material.

ACTIVITY

Evaluating methods of investigating celebratory behaviour

Look back at your answers to the activity at the bottom of p. 261. Now evaluate the suggestions you made there for investigating celebratory behaviour. In other words, answer part (d) of the Example Exam Question on p. 629/897 in terms of a physiological explanation. Read the guidance notes underneath the question and use a PC to write your answer to this question, limiting yourself to 150 words.

EXAMPLE EXAM QUESTIONS

In your work on this unit, you have already planned and written answers to all four parts of the Example Exam Question on p. 629/897, in terms of a physiological approach.

Sample questions

A Over the last few years, there has been an upsurge in television shows such as *Stars in their Eyes* and *The X Factor*, where members of the public compete to reach the pinnacle of singing success – being seen as a 'star'. Given that some of these shows involve public humiliation, when the judges are less than complimentary, why do even relatively talentless people put themselves through such an ordeal?

    (a) Describe how **two** approaches might try to explain why people are determined to 'be a star'.   (6 + 6 marks)

    (b) Assess **one** of these explanations of why people are determined to 'be a star'.   (6 marks)

    (c) How would **one** of these approaches investigate why people are determined to 'be a star'.   (6 marks)

    (d) Evaluate this method of investigating why people are determined to 'be a star'.   (6 marks)

(Note: in the answer below, only one approach is covered in part (a), whereas in an exam, you would be required to cover two approaches for the 6 + 6 marks.)

Sample answer

(a) Researchers have identified a region of the brain that functions as a pleasure centre. When an animal's behaviour is reinforced, this part of the brain is activated, producing a sensation of pleasure. In animals, dopamine is released in this area, usually as a response to pleasurable activities such as eating and sexual activity. Possibly, for these people, being applauded by the studio audience, or the thrill of being on television, is an equivalent thrill to sexual activity, and therefore causes the same release of dopamine from the 'pleasure centre'. They would find this extremely rewarding, and would therefore be motivated to seek out the same experience again, regardless of any obstacles (such as humiliation or lack of talent).

(b) A strength of this explanation is that it is reductionist, breaking down a complex behaviour (seeking celebrity status) into more basic physiological processes (stimulation of a particular area of the brain). This can then be investigated using physiological techniques that provide scientific evidence for a change in brain activity whenever an individual engages in – or even imagines engaging in – this particular behaviour. However, there are also problems with reducing a person's 'search for stardom' into just physiological changes. It ignores other possible explanations for the same behaviour, such as trying to overcome feelings of inferiority, a need for affiliation and so on. Selecting the wrong explanation may, therefore, prevent a true understanding of why people go to such lengths to fulfil their ambition.

(c) Physiological psychologists might use positron emission tomography (PET) to investigate this explanation. Radioactive glucose could be injected into the bloodstream of an experimental group of 'X factor' (or a similar show) applicants, and into a control group of people matched for age and sex who had not applied to appear on the show. Each group could then be asked to imagine themselves in a television studio, performing in front of a live audience who applaud wildly at the end of their performance. The PET scan would be able to chart the parts of the brain that are most active while participants are visualizing this scenario. It would then be possible to see whether there is a different pattern of activity in the pleasure centre of the brain and the nerve pathways leading from it, for those who have applied for the show compared to the control group. If there is, this would provide physiological evidence that they would find the experience of 'stardom' more rewarding than members of the control group.

(d) A problem with the use of PET scans in this investigation is that it involves recording over long periods and is a very technically complex procedure. This may actually appeal to the people who have applied to 'be a star', as it makes them feel they are important enough to be subjected to this type of treatment. Therefore, the procedure itself might activate the pleasure centre of these participants. PET scans could also give false results if participants' chemical balances were not normal. For example, if any of the participants had eaten within several hours of the scan, this would adversely affect the results because of altered blood sugar levels. There are also some risks associated with the procedure, for example the radioactive substance might expose radiation to the fetus of any participants pregnant at the time of the scan. As this is a psychological investigation into a fairly unimportant area of human behaviour, the benefits might not justify the costs involved.

ACTIVITY

One for you to try ...

B Insurance statistics tell us that most car accidents are caused by males in the 17 to 25 age group. This is because of a variety of factors, such as lack of experience or insufficient skill, but a key contributory factor is simply driving too fast. Driving fast has become a passion for young men, who will often save all their money to get the fastest car they can afford to buy (and insure).

Using material from this Topic and from the textbook (pp. 610–13/878–81), complete your own answers to the following questions. (You might also consult p. 172/440 for a possible physiological explanation that is different to the one offered in **A** on the left.)

(a) Describe how **two** approaches might try to explain why young men have a passion for fast driving.

(6 + 6 marks)

(b) Assess **one** of these explanations of why young men have a passion for fast driving. (6 marks)

(c) How would **one** of these approaches investigate why young men have a passion for fast driving.

(6 marks)

(d) Evaluate this method of investigating why young men have a passion for fast driving. (6 marks)

CHECK YOUR UNDERSTANDING

When you have finished working through this topic, try the questions in 'Check your understanding' on p. 614/882 of the textbook. Check your answers by looking at the relevant parts of the textbook, listed below.

1 textbook p. 610–11/878–9   **3** textbook p. 611/879   **5** textbook pp. 612–13/880–1

2 textbook p. 611/879   **4** textbook p. 611/879

When Charles Darwin first published *The Origin of Species*, some readers were horrified to think that we might be related to monkeys. Some critics lampooned Darwin mercilessly for his theory of evolution. However, it was to prove one of the most influential of all scientific theories and provided the trigger for a vast amount of research. More recently, Darwin's ideas have been developed in the field of psychology known as 'evolutionary psychology'.

In this topic, you will look at the key assumptions and concepts of the evolutionary approach, assessing them in terms of their strengths and weaknesses. You will also look at typical methods used by those favouring this approach, again assessing these in terms of their strengths and weaknesses.

THE EVOLUTIONARY METAPHOR

ACTIVITY

The evolutionary metaphor

Read from the start of Topic 2 up to the heading 'Key concepts ...' on p. 614/882 of the textbook.

1 What is the main assumption of the evolutionary approach?

2 What implications does this have for the study of human behaviour?

3 According to the evolutionary approach, what accounts for differences between people?

KEY CONCEPTS OF THE EVOLUTIONARY APPROACH

The key concepts of the evolutionary approach are outlined in the textbook on pp. 614–15/882–3, under four headings: natural selection, sexual selection, kin selection and mental modules. Read through the information in the textbook and then complete the following four activities. Write your answers on a separate sheet of paper or using your PC. You may also find it useful to work in pairs on the activities, with one person checking the other person's answers.

ACTIVITY

Sexual selection

As well as the text on p. 615/883, read the information about sexual selection on pp. 434–6/702–4.

1 What is the basic principle of sexual selection?

2 What is the difference between intersexual selection and intrasexual selection?

3 Outline three different criteria that individuals might use when selecting mates.

4 Why is it more common for males of the species to show sexually selected characteristics (such as the peacock's tail or the robin's red breast)?

ACTIVITY

Natural selection

1 What is the basic principle of natural selection?

2 What factors determine whether genetic characteristics survive or are lost?

3 What factors determine 'selective breeding' within species?

Kin selection

1 What is the basic principle of kin selection?

2 What is meant by the following terms?

- Adaptiveness
- Selfish gene (Dawkins 1976)
- Inclusive fitness (Hamilton 1963)

3 How many (genetically related) uncles or aunts would Haldane 'lay down his life for'?

Mental modules

1 What is meant by the following terms?

- Mental module
- EEA
- Evolutionary psychology
- Ultimate causes
- Proximate causes

2 One example of mental modules is the rank theory of depression, explained on p. 615/883. Think of another aspect of human behaviour (e.g. a desire to play sport) and try to explain it in terms of genetically determined mental modules.

Answering part (a) of the exam question

The text on pp. 614–15/882–3 gives you a good overview of the evolutionary processes involved in human behaviour. In the exam you have to apply your understanding to the question, and in particular to explaining the behaviour described in the stimulus material. You can do this by asking yourself questions such as the following.

1 *Relevant behaviours* – What human behaviours are described in the stimulus material?

2 *Natural selection of traits* – What physical or psychological characteristics are involved in the behaviour? How could these traits be explained by natural selection?

3 *Sexual selection* – How could these behaviours/traits be explained in terms of sexual selection? Are they used, for instance, by males or females in order to increase their reproductive success?

4 *Kin selection* – How could these behaviours/traits be explained in terms of kin selection? Are they used by individuals to increase the reproductive success of relatives?

5 *Mental modules* – How could these behaviours be explained in terms of mental modules? Does the behaviour, as demonstrated now, have its origin in the EEA – our ancestral past?

Explaining behaviour in evolutionary terms

Look at the stimulus material in Example Exam Question on p. 629/897. Think about how you might answer part (a), taking the evolutionary approach. Ask yourself each of the five questions above and, on a separate sheet of paper or using a PC, jot down some ideas in response to them.

Thinking of the example of celebrating festivals in the Example Exam Question on p. 629/897, how would an evolutionary psychologist explain public and private celebrations in terms of natural selection?

- Thinking about mental modules, you could try to explain the role of public celebrations in our ancestral past. Perhaps they served an important social role for tribal living, cementing ties within the community or establishing the status of different tribes. They may also have enhanced the power of central figures within a community (see 'Schizophrenia and shamanism' on p. 447/715).

- Celebrating personal events, such as birthdays, may have a role in sexual selection. For example, birthdays involve presents; gifts (of food, for example) have been found to have a role in sexual selection (see 'Selection for provisioning' on p. 435/703) and in the formation of valuable alliances.

Explaining other behaviours in evolutionary terms

You can get more practice at explaining our behaviour in evolutionary terms by doing the activity on p. 616/884 of the textbook. It suggests some more human behaviours whose origins might be traced back through our evolutionary past.

Answering part (b) of the exam question

The second part of the Approaches question will ask you to assess one of your explanations in terms of its strengths and weaknesses (see part (b) of the question on p. 629/897). The Evaluation panel on p. 616/884 discusses the evolutionary approach in just these terms.

ACTIVITY

Assessing the evolutionary explanation

Read through the list of the different aspects of the evolutionary approach in the Evaluation panel on p. 616/884 and decide whether each point discussed is a strength or a weakness, or has elements of both. Complete the table below to summarize both strengths and weaknesses.

	Strength	Weakness
1 Reductionist and determinist		
2 Difficult to falsify		
3 Based on research with non-human animals		
4 Has human evolution stopped?		
5 Ultimate vs proximate causes		

This table will be very useful for tackling part (b) of the Approaches question, where you have to analyse the strengths and weaknesses of the evolutionary explanation you gave in part (a). For example, in assessing the evolutionary explanation, you could evaluate the role of research with non-human animals. Try the next activity.

ACTIVITY

Personal celebrations, gifts and examples from the animal kingdom

In answering part (a) of the question on p. 629/897, you might have explained parties and other personal celebrations as part of the process of sexual selection, e.g. the quality of the expected gifts might be interpreted by the selector as a measure of the ability of the giver to provide for their mate (in evolutionary terms). Now answer the following questions.

1 What examples of research are there with non-human animals that support this explanation?

2 How justified is it to generalize from research with non-human animals to explain more complex human behaviours?

METHODOLOGY USED BY THE EVOLUTIONARY APPROACH

On pp. 616–17/884–5, several different types of methodology are discussed that can be used to investigate evolutionary causes of behaviour:

- demonstrating genetic causes using kinship studies and gene mapping
- experiments
- observations and surveys
- cross-cultural studies.

Read about these methods and then complete the following four activities. Write your answers on a separate sheet of paper or using your PC.

On pp. 616–17/884–5

ACTIVITY

Kinship studies and gene mapping

1 Why are kinship studies so useful for investigating the possible genetic cause of characteristics or behaviours?

2 Kinship studies are sometimes called 'concordance studies'. What is meant by the term 'concordance'?

3 What is 'gene mapping'?

4 Summarize how concordance studies and gene mapping have been used to investigate the genetic basis of IQ and what the main findings were. (You may find it useful to read Unit 10/18, pp. 299–301/567–9.)

ACTIVITY

Experiments

1 The evolutionary role of genes can be investigated using either field or natural experiments.

   (a) What is the main similarity between these two types of experiment?

   (b) What is the main difference?

2 Would it be possible to investigate evolutionary explanations using laboratory experiments?

3 Give one example of a natural experiment carried out to investigate evolutionary explanations of human behaviour.

4 Give one example of a field experiment carried out to investigate evolutionary explanations of human behaviour.

ACTIVITY

Observations and surveys

1 Dunbar (1995) used observational methods to investigate the evolutionary explanation of mate selection. Think of another human behaviour that could be investigated using observational methods.

2 Buss (1999) used a survey to investigate the evolutionary explanation of mate selection. Think of another human behaviour that could be investigated using a survey.

ACTIVITY

Cross-cultural studies

1 How do cross-cultural studies help us to investigate evolutionary explanations of human behaviour?

2 Outline one example of a cross-cultural study investigating evolutionary explanations of human behaviour.

3 Think of another example of human behaviour that would lend itself to being investigated by cross-cultural studies.

Answering part (c) of the Approaches question

In part (c) of the Approaches question, you have to think about how someone taking an evolutionary approach would investigate the behaviour described in the stimulus material.

1 What methodology might this approach favour?

2 Which of the types of method would be suitable for investigating the behaviour described? Kinship studies? Gene mapping? Field or natural experiments? Observations or surveys? Cross-cultural studies?

3 What practical steps would be involved in setting up the research (e.g. operationalizing variables in the experiments, designing a questionnaire for the survey)?

ACTIVITY

Investigating celebratory behaviour taking an evolutionary approach

Look at the stimulus material Example Exam Question on p. 629/897. Think about how you might answer part (c), taking the evolutionary approach. Ask yourself each of the three questions on the left and jot down some ideas in response to them.

Look at the stimulus material Example Exam Question on p. 629/897.

Unit 21/29 // Approaches

Answering part (d) of the exam question

In part (d) of the Approaches question, you need to evaluate the methods you suggested in part (c). By thinking ahead when you are answering part (c), you can pick a method that has both clear strengths and weaknesses when it comes to investigating the relevant behaviour. The Evaluation panel on p. 617/885 discusses the strengths and weaknesses of the various methods used by the evolutionary approach. You will also find some useful information about experiments, observational methods and surveys in *Psychology for AS-level* Unit 6, pp. 195–211. These pages include points about ethical issues associated with these types of research, which you can also bring in when evaluating research methods.

AO2 ACTIVITY

Evaluating methodology used by the evolutionary approach

Read through the Evaluation panel on p. 617/885 and summarize the strengths and weaknesses of the methods discussed. (Note that the Evaluation panel focuses on weaknesses, so you will need to think carefully about the strengths of the various methods.)

	Strength	Weakness
1 Concordance studies		
2 Experiments		
3 Observational studies and surveys		
4 Cross-cultural research		

AO2 ACTIVITY

Evaluating methods of investigating celebratory behaviour

Look back to the activity at the bottom of p. 267. Now evaluate the suggestions you made there for investigating celebratory behaviour. This will enable you to answer part (d) of the Example Exam Question on p. 629/897 in terms of evolutionary explanations. Read the guidance notes underneath the question and use a PC to write your answer to this question, limiting yourself to 150 words.

EXAMPLE EXAM QUESTIONS

In your work on this unit, you have already planned and written answers to all four parts of the Example Exam Question on p. 629/897, in terms of an evolutionary approach. Below are two questions: we have answered the first for you; for the second, use the material from this topic and the textbook in order to construct your own answer.

Sample questions

C When Julie was at university, she was relatively carefree. After graduation she started a career and moved out of the home she had shared with her parents for the previous 21 years. She soon began to realize that being an adult was not that easy. Living in a flat on her own was lonely, and she telephoned her mother a great deal. She also found solace in her cuddly toys, and spent much of her time talking to them, and treating them as if they were children. When visitors came she would insist that at least one of her favourite toys sat with them, and would get very angry if visitors ever made fun of her toys or mistreated them.

    (a) Describe how **two** approaches might try to explain Julie's attitude to her cuddly toys.   (6 + 6 marks)

    (b) Assess **one** of these explanations of Julie's attitude to her cuddly toys.   (6 marks)

    (c) How would **one** of these approaches investigate Julie's attitude to her cuddly toys?   (6 marks)

    (d) Evaluate this method of investigating Julie's attitude to her cuddly toys.   (6 marks)

A2 Perspectives

(Note: only one approach is covered in part (a), whereas in an exam, you would be required to cover two approaches for the 6 + 6 marks.)

(a) One explanation could be the evolutionary explanation. Babies have certain features (such as big eyes and a squashed nose) that make them irresistible to us. Film-makers such as Walt Disney have made a fortune out of exploiting these features with characters like *Bambi*. The same thing applies to cuddly toys. Many of these are given baby-type features to make people feel like wanting to look after them. Julie may feel very protective towards her cuddly toys because they are like babies to her and she is programmed to want to look after them. In the environment of evolutionary adaptiveness (EEA), it would have been important for females to look after their children in times of danger, and this mental module still exists in modern times. If Julie feels threatened in any way in her own life, it will increase this need to tend to the needs of her 'babies'.

(b) The strengths of an evolutionary explanation for Julie's need for cuddly toys are that it does help to explain why such a behaviour developed in the first place, i.e. its ultimate explanation. This may lead to more valid ways of treating behaviours that appear maladaptive by understanding their adaptive significance. The limitations of this explanation include the fact that we have no actual physical evidence to support this explanation. This makes it difficult to prove or disprove. We also cannot assume that another explanation (e.g. a cognitive one) is not responsible for Julie's preference for cuddly toys rather than other types of contact. She may have been let down in a relationship and decided that the only things she can 'trust' not to let her down are her cuddly toys that have 'stuck with her' from childhood.

(c) One way of investigating Julie's attitude to her cuddly toys would be through a cross-cultural study. If her protective attitude to her toys is a product of natural selection, based on the needs of our ancestors in the EEA, then the same behaviour should be present, at least to some degree, in all cultures throughout the world. The researchers could employ a variety of methods to test for this behaviour, from looking at the use of child-like features in advertising and popular media, through to interviewing adults about their attitude to cuddly toys. If these investigations showed evidence of cultural variability in attitudes to cuddly toys (or their equivalent in that society) then it would be impossible to claim that humans share a universal, species-typical behavioural tendency, and therefore to suggest that this originated in the EEA. If the investigations revealed a common pattern of preference across all cultures, this would indicate that this was a species specific behaviour that was independent of cultural or historical influences.

(d) Uncovering cultural similarities and differences in people's attitude to cuddly toys and child-like features in general is important for several reasons. It helps us refine our understanding of human behaviour, for example cross-cultural research in this area would help to refine our understanding of attachment in order to accommodate important differences in these practices around the world. A problem of cross-cultural research in this area is that any tests or procedures that are developed in one culture may not have the same meaning when applied in a different culture. Similarly, behaviours observed in one culture (e.g. talking to toys) may be considered perfectly normal in one culture, but abnormal in another. A greater understanding of what is normal in a particular behaviour means that any appropriate treatment for deviations to normal, acceptable behaviour can be given in a culturally sensitive way.

ACTIVITY

One for you to try ...

Look again at Sample question **A** on p. 262. Note: in the sample answer on pp. 262–3, we explained this behaviour from a *physiological* approach. Your task is now to explain it from an *evolutionary* approach. Remember that real exam questions will ask for **two** approaches in part (a), but here you are providing just one.

CHECK YOUR UNDERSTANDING

When you have finished working through this topic, try the questions in 'Check your understanding' on p. 618/886 of the textbook. Check your answers by looking at the relevant parts of the textbook, listed below.

1 textbook p. 614–15/882–3   **3** textbook p. 615/883   **5** textbook p. 616/884

2 textbook p. 615/883   **4** textbook p. 615/883

Topic 3 >> The psychodynamic approach

Sigmund Freud has had an enormous influence on the study and practice of psychology for 100 years or so. You should already have learned about his psychodynamic model in your study of abnormality at AS level. There is a subtle difference between the terms 'psychodynamic' and 'psychoanalytic': 'psychoanalytic' refers only to Freud's theory, while 'psychodynamic' refers to all theories within the broader approach, which includes psychoanalytic theory. In this topic, you will look at the key assumptions and concepts of the psychodynamic approach, assessing these in terms of their strengths and weaknesses. You will also look at typical methods used by those favouring this approach, again assessing these in terms of their strengths and weaknesses.

THE PSYCHODYNAMIC METAPHOR

ACTIVITY

The psychodynamic metaphor

Read from the start of Topic 3 on p. 618/886 of the textbook up to the heading 'Key concepts ...'.

1 What is the main assumption of the psychodynamic approach?

_____

_____

_____

2 On p. 618/886, two metaphors are suggested that describe the psychodynamic approach. What are these two metaphors?

- _____

- _____

KEY CONCEPTS OF THE PSYCHODYNAMIC APPROACH

Read p. 619/887 of the textbook, which discusses the key concepts of the psychodynamic approach, and complete the following activity. Write your answers on a separate sheet of paper or using your PC. You may also find it useful to work in pairs on the activities, with one person checking the other person's answers.

ACTIVITY

Key concepts of the psychodynamic approach

The structure of the mind

1 Briefly define the three parts of the personality.
- Id
- Ego
- Superego

2 What is meant by the following terms?
- Pleasure principle
- Reality principle

3 What is meant by the following terms?
- Primary process thinking
- Secondary process thinking

Drives and ego defences

4 What, according to Freud are the two main drives or instincts?

5 What are 'ego defence mechanisms'?

6 Give three examples of types of defence mechanism and explain how they protect the ego (you may find it useful to refer to *Psychology for AS-level* – see Unit 4, p. 131).

Psychosexual developmental stages

7 What is the role of the 'libido'?

8 What is meant by the term 'fixated' and how does 'fixation' come about?

9 How can fixation be dealt with?

Personality types

10 What traits characterize the following adult personality types?
- Oral receptive
- Oral aggressive
- Anal retentive
- Anal expulsive
- Phallic

11 Are these personality types that you would recognize?

Answering part (a) of the exam question

The text on pp. 618–19/886–7 gives you a good understanding of the psychodynamic analysis of the causes of human behaviour. In the exam, you have to apply your understanding to the question, by explaining the behaviour described in the stimulus material. You can do this by asking yourself questions such as these.

1 *Relevant behaviours* – What human behaviours are described in the stimulus material?

2 *Structure of the mind* – Which parts of the mind – conscious or unconscious – might be involved in the behaviour? Do the behaviours seem to involve the pleasure principle or the reality principle? Or do they illustrate the struggle between the two?

3 *Drives* – Which of the two Freudian drives is at work in the behaviours: sex or aggression (eros or thanatos)?

4 *Ego defences* – Can the behaviours be explained in terms of ego defences, e.g. repression, regression, displacement, denial, sublimation?

5 *Psychosexual developmental stages* – Can the behaviours be analysed in terms of developmental stages and hence be linked to a part of the body (mouth, anal region, genitals)?

6 *Personality types* – Can the behaviour be linked to specific personality types?

ACTIVITY

Explaining behaviour in psychodynamic terms

Look at the stimulus material Example Exam Question on p. 629/897. Think about how you might answer part (a), taking the psychodynamic approach. Ask yourself each of the six questions above and, on a separate sheet of paper or using a PC, jot down some ideas in response to them.

Thinking of the example of celebrating festivals in the Example Exam Question on p. 629/897, how do you think a psychodynamic psychologist might explain this?

1 Freud might explain our fascination with public and private celebrations in terms of defence mechanisms such as identification, forming an alliance with someone else and becoming like them in order to allay anxiety. Alternatively, in reaction formation, we experience denial and reversal of our feelings so that celebrating someone's birthday or their accomplishments may be a way of dealing with the negative feeling we have toward them.

2 Public celebrations, particularly when they involve one central figure, may be seen as a way of re-asserting paternal dominance. This was a technique commonly used by historical figures such as Hitler

and Mussolini, so that followers would see them not only as benevolent father figures, but also figures to be feared.

ACTIVITY

Explaining other behaviours in psychodynamic terms

Think of a range of human activities – e.g. playing musical instruments, shopping, cleaning – and practise explaining them in psychodynamic terms. What aspects of psychodynamic theory might they exemplify?

Answering part (b) of the exam question

The second part of the Approaches question will ask you to assess one of your explanations in terms of its strengths and weaknesses (see part (b) of the question on p. 629/897). The Evaluation panel on p. 620/888 discusses the psychodynamic approach in just these terms.

A02 ACTIVITY

Assessing the psychodynamic explanation

Read through the list of bullet points evaluating the psychodynamic approach in the Evaluation panel on p. 620/888 and decide whether each point discussed is a strength or a weakness, or has elements of both. Draw up a table, similar to the one on p. 266, to summarize both strengths and weaknesses.

This list you drew up in the last activity will be very useful for tackling part (b) of the Approaches question, where you have to analyse the strengths and weaknesses of the psychodynamic explanation you gave in part (a). For example, in assessing the psychodynamic explanation, you could evaluate the role of sexual influences. You could ask how plausible it is to explain the behaviours described in the stimulus material in terms of defence mechanisms or the public display of parental dominance.

ACTIVITY

Personal and public celebrations, and basic instincts

In responding to part (a) of the question on p. 629/897, you might have explained personal and public celebrations in terms of defence mechanisms and the public display of parental dominance (see points 1 and 2 in the middle of p. 271). You might consider the following as AO2 points for this psychodynamic explanation.

1 Although many of these concepts are unfalsifiable, there is some research support for the use of

defence mechanisms in everyday behaviour. Use the Internet to find some, and then make a note of this for your future use of the concept of defence mechanisms.

2 Paternal dominance may have been a central theme in Victorian society, but may be less of an issue today. Again, use the Internet to find out how modern psychoanalysis views the importance of this concept.

METHODOLOGY USED BY THE PSYCHODYNAMIC APPROACH

On pp. 620–1/888–9, two types of methodology favoured by the psychodynamic approach are discussed: case studies and experiments.

Case studies

The psychodynamic approach is interested in how an individual's personality has developed. It is natural, therefore, that case studies of individuals should be a useful methodology.

ACTIVITY

Case studies

1 What is the purpose of interviews with individuals (or 'therapy') from a psychodynamic perspective?

2 Several techniques are used during therapy to help the individual to gain insight. These are explained on p. 620/888 and in Unit 18/26 on p. 539/807. Summarize what happens during the therapy and how the therapy is intended to help the individual.
- Free association
- Word association
- Dream analysis
- Transference
- Projective tests

ACTIVITY

Experiments

1 Turn to Unit 11/19 and read the text on pp. 322–3/590–1 about 'Empirical evidence'. How did the following researchers investigate aspects of personality based on the psychodynamic approach?

(a) Myers and Brewin (1994)

(b) McGinnies (1949)

2 What are the limitations of such experiments based on a psychodynamic approach? (At least two are mentioned on p. 323/591.)

Answering part (c) of the Approaches question

In part (c) of the Approaches question, you have to think about how someone taking a psychodynamic approach would investigate the behaviour described in the stimulus material.

1 What methodology might this approach favour?

2 Which of the types of method would be suitable for investigating the behaviour described? Case studies? Experiments?

3 What practical steps would be involved in setting up the research (e.g. choosing a type of therapy, operationalizing the variables in an experiment)?

Investigating celebratory behaviour taking a psychodynamic approach

Look at the stimulus material Example Exam Question on p. 629/897. Think about how you might answer part (c), taking a psychodynamic approach. Ask yourself each of the three questions at the bottom of the previous page and jot down some ideas in response to them.

(A02) ACTIVITY

Evaluating case studies

Read through the Evaluation panel on pp. 620–1/888–9 and summarize the strengths and weaknesses of using case studies. Draw up a table, similar to the one on p. 268, to summarize both strengths and weaknesses.

(A02) ACTIVITY

Evaluating methods of investigating celebratory behaviour

Look back to your answers to the activity above left. Now evaluate the suggestions you made there for investigating celebratory behaviour. In other words, answer part (d) of the Example Exam Question on p. 629/897 in terms of psychodynamic explanations.

Read the guidance notes underneath the question and use a PC to write your answer to this question, limiting yourself to 150 words (as you would have to do in the exam).

Answering part (d) of the exam question

In part (d) of the Approaches question, you need to evaluate the methods you suggested in part (c). By thinking ahead when you are answering part (c), you can pick a method that has both clear strengths and weaknesses when it comes to investigating the relevant behaviour. The Evaluation panel on pp. 620–1/888–9 discusses the strengths and weaknesses of case studies. As for experiments, you have already thought about their limitations (in the activity on p. 268); more useful points are discussed in the Evaluation panel on p. 625/893.

EXAMPLE EXAM QUESTIONS

In your work on this unit, you have already planned and written answers to all four parts of the Example Exam Question on p. 629/897, in terms of a psychodynamic approach. Below are two more questions: we have answered the first for you; for the second, use the material from this topic and the textbook in order to construct your own answer.

Sample questions

C Look again at Sample question **C** on p. 268 (Julie and her cuddly toys). This time, we have provided answers to the four questions based on a psychodynamic explanation. Note: only one approach is covered in part (a), whereas in an exam, you would be required to cover two approaches for the 6 + 6 marks.

Sample answer

(a) Freud's psychoanalytic explanation might suggest that by keeping contact with her cuddly toys, Julie is showing a reluctance to become a proper 'adult'. This is the defence mechanism of regression, which involves taking the position of a child rather than acting in a more adult way. This is usually in response to stressful situations, with greater levels of stress leading to even more overtly regressive behaviour. If she has recently left home and is living on her own, she may feel under a lot of strain and this is one way of her staying 'child-like'. Alternatively, Freud might suggest that she is using displacement, i.e. shifting behaviour from a desired target (e.g. a real baby) to a substitute target (i.e. a cuddly toy). As she is now sexually mature, she may want to have a child, but because of personal circumstances may not be in a position to have one. The toys then take the place of her real children.

(b) The main ideas behind this explanation (regression and displacement) are not widely supported by evidence, and so are not falsifiable. It is difficult to generate hypotheses that would directly test the relationship between Julie's attitude to her cuddly toys and the action of these defence mechanisms. The explanation of regression does, however, have a parallel in the psychoanalytic theory of eating disorders, in which anorexics attempt to escape the conflicts that occur with the onset of puberty. Anorexia allows them to 'regress' back into a childhood state, so avoiding the problems (maturation and sexuality) that are part of adult life. The psychoanalytic explanation has been criticized for being reductionist as it may oversimplify Julie's attitude to her toys, and prevent us from investigating other possible explanations for Julie's behaviour. Her insistence that one of her toys sits with them when visitors come to call might be a sign of a potential mental disorder.

(c) A psychodynamic researcher might investigate Julie's attitude to her toys through the use of a case study. She might be invited to attend a psychoanalytic session, where the therapist would use free association and dream analysis. In free association, the therapist would invite her to talk about her toys, her relationship with her parents, her fears for the future and so on. She would be able to express her feelings and thoughts on these matters without censorship from the therapist.

The therapist would listen for any associations that reflect internal conflicts. For example, Julie may express a fear that her parents wanted her to leave home because they no longer loved her – her overt concern for her toys might be a way of countering that fear. Through dream analysis, the therapist would try to understand the true meaning of any symbols in her dreams, to try to get at the underlying problems that are manifested in her behaviour with her toys.

(d) A problem with the case study method – and particularly free association – is that an interviewer may pursue an interpretation based on their own expectations. This may lead Julie to provide certain answers that confirm this interpretation, even when that interpretation might not be correct. Julie may feel the need to please the therapist and so provide answers that reinforce the interpretation. This need would be particularly strong if Julie was experiencing transference – this is a distortion of the interaction between the therapist and herself, based on unresolved conflicts left over from early relationships, especially with her parents in childhood. Despite this, a case study would allow an investigator to ask far-ranging questions over the course of several interviews. This would build up a highly detailed understanding of Julie's behaviour, with the eventual aim of resolving any unresolved childhood conflicts, and thus releasing her to take on adult life.

ACTIVITY

One for you to try ...

D Although we are well-used to older men with their younger 'trophy' wives, an increasingly common phenomenon in UK and US society is the younger man with his older female partner. 'Older women' on television, such as Helen Mirren and Susan Sarandon, set many a young male heart fluttering, and who can forget the seductive charms of Anne Bancroft in the 1967 film, *The Graduate*? But why do young males fall for older women?

(Note: Remember that real exam questions will ask for two approaches in part (a), but you are providing just one here.)

(a) Describe how **two** approaches might try to explain why young males fall for older women.

(6 + 6 marks)

(b) Assess **one** of these explanations of why young males fall for older women. (6 marks)

(c) How would **one** of these approaches investigate why young males fall for older women. (6 marks)

(d) Evaluate this method of investigating why young males fall for older women. (6 marks)

CHECK YOUR UNDERSTANDING

When you have finished working through this topic, try the questions in 'Check your understanding' on p. 621/889 of the textbook. Check your answers by looking at the relevant parts of the textbook listed below.

1 textbook pp. 618–19/886–7

2 textbook p. 619/887

3 textbook p. 619/887

4 textbook p. 619/887

5 textbook p. 620/888

Behaviourism was the dominant approach to psychology for much of the early and middle part of the twentieth century, when it was supplanted by a greater interest in cognitive processes. Behaviourism differs greatly from biological approaches in that it assigns a primary role to environmental influences, rather than innate, physiological ones.

In this topic, you will look at the key assumptions and concepts of the behavioural approach (and its development, social learning theory), assessing them in terms of their strengths and weaknesses. You will also look at typical methods used by those favouring this approach, again assessing these in terms of their strengths and weaknesses.

THE BEHAVIOURAL METAPHOR

ACTIVITY

The behavioural metaphor

Read from the start of Topic 4 up to the heading 'Key concepts ...' on p. 622/890 of the textbook.

1 What is the main assumption of the behavioural approach?

2 What implications does this have for the study of human behaviour?

KEY CONCEPTS OF THE BEHAVIOURAL APPROACH

Read pp. 622–3/890–1 of the textbook, which discuss the key concepts of the behavioural approach, and then complete the following activity. Write your answers on a separate sheet of paper or using your PC. You may also find it useful to work in pairs on the activities, comparing your answers to the questions.

ACTIVITY

Key concepts of the behavioural approach

1 What is the underlying process by which classical conditioning works?

2 In the Watson and Rayner (1920) experiment involving Little Albert (see *Psychology for AS-level* Unit 4, pp. 133–4), what was:
- the neutral/conditioned stimulus
- the unconditioned stimulus
- the conditioned response?

3 What is the underlying process by which operant conditioning works?

4 What is meant by the following terms?
- Positive reinforcement
- Negative reinforcement
- Schedule of reinforcement

5 Antisocial, aggressive and anxious behaviours are often explained in terms of operant conditioning. What might the rewards/reinforcers be for:
- someone behaving aggressively
- an anxious child crying?

6 What is meant by the process of 'shaping'?

7 How might Skinner's experiment with pigeons be applied to human behaviour?

8 What is meant by the following terms?
- Generalization
- Discrimination
- Extinction

SOCIAL LEARNING THEORY

Social learning theory built on behavioural therapy, introducing the crucial concept of indirect learning. Read the text on p. 623/891 of the textbook and then try the following activity.

ACTIVITY

Key concepts of social learning theory

1 What is the difference between direct learning and indirect learning?

2 What is meant by 'vicarious reinforcement'?

3 What determines whether the behaviour observed becomes part of an individual's own repertoire?

4 What is 'reciprocal determinism'?

5 What is 'self-efficacy'?

Answering part (a) of the exam question

The text on pp. 622–3/890–1 gives you a good understanding of the behavioural analysis of human behaviour. In the exam you have to apply your understanding to the question, by explaining the behaviour described in the stimulus material. You can do this by asking yourself questions such as:

1 *Relevant behaviours* – What human behaviours are described in the stimulus material?

2 *Role of conditioning* – How might the behaviour described have been acquired through classical or operant conditioning? What would be the rewards or reinforcers in this case?

3 *Shaping* – Is this a complex behaviour? How might shaping play a part in helping individuals learn it?

4 *Generalization, discrimination, extinction* – What part have any of these processes played in the development of the behaviour? For example, is it an example of a behaviour learned in one context being generalized to another?

5 *Indirect reinforcement* – How might the behaviour described have been acquired through vicarious reinforcement? What might have encouraged the individuals to imitate the behaviour?

6 *Reciprocal determinism and self-efficacy* – Do either of these explanations seem relevant to the behaviours described?

ACTIVITY

Explaining behaviour in behavioural terms

Look at the stimulus material Example Exam Question on p. 629/897. Think about how you might answer part (a), taking the behavioural approach. Ask yourself each of the six questions above and jot down some ideas in response to them, on a separate piece of paper or using a PC.

Thinking of the example of celebrating festivals, two possible explanations that a behaviourist might give are as follows.

1 In public celebrations, there is generally a 'feel good' factor that accompanies whatever is being celebrated (such as a royal wedding or the triumphant procession of a cup-winning team). By being present at the celebrations, this allows people to share in the euphoria, a powerful positive reinforcer.

2 For many people, celebrating Christmas and birthdays is a very important part of their life. It gives them the chance to buy presents (which can be reinforcing by itself) and to experience the gratitude of those who receive them. If you are the one who buys the most thoughtful or the most expensive present, this can also bring admiration from others.

ACTIVITY

Explaining other behaviours in behavioural terms

You can get more practice at explaining our behaviour in behavioural terms by doing the activity on p. 624/892 of the textbook. You might find it useful to discuss your ideas with other students studying psychology.

Answering part (b) of the question

The second part of the Approaches question will ask you to assess one of your explanations in terms of its strengths and weaknesses (see part (b) of the question on p. 629/897). The Evaluation panel on p. 624/892 discusses the behavioural approach in just these terms.

Assessing the behavioural explanation

Read through the list of bullet points evaluating the behavioural approach in the Evaluation panel on p. 624/892 and decide whether each point discussed is a strength or a weakness, or has elements of both. Draw up a table, similar to the one on p. 266, to summarize both strengths and weaknesses.

The list you draw up will be useful for tackling part (b) of the Approaches question, where you have to analyse the strengths and weaknesses of the behavioural explanation you gave in part (a). For example, in assessing the behavioural explanation, you could consider how it might explain individual differences in how people celebrate personal events such as birthdays. Why do some people relish giving parties, while others hate the idea? Can that be explained in terms of different reinforcement experiences? Try the activity above right.

Celebrations and learned behaviour

In responding to part (a) of the question on p. 629/897, you might have explained personal and public celebrations in terms of shared euphoria or the pleasure of giving (and being seen to give). How might we assess these explanations?

1 Not everybody feels the same way about public celebrations or has the same need to buy and give expensive presents at Christmas. Is this a strength or a limitation of the behavioural explanation?

2 Such explanations don't give much importance to self-determination of behaviour. Is it inappropriate to suggest that such behaviours are 'controlled' by factors that are outside our control?

METHODOLOGY USED BY THE BEHAVIOURAL APPROACH

On pp. 624–5/892–3, two types of methodology favoured by the behavioural approach are discussed: laboratory experiments and research with non-human animals.

ACTIVITY

Methodology used by the behavioural approach

Experiments

1 Why are laboratory experiments particularly suitable for research by behaviourists?

2 What steps are involved in setting up a laboratory experiment? Read the text at the bottom of p. 624/892, as well as pp. 216–21 in Unit 7 of *Psychology for AS-level*. Alongside each step, note down important points or guidelines to remember at each stage.

Research with non-human animals

3 How do behaviourists justify the use of research with non-human animals to learn about human behaviour?

Answering part (c) of the Approaches question

In part (c) of the Approaches question, you have to think about how someone taking a behavioural approach would investigate the behaviour described in the stimulus material.

1 What methodology might this approach favour?

2 Which of the types of method would be suitable for investigating the behaviour described?

3 What practical steps would be involved in setting up the research?

Investigating celebratory behaviour taking a behavioural approach

Look at the stimulus material on p. 629/897. Think about how you might answer part (c), taking a behavioural approach. Ask yourself each of the three questions at the bottom of p. 277 and jot down some ideas in response to them.

Evaluating methodology

Read through the Evaluation panel on p. 625/893 and summarize the strengths and weaknesses of using this method. Draw up a table, similar to the one on p. 268, to summarize both strengths and weaknesses.

Answering part (d) of the exam question

In part (d) of the Approaches question, you need to evaluate the methods you suggested in part (c). The Evaluation panel on pp. 625/893 discusses the strengths and weaknesses of laboratory experiments and research with non-human animals. Your analysis can include a discussion of ethical issues – ethical issues in laboratory research are discussed in *Psychology for AS-level* Unit 6, p. 198 (along with a list of advantages and disadvantages of laboratory experiments).

Evaluating methods of investigating celebratory behaviour

Look back to your answers to the activity above left. Evaluate the suggestions you made there for investigating celebratory behaviour. In other words, answer part (d) of the Example Exam Question on p. 629/897 in terms of behavioural explanations. As before, limit yourself to 150 words.

EXAMPLE EXAM QUESTIONS

In your work on this unit, you have already planned and written answers to all four parts of the Example Exam Question on p. 629/897, in terms of a behavioural approach. Below are two more questions: we have answered the first for you; for the second, use the material from this topic and the textbook in order to construct your own answer.

Sample questions

E A worrying trend over the last few years is the number of young girls (aged 12 to 16) who are taking up smoking. They seem impervious to the threats of their parents and teachers, and although they rarely smoke on their own, they will readily light up whenever they are in a group of their friends.

    (a) Describe how **two** approaches might try to explain why young girls smoke.   (6 + 6 marks)

    (b) Assess **one** of these explanations of why young girls smoke.   (6 marks)

    (c) How would **one** of these approaches investigate why young girls smoke.   (6 marks)

    (d) Evaluate this method of investigating why young girls smoke.   (6 marks)

(Note: in the answer below, only one approach is covered in part (a), whereas in an exam, you would be required to cover two approaches for the 6 + 6 marks.)

Sample answer

(a) To understand why a young girl might start smoking, a behaviourist would distinguish between the form that a behaviour takes (in this case, smoking), and its function. There are a number of possible functions for smoking behaviour, although the fact that girls aged 12 to 16 are involved suggests that peer acceptance and approval is an important one. Being seen as 'grown up' and 'one of the crowd' is an important source of reinforcement for children of this age, and as smoking is often seen as something 'cool' that grown-ups do, young girls are keen to copy this in their own behaviour. Other girls will then want to join them, in order be with the 'grown-up' girls, and smoking becomes a way-in to this new and exciting lifestyle. The approving reactions of their peers reinforces this behaviour despite the irregular punishments from parents and teachers. Once they are in a crowd of smokers, stopping is not an option, as they would then risk ridicule (i.e. punishment) from their co-smokers.

(b) This explanation is supported by research evidence which shows the importance of positive reinforcement (in this case the approval of others) in human behaviour. The behaviourist concept of selective reinforcement explains why girls tend not to smoke on their own but only when they are with others. On their own, there is no reinforcement, but in groups, there is. Another advantage of this explanation is that, unlike psychodynamic or evolutionary explanations, it can be tested scientifically. However, while the behavioural explanation can explain some aspects of these girls' behaviour, it cannot explain all of them. Why, for example, do the punishments from their parents have no effect? And why do they persist in smoking even though there are many other negative consequences (e.g. cost, smell and negative reactions from non-smokers)? The fact that these children persist in their smoking may have nothing to do with peer pressure, but more to do with the addictive effects of nicotine.

(c) Behaviourists are most likely to use an experiment to test a hypothesized cause of behaviour. If, by varying the consequences of smoking behaviour, they could change its frequency, then the hypothesis is likely to be correct. For this example, the behaviourist could introduce extinction, meaning they would arrange for these girls no longer to experience the usual reinforcement when they smoke. In this case, every other girl would have to stop showing approval when the girl in question started to smoke. If peer approval is the most important consequence of maintaining their smoking behaviour, then withholding this approval would eventually end the smoking. An alternative solution would be to set up circumstances where social approval follows some behaviour other than smoking. If the girls' smoking behaviour decreases when the frequency of social approval for these other actions increases, then this would also be evidence that approval from peers maintained the original behaviour.

(d) There are problems with the use of extinction in this investigation. First, there would be the difficulty of getting all of a girl's friends and classmates not to offer social approval when the girl starts to smoke. Second, it would be difficult to prevent them making comments that would act as confounding variables to the investigation. There would also be important ethical considerations. The girls involved may have quite fragile self-esteem that is only kept at an acceptable level through the approval of their peers. If so, it may be considered unethical to manipulate events so that this is denied to them. It would also put pressure on their peers, who in denying approval to their friends, might find themselves in an uncomfortable interpersonal role. The use of alternative social approval would largely overcome this problem. Despite these problems, an experimental investigation allows the investigator to demonstrate causes of this behaviour by systematically manipulating each variable in turn.

ACTIVITY

One for you to try ...

F Buying clothes for some people isn't just about buying what they need, but buying into a lifestyle. Young men in particular will spend what their parents consider to be ridiculous amounts of money for a shirt or a jacket because it is from a recognized designer. Having the designer's name in a prominent position for all to see is a must, but why do so many young people feel the need to spend so much on designer clothes?

(Note: the real exam questions ask for two approaches in part (a), but you are providing just one here.)

(a) Describe how **two** approaches might try to explain why young people feel the need to spend so much on designer clothes. **(6 + 6 marks)**

(b) Assess **one** of these explanations of why young people feel the need to spend so much on designer clothes. **(6 marks)**

(c) How would **one** of these approaches investigate why young people feel the need to spend so much on designer clothes. **(6 marks)**

(d) Evaluate this method of investigating why young people feel the need to spend so much on designer clothes. **(6 marks)**

CHECK YOUR UNDERSTANDING

When you have finished working through this topic, try the questions in 'Check your understanding' on p. 625/893 of the textbook. Check your answers by looking at the relevant parts of the textbook, listed below.

1 textbook p. 622/890

2 textbook p. 622/890

3 textbook p. 623/891

4 textbook p. 623/891

5 textbook p. 624/892

Topic 5 >> The cognitive approach

'Cognition' is another word for 'thinking' and so, as you might expect, the cognitive approach is interested in the mental processes that are involved in human behaviour. In this topic, you will look at the key assumptions and concepts of the cognitive approach, assessing them in terms of their strengths and weaknesses. You will also look at typical methods used by those favouring this approach, again assessing these in terms of their strengths and weaknesses.

THE COGNITIVE METAPHOR

ACTIVITY

The cognitive metaphor

Read from the start of Topic 5 up to the activity on p. 626/894 of this workbook and then answer the following questions.

1 What is the main assumption of the cognitive approach?

2 What implications does this have for the study of human behaviour?

Try the activity on p. 626/894 of the textbook, which encourages you to examine the central metaphor of the cognitive approach.

KEY CONCEPTS OF THE COGNITIVE APPROACH

Read pp. 626–7/894–5 of the textbook, which discuss the key concepts of the cognitive approach, and then complete the following activities.

ACTIVITY

Mental and perceptual set

1 What is meant by the following terms?
- Structural understanding
- Mental set
- Functional fixedness
- Perceptual set

2 Summarize the Gestalt view of how we solve problems.

3 How does this differ from the earlier behaviourists' view?

ACTIVITY

Schemas and stereotypes

1 What is meant by the following terms?
- Schema
- Stereotype

2 How does each of these affect the way we remember things?

ACTIVITY

Bartlett's War of the Ghosts research

Bartlett's theories concerning reconstructive memory will have been part of your AS-level studies. You may find it useful to read about his work again – see *Psychology for AS-level* Unit 1, pp. 31–3 and in particular the Key Study on p. 31.

You can test Bartlett's findings about the War of the Ghosts story for yourself. First find the text of the story on the Internet. Type in 'Egulac foggy' into your favourite search engine (these words appear in the story). You will get a list of sites – mainly colleges and universities – describing Bartlett's research. Some of these include the text of the story.

Read the story. Then set it aside for a day or so and, without reading it, try to recall it as best you can. Then compare your version with the original and see what the differences are. How do they tie in with what Bartlett found?

Language and thought

One of the areas that cognitive psychologists are most interested in is the relationship between language and thought. How are language and thought connected? Does language determine thought, or vice versa? Or are they independent processes?

1 Read pp. 252–3/520–1 of the textbook about research into the relationship between language and thought. What are the positions in the language–thought debate taken by:

- Sapir and Whorf
- Piaget
- Vygotsky

2 Whorf claimed that the Inuit had many more words for snow than other peoples. What different interpretations could be put on this phenomenon?

3 Pinker (1994) argued that English had just as many words for snow. What conclusions about language and thought might that suggest?

Social cognition

1 What is meant by the term 'social cognition'?

2 What is the basic assumption of this area of psychology?

Maladaptive thinking

As well as the paragraph on p. 627/895, you may find it helpful to read the section on 'Use and mode of cognitive–behavioural therapies' on pp. 535–8/803–6 of the textbook.

Attributions of causality and social representations

One of the areas that interests social-cognitive psychologists is 'attributions of causality'. Read the introduction to Topic 1 of Unit 1/9 on p. 4/272 and pp. 10–13/278–81. Then answer the following questions.

Attributions of causality

1 What is the fundamental attribution error?

How does this affect the way we think about people and events around us?

2 What is the self-serving bias?

How does this affect the way we think about ourselves and events around us?

Social representations

1 What are social representations?

2 What are the two main functions of social representations?

3 Read the Key research panel on pp. 17–18/285–6 and summarize the social representations of smokers expressed by:

- adolescent girls who smoked
- non-smoking, adolescent girls.

4 Think of an activity that you carry out (e.g. playing sport or a musical instrument), or an aspect of your background, culture or personality. What social representations exist about that aspect of your life?

Answering part (a) of the exam question

The text on pp. 626–7/894–5 gives you a good understanding of the cognitive analysis of human behaviour. In the exam you have to apply your understanding to the question, by explaining the behaviour described in the stimulus material from a cognitive point of view. You can do this by asking yourself questions such as the following.

1 *Relevant behaviours* – What human behaviours are described in the stimulus material?

2 *Mental and perceptual set* – How do the behaviours illustrate the use of a particular mental or perceptual set? To what extent does this restrict or limit individuals' behaviour?

3 *Schemas and stereotypes* – How could the behaviours be explained in terms of schemas? Do the behaviours involve mental short cuts or stereotyping?

4 *Language and thought* – What light (if any) do the behaviours cast on the relationship between language and thought?

5 *Social cognition* – What insight can you gain from the behaviours as to how people view the world and people around them? How far can the behaviours be interpreted as typical social representations?

6 *Maladaptive thinking* – Can the behaviours be seen as implying maladaptive thinking? If so, how would a cognitive psychologist interpret this? And what would be a suitable course of action for remedying it?

Thinking of the example of celebrating festivals in the Example Exam Question on p. 629/897, how do you think a cognitive psychologist might explain this?

- *Social cognition* – Social representations theory (Unit 1/9, pp. 15–8/283–6) might explain celebratory behaviour in terms of our efforts to 'conventionalize' events through tradition and convention. These then come to exist independently of the individuals who created them.

- *Schemas* – Based on our experience, we develop the belief that celebrating people's birthdays and anniversaries is the right way to behave, in much the same way as we come to believe that we must eat turkey at Christmas and chocolate at Easter.

Answering part (b) of the exam question

The second part of the Approaches question will ask you to assess one of your explanations in terms of its strengths and weaknesses (see part (b) of the question on p. 629/897). The Evaluation panel on pp. 627–8/895–6 discusses the cognitive approach in just these terms. Now try the AO2 activity above right.

This table will be very useful for tackling part (b) of the Approaches question, where you have to analyse the strengths and weaknesses of the cognitive explanation you gave in part (a). For example, in assessing the cognitive explanation, you could consider how it might explain public celebrations in terms of social representations. How do celebrations such as Christmas illustrate shared beliefs and views?

In responding to part (a) of the question on p. 629/897, you might have explained personal and public celebrations in terms of social representations and the use of schemas. You might consider the following as AO2 points for explanations from this perspective.

1 Social representations explanations of celebratory behaviour ignore the fact that, in Western cultures, we show a preference for dispositional over situational causes for events, seeing the individual as the main causative agent in their own behaviour rather than some collective tradition.

2 Unlike some other perspectives, cognitive explanations usually lend themselves to scientific testing. It should be possible, therefore, to test the explanation that schemas exist for private celebratory events.

METHODOLOGY USED BY THE COGNITIVE APPROACH

As explained on p. 628/896, the cognitive approach uses a variety of methods, including laboratory experiments, case studies and brain scanning techniques. These methods are considered in more detail in other topics in this unit, so it is worth looking back at the following pages in this workbook:

- laboratory experiments – see p. 277
- case studies – see p. 272
- brain scanning techniques – see p. 261.

Answering part (c)

In part (c) of the Approaches question, you have to think about how someone taking a cognitive approach would investigate the behaviour described in the stimulus material.

1 What methodology might this approach favour?
2 Which of the types of method would be suitable for investigating the behaviour described?
3 What practical steps would be involved in setting up the research?

Answering part (d) of the exam question

In part (d) of the Approaches question, you need to evaluate the methods you suggested in part (c). Again, it will help to look back at those pages in this workbook where the various research methods are evaluated, i.e.

● laboratory experiments – see p. 278
● case studies – see p. 272
● brain scanning techniques – see p. 262

Evaluating methods of investigating celebratory behaviour

Look back to your answers to the activity below left. Evaluate the suggestions you made there for investigating celebratory behaviour. In other words, answer part (d) of the Example Exam Question on p. 629/897 in terms of cognitive explanations. As before, limit yourself to 150 words.

EXAMPLE EXAM QUESTIONS

In your work on this unit, you have already planned and written answers to all four parts of the Example Exam Question on p. 629/897, in terms of a cognitive approach. Below are two more questions: we have answered the first for you; for the second, use the material from this topic and the textbook in order to construct your own answer.

Sample questions

F Look again at Sample question F on p. 279 (about young people and designer clothes). This time, we have provided answers to the four questions based on a cognitive explanation. Note: only one approach is covered in part (a), whereas in an exam, you would be required to cover two approaches for the 6 + 6 marks.

(a) Describe how **two** approaches might try to explain why young people feel the need to spend so much on designer clothes. (6 + 6 marks)

(b) Assess **one** of these explanations of why young people feel the need to spend so much on designer clothes. (6 marks)

(c) How would **one** of these approaches investigate why young people feel the need to spend so much on designer clothes. (6 marks)

(d) Evaluate this method of investigating why young people feel the need to spend so much on designer clothes. (6 marks)

Sample answer

(a) A cognitive psychologist might approach the explanation of young people's passion for designer clothes from the perspective of social cognition. There are a number of aspects of social cognition that might explain this. First, the concept of stereotypes may explain that, to many young people, people wearing designer clothes are stereotyped as being successful and therefore to be looked up to. By wearing designer clothes themselves, other people will see them as successful, and look up to them. This belief may be strengthened by the fact that they think that way themselves about other people, which social-cognition theorists call being a 'cognitive miser'. This connection between clothes and success then becomes a form of maladaptive thinking, as young people feel convinced that others will see them as unsuccessful, and will look down on them if they wear anything less than designer clothes.

(b) A strength of this explanation is that stereotypes are usually seen to have some 'grain of truth' about them. The fact that many young people already think this way themselves about the clothes that other people wear tells us that they may be right in assuming that others will also think that way about them. Another strength is that seeing such beliefs as a form of maladaptive thinking means that it should be possible to challenge these irrational thoughts, and so change their way of thinking about clothes to a more reasonable level. However, the view of people as 'cognitive misers' may be undone by the fact that, once they are exposed to information that contradicts the initial stereotype (e.g. they meet a number of people in designer clothes who are not successful), they may just recategorize those people. For example, people wearing Burberry designer baseball caps are no longer seen as well-off or trendy, but are viewed in a less than complimentary way by those around them.

(c) Researchers could gather qualitative data by interviewing young people about their reasons for buying expensive clothes. They could use an unstructured interview, asking questions, seeking detail and clarification, but without forcing the person in any particular direction. From the answers to these questions, researchers could categorize data and identify themes, such as the connection between designer clothes and success, the relationship between the type of clothes worn and peer acceptance, and so on. If researchers are interested in whether people's passion for designer clothes is part of a more general type of maladaptive thinking, they could ask them to keep a journal, noting down their thoughts, feelings, and actions when specific situations arose. The journal would help to make the person aware of his or her maladaptive thoughts. The therapist would not only be interested in the person's 'symptoms' (i.e. their need to buy expensive clothes) but also in their interpretation of events (e.g. 'people won't like me unless I do this').

(d) A strength of the unstructured interview method in this study is that it would allow the interviewees to raise topics and issues which the interviewer did not anticipate and which might be critical to the investigation. They may, for example, discover that many people with low self-esteem 'hide' behind an expensive designer label, or that conformity to peers is more important than the clothes themselves. Despite this advantage, however, these methods are open to subjective interpretation and bias, as the researchers may only report those aspects of behaviour that support their own point of view. If, for example, the researcher believes that a passion for designer clothes is a consequence of stereotyping, this will affect their questioning and also bias the interpretation of any responses. There may also be interpersonal difficulties for the interviewee, particularly if the researcher is of a similar age to the interviewee's parents, who have already expressed their disapproval at their children buying expensive clothes. This may make the interviewees more defensive in their responses.

ACTIVITY

One for you to try ...

G Many young people spend long hours of every evening sitting in front of their computers playing strategy games such as *Final Fantasy* and *Civilization*. Strategy gamers will often prefer to play these games rather than pursue any other leisure pastime. They can become relatively reclusive as they ignore friends and family in order to get their nightly 'fix' in their fantasy computer world.

(a) Describe how **two** approaches might try to explain why some young people are obsessed by computer strategy games. (6 + 6 marks)

(b) Assess **one** of these explanations of why some young people are obsessed by computer strategy games. (6 marks)

(c) How would **one** of these approaches investigate why some young people are obsessed by computer strategy games. (6 marks)

(d) Evaluate this method of investigating why some young people are obsessed by computer strategy games. (6 marks)

(Note: the real exam questions ask for two approaches in part (a), but you are providing just one here.)

CHECK YOUR UNDERSTANDING

When you have finished working through this topic, try the questions in 'Check your understanding' on p. 628/896 of the textbook. Check your answers by looking at the relevant parts of the textbook or this workbook, listed below.

1 textbook p. 626/894; workbook p. 280

2 textbook p. 626/894

3 textbook pp. 626–7/894–5; workbook p. 280

4 textbook pp. 626–7/894–5

5 textbook p. 613/881; workbook p. 262